THE REMARKABLE RISE OF
Eliza Jumel

THE REMARKABLE RISE OF
Eliza Jumel

a story of

MARRIAGE *and* MONEY *in the* EARLY REPUBLIC

MARGARET A. OPPENHEIMER

CHICAGO
REVIEW
PRESS

Published by Chicago Review Press Incorporated
814 North Franklin Street
Chicago, Illinois 60610
ISBN 978-1-61373-380-6

Library of Congress Cataloging-in-Publication Data
Oppenheimer, Margaret A.
 The remarkable rise of Eliza Jumel : a story of marriage and money in the early
republic / Margaret A. Oppenheimer.
    pages cm
  Includes index.
  ISBN 978-1-61373-380-6 (hardback)
  1. Jumel, Eliza Bowen, 1775?-1865. 2. Jumel, Stephen, 1755-1832. 3. Married
women—New York (State)—New York—Biography. 4. French Americans—
New York (State)—Biography. 5. Burr, Aaron, 1756-1836. 6. Politicians'
spouses—United States—Biography. 7. Socialites—New York (State)—New
York—Biography. 8. Businesswomen—New York (State)—New York—
Biography. 9. Jumel, Eliza Bowen, 1775?-1865—Family. 10. New York (N.Y.)—
History—1775-1865—Biography. I. Title.
  E302.6.B91O66 2015
  973.4'6092—dc23
  [B]
                        2015029634

Interior design: Jonathan Hahn

Printed in the United States of America
5 4 3 2 1

For my parents, with love.

CONTENTS

PROLOGUE

*I*n 1873 New Yorkers following the courtroom battle of
the decade could read a short update in the *Commercial
Advertiser*:

> It may be gratifying to the relatives and friends of the luckless jurors
> engaged in the trial of the JUMEL will case, to know that that com-
> pany of wretched men still exists—not healthy nor happy, but alive
> and patient. It is altogether impossible to say when the fight for the
> estate will end; but it is to be presumed that the jurors profited by
> the hint they received, and by settling up all their worldly affairs,
> prepared themselves for a gradual and peaceful descent into the
> tomb. Court, counsel, and jury are becoming old and gray.[1]

The fight over the Jumel fortune began in 1865, after Eliza Jumel
died in her ninetieth year. It raged on into the 1890s. As the years
passed, Americans from Maine to California marveled at the stories
woven around the amazing Madame Jumel, who rose from grind-
ing poverty to enviable wealth. Family members told of a woman
who earned the gratitude of Napoleon I, shone at the courts of
Louis XVIII and Charles X, and fought valiantly to recoup her first

husband's fallen fortunes.[2] Claimants to her estate painted a different picture: of a prostitute, a mother of an illegitimate son, a wife who ruthlessly defrauded her husband and perhaps even plotted his death.[3] The parties agreed on but a single fact: "she was for a short time the wife of the notorious Aaron Burr."[4]

Which narrative should we believe today? Over the course of Eliza's tumultuous afterlife as the star of a courtroom drama, the facts of her life were obscured beneath libels and legends. Her real story—so strikingly unique that it surpasses any invention—has yet to be told.

The child called Betsy Bowen, who became Eliza Jumel and later Mrs. Aaron Burr, was raised in a brothel, indentured as a servant, and confined to a workhouse when her mother was in jail. Yet by the end of her life she had servants of her own, a New York mansion that stands today, a summer home in Saratoga Springs that survives as well, and several hundred acres of land. She was America's first major woman art collector, forming a collection of 242 European paintings. She raised a niece, great-niece, and great-nephew to adulthood and arranged good marriages for both the girls. She married twice herself, above her station, without family connections to ease the way. She used marriages and money to improve her social standing and the legal system to protect her financial security. When she died, her estate was worth some $1 million dollars, comparable in buying power to $15 million today. She even managed to do what Alexander Hamilton could not: she triumphed over Aaron Burr.

Her life represented an extreme rarity for her era: a rags-to-riches story, female version. One of the foundational beliefs of America was that a *boy* who grew up poor could work his way up to fame and fortune.[5] Although the truth was more nuanced—relatively few poor boys rose into the social and financial elite—the United States was still the country of self-made men.[6]

But there was no comparable myth for young women. Working hard didn't translate into opportunities for girls, because the available jobs paid badly and afforded little or no upward mobility.[7] Marrying up wasn't easy either. Potential husbands for poor girls were nearly as impoverished as the girls themselves. It took a woman like Eliza to break the mold. Intelligent, determined, sometimes difficult, she had the strength to seize opportunities and readjust facts to achieve the security and status she so desperately craved.

To understand her unique achievement, we must begin in Providence, Rhode Island, with the young girl who was known as Betsy Bowen. Watch vigilantly as she steps onto history's stage, because the echoes of a riot blur the sound of her voice.

BEGINNINGS

Most nights Betsy would have heard the buzz of voices rising from the rooms below. Occasionally men might shout a toast or bellow a bawdy song. But the bursts of noise, the clinking mugs and rattling dice, would have been the normal backdrop of her life.

She might have half awakened once or twice to the sound of footsteps on the stairs. There would be a man stumbling with drink, and a woman, giggling and whispering to him—Esther perhaps, or Debby or Black Bets, or even Betsy's mother, Phebe.[1] But then she could turn over and go back to sleep.

The night of July 22, 1782, would have been terrifyingly different.[2] Furious rioters swarmed into the house. Reports of a similar incident, in which a *"Bastille of Iniquity"* was stormed and "gutted of its contents," allow us to envision the chaos.[3] "Furniture, beds, clothing, &c." were "entirely destroyed."[4] "Petty-coats, smocks, and silks, together with the . . . feather beds" were "strewed to the winds."[5] "Mother Cary and her *innocent Chickens*" were "turned out to the inclemency of a midnight air."[6] The house "in a short time was intirely rased [*sic*] to the ground floor"—just as was the one in which Betsy had been living.[7]

Brothel riots, such as the one in Providence, Rhode Island, that ensnared seven-year-old Betsy Bowen and her mother, Phebe, were rare but not unknown in eighteenth-century America. Communal attempts to enforce social norms, they most often occurred when local authorities could not or would not act. They might happen when a customer felt cheated or a girl was thought to have been lured in against her will.[8]

The cause of the riot in Providence is unknown. But the city had changed dramatically since the outbreak of the American Revolution in ways that must have upset long-term residents. On the face of it, Providence was still a pastoral place, looking much as a clergyman had found it in 1754, with "two streets of painted houses" on the northeast side of the Providence River, surmounted by "a most delightful hill, gradually ascending to a great distance, all cut into gardens, orchards, pleasant fields, and beautiful enclosures."[9] There was "a fine harbor of shipping," "a well-built bridge," and, on the southwest side of the river, a suburb "less elegant than on the northeast, but [containing] two or three streets of well-built houses."[10] Yet this pleasant New England settlement was bulging at the seams. Wartime Providence was filled with refugees from Rhode Island's largest city, Newport, which was occupied by the British from late 1776.[11] Young men had left for the armies, and others had arrived. By 1781, American troops and their French allies were encamped outside of Providence.[12] Rhode Island College (Brown University today) had been turned into a military hospital.[13]

Already a magnet for transients, the growing city attracted yet more.[14] Men worked on farms, in the shipyards, or for the army. Women became laundresses or servants in wealthy households, took a boarder or two into their rented rooms, or sometimes sold themselves.[15] Taverns and brothels sprung up to serve soldiers and sailors, not to mention local residents looking for feminine company. Houses that hosted "females of ill fame" attracted "large Collections of Men of dissolute Character" who disturbed the city's "quiet & peaceable Inhabitants."[16]

The dwelling Betsy and Phebe had lived in, an old jail converted into a residence, had come to the attention of the authorities as early as 1780, when four women residing there—including the aptly named Judah Wanton—were determined to be people of "bad character and reputation."[17] The four were pushed out, but the women who replaced them followed the same profession.

The morning after the riot that destroyed the building, Jabez Bowen, deputy governor of Rhode Island (no relation of Phebe and Betsy), wrote a letter to the Providence Town Council. "Gentlemen," he began, "You cannot be uninformed of the riot last night and that a dwelling house in the compact part of town was entirely destroyed."

The councilmen were at least partially to blame, he implied: "We have good and wholesome laws. We have chosen officers to execute them; if they are not faithful to do their duty, they ought to be displaced with disgrace and others elected in their room who will be more faithful." In the meantime, action was required to deal with the aftermath of the riot. Bowen lived in Providence himself and knew what the town had become at night.

The council members must convene immediately, he instructed. They "should order all the people that dwelt in the old gaol to appear before them," "break up the wicked nest by ordering all that are not inhabitants [of Providence] to leave," and surprise "all [the] other bad houses." We must "all exert ourselves," he added with a flourish, "for the restoration of order and virtue in our town."[18]

Later that day, town sergeant William Compton and one of his constables stepped out, warrant in hand. "In the name of the Governor and Company of the State of Rhode Island &c You are hereby commanded to Summon & Require the Following persons . . ."[19]

Elizabeth Gardner's name was near the top. Described variously as "an Indian or Molattto [*sic*] woman"—no one was quite sure which she was—Gardner (whose first name was actually Sarah) had been a thorn in the side of the town council for more than a decade, earning her living by prostitution and producing a quiver full of children. She had been ejected from Providence before—but she always came back.[20]

Patience Ingraham appeared on the list as well. She was "to be examined on a Charge of keeping a Common, ill-governed, and disorderly House, and of permitting to reside there, persons of Evil Name and Fame, and of dishonest conversation, drinking, tippling, Whoring, and Misbehaving themselves to the Damage and Nuisance of the town and great disturbance of the public Peace." Her two female lodgers were summoned also, along with a Mrs. McCollough "at the House of Joseph Willson."[21]

Then there was another name Compton would have recognized: "Margaret Fairchild, alias Margaret Bowler."[22] A former slave who lived in Providence, Bowler had been the leaseholder at the old jail-turned-residence, but thanks to the prior night's riot, that building was gone.

On Wednesday morning, July 24, the town council met at the statehouse, a handsome brick building fronted by a spacious lawn. A long walkway terminated at the imposing central door. Theodore Foster, the clerk of the council, took the minutes as Bowler was examined. She stated

> that she was the servant of Major Fairchild, who verbally gave her her Freedom . . . about five years ago. That she hath lived in different Parts of the Town, having kept House [i.e., rented rooms to others] the whole of the time. That she hired the old Gaol House of Mr. Joshua Burr, and agreed to pay him fourteen hundred dollars paper currency Rent per Year, when she first went into it. That When the House was pulled down by the Mob on Monday Night last, there were with her, lodging in the House, Phebe Bowen and her daughter Betsy—another white woman in company with the said Phebe Bowen, called Debby—a Negro Woman called Black Bets, belong-

ing to Sandwich, and a Mulatto Girl about eighteen or nineteen years of Age, called Esther, who hath since gone to Smithfield.[23]

It was no coincidence that three of the six residents of the brothel were black or biracial.[24] The rising tide of abolitionist sentiment in New England meant that a growing number of slaves were being given their freedom. Yet employment possibilities for people of color, especially women, remained scarce and poorly paid.[25]

Phebe Bowen's prospects—and those of her daughter Betsy— were little better than those of the darker-skinned occupants of the house. Phebe was by birth a resident of Taunton, a town near Boston in the province of Massachusetts Bay. Her parents, John Kelly and Hannah Owen Kelly, were unable to support her, it seems. By the time she was four or five years old, she was living in North Providence with her maternal grandfather, John Owen. Soon she was sent to Providence proper to stay with a married sister—perhaps Owen was unwilling to be burdened with the care of a young child. If so, her sister was equally unenthusiastic. When she moved away, she left Phebe behind.[26]

From then on, Phebe was "bound out"—apprenticed—as a servant in exchange for her room and board. It was an unstable existence. Most families needed an extra hand only sporadically, perhaps when there was a new baby in the cradle or extra spinning on hand.[27] A bound-out girl's master might send her to help out in other households when he didn't need her services, offloading the costs of feeding and clothing her onto the hosts.[28] Phebe—a young, vulnerable girl whose parents were absent or already dead—had worked in five different homes by her early teens.

She told her story matter-of-factly:

After my Sister Removed from Providence, I then went out and lived with John Brown Riger, and from thence I went and lived with Abraham Whipple, and from thence I went to Dwell with James Lovet, and from said Lovets I went and lived with John Nash, and from thence back to said Lovets again and now I live at David Wilkinsons.[29]

Phebe spoke these words at a meeting of the town council in the then-brand-new statehouse on September 29, 1769. She was fourteen, impoverished, illiterate, and pregnant.[30]

The purpose of that audience was to determine her place of residence. In early America, people who could not support themselves became the responsibility of the town in which they had legal residence, gained by birth, marriage, purchase of real estate, or completion of an apprenticeship.[31] To save money, nonresidents who committed crimes or appeared likely to need financial support were "warned out" of the municipality to which they had migrated, with the threat of fines or corporal punishment if they returned. Often they were escorted to their town of origin, whose officers would be obliged to take on their care.[32]

Phebe, born in Massachusetts, had no claim to the benevolence of the authorities of Providence. Oddly, however, although she was rejected from being an inhabitant of the city, the council did not order her escorted back to Taunton. Perhaps her pregnancy was sufficiently advanced to make travel inadvisable.

Another solution was available, and Phebe grasped it. On Wednesday, November 1, in the meeting house of the First Congregational Society of Providence, she married her child's father, a sailor named John Bowen.[33] A married woman took her residency from her husband, and crucially John was a local man.[34] The right to live in Providence—for as long as he lived—may have been the most meaningful gift John ever gave Phebe.

Another sort of gift—namely, the infant John Thomas Bowen—arrived before the end of the year.[35] Two more children followed. Mary—always called Polly as a child—entered the world some two and a half years later, in 1772.[36] Betsy, the youngest—officially, Elizabeth—was born on April 2, 1775; she would joke many years later to her great-niece "that she had come near being an April fool."[37] The opening salvos of the Revolutionary War were fired less than three weeks after her birth: at Lexington and Concord on April 19, 1775.

A HOUSE OF BAD FAME

The war disrupted the American economy, halting trade between the colonies and Britain. Food shortages were common in Revolutionary Providence, and life was difficult when Betsy was a child.[1] Given that she and her mother were lodging in a brothel by 1782, it is unlikely that John Bowen provided much financial support for his family. Even had he wanted to help them, sailing was one of the worst-paid trades.[2]

The Bowen children would have to contribute to their own maintenance. John Thomas and Polly, unmentioned during the inquiry that followed the brothel riot, may have been "working out" already from time to time, at the ages of thirteen and ten, respectively. John Thomas was old enough to plow and plant on one of the farms surrounding Providence, if he were not already serving an apprenticeship.[3] Polly could have obtained temporary, live-in jobs doing housework and spinning.[4] Betsy, the youngest child, was still with Phebe, but the riot had left her and her mother homeless.

Three bills submitted to the Providence Town Council in 1784 hint at the Bowen family's precarious financial situation.[5] From February 7 to April 27, Betsy and her sister Polly lived in Providence's workhouse, boarded at the expense of the town. The reason for their stay is unknown, but the workhouse was a last resort. New England town officers preferred to support needy families with inexpensive "outside relief" consisting of small gifts of food or wood.[6]

Institutionalization was reserved chiefly for the "unworthy" poor—as alcoholics, vagrants, and the lazy or shiftless were defined.[7] These individuals would be forced to work for their room and board, relieving the town of the expense of their support.[8] Men and women arrested for minor misdemeanors (such as a drunken spree or violating an order to leave town) were funneled into the workhouse too, confined in a secured area known as "the cage."[9]

To some extent, however, the name "workhouse" was a misnomer. The building in Providence was referred to originally as a "Work house *or* [emphasis added] Alms house," and retained the supplemental function of providing short-term relief for the destitute.[10] Surviving bills for board, such as those for Betsy and Polly, reveal that a handful of desperately poor townspeople swelled the institution's population each winter.[11] These unfortunates—chiefly women and children unable rather than unwilling to earn a living—seem to have been placed in the workhouse as the most cost-efficient option to shelter them during the coldest months of the year. For Betsy and Polly, then, the institution—as lonely and desolate as it may have been—would have functioned as a refuge rather than a punishment. Perhaps Phebe had a broken bone or serious illness in 1784 and could not care for her children.

Whatever the reason for her absence, it was transitory. A year later, she and her two daughters were living with forty-nine-year-old Patience Ingraham, a widow scraping out a life on the margins of society.[12] She had been "examined, cautioned, and reprimanded" two years before "for keeping a House of bad Fame."[13] The atmosphere inside her home at night could not have been very different from what Betsy had known at the old jail.

At least Ingraham had several children under the age of fourteen who could offer Betsy companionship by day.[14] It might have been her daughters Sarah and Susannah who showed Betsy around the house, as James, the youngest child, toddled behind.[15] An inventory drawn up in 1785, which lists the contents of the house although not the layout or number of rooms, suggests that it was a modest home containing several of the multipurpose rooms common in eighteenth-century New England.[16] Upstairs were five beds—some merely mattresses on the floor—probably divided between two bedchambers, as well as a candlestand and a flour barrel filled with odds and ends. There were two spinning wheels, one broken. A small stock of linen and woolen yarn testified that the other still functioned.[17]

The layout of the first floor is conjectural, but it appears that there was at least a parlor—a room that combined the functions of best bedroom and place to entertain guests—and a family room, typically called a keeping room or hall, that could be used, like the parlor, for cooking, eating, and sleeping. Two or three beds were divided between these rooms. Several trunks and a maple desk contained clothing and bedding. Tinware, crockery, and iron cookware, described summarily in the inventory, would have been arranged near the fireplaces. A lean-to kitchen may have been attached to the back of the house; if not, all of the cooking would have been done in the parlor and keeping room.[18] The contents of the home—old-fashioned furniture and well-worn linens—were valued at barely £10.[19]

At night, guests would have gathered in the small downstairs rooms. With her new lodger, Phebe Bowen, Ingraham continued to ply the only trade she knew.

On June 25, 1785, the two women were brought before the town council "for keeping a Disorderly House." Theodore Foster entered a summary of the hearing in the town record book:

> Whereas it is Represented and made to appear to this Council that Patience Ingraham, Widow of Joseph Ingraham Deceased, hath for considerable Time Past, and Still Doth behave, in a very Disorderly Manner by keeping a Bad House of Evil Fame to the Disturbance of the Peace of the Neighborhood in which she lives; and although she hath been called before this Council and Admonished to good

Behavior, she still doth so conduct herself as to disquiet the Good People of the Town.

It is therefore Resolved as the Opinion of the Council that it be and is Recommended to James Arnold and John Dorrance Esq.ʳ, Two of the Justices of the Peace, to take cognizance of the Matter of the bad conduct of the said Ingraham and that they proceed with her according to Law.[20]

The meeting had frightening repercussions for Betsy. Her mother, Phebe, and Ingraham—the two were apparently complicit in running the "Disorderly House"—were arrested two days later and committed to the county jail.[21] The children of the two women were left to the mercies of the town council, which provided for them in the manner of the day: "It is therefore Ordered that the said Children be sent to the Work House under the direction of the Overseers of the Poor."[22]

Once more Betsy and Polly entered the institution, spending three and a half weeks there while their mother was in prison. A little comfort was provided by town sergeant Henry Bowen (no known relation of Phebe and her daughters), who had been charged with caring for the family's belongings, "Saving that he furnish them with such necessary Bedding, Cloathing &c. as may be suitable for them in their present Condition."[23] The sergeant interpreted his orders liberally. The day after Phebe's arrest, he delivered her most valuable possession to the jail: a looking glass fitted with a little drawer containing a comb, a thimble, and six shillings.[24] This object was what antique dealers call a dressing glass, consisting of a small, pivoting mirror hung between two posts, affixed to a base that housed a drawer for storing jewelry or other valuables.

About ten days later, Bowen made further deliveries to jail and workhouse: a glass decanter, a "small loose gown"—the size perhaps identifying it as belonging to Betsy—and some additional, unspecified clothing. Touchingly, there was also a spelling book.[25] Illiterate Phebe had scraped together the means to purchase it, envisioning a brighter future for her children.

While Betsy, Polly, and the young Ingrahams sweated through the July days in the workhouse, the town councilmen dictated their destiny:

> And it appears to this Council that the said Patience Ingraham, for want of Discretion in the Management of herself, her Family Affairs, and Estate, is likely to bring herself and Family to Want and Misery, it is therefore Voted and Resolved . . . that her said Children, viz Sarah, Susannah, and James, who are now in the Work House, be bound out under the Direction of the Overseers of the Poor to some good Masters as they shall think proper and according to Law. And that the children of the said Phebe Bowen be also bound out in like Manner.[26]

Supporting minors to adulthood would be financially ruinous for a town. Poor children who came to the attention of municipal officers because their parents were unable to provide for them suitably on a long-term basis (either from a perceived lack of moral fitness or insufficient economic resources) were indentured (apprenticed) to masters who would feed and clothe them in exchange for their labor.[27] The indenture—a legal contract—typically provided that a girl would remain with the family to which she was bound until the age of eighteen and a boy to the age of twenty-one.[28] Frequently the children would remain in touch with their relatives, often paying or receiving visits on Sundays.[29] By the time they were ten or eleven years old, they could work hard enough to balance out the cost of their keep.[30]

Polly was placed with Henry Wyatt, of whom nothing is known, and Betsy with a sea captain, Samuel Allen, and his wife.[31] From a distance Phebe continued to watch over the girls and her oldest child, John, who was unhappy in an apprenticeship to a carpenter. At the beginning of April 1786, she approached the town council on his behalf. Her mission was recorded in a brief paragraph in the town records:

Whereas Phebe Bowen hath represented and complained to this council that her son John Bowen, who is bound as an apprentice to Mr. Asa Hopkins, had been abused, and that he is not treated as he ought to be, [it] is thereof Voted and Resolved that it be recommended to John Dorrance and Theodore Foster, Two of the Justices of the Peace, to attend to the said Complaint, to examine the circumstances, and do what shall appear to be Right thereon.[32]

Apparently the cruelty was not sufficiently blatant to justify nullifying the apprenticeship. Nine months later, John Thomas was still with Hopkins.[33]

Phebe did not contact the council regarding Betsy or Polly. The absence of an appeal suggests that the girls' employers were not unusually demanding or harsh. The Allens, Betsy's master and mistress, were a married couple in their mid-twenties.[34] Samuel had begun his career as a second lieutenant on the sloop *America*, one of the many privateers fitted out in Rhode Island to prey on British merchant ships during the Revolutionary War.[35] By the 1790s, he owned a share in most of the trading vessels he commanded.[36]

His wife, Charlotte, captained their household when he was away at sea. Betsy would have assisted her with housekeeping tasks: the Monday laundry; the Tuesday ironing; the daily cooking, baking, mopping, sweeping, and dusting.[37] She would have helped with chores such as jelly and candle making, and, if the Allens owned a cow, learned to milk, churn butter, and make cheese.[38]

In quieter moments, Charlotte would have shown Betsy how to sew, mend, and spin—at least whatever Phebe, with her carefully guarded thimble, had not already taught her of these essential tasks. Girls of all classes were expected to master plain sewing (i.e., simple stitching and mending, as distinguished from embroidery and other decorative needlework). Seven- to ten-year-olds sewed bed and table linens and more complex items such as nightcaps and shirts.[39] In addition, they learned to spin wool and flax into yarn that would be used to make woolen and linen cloth.[40]

But probably Betsy's primary duty was child care. As the Allens' year-old son James began to crawl and then walk, she must have spent much of her time running after him, keeping him away from the beckoning flames in the fireplaces once the New England autumn set in. If Charlotte paid calls on friends, Betsy would have accompanied her, carrying the child.[41]

How much freedom she was allowed would have depended on her mistress. Some women had a near-motherly solicitude for the indentured girls they employed. Seventeen-year-old Harriet Trumbull of Lebanon, Connecticut, wrote to her mother in 1801: "I am very glad you have got a little girl, as I think attending to and teaching her will be a great amusement to you, I hope she will prove very good, and of great use to you, both now and when she grows older, I long to see her and teach her to read and work."[42]

Elizabeth Drinker of Philadelphia, a wealthy Quaker, also took care in bringing up the children bound out to her family.[43] She was devastated when one of them, Sally Brant, became pregnant, subsequently bearing a short-lived child before her indenture expired. Of Sally's mother she wrote, "poor Woman, my heart aches for her."[44] But ultimately there was always the tension of a class difference, a recognition that the girls were there to serve and indulgence could only go so far. In 1806 Drinker sounded a critical note when writing of a thirteen-year-old girl who was bound to her: "Rose's father called to see her forenoon. I gave him but a poor account of her, wish'd it could be better, her Sister Mary came in the Afternoon – Rose is no changeling."[45]

The specifics of Betsy's interactions with her mistress are lost. But living in the same household as those she served, in an atmosphere full of unspoken boundaries, she would have been conscious of how much her place in the world differed from that of her mistress Charlotte.

3

A DEATH IN
THE FAMILY

"Thursday evening last John Bowen, a seafaring man of this Town, being in a small fishing Sloop off the Harbour of Newport, was knocked overboard by the Boom, and drowned."[1] The passing of Betsy's father on May 18, 1786, six weeks after her eleventh birthday, merited but a single sentence in the *Providence Gazette and Country Journal*.

John's body was returned to Providence for burial. His assets were so negligible that the town supplied a sheet for a shroud, candles for the night watch, and an undertaker to inter the corpse.[2] Item: Seven shillings for digging the grave. Item: Three shillings sixpence for use of a horse and carriage. Item: Three shillings for attending the funeral. For a total of thirteen shillings and sixpence, duly paid by the town, the body of John Bowen was committed to the earth.[3]

Phebe's right to remain in Providence after her husband's death was questioned a few years later, when she embarked on a new relationship with a widower named Jonathan Clark. A cobbler by trade, Clark was born in Weymouth, Massachusetts, and apprenticed in nearby Dorchester.[4] After serving briefly in the Continental Army, he had settled in Boston and fathered six children.[5] He had no claim to be a citizen of Providence.[6]

The town council examined him twice about his residency in 1790. At the second hearing, in May, he claimed that he had married Phebe.[7] But if he had hoped this would give him the right to stay in Rhode Island, he was disappointed; a wife's residency was determined by that of her husband. The Clarks were ordered confined until the town sergeant could send them to Boston, deemed Jonathan's last place of legal settlement.[8] On June 30 the town constable hunted down "Phebee Clarke" and conducted her to the cage (secured area) of the workhouse.[9]

This was the beginning of a cat-and-mouse game between Phebe, Jonathan, and the municipal authorities. The couple would be warned out, sneak back in, be caught and incarcerated briefly. Then the process would repeat itself.[10] On October 12, 1790, a wedding was recorded in the register of King's Church in Providence: "Jonathan Clark and Phebe Bowen, married by Rev. Moses Badger."[11] Clark's earlier claim of having married Phebe had been an improvisation, designed to give the town council a good impression.

During the first half of the 1790s, the Clarks sojourned briefly in at least four Massachusetts towns: Rehoboth, Taunton, North Brookfield, and Rutland, none more than fifty miles from Providence.[12] With Phebe's children living in Rhode Island's capital, they never wandered too far away.[13] In 1797 they attempted yet again to reestablish themselves in Providence, but were given three hours to depart.[14] Now, for the first time, they left New England. By May 1798, they were in Williamston, North Carolina, paying $3.33 a month to rent a house.[15]

Life remained a hand-to-mouth affair, and Phebe and Jonathan soon became embroiled in a dispute with their landlord. Polly Bowen, living with her mother and stepfather—at twenty-six, she was eight years past the likely completion of her indenture—drew up a list of "goods and clothing rob'd & stolen from me by Edward Griffin & Co., on July 4th, 1798."[16] Her belongings may have been seized to cover back rent. In September 1798, Jonathan Clark and a man named Stephen Fagan went to court to settle a quarrel over land.[17]

Clark lost, and he and Phebe appealed. But before the case could be reheard during the December term, husband and wife were dead, victims of a yellow-fever epidemic that was sweeping the eastern seaboard.[18] John Thomas Bowen may have perished with them; he was said decades later to have "died in the south of fever" when still "young and unmarried."[19] He would have been twenty-nine years old. Phebe was only in her early forties at the time of her death.

Presumably Polly arranged for Phebe and Jonathan's burial, and maybe John Thomas's as well. Was Betsy in North Carolina to mourn them with her? The question of how she passed her early adulthood would be examined three-quarters of a century later in bitterly fought courtroom battles. For the moment, we will pass over the crucial years in silence and turn to her future husband, an ocean away. Like Betsy Bowen, Stephen Jumel grew up in a world on the brink of revolutionary change.

4

THE MAKING OF
A MERCHANT

*I*n eighteenth-century France, rivers were destiny. Mont-de-Marsan, where Stephen Jumel was born in 1765, owed its prosperity to three of them. On a map, the city looked like a westward-pointing thumb. The river Douze ran west along the north border of the thumb; then doubled back on itself, encircling the outer edge of the thumbnail. The southern border of the thumb was formed by the westward-flowing Midou. On the southern edge of the digit, just where the fleshy part of the thumb ended and the nail began, the Midou joined the Douze to form the Midouze.

As rivers go, the Midouze was modest. Shallow and sandy, it was nearly unnavigable during the driest weeks of summer. But most of the year, flat-bottomed barges floated southwestward down the Midouze to its junction with the Adour River, then continued southwest on the Adour to bustling Bayonne, an Atlantic seaport near France's border with Spain.[1]

The riverine highway made Mont-de-Marsan a transit hub. Goods from the surrounding regions of southwest France were assembled and shipped onward to the coast. Wool came from sheep that grazed the heather-covered moors to the northwest. Pine plantations supplied pitch, tar, turpentine, and wood. Bags of grain were loaded onto the barges too: millet, barley, sorghum, rye, and corn—crops tolerant of the poor, dry soil. The southeast supplied brandy, especially the prized Armagnac that bore the name of the area from whence it came. From even farther east, the broadcloth of Toulouse was sent to Mont-de-Marsan and passed down the Midouze to Bayonne.[2] Little favored by nature, barren of industry, Mont-de-Marsan was dependent on trade.

From the time Stephen Jumel was old enough to explore his hometown, he would have made a beeline for the hum of activity near the docks. There a young boy could immerse himself in the hubbub of commerce—dart among sweating porters hauling barrels and sacks, beg a ride from one of the boatmen poling barges and rafts, or eavesdrop on prosperous merchants supervising the arrival of cargoes.

The port was only about a ten-minute walk from home, an easy adventure for an active child. Stephen's family lived at 16, rue du Bourg, the main street of the commercial quarter of Mont-de-Marsan.[3] Located south of the so-called old city, which was nestled inside the thumb formed by the Douze and Midou, the rapidly growing *bourg*, or commercial sector, contained shops, craftsmen's workshops, and the lively port. There were also warehouses, merchant's houses, and humbler residences—the homes of artisans, boatmen, and tradesmen.

Stephen's family had deep roots in this mercantile economy. His paternal grandfather kept an inn, invested in land, and traded in salt, cereal grains, and cloth—activities continued by Stephen's paternal uncle.[4] His maternal grandfather was a tailor who had his own shop.[5]

Stephen's parents, also shopkeepers, owned and operated a *droguerie*.[6] Literally, the word means "drugstore"—but there is no exact modern equivalent of an eighteenth-century *droguerie*. It was a store that carried a broad range of imported products that fell into two basic categories: drugs (the raw ingredients for medications prepared by pharmacists or doctors) and chemicals (organic and inorganic products used in the craft industries, especially by dyers and furniture makers).[7]

The Jumels' *droguerie* would have been a treasury of products from around the world: exotic items that were funneled into Bayonne, hauled up the Midouze on barges tugged by oxen and men, and tucked into every nook and cranny. Carpenters could have found isinglass (fish gelatin used to make glue) and lac (secreted by insects in India) to dissolve in alcohol to produce shellac. For dyers the Jumels would have stocked a range of West Indian woods: brazilwood for rich reds; fustic for a gamut of yellows; logwood for purples, grays, and blacks.[8]

The selection of drugs would have been even more extensive. Since eighteenth-century doctors could do little but try to expel disease, the range of purgatives was staggering. From China came gnarled, yellow pieces of rhubarb. From the West Indies, castor beans, mottled and striped. From Mexico, jalap root, riddled with resinous veins. From Lebanon, senna leaves, pointed like a lance. If a purgative didn't work, there were always expectorants—most important, ipecac from the Americas, its varieties distinguished by the color and striations of their roots.

The rich and pungent scent of the shop would have been among Stephen's earliest memories. His family lived in the building that housed the store.[9] Stephen's father, Dominique Jumel, and his mother, Jeanne Sonier, married on November 22, 1759.[10] Dominique was thirty and Jeanne, twenty-two. Their first child, François, was born a year later, on November 26, 1760. A daughter, Madelaine, arrived a year and a half after François, on May 13, 1762. Stephen, the last born, joined the family three years later, on May 7, 1765.[11] Named Étienne after his father's brother, he adopted the name Stephen—the English equivalent—after moving to the United States.[12]

Stephen's first language would have been Gascon, a dialect that was the spoken language of southwest France. Soon he would have absorbed French as well—the written language and the tongue spoken in school.[13] Charity schools offered poor children the bare rudiments of literacy, but as shopkeepers, several steps up the social ladder, Stephen's parents could have afforded to send him to a school-master, beginning around the age of six. Together with his brother and sister, and probably neighbors' children as well, he would have learned his catechism and how "to read, write, and count."[14]

He would have spent happy hours running about the countryside, too. A year before Stephen's birth, Dominique Jumel had inherited a farm from his father, François.[15] Located in the parish of Parentis, about four miles north of Mont-de-Marsan, it would have been oper-ated by tenants. However, Stephen must have paid frequent visits. As an adult he proved expert at managing a country estate—planting a vineyard, raising sheep, even preparing poultry feathers to make a mattress—surely skills he absorbed in his youth.[16]

He received another education while helping out in the shop. By the time Stephen reached his teens, he would have come to recognize the products sold in the store—their colors, shapes, sizes, textures, and smells. His parents would have taught him to keep daily jour-nals of sales and inventory, assess the quality of products and avoid fraudulent merchandise, build relationships with customers, and dis-play stock to boost sales.[17]

While the young Stephen was assisting his parents, his older brother François was launched on the world. At sixteen François journeyed to Bordeaux, about ninety miles northwest of Mont-de-Marsan. There he embarked on the ship *Le Triton* for Saint-Domingue, France's richest colony.[18] The world's largest producer of sugar and coffee, thanks to the backbreaking labor of four hunded thousand slaves, Saint-Domingue (today's Haiti) was the promised land for ambitious young Frenchmen who hoped to acquire property and riches.[19]

Yet much of the best land was already in private hands by the third quarter of the eighteenth century. Increasingly, new arrivals became and remained struggling *petits blancs* (little whites), as the slaves termed poor and landless white Europeans.[20] François, how-ever, had a leg up on the competition. He would be joining rela-tives already established on the island. His maternal uncle, Jacques Sonier, had married into the Sterlin family, whose members owned land in Saint-Domingue. As a result of his union with Angelique-Geneviève Sterlin, Sonier possessed five coffee plantations in the island's Northern Province.[21]

The Jumels' oldest son would help his childless uncle and aunt manage their properties. Their plantations were small, but if François were hardworking and kept an eye out for opportunities, he would be able to acquire additional land of his own.[22]

Having settled their eldest son on the path to a livelihood, Dominique and Jeanne Jumel turned their attention to their youngest child. They would send Stephen, like François, to busy Bordeaux, but unlike his brother, not onward to the West Indies. Instead, Stephen would be prepared for a mercantile career in Bordeaux itself, a city whose lifeblood was commerce.

In all likelihood Stephen set out for the city around 1781, when he was sixteen years old, a typical age for apprenticeship as a merchant and the same age at which his brother began his career.[23] By then the "port of the moon"—as Bordeaux was called, after the crescent-shaped bend in the Garonne River that formed its harbor—already deserved the title of "the most beautiful city in France" bestowed on it by the novelist Stendhal a half century later.[24] Along the curving right bank of the Garonne, grand stone buildings with unified façades overlooked the busy quays. In the center of the arc, two commanding edifices flanking the Place Royale reflected the city's priorities: on one side, the stock exchange; on the other, the Hôtel des Fermes, where taxes and customs duties were collected.

The river in front of them was "so crowded with vessels of different nations" that it looked like a forest in perpetual motion. Small boats darted here and there, and flags snapped in the breeze—Russian, Prussian, and Swedish; Spanish, English, and American. On the quays, teams of enormous oxen dragged sledges piled with wine barrels.[25] The casks would be loaded onto waiting ships.

Stephen's life was centered on the commercial quarter known as the Chartreux, named after the local convent of the Chartreux (in English, Carthusians). The neighborhood's wealthiest merchants lived in tall mansions fronting on the Garonne, while the port's supporting players—boatmen, coopers, carpenters, and stevedores—resided in the medieval streets behind.[26] Regardless of who lived aboveground, vaults beneath every house were stacked with wine casks, the buried treasure from which Bordeaux fortunes were made.

By the summer of 1789, Stephen was working for d'Egmont frères, a firm of merchants headquartered on the prestigious Quai des Chartrons, at the corner of the rue Denise. A pocket-sized, leather-bound notebook survives, in which he recorded the number of wine barrels removed from wine cellars and the clients to whom they were delivered.[27] Surnames that can be identified suggest that the firm had contacts at the highest levels. "Texié" was probably Pierre Texier, an immensely successful French Protestant ship owner; "Laffargue," the merchant Pierre Laffargue; and "Brun," the merchant Mathias-Basile Brun—all epitomizing the most elevated echelons of mercantile Bordeaux. The aristocracy is represented with "de Pontac"—probably the marquis de Pontac—and the army with references to the cavalry, artillery, and engineers. A list of churches suggests that clerical Bordeaux also did business with d'Egmont frères.

Stephen may have been in business for himself already, aside from his work for the d'Egmont firm. "Remov[ed] eight barrels from my wine cellar," he noted after a client's name on July 30, 1789. In other words, the vintage belonging to this client of d'Egmont frères had been stored in a cellar that Stephen owned.

Although it seemed that Stephen was safely on track to a successful career in Bordeaux, the city would soon grow less hospitable to merchants. In 1789 France was a pressure cooker, bubbling with political turmoil and social unrest. The crown was all but bankrupt after endless dynastic wars and costly support for the American Revolution. The peasantry was sinking ever deeper beneath catastrophically high taxes, while the nobility, lightly taxed, refused to pay more. Unable to achieve fiscal reform, Louis XVI resorted to desperate measures. He summoned the Estates General, a consultative body that hadn't met since the seventeenth century, in the hope that it would rubberstamp, and thus legitimize, the financial restructuring he had been unable to accomplish.

The Estates General turned out to have a mind of its own. Although the three estates were supposed to meet separately, some nobles (members of the First Estate) and clergymen (belonging to the Second Estate) broke ranks and joined the Third (representing everyone else). After being banished from their meeting room for the breach of protocol, the renegade representatives gathered beneath the high roof of the cavernous indoor tennis court at Versailles. There, on June 20, 1789, they vowed not to disband before establishing a constitution for France. The French Revolution had begun.

A partially illegible line, faded with age and abrasion, is written on the last page of Stephen's notebook. In the brief memorandum, the young businessman recorded that a display of lights took place at Bordeaux on July 1, 2, and 3, in honor of the royal audience that Louis XVI gave (grudgingly) to the rebellious Estates General on June 23. The presence of this notation, in an otherwise businesslike notebook, testifies that Stephen recognized the momentous nature of the event.

Probably it pleased him. Urban professionals, including merchants, lawyers, bankers, and doctors, were early supporters of the Revolution. Moderate in their political opinions, they were interested not in overthrowing French society, but in sensible economic reform. It was no accident that France's Declaration of the Rights of the Man and Citizen, proclaimed on August 26, 1789, guaranteed "life, liberty, and property," rather than the more idealistic American triad, "life, liberty, and the pursuit of happiness."

Stephen may have joined Bordeaux's National Guard, which was founded on July 20, 1789, under the rousing name of the *Armée Patriotique*. It enrolled as many as twelve thousand volunteers—chiefly educated and prosperous men—in its first twenty-four hours of existence.[28] On August 13, Stephen jotted down in his notebook a list of supplies needed for making a drum (two goatskins, wood for drumsticks, etc.), appending prices after a few of the items. The finished product would have been the sort of instrument popular at patriotic festivals during which the National Guard paraded proudly.

⸻

If the early days of the Revolution promised rational and measured change to members of the professional classes, there were intimations that violence lurked beneath the surface. Bread shortages caused by the dismal harvest of 1788 sparked riots in the summer and fall of 1789. Aristocrats, nervous, began to emigrate. On October 5, a turbulent crowd of Parisian market women marched on Versailles, demanding bread. That night they invaded the palace through an unlocked gate, threatened the life of the queen, and demanded the king's return to the capital, where the National Assembly was attempting to remake France. The next day the unruly mob escorted the royal family willy-nilly to Paris. There on October 10, Louis XVI, King of France, was renamed King of the French. The people had found its voice.

Over the next two years, change accelerated. Class distinctions were attacked, and threats to the very existence of the monarchy grew. The property of the Catholic Church was nationalized on November 2, 1789. Hereditary aristocratic titles were abolished eight months later. On September 14, 1791, King Louis XVI was forced to accept a constitution.

Across the ocean in Saint-Domingue, slaves inspired by the talk of *liberté* began a revolution that led to the founding of the country of Haiti. Jacques Sonier, Stephen's uncle, died just before or during the massacres that marked the first months of the rebellion, and his widow, with Stephen's brother, François, fled back to France in 1792.[29] They returned to yet more chaos. The French monarchy was abolished in September, and the king went to the guillotine on January 21, 1793. By fall, dozens of guillotines were casting their shadows over France. Masterminded by the radicals known as the Jacobins, the Reign of Terror had begun.

Growing extremism in Bordeaux paralleled that on the national stage. In September 1793 the city's municipal council, run by merchants and lawyers, was forced from power by a mob.[30] On October 17 "representatives of the people," sent by the Jacobin-dominated National Convention now ruling France, arrived in Bordeaux and brought the Terror with them.[31] The have-nots (or sansculottes, literally, "those without breeches"—workers and peasants who wore loose trousers instead of breeches of silk or satin) at last had their chance to rule. In these leveling times, any citizen with money or power fell under suspicion. Merchants became "enemies of equality" and commerce "usurious, monarchial, and anti-revolutionary."[32] A guillotine was erected on Bordeaux's patriotically named Place Nationale (today's Place Gambetta). Efficiently it removed 301 heads before the Terror ended with the overthrow of its prime mover, radical legislator and orator Maximilien Robespierre, in Paris on July 31, 1794.[33]

Stephen Jumel did not hear the ominous drumbeats announcing the executions nor the thump of the steel blade as it fell. After October 12, 1789, the entries in his notebook break off abruptly. He had left Bordeaux, and probably France as well; he did not attend his sister's November 24, 1790, marriage in Mont-de-Marsan.[34] By 1795 he was established in the United States.

TRANSITIONS

On May 1, 1795, New York City was on the march. By tradition, leases of property in the metropolis expired on April 30. The ritual that followed amazed foreign visitors:

> As the inhabitants in general love variety, and seldom reside in the same house for two consecutive years; those who have to change, which appears to be nearly the whole city, must be all removed together. Hence, from the peep of day till twilight, may be seen carts, which go at a rate of speed astonishingly rapid, laden with furniture of every kind, racing up and down the city, as if its inhabitants were flying from pestilence, pursued by death with his broad scythe just ready to mow them into eternity.[1]

Even an entire house might be moved when a lot lease expired. With a wheel tucked under each corner and furniture inside, the whole would be dragged away by sweating horses.[2] Annually the city convulsed on May 1 and then returned to normality.

When the dust settled in the early summer of 1795, New York was revealed to have a new resident: "Jummel, merchant, 44 Reed."[3] In afteryears, Stephen's English would be fluent enough to ensure that the clerks had the correct spelling of his surname when the data for the directory were compiled. Pronunciation was another matter. In French the two syllables of the name are given equal weight (jyu-mel), and the first consonant is pronounced more like the *s* in "pleasure" or "vision" than an English *j*. Probably, though, most Americans pronounced it in the same way that it is Anglicized today, with a longer, heavily stressed second syllable (ju-mell´). Indeed, in shipping reports in early nineteenth-century newspapers, the name is occasionally misspelled "Jumell," suggesting the currency of this pronunciation.

Reed (later Reade) Street, the inexpensive neighborhood where Stephen settled, was on the uppermost border of the built-up area of New York City, just north of today's city hall. House numbers were not assigned to the street until 1794, and even then much of the land to its north was still occupied by a patchwork of farms. The city hospital and a military barracks were nearby—purposefully isolated on the outskirts of the city. Stephen's neighbors were mainly day laborers and cartmen—the Teamsters of the day, each supplying his own single-horse cart.[4] Reed Street sheltered modestly paid artisans as well, including house painters, masons, and carpenters.[5]

At number 44 Stephen joined two other newcomers to New York whose names suggest that they were also of French origin. Merchant John Pichon arrived first at 44 Reed, appearing in the city directory in 1794, followed in 1795 by Stephen Jumel and a surgeon named Rennet Lisbeaupin (probably a misspelling of "René Lesbeaupin").[6] All three moved on in 1796, Stephen to successively more fashionable addresses. There was no better decade than the 1790s in which to launch a career as a merchant in the United States.

The commercial opportunities that Stephen would exploit were the direct results of the revolution he had fled. Crowned heads across Europe, trembling at the sight of an absolute monarch dethroned, were willing to fight to restore a king to France and prevent the infection of revolution from spreading beyond its borders. By 1793 the young French Republic was at war with Austria, Prussia, Great Britain, the Netherlands, Spain, Portugal, Sardinia, and the Kingdom of the Two Sicilies (Naples and Sicily). England and France preyed on each other's merchant fleets, seizing vessels plying the trade routes to and from their respective colonies in the Caribbean.

Neutral nations—including Denmark, Sweden, and above all the United States—became the key players in keeping transatlantic commerce alive.[7] During the French Revolutionary Wars and Napoleonic campaigns that followed, the belligerents traded with their possessions largely through the intermediary of American shippers, who profited handsomely. The value of exports from New York rose dramatically, from $2.5 million in 1792 to $26.3 million in 1807.[8] It was a good time to be an American. On May 29, 1797, Stephen Jumel became a citizen of the young United States.[9]

6

REINVENTION

*D*uring Stephen's early years in business, migrants continued to stream unstoppably into New York. Between 1790
and 1800, the city nearly doubled in size, ballooning from thirty-
three thousand to sixty thousand residents.[1] Just keeping track of
them all was a challenge. "The increasing population of our city,
with the passion for removal on May-day, render the annual publication of a directory absolutely essential," opined the *Daily Advertiser*.[2]

David Longworth was happy to fill the need. By the beginning of
July 1803, the latest edition of his *American Almanac and New-York
Register* was rolling off the presses.[3] Page ninety-eight contained the
following line: "Brown, Eliza, 87 Reed."[4] Betsy Bowen of Providence, Rhode Island, had become Eliza Brown of New York City.

The transition from Betsy to Eliza marked the start of a new
phase in life for the twenty-eight-year-old woman from Providence. In eighteenth- and nineteenth-century novels, changing one's
name was an act of reinvention, celebrating the start of a new, self-
fashioned existence.[5] American women embraced the fictional practice in real life. To women of the early nineteenth century, whether
they worked for a living or were comfortably middle class, the lilting
"Eliza" and Italianate "Maria" seemed more elegant than the sen-

sible "Betsy" or "Mary."⁶ Contemporaries noticed that even poor girls who staffed the lowest class of brothels adopted refined sobriquets; they were "almost all 'Ann Eliza's,' 'Ann Maria's,' 'Melissa Matilda's,' &c."⁷

Eliza Brown, as we must call her now, changed her surname as well as her first name. Possibly the shift from "Bowen" to "Brown" was plotted to suggest a relationship with the respected and wealthy Brown brothers of Providence, known for their mercantile success and generous philanthropy. Her city of origin, which she never disguised, could have made a connection with the distinguished Brown family seem plausible.

Eliza's new lodgings were on the same street where Stephen had settled in 1795, soon after his arrival in New York City. Nine years later, more of the surrounding farmland had been built up, but Reed Street remained an inexpensive address, still attracting artisans, cartmen, and laborers. At number 87, Eliza boarded with Sebe and Hannah Brinckerhoff, a couple in their early thirties.⁸ A house carpenter by trade, Sebe speculated in land as well, perhaps developing the properties himself.⁹ He and Hannah were raising four children by the time Eliza joined their household, from eleven-year-old Osselchy (named after Sebe's mother) down to tiny, three-month-old Richard.¹⁰

From the Reed Street address, Eliza had to walk only one block east to reach Broadway, Manhattan's main north–south artery. From there, a five-block stroll south took her to Barclay Street, where she could make a left to skirt the edge of what would soon become City Hall Park—ground was broken for the new city hall on May 27, 1803. If she turned left again almost immediately, she would find herself on Park Row, in front of the handsome Park Theatre, completed in 1798 at a cost of over $130,000.¹¹

From a niche in the building's pediment, a bust of Shakespeare watched over theatergoers passing beneath the arched portico below. Inside, painted cupids fluttered over a high dome, while flickering candles in an immense chandelier created a dramatic play of light and shadow. A blue mohair curtain decorated with a golden lyre hung between faux marble columns on either side of the stage.¹²

Soon Eliza would become familiar with the view from the stage. According to William Dunlap, the Park's general manager until 1805, "She had been a supernum[er]ary [i.e., extra] at the Theatre before Jumel married her."[13] This bare statement is all that we know for certain of Eliza's theatrical career.

What attracted her to the stage? We can only speculate. A drama critic of the day identified the appeal of acting "among the middling ranks of mankind" as "a hope of genteel income and a profusion of public panegyric."[14] Dunlap met many young people with such aspirations. "The frequent applications of *would-be* authors and actors is a source of trouble to all managers," he wrote. "Sometimes the applications are vexatious, sometimes ludicrous."[15] That Eliza made it onto the boards suggests that she showed more promise than the average supplicant. She must have presented herself with poise, moved gracefully, and been quick to learn gestures and stage directions.

At the Park Theatre, she would have been able to admire the "tall and elegant" Elizabeth Johnson, who excelled at depicting tragic heroines and well-born ladies of fashion, and the versatile Frances Hodgkinson, who "surpassed all her contemporaries in rustic comedy and singing parts, in chambermaids and soubrettes." Then there was Charlotte Melmoth, a superb tragedian, although limited to "matronly characters" due to "her unfortunate bulk," and Hodgkinson's mother, Hannah Brett, "a valuable actress of old women and coarse chambermaids." The industrious John Martin could turn his talents to any role, while the handsome and dignified Joseph Tyler "bore away the palms from all competitors" in playing elderly characters requiring an aristocratic bearing."[16] In the theater Eliza would have learned to adopt the manners of the upper classes and transform herself in daily life as thoroughly as if she were playing a new part.

Even as an insignificant extra, she could have attracted admirers who appreciated her oval face and straight nose; the blue eyes that contrasted pleasingly with her dark brown hair; and the trim figure that at five feet, four inches, was neither unpleasingly lanky nor distressingly squab.[17] But her early theatrical employment would leave a lasting blot on her reputation. Actresses were tarred in the court of public opinion because inadequate salaries led some to supplement their incomes with prostitution. Tom Ford, a supernumerary in Boston who gave up his salary to the captain of the extras in return for introductions to attractive ballet girls, was not the only man hanging around the theater who hoped to enjoy more than a theatrical performance.[18] The reputations of women who aspired to the dramatic arts were blighted further by persistence of the notorious "third tier." In a tradition adopted from English theaters, prostitutes populated the uppermost boxes of American playhouses, drawing attention from the stage.[19] By extrapolation, their presence contributed to the raffish reputation of the actors and actresses below.

In spite of the disadvantages it entailed, Eliza's work as a supernumerary hints at important aspects of her character. She was ambitious: what super would not envision herself stepping into the lead? She was bold: she entered into employment most women would shun. She liked attention: throughout her adult life, she favored actions that could bring her public recognition. She was confident: she maintained her enthusiasm for the theater in after years, although it might remind people of what she had been.

Extras were employed irregularly and paid negligible wages—as little as twenty five cents per night as late as 1839—so Eliza must have had an additional source of income.[20] She was supporting both herself and a thirteen-year-old boy. Her young companion, William B. Ballou, was a fellow Rhode Islander, a member of a large clan descended from Maturin Ballou, one of the founders of Rhode Island.[21] William's father, David, a ship carpenter, began to trade with the West Indies after the American Revolution. He was prosperous for a time, owning real estate in North Providence and a store in Pawtucket, Rhode Island. With his wife, Lucy Martin, who came from nearby Rehoboth, Massachusetts, he had eight children, of whom five survived infancy. William, the sixth child, was born on December 6, 1790.[22]

After Lucy died in 1800, David, suffering from business reverses, broke up the household. He left Providence, placing his youngest children with others who would raise them.[23] Eliza took on William's care.[24] As a single woman, she was a curious choice of caretaker. It is worth speculating whether she might have tended the boy when he was an infant. In 1789, when Eliza was fourteen, her mistress Charlotte Allen died.[25] Bound-out girls were removed from a household if there wasn't a woman to supervise them, so Eliza would have been placed elsewhere after Samuel Allen was widowed.[26] If she had worked in David Ballou's household and cared for young William, she would have been a plausible person to turn to later, when the boy needed a home after his mother died. Perhaps she was given money to care for him. She could have earned extra money doing housework or child care, conceivably assisting Hannah Brinckerhoff in exchange for her lodging. If so, her nights on the stage would have offered a respite from the drudgery. Once she entered the door of the theater, she could dream of a more brilliant future.

MARRIAGE

*M*aybe it began with a visit to the theater, Stephen's attention caught by an attractive face paired with sharply intelligent eyes. "Connections formed on the Stage sometimes enable those to become independent, who, if they had been left to the reward of their own abilities, must have pined in want."[1] More likely Reed Street was the link between the two—Stephen visiting a former neighbor, finding Eliza there chatting or taking tea.[2] Whatever the origin, the acquaintance flourished.

By the beginning of January 1804, Stephen had begun to employ a manservant to shave him and dress his hair.[3] The need for a valet—as well a purchase of hair powder a few years later—suggests that he wore his dark locks powdered, a convention that persisted among upper-middle-class Americans into the first decade of the nineteenth century.[4] Was Stephen paying more attention to his appearance because there was a woman in his life? At the beginning of February, he spent an extravagant thirty-five dollars on a "lady's pelisse" (the term referred to a coat or cloak, sometimes trimmed or lined with fur).*[5] Eliza's name appears for the first time in his

---

* By comparison, Stephen would rent an entire house for just under twenty-three dollars a month in May 1804.

papers a month later. In early March, he engaged two tutors, one for her and one for William Ballou. Each received three months of tuition in French.[6]

Monday, April 2, 1804, was Eliza's twenty-ninth birthday. One week later, on "a fine mild day," she and thirty-eight-year-old Stephen were united in a Catholic ceremony.[7] (Like most Frenchmen of the period, Stephen was Catholic. Eliza was not; her parents were married in the Congregational Church.) Father William W. O'Brien, pastor of Manhattan's only Roman Catholic church, officiated.

Writing in Latin, he penned the marriage certificate of "Stephanus Jumell" and "Elizabethum Browne":

> To all readers of this notice:
>
> Greetings in the Lord
>
> I, enfranchised Catholic apostolic priest, pastor, and rector of the Church of St. Peter the Apostle, by these present notify and witness to all, on this day, the 9th of April 1804, have joined in matrimony Stephen Jumel and Elizabeth Brown. The witnesses present were Blasius Philip Lapeyre and William B. Bellow [*sic*]. In this fact I have fixed by hand the proper sign and seal.[8]

In spite of this sober certificate, a highly colored narrative about the genesis of the marriage has become one of the most enduring stories told of Eliza. It is first recorded in a rambling letter that a prominent New Yorker named John Pintard wrote in 1821. Gossiping to his oldest daughter about the couple, Pintard stirred in a juicy piece of scandal:

> Stephen Jumel was a French merchant who came to this country at the earliest stage of the French Revolution. It was said that he had been a priest. At any rate he was successful in commerce . . . M[rs] J . . . was his *chere* [*sic*] *amie* [i.e., mistress]. In a fit of illness, w[hic]h she was adroit eno[ugh] to consider her last, she c[oul]d not die in peace until she was lawfully married. To quiet her conscience Jumel married her & Madam recovered, & made him a good wife.[9]

The anecdote has the flavor of a scene from a melodrama. A director might stage it something like this:

Eliza is on her deathbed, restless and pale, muttering a few broken words. Stephen, at the bedside, leans over to hear her. She clutches his hand feverishly, almost deliriously; a fixation has her in its grasp: "If you ever loved me, let me die a wife, not a mistress. If you ever loved me . . ." She repeats the same words over and over.

What harm could it do? Stephen calls a clergyman. In the candlelit bedchamber, the priest performs the ceremony. Eliza is propped up against the pillows, barely able to whisper her vows. After the ceremony is completed, Stephen tucks the covers around her. He sits by the bedside until she falls into a troubled sleep.

The next morning, Eliza wakes and stretches. Her cheeks blush with natural color. The new Mrs. Jumel is on the mend.

How seriously should we take Pintard's story? Certainly a healthy dose of skepticism is indicated. The fact that Stephen began paying for French lessons for Eliza and William a month before the marriage suggests that he had a long-term relationship in mind. The timing of the ceremony, precisely a week after Eliza's birthday, also suggests premeditation.

Yet it is unlikely that Pintard invented the anecdote from scratch; rather, he was retelling a good story. Throughout the letter, he mixed firsthand knowledge with tittle-tattle. For instance, he wrote that Stephen participated in an attempt to found a Roman Catholic convent in New York. This was indeed a project with which Stephen was involved; he sold the founders land for the institution.[10] Yet Pintard also threw out the baseless, offhand comment, "It was said that he had been a priest." (The stereotypical American vision of Frenchmen was that they were hairdressers, dancing masters, or clerics.) The anecdote about Stephen and Eliza's marriage should be considered similarly: as a rumor that did not necessarily have any basis in fact.

Nonetheless, it is a valuable indicator. The fact that gossip about Stephen's marriage circulated among well-connected New Yorkers is a sign that his choice of bride violated values and conventions—specifically, rules governing courtship and marriage.[11] Merchants typically married daughters of fellow merchants, or the offspring of professional men or gentlemen of leisure. But no one knew where Eliza had come from or who her family was. Worse, some New Yorkers must have recognized her face from her appearances on the stage. They would have whispered to others that Stephen had married an actress, a woman with no assets but her appearance. She was "pretty but not very handsome," Pintard wrote some years later, implying that her attractiveness could not have been expected to outlive her youth.[12] It was something a man was unlikely to say except about a woman whose social status was far below his own.

Gossip might have grown not just from the inequality of the marriage, but also from its quiet nature. The Jumels married at home—whether at his residence or hers is not recorded.[13] That in itself was not unusual; many marriages were performed privately at the domicile of the bride and her family.[14] But typically a small group of relatives and close friends would attend. Afterward they would enjoy a dessert, tea party, or festive meal, even though preparations were not elaborate, since a wedding might take place as little as a week after the engagement.[15]

There is no indication that friends were invited to celebrate the Jumels' marriage. William Ballou was one of the witnesses, which was certainly appropriate, given his close connection to Eliza. Although Stephen had no relatives in the United States, he could have invited a friend or business associate to support him. Instead, the second name on the certificate is that of an unknown—Blasius Philip Lapeyre. The name Lapeyre does not appear in the New York City directories before, during, or after this period, even when variant spellings are considered. Nor is there any reference to such a person in American newspapers or genealogical records.[16] The most likely assumption is that he was a servant who worked for Stephen transiently and then moved on.

If Eliza's landlords, the Brinckerhoffs, or any of Stephen's acquaintances had attended the ceremony, there would have been no need to call in a domestic as witness. Nevertheless, it is unnecessary and indeed, implausible, to assume that a dramatic ruse on Eliza's part accounts for their apparent absence. More probably the two were already living together and weren't anxious to advertise a ceremony that followed rather than preceded cohabitation. The French lessons Stephen was subsidizing in advance of the ceremony, not just for Eliza but William as well, are suggestive of an intimate, ongoing association.

When Eliza's French tutor visited Stephen's counting house in early June 1804 to collect his fee, he referred to her as "Miss Brown" rather than Mrs. Jumel, suggesting that she and Stephen had not publicized her change in status.[17] But as word leaked out, the marriage of a successful merchant to a young woman of unknown antecedents must have led to speculation. Iniquitous rumors like the one Pintard reported could have been generated to explain a seemingly inexplicable event. Alternately, since the story is not recorded until Pintard tells it in 1821, it might have sprung up years after the marriage, at a moment when Eliza was attracting censorious attention for living apart from her husband.

Broadly speaking, the yarn reverses the popular fictional device of a fortune hunter tricking an innocent girl into marriage. Eliza is placed in the man's role, deceiving the credulous Stephen. The story could have been inspired by Eliza Haywood's widely read novel, *The History of Miss Betsy Thoughtless* (1751), which features a deathbed ceremony followed by the instant recovery of the male suitor who perpetrated the fraud.[18] Someone who disapproved of Eliza might have inverted the scene from the novel to stigmatize her. She became the deceiver; Stephen the deceived.

Regardless of what the world thought of their union, Eliza could take pleasure in becoming a woman of means. The marriage was an extraordinary step upward in social status for someone who had lived in a workhouse and labored as a domestic servant. Children like Eliza who were bound to service because their parents were unable or unfitted to support them were at high risk of becoming poor transients as adults. Up to 40 percent of persons warned out of Rhode Island towns in the second half of the eighteenth century had been bound out in their youth by the overseers of the poor.[19] In eighteenth-century Pennsylvania, 84 out of a group of 110 indentured servants—more than three-quarters—needed public assistance at least once during the thirty years after completing their service.[20]

Scattered anecdotal reports about women apprenticed as servants in their youth suggest that they led modest and often difficult adult lives. Among the women who had been bound to Elizabeth Drinker of Philadelphia in childhood, at least two were impoverished in later years and a third married a blacksmith who didn't always have stable employment.[21] A fourth, Sally Brant—the girl who had borne an illegitimate child while serving out her indenture—later married but did not have an easy life, judging from Drinker's subsequent references to her (in 1803, "poor Sall, she has her troubles," and in 1806, "poor girl she has enough to do").[22] A grimmer example was an orphan girl bound out in Pennsylvania in 1759 who wasn't even taught to read and write, although she had been promised those skills as part of the indenture. By the end of her service, a clergyman wrote, she had "been so completely debauched that she prefer[red] to remain with her mistress" and was "satisfied with her brutish life."[23] In Providence, Rhode Island, the town councilors complained that bound-out girls were "entice[d] away" from their masters into prostitution, "to the great injury of themselves and their employers."[24]

That virtually no eighteenth-century American women indentured in childhood have entered the historical record is a reflection of the difficulty they would have had in achieving the literacy necessary to leave memoirs or the training required to build successful careers. A rare exception is Deborah Sampson, born in Massachusetts in 1760 and bound out at the age of ten, several years after her father deserted the family. After completing her service, she disguised herself as a man to serve in the Continental army during the Revolutionary War. Later she gave lectures about her wartime experiences and became a minor celebrity regionally. But even for her, social mobility was limited. She married a small-town farmer and did not rise above the lower-middle class.[25]

Given the circumstances into which she was born, Eliza's marriage to a wealthy man was strikingly unusual and possibly unique.

8

MRS. JUMEL

*S*oon after the marriage, Stephen purchased a gig—a two-wheeled vehicle pulled by a single horse—from the coach makers Donaldson and Blackgood.[1] The high price of the model Stephen chose—$471—suggests that his conveyance was handsomely finished. Perhaps there were silver- or gilt-plated mounts on the harness, as on a model Donaldson had built a few years earlier.[2]

The purchase was a gesture Eliza would have appreciated. "To the minds of Americans," wrote a visitor to our shores, "that which without exception denotes the greatest superiority is the possession of a carriage. Women especially desire them to a degree that approaches delirium; and a woman who owns one is very certain that no other woman who lacks a carriage will ever be considered, or ever become, her equal."[3] Did a gig count? If not, no matter—soon the couple acquired a larger vehicle.[4]

Eliza was acutely conscious of such markers of status. She made charitable contributions under her own name, even though her money came from Stephen. When the Society for the Relief of Poor Widows with Small Children was soliciting donations in 1810, "Mr. Stephen Jumel" gave ten dollars, but "Mrs. Eliza Jumel" contributed thirty. She was the second-most-generous donor to the campaign.[5]

In 1807 she affiliated herself with the wealthiest and most prominent members of New York society by becoming an Episcopalian. In her decision to adopt a new religion—notably, not the Catholicism of her husband—it's hard to believe that she did not weigh worldly needs in the balance. The Episcopal Church, as the Anglican Church was renamed in the United States after the Revolution, wielded influence far out of proportion to the size of its membership (Episcopalians, Presbyterians, and Congregationalists combined constituted only about 9 percent of the American population.)[6] In the first half of the nineteenth century, 45 percent of U.S. presidents were Episcopalian. So were 39 percent of the Supreme Court justices appointed between 1789 and 1839. Among signers of the Declaration of Independence, 61 percent had belonged to the Anglican Church.[7] As late as 1842, an English visitor to New York commented that "the most respectable part of the citizens attend the Protestant Episcopal churches."[8] For a woman who wanted to be accepted by the establishment, Episcopalianism—rather than Stephen's Catholicism—was the logical choice.

Both Eliza and William Ballou were baptized at Manhattan's Trinity Church.[9] When she attended services, Eliza could worship near the pew that George Washington had occupied and walk in the cemetery that boasted Alexander Hamilton's grave.[10] The church was only a few blocks north of the Jumels' rented house at 5 Beaver Street. It remained within walking distance when they moved south to 28 Whitehall, another rental, in 1808. A niece of Eliza's recalled visiting the couple at the second of the two houses when she was three or four years old. One of the treasures it contained remained vivid in her memory sixty years later: "I remember going there and turning the handle of an organ or musical instrument that, if the crank was simply turned, played tunes."[11]

Stephen, who would prove to be a generous and warmhearted man, took William Ballou into his household and made a place for him in his business. From 1805 onward, William's signature appears occasionally in Stephen's receipt books or letter book, marking occasions when the young man witnessed a transaction or hand-delivered a letter.[12] By 1810, aged nineteen or twenty, William was importing a small amount of "silk goods" himself.[13]

Stephen helped others connected to his wife as well. Eliza's sister, Polly, was living in New York by the turn of the century. Like Eliza, she had updated her name, calling herself Maria Bowne. On September 6, 1801, she had given birth to an illegitimate daughter, Mary Ann Walter Bowne.[14] The inclusion of Walter and the altered spelling of Bowen were significant. Although no one spoke of it publicly until after Mary's death, her father was the merchant Walter Bowne.[15] Born in 1770 of a prominent Quaker family in Flushing (part of New York City's borough of Queens today), he would one day be mayor of New York.[16] His relationship with Maria probably terminated before his 1803 marriage.[17]

In late 1805 Maria was pregnant again, with a child fathered by a man named William Jones. She married Jones on December 19, 1805; their first child, William Ballou Jones, was born four months later.[18] Although his first name was the same as that of his father, his full name suggests a tribute to William Ballou as well. A second child, born January 28, 1808, was named Eliza Jumel Jones, honoring both Eliza and her husband.[19]

Stephen and Eliza assisted the Joneses financially. In May 1809 Stephen paid school tuition for "Mary Jones," Maria's illegitimate child, who was using her stepfather's surname.[20] Mary's half siblings, William and Eliza Jones, and their younger sister, Louisa, born in 1809, were baptized at Trinity Church in September 1810, possibly at their aunt Eliza's prompting.[21] In another indication of the ties between Eliza and her sister's family, William Jones opened a short-lived boardinghouse at 24 Pearl Street in 1812, immediately across the street from Stephen's business premises at 23 Pearl.[22]

Seeing the Jones family growing up around them, Eliza and Stephen may have felt a private sorrow. The years passed, but they had no children. The youngest member of their household, William Bal-lou, moved into rented lodgings, paid for by Stephen, in 1810.[23] Later that year he married a dressmaker's assistant.[24]

It was probably around this time that Eliza and Stephen took her oldest niece, Mary Jones, into their home. By spring 1813 Mary had become "Miss Jumel."[25] They would raise her as their daughter.

BLOOMINGDALE

*T*he Jumels' shared life as a couple remains hazy. According-ing to a narrative written in 1908 by historian Hopper Striker Mott, they socialized with a community of French émigrés established in Bloomingdale. Mott painted a romantic picture of the habitués of this pretty, rural suburb that has since become the Upper West Side of Manhattan. The social center of the community was Chevilly, a house occupied by "Mme. d'Auliffe, *dame d'honneur* to Marie Antoinette," who lived there with her three little daughters.

> Among its constant visitors was the marquis de Cubières, a gal-lant of the vanished court, who was a fine type of the gentleman of the ancient *régime*, though, perhaps, never quite reconciling him-self to the institutions of republican America. He named his horse "Monarque," and, mounted thereon, he might have been seen mak-ing frequent pilgrimages out into the country from his home in Broad Street, to visit his friends at Chevilly. Another welcome guest was Col. August de Singeron who had commanded the Cuirassiers of the Guard at the Tuileries on the fatal Tenth of August.[1]

Diplomats, too, entered the drawing room of Chevilly:

The great Talleyrand was always a welcome arrival. Another Frenchman who at this time made New York his home was the famous General Moreau, the rival of Napoleon in popular favor and the victim of that eminent man's jealousy. The Moreaus lived at 119 Pearl Street . . . We can well imagine he was also a guest at Chevilly, for he had property interests nearby.[2]

Even royal princes frequented this Paris in exile. "When the young duc d'Orléans"—who became in 1830 King Louis-Philippe of France—"and his brothers, the duc de Montpensier and the prince de Beaujolais, came to New York, they soon found their way to Chevilly, where madame and her little circle made the fugitives feel less poignantly the loss of country, rank, home, and kindred, surrounding them with an atmosphere that reminded them of Versailles." The future king "was often actually in need, as were the young princes who accompanied him, and to gain a livelihood taught school during his stay in Bloomingdale."[3]

In these lofty if sometimes purse-pinched circles, "M. Jumel, although not to the manor born, was well received because of his kindliness and the popularity of his famous wife. He owned land in Bloomingdale, on which they lived, the house being located between 77th and 78th Streets on the east side of present Amsterdam Avenue."[4]

This charming picture of aristocratic life in the early republic turns out to be a muddle of epic proportions. The most noble Simon-Louis-Pierre, marquis de Cubières, said to have trotted out into the country from his home on Broad Street, never visited the United States at all.[5] Equally incredibly, Colonel August de Singeron, that brave French officer, was plucked from an 1829 article in a New York literary magazine and set down at Chevilly, which was not mentioned in the original source. In the article, delusively titled "Reminiscences of New-York," he is described improbably as having "turned pastry cook and confectioner" after arriving in the United States, fashioning gilt gingerbread figures of Louis XVI and Marie Antoinette, and marzipan stamped with the façade of the Tuileries Palace.[6] Yet no one named Singeron appears in New York's city directories, as a confectioner or otherwise, during the French Revolutionary or Napoleonic periods. Although an officer named Lavaur, who was a member of Louis XVI's guard, fled to the United States after the August 10, 1792, attack on the Tuileries, he returned to Europe in 1796 and there is no evidence that he worked as a confectioner or visited Chevilly.[7] Possibly his story inspired the creation of the fictional Singeron, whose name may have been a play on the French word for monkey (*singe*), matching his description (or rather, caricature) as a short, red-haired man whose "broad shoulders overshadowed a pair of legs under the common size" and whose "voice was an exaggeration of the usual sharp tones of his nation."[8]

Of the other supposed visitors to Chevilly, only Charles-Maurice de Talleyrand-Périgord, who lived in the United States between April 1794 and June 1796, can be proved to have set foot there.[9] Although he spent much of his time in Philadelphia, he was in New York from June through November 1795 and stayed at Chevilly for several weeks in late April and early May 1796, before he sailed for Europe.[10] Eliza and Stephen couldn't have socialized with him as a couple, however, since they were not married until 1804—nor is there any record of him having met Stephen. Similarly, the visit of the duc d'Orléans and his two brothers to the United States lasted well under two years and occurred long before the Jumels' marriage. Orléans arrived in North America on October 24, 1796, and his brothers, the duc de Montpensier and the comte (not "prince") de Beaujolais, joined him in early February 1797. They used Philadelphia as their base for trips into the American interior, spending only three weeks in New York City.[11] Although they could have stopped in at Chevilly then, there is no proof one way or the other. As for the story of the future king teaching school in New York, it was not recorded until 1875 and proves to be purely imaginary.[12] Louis-Philippe did teach school for eight months to support himself in exile, but that was in Richenau, Switzerland.[13]

Chevilly's hostess, "Mme. d'Auliffe, *dame d'honneur* to Marie Antoinette," was the victim of perhaps the greatest misunderstanding of all. The major French biographical dictionaries, including Michaud's *Biographie universelle* and the *Nouvelle biographie générale* published by Firmen Didot frères, reveal no family bearing the name Auliffe. This is not surprising, since the French refugees settled at Chevilly turn out to have been not the Auliffes but the Olives. The origin of the error must have been a misunderstanding of the name as heard by an American, Olive (pronounced oh-leev in French) being written down incorrectly as Auliffe (oh-leef).

Letters written by Nicholas Olive, a wealthy merchant, to his three daughters from Chevilly in 1800 and 1801 make clear that he and his wife, and not the mythical madame d'Auliffe, were living on the property.[14] Although they welcomed visits from other French émigrés after arriving in the United States in 1793—Olive was a shareholder in Castorland, a settlement in northern New York State founded as a refuge for royalists fleeing the French Revolution—they returned to France in 1802 and could not have been the center of New York's French community during the Jumels' married years.[15] Nor could they have hosted General Jean-Victor-Marie Moreau, who was only in the United States between 1805 and 1813, and didn't settle in New York City until 1808. At least their true identity helps to explain the appearance in the story of the marquis de Cubières, despite his never having visited New York. Olive died shortly after he and his wife returned to their homeland in 1802, and his widow married Cubières in 1805.[16] As the chronology became garbled with the passing of years, he and not she was transplanted to the United States.

In later years the Jumels would socialize with the Cubières family in France, suggesting that Stephen had been on friendly terms with Nicholas Olive in New York and stayed in contact with Olive's widow, the future marquise de Cubières. Thus a tiny nugget of truth was buried beneath the legends. Another kernel of fact underlies the story of the house in Bloomingdale that Eliza and Stephen supposedly inhabited. In fact, they did own land in Bloomingdale briefly, but didn't purchase the six-acre property until 1811, never lived on it themselves, and sold it in 1813.[17]

With Mott's romantic stories removed from the picture, Eliza's life on a day-to-day basis remains shadowy. Only Stephen's business accounts and not the household accounts have survived, and therefore the staffing of the house is unclear, but it is probable that the Jumels had servants who did the cooking and cleaning. At a minimum they employed a coachman by 1812.[18] Eliza and her adopted daughter could drive out together, and she and Stephen could take the carriage on formal occasions. Dressed in her best, she might wear the diamond earrings and pin her husband purchased for her in 1809.[19]

If a new dress was needed, Eliza had a mantua maker visit her home to take her measurements and sew the gown, the typical practice among middle-class women.[20] On Sundays she would attend church, but perhaps not with her husband and daughter. Unlike her step siblings, Mary was never baptized in the Episcopal Church, suggesting that Stephen preferred that his adoptive daughter share his religious affiliation. By 1812 he was renting a pew at the Catholic Church of Saint Peter the Apostle.[21]

Eliza would say many years later that her favorite occupation was reading.[22] Traces of this interest survive in a handful of books from this period that list her as a subscriber (the publication of books in the early nineteenth century was often funded by collecting subscriptions in advance). She appeared on a long roll of men and women (headed by Thomas Jefferson and John Adams) who subscribed to Donald Fraser's *Compendium of the History of All Nations*, which traced the rise and fall of "empires, kingdoms, and states" from the creation of the world to the present.[23] If this acquisition was made for her own edification, she may have had Mary in mind when she subscribed to a second Fraser production: *The Mental Flower Garden: or, An Instructive and Entertaining Companion for the Fair Sex*. This miscellany included "a variety of entertaining and moral Dialogues, partly *original*, calculated for Misses from Eight to Twelve Years."[24] Together Eliza and Mary could have enjoyed the *Mental Flower Garden*'s essays, devotional poems, and "interesting sketches of Female Biography."

For Sabbath reading, Eliza had her issues of the *Churchman's Magazine*, an Episcopal publication designed "to promote the knowledge and the practice of the truths and precepts of Christianity," and an abridged version of John Foxe's *Book of Martyrs*, which immortalized heroes and heroines who had died for their faith.[25] For Mary, Foxe's often-gory narratives could have functioned as Plutarch's *Lives* did for another young girl: "like a long continued fairy story."[26]

The Jumels' adopted daughter received the education of an upper-middle-class girl who would not have to earn her own living. In April 1813 Peter Smith was paid sixteen dollars "for Miss Jumels [*sic*] tuition on the Pianoforte," and he continued to instruct her through the fall of 1814.[27] Mary received painting and drawing lessons, too, in 1814 and early 1815.[28] Nor were social skills neglected. In April 1815 Charles Bérault was paid fifty-four dollars for teaching dancing to "Mademoiselle Marie."[29] Eliza may have sat in on the piano lessons; at some point she acquired a modest competence on the keyboard, an accomplishment expected of genteel women.[30]

The money for these luxuries came from Stephen's shipping business, which flourished during the challenging decade leading up to the War of 1812. During the first dozen years of the nineteenth century, his ships navigated the waters of a world at war.

THE FORTUNES
OF WAR

On May 21, 1804, Stephen's brig *Minerva* docked in New York after a sixty-day passage from Bordeaux.[1] From her berth on the west side of the Old Slip, a visitor could have marveled at the "busy hum" of commerce pervading this "Tyre of the New World." Wharves were "crowded with commodities of every description." "Carts, drays, and wheel-barrows" rattled to and fro. "Hogsheads of sugar, chests of tea, puncheons of rum, and pipes of wine; boxes, cases, packs and packages of all sizes and denominations, were strewed upon the wharfs and landing-places, or upon the docks of the shipping. All was noise and bustle."[2] With her cargo of wine, brandy, dry goods, and oil, the *Minerva* had arrived at one of the busiest ports on earth.

The cheerful bustle belied the dangers that the crew had experienced at sea. The *Minerva* had been boarded three times during her two-month passage: first by a British privateer, then by a French frigate, and finally by a naval schooner, also French, whose crew had commandeered a supply of wine.[3] The probability that the vintage would be paid for was nil, but comparatively speaking, the *Minerva* was lucky. The whaler *Hannah and Eliza* had to return to port because ten of her crew members had been impressed into the British navy.[4]

The *Minerva*'s thrice-disrupted voyage was the norm. France and Britain were at war almost uninterruptedly between 1793 and 1815, and American shippers and sailors were caught in the middle. England tried to prevent France and its allies from exporting goods or importing necessities. France tried to prevent England from doing the same. Neutral vessels (chiefly American) risked seizure by the British if they carried French merchandise and by the French if they carried British goods.[5] Sometimes their crewmen were forced into the British naval service.[6]

Stephen navigated these dangerous waters with flair. With his clerk, Benjamin Desobry, whom he took into a minority partnership at the beginning of 1805, he specialized in the trade between New York and Bordeaux.[7] Between 1793 and 1815, he sent more bottoms to "the port of the moon" than any other American merchant.[8] Even that statistic undercounts his activity, as it excludes shipments he sent in vessels owned by others and cargoes directed to nearby ports—most commonly, San Sebastián, in Spain—when Bordeaux was inaccessible due to British blockades.[9]

Outward bound from New York, Stephen's craft carried foodstuffs and agricultural commodities to Europe. Some of the items came from the United States: cotton and tobacco, beeswax to make candles, and staves for constructing barrels.[10] But products from the Caribbean constituted the bulk of his cargoes: coffee, sugar, cocoa, pepper, and dyewoods such as logwood and fustic.[11] Once purchased by an American merchant, they became, at least on paper, the property of a neutral, with a fighting chance of reaching Europe without being seized on the way.

The profits from these commodities, eagerly awaited in Europe, were used to purchase return cargoes of high-end merchandise.[12] Stephen imported an extensive array of dry goods, ranging from fabrics (silks, taffetas, linens, and lace) to ready-made items (handkerchiefs, stockings, shoes, and gloves). Elegant accessories arrived as well: satin ribbons, silk shawls, artificial flowers, and silk suspenders; pocketbooks for men and women and silk laces for stays. Vinegar, wines, and spirits (claret and cognac above all) came from the vineyards of his native southwest France. Olive oil (then called sweet oil) arrived in quantity too, along with other specialty foodstuffs from the Mediterranean: almonds, olives, capers, anchovies, and fruits preserved in brandy. As suggested by the inclusion of anchovies and capers—hardly popular with American cooks—most of the goods were designed for reexport.[13] The lightly populated United States could not absorb such bounty, which went instead to colonists of European heritage prevented by war from trading directly with their mother countries. This explains the arrival of otherwise puzzling sundries, such as "five trunks' hats for Spanish monks," "brown linen for the Spanish and French islands," and "four thousand strong canvas coffee bags, suitable for the West India plantations."[14] Like the Caribbean goods Stephen shipped to France, these items purchased in Europe would travel as American property, increasing the likelihood that they would reach their destinations.

In this import-reexport trade, there were huge profits to earn, but equal risks to surmount. The travails of the brig *Stephen*, which bore the name of her owner, are instructive in this regard. She was seized four times in fewer than five years—on one occasion, by the officials of her own country!

The *Stephen*'s troubles began in November 1807. Homeward bound from Bordeaux, she was taken by a privateer and condemned in a British prize court.[15] Her captain repurchased her on Stephen's instructions, to get the cargo (which was exonerated) home to New York.[16] "God guide him!" Stephen wrote, as he passed on the glad news of the vessel's imminent departure from England.[17]

The *Stephen* returned home to an altered political situation. On December 22, 1807, the Jefferson administration had instituted the Embargo Act in retaliation for British impressment of American sailors and British and French interference with neutral commerce.[18] The draconic edict, which would bankrupt more than a hundred American merchants, barred U.S. vessels from trading with foreign ports.[19]

With her usual destinations off-limits, the *Stephen* was sent to New Orleans. She carried cheese, flour, butter, lard, and a modest selection of previously imported goods.[20] Stephen and his partner wrote optimistically to her captain on the eve of the brig's departure: "Your voyage being, as we may call it, a coastways one, we are little apprehensive that you should experience anything strange at the hands of any of the belligerent cruisers. Your vessel, cargo & freight are all American property; so we do not suppose any of them would be tempted to lay obstructions in the way of our territorial navigation."[21] Their confidence was misplaced. The *Stephen* was seized by a British warship in the Mississippi River delta. A few days later her passengers and crew retook her—at the cost of two English lives.[22]

Jefferson's embargo on all foreign trade was discontinued in March 1809, replaced by a more-circumscribed Non-Intercourse Act directed against the French and British Empires.[23] This was lifted in June with respect to Britain but not France, permitting the *Stephen* to return to the transatlantic trade.[24]

August 1809 found her sailing sedately for Liverpool.[25] Just after her arrival, "a dreadful gale of wind compelled her to cut both cables and run on shore."[26] The accident necessitated time-consuming repairs. When she returned to New York in March 1810, she was seized by the customs inspector for violating the Non-Intercourse Act, reinstated against Britain just after her departure from the United States. Jumel & Desobry had to appeal to Albert Gallatin, secretary of the treasury, to have the *Stephen* released.[27]

Nor had her troubles ended. After a handful of uneventful voyages, the *Stephen* was in John Bull's hands yet again. In January 1811 she was apprehended on a voyage from Liverpool to New Orleans and taken as a prize to British-owned Bermuda. The commander of the corvette that seized her wanted to try the claim from the prior capture she had escaped![28]

The *Stephen*'s captain, James Berry, wrote dolefully from the island, "this is one of the worst places I ever was in." He feared that the authorities would "put off the tryall as long as they please," although it was "well known" in the customs houses at New York and New Orleans "that there was not an article on board either of freight or owner's property but what property belong[d] to citizens of the U.S. at the time of the former Capture and Should they Condemn us it will be very unfair and what ought to be look[d] into by our Government." Below his signature, Berry added a polite postscript: "Please to excuse the paper as it is the best I can find."[29]

"Very unfair" or not, the brig was condemned.[30] Berry must have managed to repurchase her, however, as in July she was sailing from New Orleans to New York. She was detained for three hours by the British sloop of war *Atalanta*, but—for once—"treated politely."[31] Perhaps her luck had turned.

The calamitous voyages of the *Stephen* raise the question of how merchants could make a living in those taxing times. Indeed, many could not—but successful voyages were so profitable that the risks were worth taking. Marine insurance, available for vessels and cargoes, helped to balance out the inevitable losses.[32]

Skillful businessmen maximized the probability of success by constantly changing their vessels' destinations, as dictated by political realities. In spite of Stephen's preference for the Bordeaux run, over the years he sent cargoes to ports as diverse as Corunna (Spain) and Archangel (Russia).[33] He chose accomplished captains, permitted them to trade on their own behalf, and allowed them the leeway to employ their own skill and judgment. Stephen's wisdom is apparent in a letter to Captain John Skiddy, embarking on the *Eliza* for Tonningen, in Denmark (today Tonning, in Germany): "As in these stormy times for American commerce, it is impossible to foresee all the occurrences that may happen, we cannot likewise pretend to point out to you the remedy against every one. You have our entire confidence, your own property runs the same chance as ours, you will do for us as you will do for yourself, and we have no doubt that your prudence will direct you to those means of safety which we shall have reason to approve."[34]

Skiddy, Stephen's most capable captain, kept the ship safe from the perils of the sea. But the journey was rife with frustrations and delays. The brig left port without full insurance, which had turned out to be unexpectedly difficult to obtain.[35] The return trip to the United States proved even more troublesome. Skiddy arranged through Jumel & Desobry's London bankers for insurance at a rate of 15 percent. On the same day, his employers obtained a policy at a 7 percent rate in New York.[36] The partners negotiated politely but firmly for months to straighten out the mess caused by the duplicate contracts.

If anyone could be blamed for the boondoggle, it was Skiddy. He had misjudged the situation when he had purchased the insurance, but it was not an easy call. Stephen understood that even the best men made mistakes, and he turned down the bank's offer to charge the costs of the error to the captain. He "was certainly intrusted with our confidence and is still worthy of it," Stephen informed the bankers, Batard, Sampson & Sharp, and "you were of course fully justified in giving faith to what he wrote you; but observe well that he has never mentioned to you that he had our instructions for requesting you to insure our property . . . We have reason to regret that you have not considered the matter in that way; but to go further and do anything that would in the end fall to his charge, we never had an idea; because we are sure that he has acted for the best, in his opinion."[37]

In truth, Skiddy's error was aggravating, but Stephen had an unerring sense for the human compromises that successful trade required. Over months of persistent attempts to reach a resolution of the insurance tangle, he and his partner were never less than patient and courteous when addressing "their friends in England." They even managed a touch of humor over the unfortunate affair. One letter to the bankers opened disarmingly, "We are doomed to experience further troubles respecting the double assurance on the cargo of the ship *Eliza*, Skiddy."[38]

Stephen was equally adept in his dealings with a network of fellow merchants that stretched from the eastern seaboard to the Baltic. Most of Stephen's contacts were of French origin, and their shared language and culture knitted powerful bonds.[39] His most important business relationship, with a Bordeaux merchant named Jean Pery, lasted some twenty-five years.[40] Virtually all of his Bordeaux cargoes passed through Pery's hands—transactions that in time involved a second generation of the Pery family.[41]

Despite Stephen's imagination and skill, trade with Europe became increasingly unrewarding as the first decade of the nineteenth century closed. The *Margaret Tingey* and the *Sally Tracy*, both bound for Bordeaux, were condemned by the British in 1808.[42] The *Collector* sailed for San Sebastián in 1809 and was never heard from again.[43] The *Prosper*, belying her name, was confiscated by the French on entering the port of San Sebastián in 1810.[44] The *Maria Louisa* was wrecked on Gardiner's Island (near New London, Connecticut) on her return from Bordeaux in 1811.[45] The *Gold Coiner*, afloat notwithstanding the War of 1812, was captured by the English in 1813.[46]

Given the paucity of promising opportunities at sea, Stephen employed a portion of his capital elsewhere. He and Desobry purchased stock in a variety of start-up ventures: the Hudson Manufacturing Company, the New Brunswick and Hudson Banks, a projected turnpike in New Jersey, and a planned toll bridge in Hartford.[47] Above all Stephen made investments in land. He bought (or in one case, accepted in payment of a debt) two lots in lower Manhattan, 110 Greenwich and 57 Pearl Street; three hundred acres of farmland in Westchester; one thousand acres in Otsego County; and the six-acre property in Bloomingdale.[48] Most important for Eliza, in 1810 he acquired a country seat.

MOUNT STEPHEN

*S*even days a week, the Albany stagecoach clattered and swayed northward from New York City.[1] Once the metropolis was left behind, its passengers, crowded onto backless benches, saw little but fields, woods, and the occasional farmhouse.[2] Occasionally the coach would draw to one side, giving way to lowing cows or bleating sheep being driven south to the city's markets.[3]

North of the valley of Harlem (125th Street today), the pace slowed as the elevation increased. On the coldest days, steam would rise from the horses' backs as they strained their way up Harlem Heights. From his seat on the front bench of the coach, the driver would have been the first to spot a prominent local landmark: a stately, white mansion, its imposing portico formed of tall Tuscan columns surmounted by a triangular pediment. Commanding a bluff overlooking the Harlem River, the house, called Mount Morris by its original owners, was vacant except for its ghosts.

Could it have spoken, it had a story to tell. Built in 1765 as a summer home by a British Army officer, Colonel Roger Morris, and his wife, local heiress Mary Phillipse Morris, the mansion had been commandeered as a military outpost during the American Revolution.[4] For thirty-four days, it had served as General George Washington's headquarters during the battle for New York.[5] Subsequently it had housed British and Hessian officers.[6]

After the war, the house was seized and sold by a committee on forfeiture as the former property of a Tory.[7] Since then it had passed through several hands. Although run briefly as an inn from 1786 to 1787, mainly it had stood vacant or been occupied by farmers who rented the surrounding land.[8] The mansion stood in lonely splendor, waiting to recover its former glory.

In March 1810 Stephen and Eliza purchased 104 acres of the old Morris estate at auction for $9,927.50.[9] Their newly acquired lands included a mix of woodlands, meadows, and grasslands for pasturage. The mansion and thirty-six acres of land surrounding it—the "homestead lot"—passed into their possession a month later, for an additional ten thousand dollars.[10] In total, their acreage extended some three-quarters of a mile from south to north (approximately between today's 159th and 174th Streets). On the east it was bordered by the Harlem River and on the west by the Kingsbridge Road (today known as Saint Nicholas Avenue up to 168th Street and as Broadway north of 168th). The strip of property was unbroken except for a narrow horizontal band owned by the Wear family that bisected it a quarter mile north of the mansion. A single plot stretched southwestward from the Kingsbridge Road to the Hudson River (approximately between today's 172nd and 175th Streets on the east and 171st and 174th Streets on the west). It contained forty acres of farmland.[11]

The house that stood amidst the woods and fields would become Eliza's pride and joy. Although in need of repair when the Jumels purchased it, the mansion would have looked graceful and welcoming, much as it was described in a 1792 advertisement (and still appears today):

> It has . . . a large hall thro' the center; a spacious dining room on the right, with an alcove, closets, and a convenient pantry and storeroom adjoining, and beyond these, a light, easy mahogany staircase. On the left is a handsome parlour, and a large back room, particu-

larly adapted and fitted for a nursery. A passage from the rear of the hall leads to an oblong octagon room, about 32 feet by 22, with six sash windows, marble chimney pieces, and a lofty airy ceiling. On the second floor are eleven bed chambers, four with fireplaces and marble hearths; and a large hall communicating with a gallery under the portico, and from which there is a most inviting prospect. On the upper floor are five lodging rooms, three of which have fireplaces; and at the top of the house is affixed an electrical conductor. Underneath the building are a large commodious kitchen and laundry, a wine cellar, storeroom, kitchen pantry, sleeping apartments for servants, and the most complete dairy room, the floor a solid flat rock, and which, with common attention to cleanliness, cannot fail to render the place constantly cool and sweet.[12]

Outbuildings included "a large barn, and most excellent coach house and stables." Spectacular views stretched from the New Jersey Palisades to the Long Island Sound and from Westchester to Staten Island. All in all, the property was, as advertised, "an eligible retreat for a gentleman fond of rural amusements and employments . . . who wishes to pass the summer months with pleasure and comfort."[13]

Working from this promising raw material, Eliza and Stephen turned the estate into a showpiece.[14] A handful of purchases that seem to relate to the property appear in Stephen's receipt books: 1,500 asparagus roots, purchased in January 1813; 350 boards to be delivered by the ferry boat to Manhattanville (in today's Harlem) in November 1813; a flock of merino sheep, purchased in November as well.[15] The Jumels planted a vineyard of French grapes and improved the ornamental gardens around the house.[16] They enjoyed homegrown fruit—peaches, pears, apricots, cherries, and plums—and savored oysters, clams, and fish from the Harlem River.[17] An advertisement for a brindle cow gone astray in October 1810 suggests that fresh milk and butter appeared on their table as well.[18]

Walking their lands, Eliza and Stephen could admire a thriving expanse of timber, including chestnut, hickory, cedar, and oak. Fields of clover nourished sheep and soil. By 1814, the property produced fifty tons of hay per year. A smokehouse and ice house made it possible to preserve food grown or raised on the property.[19]

Eliza renamed this arcadia Mount Stephen, in honor of her husband.

FRANCE BECKONS

There was no greater contrast to the rural tranquility of Harlem Heights than the bustle of Broadway in lower Manhattan. For more than two miles, the avenue was lined with retail stores and booksellers, which occupied "the lower stories of most of the houses." Large display windows overflowed "with china and glassware, plate, millinery, fruit, confectionary; in short, everything." Even more astounding were the crowds that filled the thoroughfare: "the throng resemble[d] the dense multitude issuing from the door of a church." Broadway was the lounge of "the fashionable, the gay, and the idle"—especially women distinguished by the "richness and variety" of their dress. The "superb buildings with their marble fronts [were] completely eclipsed by the teeming fair ones, from morning till ten o'clock at night."[1]

In 1812 Eliza and Stephen secured a foothold on this fashionable avenue. Their acquisition, a parcel at the northeast corner of Broadway and Liberty Street, was twenty-six feet wide on the valuable Broadway frontage and extended one hundred and ten feet down Liberty Street. Stephen purchased the property, located three blocks north of Wall Street, for $14,700 at auction.[2] Generating generous rents for years to come, it would be his and Eliza's most valuable possession.

They began maximizing the value of the land immediately. By May 150 Broadway was under construction.[3] The three-story brick building had a storefront on the Broadway façade and a separate entrance to living spaces above.[4] Storage vaults extended beneath the Liberty Street frontage. A three-story brick house at 69½ Liberty Street (later renumbered 71), was either built or upgraded concurrently.[5]

James B. Durand, a dry-goods merchant and close associate of Stephen's, would lodge in the 150 building for many years.[6] He rented the storefront more briefly, until 1817; the location was "one of the best in this city for business."[7]

As for the Liberty Street house, Stephen, Eliza, and Mary may have occupied it, but only for a short time.[8] In April 1814, on the opposite side of the Atlantic, Napoleon was overthrown and banished to Elba. By fall the Jumels had decided to relocate to France.[9]

Eliza's opinions about the move are not recorded. But the books she read during a period of several months preceding their departure are revealing. Documented in a rare, surviving circulation ledger from the New York Society Library, an institution she joined in 1807, her selections—many written in French—hint at an eagerness to embark on life in a foreign country.[10] Of equal interest, her reading patterns reveal that this child of an illiterate mother had become a woman of considerable intellectual attainments. She polished off complex titles—in a second language, no less—in as little as three or four days.

On November 28, 1814, Eliza checked out the first volume of a collection of plays in French—by whom is not recorded. On returning it two days later, she borrowed an English translation of *Alf von Dülmen*, a Gothic novel by the German writer Benedikte Naubert.[11] The two-volume work of historical fiction, featuring a secret tribunal

and crumbling castle, represented a rare excursion into light reading for Eliza.[12] After returning it, she read four volumes of Molière
plays—some, if not all, in the original language—between December 3 and December 19. Then, as Christmas approached, she went
home with yet another foreign-language title, a French translation of
Pliny the Elder's *Natural History*. This tome she returned the same
day, possibly having confused the author with Pliny the Younger,
whose letters, in English, she borrowed instead. She spent two weeks
studying the translation from the Latin by John Boyle, fifth earl of
Orrery and Cork; then exchanged it for William Melmoth's equally
fine translation, which occupied her for another seven days.[13]

Biography, history, and the writings of ancient Greek and Roman
authors were favored at this time period, so Eliza's choice of Pliny
was not atypical for her era.[14] But the number of plays she read and,
above all, the quantity of books in French, were striking. In the new
year, she polished off a volume of plays by Racine—again in the
original language—between January 14 and January 17.[15] Also that
month she read one of the most popular French novels of the eighteenth century, Bernardin de Saint-Pierre's *Paul et Virginie*. The
timing of the latter selection is suggestive. The Park Theatre had
performed an English-language adaptation of *Paul et Virginie* on
New Year's Eve, as part of a triple bill that included a comedy and
a melodrama.[16] It is tempting to speculate that Eliza attended the
performance with her husband and daughter, prompting her to read
the novel.

She ended the month with an excursion into religious matters,
checking out an English edition of *The Christian's Defense Against the
Fears of Death*, the best-known work of the French Protestant theo-
logian Charles Drelincourt.[17] Although on February 8 she exchanged
it for the first volume of a popular French miscellany—filled with
fables, bon mots, and anecdotes about famous men—Drelincourt's
words must have spoken to her.[18] She borrowed the *Christian's
Defense* a second time between February 13 and February 24. Years
later a relative said that she found attending funerals difficult; she
may have struggled to accept the finality of death.[19]

The last book Eliza took home in February was a dense volume of theology: George Anderson's *An Estimate of the Profit and Loss of Religion.*[20] Far more than her reading of the accessible Drelincourt, her choice of Anderson's polemic reveals her as a woman willing to grapple with the rigors of religious philosophy. But once she had returned the volume on March 3, the cycle of checkouts and returns ended. Probably the weather had warmed enough to lure her into the countryside, and she had gone to spend the spring at Mount Stephen. Where she obtained books while in rural seclusion is unknown.

Stephen wound up his commercial affairs as he, Eliza, and Mary prepared for departure. He and Benjamin Desobry had dissolved their partnership at the beginning of 1811 in the increasingly difficult trading environment, but Stephen had stayed in business independently.[21] He would remain active as a merchant in France, selecting goods for shipment to New York and Havana (the gateway to the South American market).[22] Although he would supply Desobry with carefully chosen French fabrics and accessories, he would no longer own ships and would not form another partnership.[23]

Before the Jumels left New York, Stephen set up a trust for Eliza. If he predeceased his wife, she would receive a life interest in the mansion at Mount Stephen and the thirty-six-acre homestead lot. The property would revert to his heirs after her death.[24] This precaution ensured that if Stephen died during the voyage, Eliza would have a permanent home. For the time being, the mansion and its acreage would be leased.[25] The couple's other properties were offered for sale but failed to attract buyers, so they were retained and left to the care of an agent.[26]

At the end of May, Eliza, Stephen, and Mary began the final preparations for their journey. Stephen's passport survives and provides, with one later exception, the only physical description we have of him. True to his ancestry in southwest France, he had a "dark" complexion and "dark" hair. His height was given as 5 feet, 5 inches, making him an inch taller than Eliza.[27]

The Jumels would sail for Bordeaux on the ship *Maria Theresa,* captained and part-owned by the faithful John Skiddy.[28] On May 31 Stephen advertised for a woman "desirous to go to France" to take care of Eliza during the voyage. "The preference will be given to one not subject to seasickness," Stephen added optimistically.[29] Often servants were too sick to be of assistance during the first weeks of a voyage.[30]

Once the ship sailed, on June 3 or 4, 1815, it was clear that Stephen and not Eliza was the one who needed an attendant. Seasick throughout the voyage, he stayed in the fresh air on the bridge even at meal times, "wishing that a wave would carry [him] away."[31] In contrast, Eliza appears to have been an excellent traveler. There is no record of her having suffered from seasickness during this or any future voyage.

AN IMPERIAL
INTERLUDE

W hile Eliza, Stephen, and Mary were crossing the Atlantic, the armies of Europe were fighting a great battle. In early 1815 Napoleon I of France escaped from Elba and attempted to return to power. After an anxious period known as the Hundred Days, when it seemed as if the empire might rise again, he was defeated definitively on July 18 near the Belgian village of Waterloo.

Afterward the fallen emperor fled to the Tuileries Palace in Paris. At that critical moment the Jumels reached France—or so it was said. Eliza's great-niece would tell and retell a dramatic tale years later. It went like this:

The ship docked. Stephen, being "an ardent Bonapartist," immediately "sought out an interview with the fallen emperor." Merchant and ex-monarch met in Paris. Stephen offered Napoleon his own ship. He "proffered him safe conduct to America and an asylum there."[1]

The grand gesture was made in vain. Napoleon expressed "his heartfelt thanks" to "M. and Madame Jumel," but "declined to attempt an escape."[2] Nevertheless, "in recognition of such an offer," he "gave his traveling carriage to the Jumels." They tried "to drive out of Paris," but were "arrested at the *barrière*, the carriage taken from them by the new government, and they themselves held as prisoners until the American Minister came to their rescue."[3] The emperor gave his army chest to Eliza before his departure for Saint Helena, a relic she brought back with her later to the United States.[4]

What are we to make of this narrative? At a minimum, the chronology is garbled. The Jumels sailed into Bordeaux, rather than one of France's more northerly ports, and didn't arrive until July 8.[5] They could not have met with Napoleon in the Parisian region, which he left for good on June 30.[6] In addition, the ship they sailed in no longer belonged to Stephen, but rather to Captain John Skiddy and two New York merchants.[7] If Stephen was involved, it would have been as an intermediary, offering Napoleon passage on the *Maria Theresa* in Skiddy's name, probably for a cut of the potential charter fees.

However, the strangest-sounding element of the Jumel family story—the idea of offering Napoleon a safe harbor in America—is less incredible than it sounds. After Waterloo the emperor planned to seek refuge in the United States. Originally he, his family, and his staff hoped to make the crossing on the French frigates *Saale* and *Méduse*, stationed on the Atlantic coast near Roquefort, just north of Bordeaux. An alternative scheme envisioned the use of the corvettes *Indéfatigable* and *Bayadère*. A group of French officers even floated the possibility of helping Napoleon escape on a whaleboat, from which he could flag down and charter a merchant ship to carry him to the United States.[8]

To facilitate a retreat by sea, Bonaparte traveled southwest from Paris to the Atlantic coast. He arrived in Rochefort on July 3, five days before the *Maria Theresa* approached nearby Bordeaux.[9] But by the time the vessel, with the Jumels aboard, entered the Garonne (the waterway leading to Bordeaux), several British frigates and three sloops of war had been patrolling the mouth of the river for several days. Their object was "to prevent Napoleon Bonaparte quitting France in any American ship or vessel."[10]

It is not impossible that Stephen and Captain John Skiddy saw an opportunity for profit in carrying the ex-emperor and his suite to the United States. They could have reached out to the dethroned sovereign as soon as the *Maria Theresa* entered Bordeaux on July 8. But it is highly unlikely that they did. By the second week of July, the British blockade was too tight. When an American brig, the *Pike*, exited the Garonne on July 12, she was forced to heave to under cannon fire from the British and submit to a search for the fallen emperor.[11]

The story makes an improbable assumption about Stephen's political sympathies also—especially in the light of the other family legends that had him and Eliza socializing with French royalist refugees in New York. It is hard to envision him as a fervent supporter of the Bonapartist regime given that he left France before the emperor took power and did not make plans to return to his homeland until Napoleon's initial defeat in 1814. His former ship, the *Maria Theresa*, even bore the name of the daughter of Louis XVI, famed for her fervent loyalty to the Bourbon monarchy. If Stephen approached the former emperor at all, the motivation would have been strictly business.

In any case, the idea of a flight to America was soon moot. Having vacillated so long that an escape by sea became impractical, Bonaparte boarded the British ship of war *Bellerophon* on July 15, 1815, placing himself, as he put it, under the protection of British law.[12] The First Empire was gone for good.

14

PARIS

The Jumels' documented actions after arriving in France were more personal than political. Stephen's brother François came to dine with them in Bordeaux when they first arrived.[1] They may have visited Stephen's hometown of Mont-de-Marsan next, or first traveled to Paris, where Mary was placed in a girls' school run by nuns. Then, to escape the hottest days of summer, Eliza and Stephen went to take the waters in the foothills of the Pyrenees.

"We received your dear letter with great pleasure," Stephen wrote to Mary in French from the resort town of Bagnères de Bigorre on August 19, 1815. He and Eliza were happy to learn that she was staying busy: "right now that is as it should be, as your time is very precious." He passed on a little news he thought might please her. Reverend Fenwick (a priest at the Church of Saint Peter the Apostle in New York) had written him and asked if Mary was still charming and good. "I told him you were in a convent school," Stephen wrote, "and there was no question but that you were doing your duty."[2]

In the fall Eliza and Stephen settled in Paris. As they passed in a carriage through narrow streets lined with tall, stone *hôtels*, so different from New York's three-story wood or brick houses, Eliza would have seen every conceivable trade or occupation "carried on along the causeways of the bridges and quays, at the corners of the streets, or on its pavements, under the archways and passageways, through every quarter of the city." Lemonade sellers served "thirsty tradesman or wearied messengers." Vendors, crouched "over little stoves," offered bubbling soup and newly baked cakes. Dog groomers clipped poodles in the middle of the sidewalk, while flower sellers offered bouquets for human adornment. "Learned monkeys, popular orators, humorous storytellers, excellent fiddle players, and tolerable ballad singers" entertained passersby.[3]

After fifteen years of Napoleonic building campaigns, the city presented dramatic contrasts of old and new. Broad avenues cut through medieval streets, and handsome monuments, some only half-completed, rose near mansions already old when the Sun King, Louis XIV, cast his beams over France. Boulevards, "forming a splendid girdle round" the city, were lined with veranda-fronted cafés and double rows of trees.[4] Families strolled in spacious "public walks and gardens," during "the fine evenings of summer, on Sundays and holidays."[5] Soon Eliza would join them, riding in her carriage along the wood-lined Champs-Élysées (Elysian Fields), where she could imagine herself once more in the countryside near Mount Stephen. When she was ill or out of sorts, the trees and fresh air of the famed promenade comforted her.[6]

After several short stints in furnished lodgings, the Jumels were established at 40, rue de Cléry by late summer 1816.[7] Their closest friends were the Cubières family: the former Marie-Françoise Olive, whom Stephen had probably known in New York when she was married to Nicolas Olive; her adult daughters Adèle and Henriette; and her second husband, Simon, marquis de Cubières. A handful of surviving letters hint at the intimacy between the two families.

From Madame de Cubières: Would Madame and Monsieur Jumel dine with them *en famille*, if Madame Jumel's health permits?[8]

From twenty-six-year-old Adèle, on a Sunday evening: If Madame Jumel hasn't gone to the theater, would she and her family spend an hour or two at the Cubières home?[9]

From eighteen-year-old Henriette to her "*chère* Mary": Would "Madame your aunt" be kind enough to permit Henriette and Adèle to dine with the Jumels? "Maman being in the country, we are free to be able to spend part of the day with your family."[10]

Simon and Marie-Françoise Cubières were an extraordinary couple. Simon, in his youth, served the French crown, first as a page at Versailles, then in a cavalry regiment. He was appointed one of the king's masters of the horse, a largely honorary post involving the management of the royal stables, a position to which he was reinstated at the Restoration. But the way he spent the hours not occupied by his official duties made it clear that he was far more than a mere courtier. Gifted with a wide-ranging intellect, Cubières delved into literature and the arts, physics, chemistry, and above all, natural science. He built a noteworthy collection of rocks and minerals, including lava he retrieved from the crater of Vesuvius. He made an ascent in a balloon—and then tried to devise better methods for steering it. He visited England to investigate modern industrial methods, and at the same time explored the art of landscaping that British gardeners had pioneered. Returning to France, he brought rare seeds with him, cultivating them in a nursery he owned at Versailles.[11]

An habitué of artists and antiquaries, Cubières turned his expertise in the fine arts to good account in the years following the deposition of Louis XVI. After Napoleon I conquered Italy, Cubières was one of the commissioners assigned to follow the French armies, selecting paintings and sculptures to ship back to Paris. During the First Empire he served as curator of the statuary in the gardens of Versailles and the Trianon, a position he retained after the restoration of Louis XVIII, in conjunction with his renewed responsibility for supervising the stables at the Tuileries Palace in Paris. In spare moments Cubières found time to write prolifically: a treatise on shells; a history of the tulip tree; a memoir on bees; another on the Louisiana cypress; an examination of "the services rendered to agriculture by women."[12]

Cubières's wife, Marie-Françoise Olive, née Marchal, was his match. Described by the marquise de Gouvernet as "a beautiful Raphael Madonna, so good, so gracious!" she shared her second husband's avid interest in botany.[13] Her first husband, Nicholas Olive, left a loving description of her, dating to their days in exile in New York. The couple had gone on a party of pleasure to the bucolic, northernmost tip of Manhattan Island, exploring the region occupied today by Inwood Hill Park. In a letter, Olive informed his daughters, then little girls at school, that their "chère maman" was "the only one who turned this little voyage to profit."

> You have seen her running through the woods with an ardor that cannot exist without a passionate interest—that of finding a bush, a tree, a plant she does not know in order to search out the seed to carry it off to France, wishing to bring back only those not there already. Thus she knows how to make use even of her leisure—a touching example of a virtuous ambition that she was enjoying in climbing the east bank of the beautiful Hudson River![14]

The marquis and his family had an apartment in the écuries du Roi—the king's stables—which were located at the Tuileries, a 368-room palace facing the Louvre. Although the Tuileries burned in 1870 and only its gardens survive today, during the Restoration the palace housed the royal family, including the elderly Louis XVIII; his younger brother, the comte d'Artois (the future Charles X), and the latter's sons, the duc d'Angoulême and duc de Berry, and their families.[15]

Friendship with the Cubières family brought the Jumels in contact with other members of the French court. They became close to the family of comte Joseph d'Abzac de Falgueyrac, who had been, like Cubières, a military officer under the ancien régime and was related to one of Cubières's colleagues at the *écuries du Roi*.[16] The comte and comtesse Tascher de la Pagerie were acquaintances too, a connection that inspired a long-standing legend that Eliza and Stephen moved in Bonapartist circles.[17] The count was a cousin of Napoleon's first wife, Empress Josephine, and had fought briefly for the empire. But by early 1814, he had adopted the royalist cause, receiving the rank of field marshal in Louis XVIII's army.[18]

Mary's education opened other social doors to Eliza. Monsieur Noël, secretary general of the administration of the forests of the Crown, solicited her help in picking up his daughter from school: "You will do me a great service, Madame, if you will be so kind as to send for my daughter with your own. I shall have the honor, Madame, of calling to thank you Sunday morning, that being my first venture out of the house."[19] Eliza's possession of a carriage gave her status in Paris, just as it had in New York.

Aside from her friendship with the Cubières family, Eliza's most important means of entrée into French high society was religion.[20] Once in France she considered converting to Catholicism, the religion of the aristocracy and the court. She appears to have attended Sunday mass at the Royal Chapel of the Tuileries at least occasionally.[21] There the master of ceremonies, in full court dress, would have escorted her to a seat from which she could stand, sit, and kneel, following the example of the Royal Family.[22] She may also have enjoyed ethereal sacred music at the church of St. Sulpice, and evening sermons at the church of the Madeleine in the aristocratic rue Saint-Honoré.[23]

A highborn friend, the marquise de la Suze, made it her mission to bring Eliza into the arms of the mother church. She arranged an introduction for her to the abbé Fraysinnous, one of the greatest preachers of the day. Be sure to arrive by noon "because his time is precious," she told Eliza in October 1816, "and he will receive you with the great interest you must always inspire. Be assured: that which you have made me feel is sincere indeed."[24]

On the feast of Epiphany, January 6, the marquise concerned herself with Eliza's spiritual health. "Here is a little prayer that all the faithful are saying right now," she wrote. "As I have no doubt that all those you have addressed to him are very acceptable to him at present, I beg you and engage you to begin immediately and say it exactly for nine days with this fervor that surely will bring you grace, if you are always faithful to your good inspirations." The writer's ardent spirit shines through the next lines: "Ah, madame, how happy and grateful I am for what God has done for me in having led you to the happiness that you will soon feel and that will be the consolation of my life as well. To bring a soul back to this merciful God, what pleasure! Hasten, madame, this moment so joyous for you and for me, who is so tenderly attached to you by all the repeated proofs that you give me of your friendship."[25]

The marquise de la Suze had an apartment in the Abbaye-aux-Bois, a deconsecrated abbey in southern Paris. The complex of buildings housed secular residents as well as a church where the abbé Fraysinnous preached and two communities of nuns. One was a nursing order, but the other, a community of Augustinian sisters, ran a convent school on-site.[26] This "boarding school for young ladies"—which included a garden where the girls took their recreation—was probably the institution Mary attended.[27] She and a young English pupil, Anna Selena Hooke, used to run around the garden of their school each morning.[28]

Although it may seem strange that she was a live-in student when Eliza and Stephen resided in the same city, the two-mile trip from 40, rue de Cléry, to 16, rue de Sèvres, south of the Seine, was not the eight-minute car ride it is today. It must have involved closer to an hour in a carriage, bumping over the cobblestones of narrow, crowded streets. Eliza and Stephen visited the school for special events and took their adoptive daughter out for excursions, as a letter from Mary to Eliza makes clear. The students were giving a concert next Thursday, she wrote to her "dear Mama" on December 8, 1816,

and the mistress told me to ask you to come, but I told her I thought you would not, because you do not like evening rides especially so far; but as Wednesday will be a recreation day, it would give me great pleasure if you would come and see me, and to bring me my gauze frock with my shoes and gloves, and my lace vandyck [a detachable collar with sawtooth edging] and my little vandyck of muslin, because I have none to put on; do not forget to send them as soon as possible. Give my love to my dear papa, and tell him not to forget his promise in sending for me the first time that the piece [i.e., play] of Abraham is to be played, and that I wait with impatience for that day, for it looks so dreary in this place that the last three English young lady [*sic*] are always crying and have at last run away from the school, but it does not look so very dreary, they have only cut the tops of the trees in our garden, which makes it look as if they wanted petticoats. As it will be very cold when we have to stay upstairs changing our dress, if you would ask Miss Laurou to let us have a fire in my room, because these [*sic*] two or three young ladies that have permission to have fire in their rooms. My dear Mama, I embrace you with a thousand kisses. Believe me to be your fond and dutiful daughter.[29]

She signed herself "Mary Eliza Jumel," adding her adoptive mother's first name to her own.[30]

THE COLLECTOR

*W*ithin a year after her arrival in Paris, Eliza was so busy that even her closest friends had trouble keeping in touch with her. Adèle de Cubières called without success to let her know that there would be English horse races on the plain of Sablons. Ultimately she wrote a note instead: "We have been so unfortunate in never finding you at home that I thought the best way of making sure you have a thing you seemed fond of was to write to you."[1]

In June 1816, on Pentecost Sunday, Adèle scolded Eliza for her neglect. She wrote humorously but her bruised feelings are evident:

> You have forgotten us so completely, madame, that I really don't know whether I would do better to go see you or just write you. Perhaps it would be appropriate to abandon you in turn, but I would get little return for my friendship in that. Besides, good faith demands that we keep the promise we made to you to arrange for you to see the trousseau of Her Royal Highness Madame the Duchess of Berry, which is, people say, beautiful *Beyond* [*sic*] *description*.

Adèle wrote the last two words in English and emphasized them to make her point. Then she stressed the time and date:

The present is therefore to alert you that tomorrow, *Monday, June 3*, the *last day* of the exhibition, we will come get you between *two* and *three o'clock* in the afternoon. We will have admission tickets for you and Monsieur Jumel, and we are going to Paris [from their country residence] just for this, because Maman's plan was not to go there until Monday evening or Tuesday morning.

Adèle's message delivered, she moved on to other topics:

It's really a pity that you didn't come to the country today. The weather couldn't have been lovelier, and also we have arranged a beautiful country ball near our house. After having danced a great deal, we will set off fireworks at ten o'clock, and there will be a lot of *fashionable Ladies* [sic].

The teasing words, again in English and emphasized, were apt. Eliza relished connections in high society. Although she might have stayed in town to celebrate Pentecost under the guidance of the marquise de la Suze, she would have regretted the lost opportunity to expand her circle of acquaintances.

Adèle closed the letter with a final pinprick: "Adieu, bad Madame Jumel, I am sending you only a little kiss because I am truly annoyed." As for Stephen, "He must take half of my severity for himself, since he has not come any more often than you."²

Although it is unmentioned in any letters from the period, Eliza had thrown herself into an all-absorbing project. Over a period of approximately eighteen months, she assembled a collection of more than 240 paintings.³

She was in the ideal place to do so. Through late September 1815, she could have admired an unparalleled assemblage of masterworks in the high-ceilinged rooms of the Louvre. She had arrived in Paris just before the treasures of Europe, gathered by the Napoleonic armies, were packed up and returned to the countries from which they had been looted. According to one visitor's count, a budding connoisseur could have found fifty-seven Rubenses, thirty-three Rembrandts, twenty-six Raphaels, twenty-four Titians, eighteen Veroneses, nine Correggios, and seven Leonardo da Vincis lining the walls of the museum.[4]

The city was rich in artistic spoil even after Raphael's *Transfiguration*, Rubens's *Descent from the Cross*, and the Apollo Belvedere were homeward bound. At the Musée des Monuments français, medieval sculptures and tombs, rescued from cathedrals ransacked by the Jacobins, crowded a former church and convent.[5] Titian's *Danae* hung at the Luxembourg Palace and the portraits of the marshals of France decorated the gallery of the Tuileries.[6] Dealers offered collections nationalized during the French Revolution and others bought from Bonapartists fleeing the Bourbons.[7] Art sales were held in the homes of defunct collectors and in the auction rooms of the seventeenth-century Hôtel de Bullion. The marquis de Cubières, with his knowledge of art and artists, could have introduced Eliza to these fascinating realms.

Her acquisitions reveal that she absorbed expertise as rapidly as the proverbial sponge. In its completed state, the Jumel collection was an encyclopedic selection of works dating from the sixteenth through the early nineteenth century. All the major categories of subject matter were represented: scenes from mythology, the Old Testament, and ancient history; landscapes, cityscapes, and seascapes; devotional paintings, genre scenes, still life paintings, and portraits; even a few allegories and animal paintings. Mannerist, baroque, rococo, and contemporary paintings came from the French, Italian, Dutch, Flemish, and Spanish schools.

The authenticity of certain works in Eliza's collection remains a vexing question. She was not a deep-pocketed collector. The bigger names in her collection were represented by copies of varying quality or originals in crying need of restoration. Thus her *Cleopatra*, said to be by the Italian Baroque artist Guido Reni, was almost certainly a poor imitation in the style of Reni that was on and off the Paris art market in 1816 and ultimately sold for barely twenty-four francs.⁸ A "Rubens" *Battle of the Amazons* was presumably a copy of a well-known painting of the subject in Munich that was traditionally attributed to Rubens. But the fact that a work was not an original did not necessarily make it a bad painting. Before the invention of photography, replicas of Old Master paintings were prized for their beauty and educational value.⁹ Eliza's *Incredulity of Saint Thomas*, which she claimed as a work of the Italian master Guercino, may have been an excellent copy made by Joseph-Marie Vien, a past director of the French Royal Academy of Painting. The Vien canvas was sold in Paris in October 1816 for 109 francs, a handsome price for a work known to be a copy.¹⁰

Two of Eliza's most highly praised paintings were by living artists, contemporary art being a niche where it was still possible to buy high-quality works for minimal sums. An attractive genre scene by Jean-François Garneray, painted around 1793, showed a young woman plucking a guitar as a boy played with his cat under the eye of an elderly woman.¹¹ Eliza also owned one of Jean-Frédéric Schall's jewel-like little paintings, creations that summoned up the pleasures of the ancien régime with their graceful dancers and amorous couples. Her acquisition, full of delicate charm, was a picture of a girl with a dog.¹²

Her budget stretched to Old Master paintings by artists who were out of fashion or whose works were not in high demand. For example, she owned a painting titled *Rejoicing of Africans* by the seventeenth-century Dutch artist Frans Post, who visited South America and painted the plantations of Brazil. His canvases sold for a reasonable sixty or seventy francs at the time Eliza was in Paris.¹³ She possessed four French rococo portraits by Jean-Marc Nattier as well—*Louis XV in the Dress of Bacchus* gives their flavor—and genre scenes and an allegory by his contemporary Jean Raoux.¹⁴ The titles—*Lovely Courtesan: Summer Scene*, for example—suggest a sun-drenched charm. All these paintings were probably bargain-priced, painted in a mode dismissed as reactionary and corrupt since the rise of neoclassicism and the French Revolution.

The question of why Eliza began collecting is unresolved. However, her turn toward the fine arts was consistent with her evident eagerness for self-cultivation: reading, studying the piano, improving her facility in French. It accorded equally with her desire for acceptance by the upper classes. A sophisticated and wide-ranging collection would help Eliza distinguish herself from parvenus such as a businessman's wife who displayed a cast of a bronze by "Bologny" (i.e., Giambologna) and announced that she was going to put pantaloons on it before receiving guests.[15] In contrast, Eliza's knowledgeable appreciation for art demonstrated cultivation and taste. Her envisioned peers were not the nouveaux riches, but rather British aristocrats who were purchasing masterpieces in Paris: the likes of Quentin Crauford, the Duke of Devonshire, the Duke of Hamilton, and Sir Charles Stuart.[16] Her home, like theirs, could become a lodestone for wealthy and cultivated visitors.

That said, Eliza may have had more than one motive. The chronologic and stylistic scope of her collection, the inclusion of something to suit every taste, raises the question of whether it was compiled, at least in part, with future resale value in mind. Quality rather than quantity would have been a more sensible choice for a collection designed to have sustained value on the European market. However, if she envisioned returning to the United States, where few people had seen authentic works by the Old Masters, a diverse collection, with a solid sprinkling of works by (purportedly) well-known artists, might have commercial potential. If this was her aim, she would soon have the opportunity to put her strategy to the test. In April 1817, after less than two years in France, Eliza decided abruptly to return to New York alone.

SEPARATE LIVES

At Le Havre Eliza boarded the *Maria Theresa*, John Skiddy in command.[1] Puzzled and unhappy, Stephen saw her off. She seems to have made illness the excuse for her departure. In any event, there is nothing in Stephen's letters to her (hers to him from this period do not survive) to suggest that a quarrel or traumatic event precipitated the separation. "My dear wife," he wrote in a parting letter, "It is so hard not to make the voyage together, but your health and the opinion of the doctor demanded your journey, and as for me, I did not want to disappoint you, fearing for your health."[2]

Stephen wrote to Eliza weekly during the first month after they parted, fighting loneliness and striving to understand her decision to leave. "Since your departure, my bedchamber has become insipid to me," he wrote sadly from Le Havre on April 18, a few days after the *Maria Theresa* sailed. "I stayed on the jetty until I could no longer see the ship."[3] In a letter of May 5, Stephen mentioned that he had paid a visit to the marquis de Cubières: "The whole family is as charming as ever and hopes to see you in a year."[4] Apparently Stephen described her voyage as a visit to her homeland, not a permanent separation. He himself may not have been sure of her intentions.

If she had been considering a departure for some time, neither her husband nor her friends had suspected it. "The ladies never dreamt that you would return to New York," Stephen wrote, "*and no more did I*"—the emphasis on the last words is his.[5] The "illness" that prompted her journey was homesickness—or at least that was the rationale she gave. In the early nineteenth century, nostalgia for one's native land was viewed as a condition that could cause serious—even fatal—physical infirmity. The only sure treatment was for the sufferer to return to his or her native surroundings.[6] "You were homesick for your country," Stephen wrote on May 5. "For the sake of your health, I didn't want to turn you from your ideas, but you will be sorry for it."[7]

In spite of his feeling of abandonment, Stephen remained deeply affectionate toward his wife. He reminded her not to work too hard in the garden, as she "always does when I am not there," and "not to work too much to put the house in order," so as not to worsen her health.[8] The potential expense of maintaining separate residences worried him. "Take care of the paintings and don't spend too much," he cautioned her, "as we have to maintain two households. And if you buy supplies, keep an account of them."[9] He didn't like being surprised by unanticipated expenses. On the sea voyage, Eliza had paid for the passage of a fellow passenger, with no certainty of being reimbursed. Although she enjoyed making such lavish gestures, Stephen was unhappy when he received the bills.[10] In speaking of purchases he would make for the mansion, he warned her not to count on having as much as she wanted.[11]

Although a wealthy man, Stephen had many demands on his purse. He made yearly allowances of 1,500 francs to his brother, 500 francs to his sister, and 250 francs to his niece Felicie, his sister's youngest child; he also paid Felicie's tuition at boarding school.[12] He was equally generous to his wife's family. Eliza sent her oldest nephew, William Ballou Jones, to be educated in France in the late summer of 1817; Stephen paid for his schooling. In addition, he paid, at least for a time, for the American education of William's sisters,

Eliza and Louisa Jones, and their brother Stephen, born in 1810.[13] Mary's boarding school was yet another recurring charge.

Eliza and Stephen's adoptive daughter remained in Paris to complete her education. When Stephen visited "poor Mary" on May 3, the schoolmistress informed him that she was making rapid improvement. He planned to see her again soon to judge for himself, he told Eliza: "I will have her play the harp for me, so I can see her progress and have her do the same on the forte piano, so I can see if she is forgetting it in learning the harp, and I will give you my opinion with my usual frankness."[14]

Eliza wrote to Mary about ten days after reaching New York. "My dear Mary," she began, "You have heard of my arrival before this as I wrote to your papa on my arrival, but the vessel departed so soon that I had no time to write to you and as you know I am not fond of writing which will be another excuse: but, believe me, my dear Mary, my thoughts are always of you, altho' I do not write often."[15]

A change of scene had worked its magic: "My health is restored to me, which is a great consolation, as I know it will be to you."[16] Plus, the two of them would soon be reunited:

> Do not forget, my dear Mary, the sacrifice I made was for your own good, which I hope you will profit by it [*sic*]; in one year to finish your education and to return to your mama, who loves you dearly. I am engaged [at] the present time in setting your room in order. It is admired by every one that see it. Your curtains is of blue sattain [*sic*] trim'ed with silver fringe, and your toilet [dressing table] the same. Altho at this distance still my thoughts is of you. I shall be very interested, when the day of pri[z]es arrives, to know how many my dear Mary has gained and for what lessons. Until then I remain impatiently, your affectionate mama
>
> Eliza Jumel[17]

Eliza's words to Mary imply that she planned on remaining in the United States rather than returning to France, and that she intended to bring Mary back to New York as well. Exactly how she presented her plans to her husband remains an open question. When she left, she took her collection of paintings with her along with some furnishings for the mansion on Harlem Heights.[18] Stephen sent other furniture in the weeks after her departure, including mirrors, armoires, a sofa, and chairs. She was planning at a minimum an extended stay.[19]

Once reinstalled at Mount Stephen, Eliza threw herself into upgrading the property. She hired laborers to work the land, planted fruit trees, and ordered "8 to 10 bundles of short shingles of the best quality," possibly to repair the mansion's roof.[20] Since Mary's redecorated room was admired by others, presumably she socialized with neighboring landowners on Harlem Heights.

John R. Murray, who had a house and farm north of the Jumel property, may have been Eliza's most important contact. A merchant and banker with a deep appreciation of European painting, cultivated during a grand tour taken at the turn of the century, he served as the vice president of the American Academy of the Fine Arts.[21] Founded in New York in 1802, this once sleepy institution had transformed itself during the two years Eliza had spent in France. In 1816 the city's former almshouse near city hall had been renovated to house it and several other cultural institutions.[22] There the academy had initiated a program of regular exhibits. The fall 1817 show would celebrate Eliza's emergence as an art collector.

Ninety-seven of her paintings—more than a third of her collection—formed the core of the exhibition. Possibly Murray, as Eliza's neighbor, had learned of the 242 artworks she had brought back from France and suggested that the members of the organizing committee contact her. Or she may have heard of the forthcoming exhibition from him and approached the committee herself.

Records of the show reveal that Eliza was a canny businesswoman. She began by offering terms the committee members "thought beyond their powers"—perhaps she asked for a rental fee?—and then negotiated to reach a mutually satisfactory agreement.[23] The academy agreed to insure the paintings and cover all costs associated with their delivery and return.[24] Thus Eliza would benefit from the exhibit even in the absence of a rental payment; she saved herself the cost of insuring the artworks at the mansion. She would still be able to admire them at her leisure, since the agreement included "a card of admission for her and her party."[25]

The exhibit opened to the public on September 1.[26] As the best-represented collector—having supplied nearly half of the 229 works on display—Eliza must have been pleased to see a laudatory note that appeared in the *Evening Post* the next day:

> On the opening of the third exhibition of the American Academy of the Fine Arts, yesterday, we were surprised and gratified to find an entire new face put upon the gallery . . .
>
> The present collection is principally European. The number of paintings brought into this country is truly astonishing. Most of the pictures will give pleasure, and some of them will excite a more powerful sentiment.[27]

The editors of the *New-York Columbian* approved of the exhibition too. It "has very truly been announced as entirely new, and a great part of the pictures were never until now taken from the packages in which they were imported from Europe." Besides welcome novelty, there was "much to gratify the lovers of painting"—in particular, "Mignard's picture of *Mademoiselle de Montespan with a Cupid*; the *Incredulity of St. Thomas*; *Cleopatra*; *Hercules and Omphale* by Le Moine; the *Crucifixion* by Flamael; the *Battle of Cavalry*, and above all that exquisite painting, the *Hunting of the Hare*, by Snyders."[28] Seven of the eight paintings singled out by the *Columbian* were from Eliza's collection.[29]

Although Stephen's friend and fellow merchant, James B. Durand, who represented Eliza in her negotiations with the academy, referred specifically to "*her* [emphasis added] collection of paintings," the press and even some of the academy members assumed that her husband had acquired them, writing that the borrowed paintings were "part of the collection of Mr. Stephen Jumel."[30] The error is telling. That a woman might be an art collector on a large scale was such an unlikely concept that it didn't occur to most people as a possibility.

Before the 1820s, only a handful of Americans—almost all male—had made their mark as art collectors. Between 1795 and 1835, Boston merchant Thomas Handasyd Perkins purchased European paintings in Paris and patronized American artists at home.[31] Another Massachusetts native, James Bowdoin III, put together a collection of 70 paintings and 142 drawings, mostly acquired during diplomatic postings in the first decade of the nineteenth century.[32] Martha Coffin Derby of Portland, Maine, and Boston, one of the rare women to make a name as a connoisseur, gathered paintings and plaster casts while touring Europe in 1801 to '03 and patronized contemporary artists.[33]

In Baltimore, Robert Gilmor Jr., a merchant's son given a classical education, collected both old master and American paintings.[34] Charleston could boast of Joseph Allen Smith, who shipped canvases, plaster casts, and impressions of gems from Italy.[35] New Yorkers could point to Dr. David Hosack's art collection and small groupings of pictures assembled by merchants, bankers, and artists.[36] But these aficionados were exceptional. Although genteel Americans had taken pride in displaying art in their residences since colonial times, even the wealthiest families owned only modest selections of pictures and statuary. Vanishingly few citizens of the young republic had paintings in their homes other than family portraits.[37] In this environment, Eliza was remarkable. Not only was she America's first major woman art collector, but the size and scope of her holdings were unmatched by the country's connoisseurs of either gender. In less than two years, she had assembled the largest collection of European paintings yet brought to these shores by a private citizen of the United States.[38]

Eliza's pictures received considerable, although not always favorable, attention. The most detailed commentary on the exhibition was provided by a local artist, the British-born John Rubens

Smith (1775–1849). Writing under the pseudonym "Neutral Tint," he discussed nearly every artwork on display. His multipart review appeared in the *National Advocate*, a New York City newspaper, between September 12 and November 8, 1817.[39]

Crotchety and opinionated, Smith was sparing in praise and endorsed few works in the exhibition without reservation, regardless of ownership or authorship. For example, of Eliza's *Lady with a Lap Dog* by the French rococo artist Jean-Marc Nattier, Smith conceded: "Good painting and drawing, particularly in the arms, and is a good picture, for 'days of yore,'" but "the obsolete fashion of the dress might have excluded it from a place in this fashionable resort."[40] Eliza's perspective views of Florence, Prague, and Lisbon by "Crevinbros" (in fact, the early eighteenth-century Dutch artist Charles-Léopold Grevenbroeck or his brother Orazio) likewise received grudging acknowledgment: "There is, or rather *was* once, a very fine effect of light and shade in these pictures previous to their being retouched and badly cleaned; they still retain evidence of much good execution and perseverance, and stamp the painter a man of no ordinary mind, and are, no doubt, faithful representations."[41]

Eliza's *Dogs Pursuing Hares* by the seventeenth-century Flemish animal painter Frans Snyders—a work previously singled out by the *New-York Columbian*—received the rare tribute of unmixed admiration: "Here is, at length, a good picture, to gladden our eyes, almost bedimmed in exploring rubbish."[42] Another "Good!" rewarded her *Astronomy* by "Courtin" (probably Jacques-François Courtin, an early eighteenth-century French artist who trained in Rome). "It has all the harmony, without the frippery, of the French school; beautiful, clear flesh tints, with an accurate knowledge of the figure. The harmoniously blended reflections in the white silk dress is [*sic*] an object of study. Though no advocate for *dark* backgrounds, this is highly appropriate."[43]

Smith's comments on *Astronomy* reveal his preferences for well-lit subjects, anatomical accuracy, and naturalistic depiction of figures and landscapes. He was unfailingly dismissive of the expressive distortion of the mannerists and an unbending critic of dramatic chiaroscuro (strong contrasts of light and dark). Thus Eliza's *King David*, then attributed to Gerrit Honthorst, but today thought to be by the French Baroque painter Simon Vouet, was dismissed as "florid, yet cold—black in shadow, with rusty iron stair rods for harp strings."[44]

Smith was even more severe about Eliza's *Hagar, the Angel, and Ishmael in the Desert*, a highly mannered work attributed to the late Baroque Italian painter Francesco Trevisani. Although it had "*some* good drawing and handling," it was "so discordantly cold, frittered in effect, and theatrically arranged throughout, as to destroy all interest in the subject. Could anyone imagine that a being perishing for want would drink with such an affected air?" The angel, he added, had "caught the cramp in her hand by sympathy, from the distressing manner in which the fellow holds the jug."[45]

Other works from Eliza's collection were rejected more tersely. With reference to *A Religious Composition* of undetermined authorship, Smith wrote: "Read a ridiculous composition, and save all further comment." Of *Religion* by Pietro da Cortona, he sniffed, "we should rather say, 'Heresy, or a Drunken Beggar in a dirty, deserted Palace.'" *A Boy with a Pigeon*, which Eliza claimed as a work of Spanish seventeenth-century painter Bartolomé Murillo, Smith wrote off as "a pigeon in a swill-tub—too contemptible to notice." *Several Figures with a Dead Body* was "execrable; the sooner they are all buried the better."[46]

It comes as a relief to learn that Eliza's *Vase, Flowers, and Fruit*, given to the Flemish still-life painter Jean-Baptiste Monnoyer, was "the work of a masterly hand," and her *Amorous Courtier, from La Fontaine's Tales* by the French rococo painter Jean Raoux, was "a fine picture, extremely well painted."[47] Similarly, her *Girl with a Dog* by Schall was "a pretty piece of clear execution; perhaps, upon the whole, somewhat too cold, but a fine sample of miniature painting in oil."[48]

The exhibition remained open until November 12, a run of just over two months.[49] Afterward, at Eliza's request, the paintings she had contributed to the exhibit stayed on display in the galleries until April 1818, when they were removed so that the annual summer show could be mounted.⁵⁰ That the officers of the academy felt they were worth retaining was a vote of confidence in Eliza's taste.

In late 1817 Eliza had intimated to Stephen that she planned to return to France. Then he had received no letters for several months, and he was unsure if she had changed her mind. "In your last," he wrote, "you indicate that your desire would be to come to France. I desire that as well . . . But consider whether in coming to France to stay, you will find what you want. We will need to buy a property here in order to spend the summer in the country." They would also need to think about what Mary's future would be.⁵¹ She was reaching marriageable age.

Stephen was right to question whether Eliza had thought through her decision. When he received three long-delayed letters from her in late May or early June, he was upset to learn that she had already reconsidered:

> I see by your letter of [April 24, 1818,] that it is no longer your intention to return to France to stay. Nevertheless, when a wife loves her husband, she must be where her husband is. But if you think differently, that [illegible] me. You knew that if my intention was to finish my days in France, you would have to stay here with me too. [If you disagree] I will be sorry for the rest of my life, having always done everything in my power, up to this moment, to make you happy."⁵²

Rather than rejoining Stephen, Eliza asked him to move back to the United States or at least send Mary to her. Perhaps she had intended from the beginning to use her absence to persuade her husband to leave France. If so, the tactic was unsuccessful. "You must know the reason, what the sea does to me," Stephen wrote. "You witnessed it." Seasickness isn't "a life-threatening illness," he acknowledged, "but what suffering! And everyone [illegible] laughs."⁵³

Beside the discomfort that an ocean crossing would entail, Stephen, fifty-three, was beginning to feel his own mortality: "I do not have long to work," he wrote, "and from one moment to the next, I might leave for Père Lachaise" (a reference to the famous Parisian cemetery). As he struggled to support Eliza and their dependents ("I am overloaded with work. I am always busy in the factories and I need more patience than ever"), she remained at a distance and was spending more and more money. She had even kept several laborers employed over the winter when there was little work to be done on the land. "I don't know what you were thinking," Stephen wrote. "You tell me you aren't spending any money at all," but Benjamin Desobry and James Durand had informed him of her expenses, and they were higher than she had acknowledged. "To do everything a property demands, you would need a fountain of money," he cautioned her. He would allow her to spend one-half of their income, but that was the most he could afford: "Mʳ Desobry will be able to tell you nearly to the dollar" how much that would be. In the meantime, he would send Mary to her, as Eliza had requested. He had arranged for her to travel with a close friend of his who was leaving for the United States with "his wife, who is very respectable."[54]

Stephen closed the letter with a cry from the heart: "Adieu. I think night and day of seeing you again. I am sending you a thousand kisses and kissing Mary for you." Sadly he signed himself "your faithful husband, Stephen Jumel."[55]

→ 17 ←

INDECISION

*M*ary reached New York on August 21, 1818, a tedious sixty days after leaving Le Havre.[1] If Eliza had hoped that her husband would accompany their daughter, she was disappointed. Stephen, having received no recent letters from his wife, wrote from Paris on July 16, "I assume that you think that I am en route." But he was staying in France, he told her. It was up to her to return. He was having their lodgings at 40, rue de Cléry furnished to receive her when she was ready to join him. There were two bedrooms, a "beautiful dining room," an antechamber, "a handsomely furnished reception room," an indoor lavatory (a luxury introduced from England), three bedrooms for servants, a kitchen, a coach house, a stable, and two cellars—one for firewood and the other for wine.[2]

A letter Eliza mailed in July left him unsure of her plans. "I still don't know your intention—if you are going to decide to cross over again to France," Stephen wrote on November 9. "These are not voyages to make every year." But he would leave her free to make her own decision:

> My intention is to finish my days in France. I don't want to set down the law and say you must come back. But consider that separating

like this isn't right at all. Think now about what you have to do. I don't want to tell you to sell the country house either, in case once [it is] sold, you are not able to have a similar property. Think about everything. I leave you mistress to do as you wish.

My love to Mary, and ask her to write me often. I know the trouble you have had with her mother. I know everything, even the loss of your horse, of the carriage. But all that is nothing. Think only of him who says to you that he is your faithful spouse for life.[3]

Stephen's last paragraph suggests that Eliza's life in New York was not without its trials—her relationship with her sister was sometimes rocky and she suffered frequently from migraine headaches.[4] But she remained unwilling to return to France. In a letter of December 8, Eliza asked Stephen to obtain a forte piano and a harp for Mary. The request, carrying as it did an assumption that his wife and Mary would be staying in New York, prompted a rare expression of frustration from him: "Bed very uncomfortable for certain persons and for others it is nothing."[5] But he would look for two instruments and send them to New York: "You will be able to teach the birds that are outside the house."[6] Eliza should not, however, purchase a seven-hundred-dollar piano that she had mentioned to him. "Neither you nor Mary is famous for your playing. And you know how weak poor Mary is. It is not my fault. She has spent enough money, and I still pay in patience."[7] For the first time, Stephen's kindness and tolerance gave way to open criticism.

"Think of all I have purchased," he continued, "the crates, the packing, the carriage from Paris to Le Havre . . . the freight from Le Havre to New York. The storage in New York. The carriage from there to the country. The loss of the broken mirrors. You cannot imagine all of the expenditures . . . You must remember to economize." For the first time, his closing—"I remain your faithful spouse"—feels almost perfunctory.[8]

By late March Stephen had regained some measure of composure. In response to a letter Eliza had written him on February 6, he acknowledged, "I don't doubt that you think about me . . . You must.

There isn't a moment that I don't think about it [i.e., their situation]. But my resolution is to stay in France, if we are at peace, as we are now. I think, as you do, that if your health is not good in France, I would not like to force you to come here."⁹ But it was more than just her health, Stephen recognized: "You love the United States, and I, I don't love crossing the ocean because all countries are agreeable to me."¹⁰

At Mount Stephen Eliza kept a carriage, coachman, and house-maid.¹¹ She took pleasure in planning improvements to the property. This year she wanted to plant peach trees and additional grapevines.¹² But her husband was increasingly worried about her expenditures. America was experiencing its first full-scale financial crisis, the Panic of 1819. Excellent harvests in Europe had reduced demand for American commodities. Grain imports by Great Britain had decreased 75 percent between 1818 and 1819.¹³

The fiscal situation was worsened by a shortage of specie. U.S. and European banks were buying up gold and silver in response to demands by their respective governments that notes be exchangeable for hard currency.¹⁴ Merchants were affected by the currency shortage, tight credit, and falling prices. Deflation, unemployment, and falling wages reduced demand for, and affordability of, imported goods.¹⁵ Customs duties collected in the United States plunged from $36 to $13 million between 1816 and 1821.¹⁶

"I preach economy," Stephen wrote, "and truly it is something that must be done, because I have not earned a *sol* [a small French coin] from my investments in the United States since my departure. I have even lost money on some, because the business crisis has been so bad. There have only been losses on top of losses . . . Do what is necessary, but no luxuries as in the past, because, truly, it is completely impossible for me to make any expenditures."¹⁷

Stephen put his foot down on Eliza's plans to move into their house at 150 Broadway, which his friend and fellow merchant James Durand was renting. Mary had told him in a letter of June 7 that "maman had been to New York to ask Mr. Desobry to give preference to her for the house Mr. Durand occupies. But the latter has orders from me to rent the house, and the rent must serve to cover the expenses of Madame Jumel. Voilà the orders given to Mr. Desobry." Stephen encouraged Eliza to be happy where she was: "You can live tranquilly at Mount Stephen, because I know you love [to live in] retirement. God knows you have everything you need in the country house." Her daily life must have felt increasingly remote to Stephen. "Tell Mary to continue to write to me in French," he asked Eliza in July 1819. "She is absolutely right when she tells me I have forgotten English, because truly I have hardly spoken it for two years."[18] All of Stephen's letters to Eliza were written in his native tongue.

The financial situation in the United States continued to deteriorate over the course of 1819. The Pery firm in Bordeaux, in which Stephen had a heavy investment, was owed one hundred thousand francs (twenty thousand dollars) in New York. The debtor was Stephen's longtime business associate and tenant, Durand, and there was no certainty whether the money would be repaid.[19] A business in Martinique owed the firm nearly as much.[20] "It's a plague," Stephen wrote. "I will be obliged to go stay with my family in Mont-de-Marsan in order to not spend a thousand dollars a year. Imagine the business situation. We will have to wait on events with patience to know what I will lose."[21] He could no longer afford to keep young William Jones in France.[22] This missive of September 1, 1819, is the last of Stephen's surviving letters to his wife from the time period.

Eliza continued to vacillate over whether to return to Europe. "For two years Mad^e Jumel and Mr Desobry have been telling me that she is going to come," Stephen wrote to a business associate in 1820.[23] But early that year, his wife was leaning toward departure. Perhaps she felt lonely living year-round in the countryside, as her desire to occupy the Broadway house might suggest. Or she may have found it difficult to maintain the living standard she preferred, given the strain on Stephen's finances from the weak economy.

Eliza began to try to lease Mount Stephen. She had a potential renter for the mansion in mind: Joseph Bonaparte, who had reigned as king of Spain for five years while his brother, Napoleon I, was conquering Europe. Joseph had taken refuge in the United States after the fall of the First Empire and in 1816 had purchased a country estate in Bordentown, New Jersey. The beautifully decorated home, known as Point Breeze, had burned to the ground in an accidental fire in January 1820.[24]

Eliza was in contact with Bonaparte's agent about the possibility of the dethroned monarch renting the Jumel mansion.[25] Had the deal gone through, she would have savored the social triumph—but the ex-monarch decided to rebuild Point Breeze. On March 25 he wrote to Eliza politely from Philadelphia:

Madame:

I am sorry for all the trouble you have taken in sending me a list of the furniture, and your kind offers of your beautiful country place, but since I have decided not to leave my estate in New Jersey, I can only reply by thanking you and renewing my compliments.

Joseph Bonaparte[26]

Eliza kept the brief note for the rest of her life.

Napoleon's brother failing her, Eliza advertised the property for let in 1820 and early '21, lauding the virtues of the "roomy and convenient mansion house," "collection of superb Paintings," "spacious ornamental garden," and "vineyard of the best table grapes."[27] But she was unsuccessful in securing a tenant. There is no indication that she considered selling the estate, which would be hers for life if she survived Stephen. Ten years his junior, she could expect to outlive him and have the opportunity to return to her native land.

Ultimately Eliza had to arrange to auction the furniture and pictures—it would have been impractical to ship them back to France—and trust that an agent would be able to lease the vacant dwelling.[28] An itemized list of the artworks was printed in advance, grandly titled *Catalogue of original paintings, from Italian, Dutch, Flemish and French masters of the ancient and modern times, selected by the best judges from eminent galleries in Europe, and intended for a private gallery in America.*[29]

When the sale took place on April 24, 1821, it attracted more rub-berneckers than serious purchasers. Thanks to her return to Mount Stephen without her husband and the exhibition of her paintings at the Academy of the Fine Arts, Eliza had become the subject of gos-sip. It was probably around this time that the rumor began to circu-late that she had tricked Stephen into marrying her. John Pintard, who, as we have seen, was the first to record the tale, wrote that the auction "attracted all the Ladies, as well to look at the pictures as at their decayed mistress." His wife and younger daughter Louisa went "to see what is to be seen, with little inclination and less money to buy." Although they acquired nothing, they "passed a very pleasant day & returned in the evening high[ly] delighted."[30]

Too many other attendees left empty-handed as well. The Ameri-can economy was still fragile after the Panic of 1819.[31] The mixed reception of the artworks at the 1817 exhibition may have affected their salability in particular. According to Pintard, Eliza's paintings "were considered *pas grandes choses*" (i.e., nothing much) when they were exhibited at the Academy of the Fine Arts.[32] The comment sug-gests that John Rubens Smith's cranky reviews had biased poten-tial purchasers against them. A tale that the paintings had belonged to Cardinal Joseph Fesch before Eliza acquired them—a story she must have circulated in an attempt to boost their sale value—wasn't enough to create strong demand.[33] (There is no indication that more than one or two, at most, were owned previously by that avid art collector, an uncle of Napoleon.)[34]

Two months later Eliza put the remainder of her once-cherished possessions, imported from France at great expense, up for sale at the Park Hall Auction Room. At 10 AM, potential purchasers could bid on

a splendid assortment of elegant Furniture, Paintings, Looking Glasses, &c. the property of the family going to Europe, consisting of 2 large canopy bedsteads, mahogany and gilt, 3 dozen elegant mahogany chairs, satin backs and bottoms, latest French fashion; 2 large looking glasses, 1 elegant cut glass chandelier, 2 down beds [i.e., mattresses], 2 hair mattresses, 1 hand organ, 1 marble statue, 2 glass stands, 2 bathing tubs, a large collection of original paintings of the most celebrated European masters, &c. &c. Sale peremptory for cash.[35]

Eliza's "elegant barouche and pair of horses" was also available, and would be auctioned at Byrnes Repository in Walker Street.[36]

Ten or twelve of the paintings and possibly some of the furnishings returned unsold to the mansion on Harlem Heights.[37] But it would not have been Eliza who reinstalled them. On June 16, two days after the auctions, she and Mary sailed for Europe.[38]

PLACE VENDÔME

*I*n a letter book Stephen used during the 1820s, a short sentence is penned among notations relating to business: "I love my dear uncle Stephen very much."[1] The tribute was written by Stephen's youngest niece, Felicie Lagardere.

During Eliza's four-year absence in the United States, Stephen was in regular contact with his extended family in Mont-de-Marsan. As early as 1809 he had sent money from New York to pay for a house for his brother François.[2] More recently he had become close to his sister Madelaine's daughters, Felicie and Rose, and the latter's husband, Jean Lesparre Jeantet. He trusted Lesparre, a cloth merchant, to handle business matters for him in Mont-de-Marsan, and wrote to him regularly when away from his hometown.[3]

In late May 1821, as Eliza wound up her affairs in New York, Stephen made an important contribution to his own family's welfare. Twenty-four-year-old Felicie had only a modest dowry, an income of three hundred francs per year. Stephen made possible her marriage with a wealthy landowner by promising the couple fifteen thousand francs, to be paid a year after his death.[4]

Before the summer ended, Eliza, now forty-six, had rejoined her husband. In 1821 or '22 the Jumels moved to 16, place Vendôme, a more elegant address than the rue de Clèry. Planned at the beginning of the eighteenth century by Jules Hardouin-Mansart, who designed much of the royal domain of Versailles, the square was lined on all sides by attached townhouses boasting mansard roofs and uniform façades. In the center, a 133-foot-tall column covered with bas-reliefs commemorated the French conquest of the German states during the Napoleonic wars. Although the monument was crowned originally with a statue of Napoleon, the white flag of the restored Bourbon monarchy was fluttering gaily from its peak by the time the Jumels settled in the place Vendôme. A "delightful" view of Paris and its suburbs was available from a gallery encircling the top of the column.[5]

Number sixteen, the townhouse the Jumels rented, had been inhabited for a time in the eighteenth century by Antoine Mesmer, a pioneering advocate of hypnotism (originally known after him as "mesmerism").[6] During the Napoleonic period, it was leased to senior officials passing through Paris.[7] The French Ministry of Justice was (and is still) located on the opposite side of the square, visible from the Jumels' windows.

Eliza circulated in Parisian society, renewing her earlier connections. The marquis de Cubières had died of a stroke on August 10, 1821, but Eliza stayed in contact with his widow and daughters.[8] Adèle wrote to her from the country one day: "Maman is definitely going to Paris tomorrow. She has promised to dine there, but Henriette and I will have the pleasure of dining with you if that suits you, as long as it can be around four o'clock." Their mother wanted to return home the same evening. "As soon as we arrive, we will hurry to join you," Adèle added, "so then we can do our shopping together."[9]

Another evening might have found Eliza visiting a neighbor in the place Vendôme: "M^de Butler presents her compliments to M. and Madame Jumell [*sic*] and Mademoiselle their Niece, and requests the pleasure of their company at her house next Tuesday evening."[10]

Now that Mary was an adult—she turned twenty in 1821—she could join Eliza for more than family parties. Rosalie Pinel, a close friend of the marquise de la Suze (who persisted in her attempts to convert Eliza to Catholicism), arranged an escort for them for a special event: "I have the promise of two tickets for six o'clock, for you and Miss Mary, and besides that, a cavalier whom you will find most agreeable and who will be delighted to accompany you. He is Mons. the General Controller. He will be in uniform."[11] Since a uniformed official had the entrée to court, they may have been attending a levee or official function.[12]

An evening at the opera offered another opportunity for a brush with royalty. In an undated letter, Adèle wrote excitedly to Eliza, "We have just learned, madame, that the king will go Tuesday to the Grand Opera . . . I hasten to tell you of it, because the boxes are very quickly sold out as soon as this news is known in Society." Would Mr. Jumel please engage a box right away? she asked. "I have the honor to remind him that the king, at present, does not go to the fine Royal Box that we so greatly admire, but that they have set aside for him a big one where gather all the princes and the service, right in the middle of the auditorium at the front of the theater."[13]

"The service" referred to the well-born gentlemen, military officers, and civil servants in immediate attendance on the king. Posts in the king's train were sought-after honors, because their occupants received admission to court, as well as reflected glory from proximity to the monarch.[14] Thus madame d'Egvilly informed Eliza with pride that her husband, who bore the title of *maître d'hotel* (making him a sort of glorified steward in the royal household), could not accept an invitation because he was at the Tuileries Palace: "He is on duty serving the king and cannot budge from the château."[15]

Eliza wished that she could brag in the same way about her own husband. An undated sheet survives on which she drafted a letter to Louis XVIII:

Sire:
Every time I have had the honor of seeing your Majesty, the graciousness with which you have deigned to notice my carriage and the great kindness with which you bow to me, makes me feel like

writing to you. But once out of your presence, courage fails me. The return of your Majesty—day [*sic*] I have so ardently wished for—caused me so much joy that I seem to be inspired with new courage to present a petition in favor of my husband.

My husband left France at the beginning of the Revolution and established a home in New York (U.S.A.) with the resolution of never again seeing his native land until the return of the Bourbons. He became a merchant and has been very fortunate in his business, becoming one of the most influential men in New York. He is so patriotic that he has been unwilling to have commercial relations anywhere except with France. He was the first to introduce La Soirée [she means *la soierie*, i.e., silk goods] at wholesale in the United States, and in doing this has created a demand for French merchandise, in consequence bringing about an enormous trade, so that the most celebrated manufacturers of France have worked for him and have sent millions . . . through his business.

He has had the misfortune to lose two of his ships, all loaded, which were seized by Napoleon and held at the Port of Bayonne—for which he has never been reimbursed.

His kindness of heart and his directness in business have made him known and loved throughout the United States. He has frequently been offered very honorable and lucrative positions, which he has always refused, saying he still hoped again to see his own country.

What a joyous day for him when he got the news of the return of the Bourbons. Immediately he made haste to sell his ships and his stocks and to leave his temporary home, which was for him a sort of exile, since it was so far away from his dear country.

We came to Paris, and he, seeing a great deal of misfortune, was moved by his kindness of heart to set up several manufacturers, who today are prosperous. At the same time he himself has met with nothing but losses. His lofty nature will not allow him to ask for a place at Court for himself, as he thinks he has not yet done enough for his country to deserve such a favor.

But, accustomed to being received as persons of high position, and our fortune admitting of our living in excellent style, and having also the good fortune—since our stay in Paris—of knowing many ladies of the Court, I often find myself embarrassed. When I see that I have no title and my husband no cross [i.e., the cross of an officer of the Legion of Honor]—in spite of all he has done for his country and of his devotion to the King—I feel utterly discouraged, and beg him to go back to his adopted country. But knowing your Majesty's extreme kindness, I am anew inspired with the hope that you will not ignore a subject so worthy as Stephen Jumel. Whatever post your Majesty might deign to offer—even without remuneration—it would be his greatest delight to fill it, and your Majesty would find in Stephen Jumel a faithful subject and one wholly devoted to his King, and in his wife, eternal gratitude.[16]

The letter is revealing. It seems that nothing could fill the void left by the poverty and exclusion of Eliza's youth: not a thoughtful husband, not a loving niece become daughter, not an elegant home, not a carriage and pair, not even a bow of recognition from a king. Whatever she craved, once acquired it was not enough, and again she would feel "embarrassed" and "utterly discouraged."

In pursuit of the fashionable life, the Jumels summered in Dieppe in 1824. A port on the English Channel, the city had begun to attract attention as a seaside resort in the last years of the First Empire, thanks to visits by Napoleon's stepdaughter, Hortense Beauharnais, whom he married to his second-youngest brother, Louis. Once peace arrived, proximity to England turned Dieppe into a popular vacation destination for visitors from across the channel. "You see nothing but Englishmen in this city," Stephen commented.[17] Throughout the summer, a steamboat from Brighton arrived daily, carrying "from fifty to sixty passengers, carriages, and horses."[18]

In 1824 a three-week visit by Marie-Caroline, duchesse de Berry—a member of France's royal family—prompted French aristocrats to join the English tourists. Eliza, Stephen, and Mary followed in their wake. "We spent a most delightful summer in Dieppe," Mary wrote to her birth mother, Maria Jones. "The sea bathing was very agreeable, the balls and parties were charming, and the Princesse De Berry [*sic*] with all her attendance aded [*sic*] to the gaiety and brilliance of the place."[19]

Stephen was equally enthusiastic. "People enjoy themselves very much; everybody bathes," he wrote to his nephew-in-law Lesparre. "As for me, I took sixty baths this year," during a stay of "more than two months."[20] Stephen decided to purchase a summer home in Dieppe on the modish place des Bains. The three-story structure had a central block with ten windows on the façade, flanked with two wings, each sixty-eight feet in length. Stephen, Eliza, and Mary would inhabit one of the wings. The center section could be rented out; it was big enough "for three families, with their cooks, stables, etc., etc., with a place for two horses for each family, and a carriage house."[21] In addition to Stephen's two horses (used to pull Eliza's carriage), "there will be room enough for ten or twelve others," he told Lesparre. "In the yard it will be possible to put thirty carriages, which can be brought in and taken out."[22] Offering storage for vehicles would be a useful source of revenue.

By late October he had already spent twenty to twenty-five thousand francs (four to five thousand dollars) on wallpaper and furniture for the house. If Lesparre visited, he would find all the amenities: "a nice pleasant room, soft water in the yard, excellent water which comes from four leagues across the mountains, through which a canal has been dug to Dieppe." In clear weather, the coast of England was visible from a belvedere at the top of the house, and "the vicinity [was] all beautiful." The land was well cultivated, there were "excellent fish," and Rouen, with its cloth mills, was only twelve leagues away.[23]

Despite these assets, Stephen showed caution in making the purchase, knowing how easily Eliza became dissatisfied. "I have two years to cancel the contract," he told Lesparre. "If Mrs. Jumel is not comfortable in it, I will be able to relinquish it."[24]

That Eliza was uncomfortable about something was certain. The evidence comes from a curious note in the diary of American writer

Washington Irving, living at the time in Paris. On November 27 Irving paid a visit to a fellow expatriate, a wine merchant from New York named Dominick Lynch. While Irving was there, another visitor arrived: "Mrs. Jumel called to see Bremner"—probably Benjamin Bremner, also a New York merchant—and "told a long story of Stephen Jumels [*sic*] being deranged."[25]

The fact that Eliza was consulting a merchant suggests that she was concerned about financial decisions Stephen was making. In September he had mortgaged the Broadway and Liberty Street buildings for six thousand dollars, probably to fund the Dieppe acquisition.[26] Eliza had counted on the income from the downtown properties— their most valuable real-estate investment in America—to support them comfortably when Stephen retired. Now the nest egg was encumbered with debt—all to purchase a home in France, when she preferred life in the United States.

In retrospect, late 1824 was not the moment to tie up capital, although Stephen could not have known it at the time. Within a year the European economy would crumble. Stephen Jumel's finances would collapse with it.

THE PANIC OF 1825

*I*n 1825 Europe's financial systems failed. The London stock market peaked early in the year and then share prices dropped precipitously.[1] Investors who had purchased stock in a host of risky ventures—mines, water companies, canals, and bridges—turned out, too often, to have been poorly informed and ill-advised.[2]

The effects of bursting speculative bubbles were apparent on both sides of the Atlantic. As the editor of *Niles' Weekly Register*, an American financial paper, wrote in early September, "those who had [money], did not know how to employ it, and so they made mighty investments in the wildest and most visionary projects that ever had their day. These, in general, have returned little or nothing, and money has become 'scarce,' the prices of stocks have considerably fallen in both countries [i.e., Great Britain and United States], and no small pressure begins to be felt, which will probably increase and become very onerous on traders and dealers of all classes."[3]

The collapse of the cotton markets added to the turmoil, as oversupply replaced fears of a shortage. "During the quarter which ended on the 30th June, nearly twenty-five millions of pounds of cotton were exported from New York," reported the *Weekly Register* on September 24.

But it would have been better for New York, if none of her merchants had touched cotton at all. The fifty thousand, and hundred
thousand dollars, that speculators in the article made in a day, while
the bubble was floating, are dissolved—leaving behind only wrecks
of fortune and bankruptcy, with the ruin of innocent persons . . .
John Bull has got the cotton, the American merchants have lost a
large part of the value of it, and the planters have been seduced into
an extended cultivation to reduce the price, and bring themselves
into trouble: and so endeth this chapter of iniquity.[4]

But it wasn't the end. On December 3, the *Weekly Register* noted
that the business climate continued to worsen:

The recent wild speculations in cotton, superadded to the various
gambling projects of stock-jobbers, which built up various mon-
ied institutions without any money at all, the whole being puff and
paper, has produced a very unpleasant state of things in several parts
of the United States, and the demand for money far exceeds the
usual supply, in several of our chief cities . . . And there is a shaking
of *confidence* which is more injurious than the losses actually sustained . . . banks that are fully able to meet all their engagements in
a regular way, merchants that can surely pay all their debts, if aided
by their usual facilities, and mechanics that are 'as good as old gold'
with the accustomed order of business—neither of these may be
competent to meet a sudden derangement, and one goes on to break
down another, until the ruin becomes general.[5]

In the second week in December, the collapse of the Plymouth
Bank in Devon and two of the largest London banks spurred a run
on banking institutions across England.[6] Depositors demanded to
withdraw their funds, and currency reserves were soon exhausted:

Expresses were hourly arriving at London to obtain gold. The people . . . lost confidence in paper, and assembled in great numbers
about the banks to obtain money for it. At Plymouth, the uproar was

dreadful. There was literally a whole population, with food in abundance staring them in the face, and yet without means of obtaining it, for . . . gold alone would the sellers take, and gold was not to be had. By break of day, all the banks were surrounded by mobs, and the civil power was mustered in front of them.[7]

By early 1826 nearly 10 percent of England's banks had failed.[8]

Like other businessmen who depended on the London financial markets, Stephen felt the shortage of cash and credit, and had difficulty collecting money owed him by fellow merchants. On February 16, 1826, he wrote to his nephew-in-law Lesparre, "I am more than sorry not to be able to give to my sister what I used to give her."[9]

Although the English banks were beginning to recover by early spring, ripples from the crisis spread across the channel and even across the Atlantic. France went into a recession.[10] "The great merchants and bankers in Germany, Prussia, the Netherlands, &c. were giving way, and for enormous amounts. The like, perhaps, was never heard of before."[11] Bankruptcies of British merchants continued—1,827 for the half year ending June 1826, compared with 489 for the same period of 1825.[12]

French, German, and British exports to Latin America plunged because of the collapse of the credit markets needed to finance shipments.[13] Funds for capital investments dried up, dooming manufacturing and mining ventures in Central and South America and destabilizing the economies of the newly independent countries they served. The governments of Peru, Colombia, Chile, Argentina, and Mexico fell into default on their sovereign debt.[14]

In May 1826, as the turmoil continued around them, Eliza, Stephen, and Mary packed their trunks in Paris. After a brief stop in Dieppe, they traveled on to Le Havre. On May 26, three days after their arrival in the busy port, Eliza and Mary sailed for New York.

Their departure on the ship *Lewis*, captained by Robert Macy, was as abrupt as Eliza's previous retreat to the United States. "Mrs. Jumel made up her mind to sail as soon as the ship arrived," Stephen wrote to Lesparre. "If my business had permitted me to do so, I would have sailed, but I hope to be able to do so in May next."[15]

The exact reason for Eliza's voyage—one might even say flight—remains unclear. On the face of it, she went to the United States to look into the condition of their investments and collect monies due to them. She took with her a power of attorney authorizing her to manage Stephen's affairs in the state of New York and, at her discretion, sell any real estate he owned there.[16] But there may have been other tensions that prompted the precipitous journey.

A letter she sent to Stephen in July 1826 is tantalizingly vague. "I am very flattered that you are thinking of me," she wrote in French, the language she used in corresponding with her husband, "but at the same time troubled to know that you are suffering from repentance. You are wrong to stay at home so much, because that could harm your health, and if that was the case, judge my despair."[17] The question of what Stephen was repentant for remains unanswered. Did he regret poor business decisions that threatened their future . . . or a quarrel that culminated in Eliza's departure?

There were earlier signs that problems may have been simmering between them. In January 1825 Stephen had changed the legal status of the mansion in New York and the thirty-six acres of land immediately surrounding it. Since 1815 the property had been governed by a trust that gave Eliza the use of the estate after his death and would return it to his heirs when she died. But at the beginning of 1825, he revised the trust to give her immediate possession of the house and acreage. Although a trustee would need to sign off on her business decisions, the property was effectively hers from that time onward—to manage as she wished for the rest of her life and leave to her heirs after her death.[18]

The precipitating factor for the transfer of ownership might have been Stephen's purchase of the Dieppe house. Far less enthusiastic about life in France than he, Eliza may have insisted on having the option of an independent life in the United States. Or if he planned to leave his new property to his French relatives after his death, she might have prodded him to give the New York mansion to her.

Another trust, set up a year later, on January 18, 1826, settled the Broadway and Liberty Street houses on Eliza as well. Their rents would be hers, free from any debts her husband might owe, although, unlike the mansion, the two downtown properties would revert to Stephen or his heirs after her death.[19] Given that Stephen was cash-strapped by this point, it seems likely that this second transfer was made to protect these assets from his creditors rather than with the intention of providing more lavishly for his wife.

Regardless of the underlying reasons for the conveyances, by midsummer cash was Stephen's immediate need. Eliza began trying to collect it as soon as she arrived in New York. She attended first to the downtown houses, which had been rented out at below-market rates by their American agent, Frederick Brunel. Even though rents had begun to drop because of the currency shortage, she persuaded the current tenant of the Broadway store, a Tyrolean-born shop-keeper named Michael Werckmeister, to take a seven-year lease at $2,100 per year—"and if I had been here a year ago, I would have had at least twenty-five hundred," she added in a letter to Stephen.[20] As for the neighboring house on Liberty Street, she gave notice to its undesirable tenants. "It is in very bad condition, I mean excessively dirty," she told Stephen, " and before I will be able to offer it for rent, I will be obliged to paper and paint it, and without any other expense, I will make it look as it should, and there isn't any doubt that I will have double the present rent."[21]

In August Eliza traveled to Cherry Valley, about fifty miles west of Albany, where she and Stephen had lands that had been transferred to them in payment of a debt. Their title to the properties—owned previously by Cadwallader D. Colden, a politician and land speculator—was problematic, Eliza discovered. "We don't have the deeds," and because of that "no one wants to buy [the farms] from us," she told Stephen. The paperwork had been managed poorly by Benjamin Desobry, with bonds and mortgages remaining on the lands. "We are presently at the mercy of Colden," Eliza explained, "because he can foreclose the mortgage on us whenever it seems good to him; voilà the manner in which Desobry arranged it."[22]

Their agent in Cherry Valley, who managed the properties and collected the rents, was a prominent lawyer, James O. Morse. He was also "a rascal," according to Eliza. "Mr. Morse does everything for his own interests [and] is continually in litigation with those who live on our lands, [who] being poor and not being able to pay, all the expense falls on us. He renews [the leases of] the farms every year, and being a lawyer, he arranges everything himself, and all our interests fall into his hands."[23]

While in Cherry Valley, Eliza tried to collect on debts owed to Stephen by a local firm, Hoffman and Glass. When she presented her husband's bills of exchange, Hoffman opened his books and showed her records indicating that he had already paid them. "He told me that you and he had the habit of exchanging your bills," she wrote Stephen, "and there were several of yours that he found not long ago and burned. In saying that, I tried to stop him, but he tore yours in pieces, saying that, supposing he owed them, they were outlawed— that is to say, six years having passed, they could no longer be used to claim the debt." Eliza was powerless against Hoffman, and her frustration is palpable. "It seems that everything conspires to prevent me from being able to procure money to send you," she wrote.[24]

She complained too about the integrity of their New York City agent, Brunel. Stephen should keep track of any payments Brunel sent, Eliza told him, because whenever she asked about money, the agent told her, "I just sent it the other day" (i.e., to Stephen).[25] Yet in their absence Brunel had been retaining large sums of money. Three years before, he had foreclosed on a mortgage on one of their farms in Cortlandt, in Westchester County, netting eight hundred dollars that should have been sent to the Jumels. He didn't tell Eliza about the foreclosure until she was leaving to inspect the land and would have discovered it for herself.[26] Frustrated by another instance of this type, Eliza told Brunel that she "was going to demand from him the interest on the money that he had kept so long." As she reported to Stephen, "He responded that if I demanded the interest, he would raise his commissions." Would Stephen tell her whether or not she should insist on the interest? she asked.[27]

Brunel also had a collusive arrangement with a farmer leasing some of the Jumels' land on Harlem Heights: "Mr. Naudine [i.e., Nodine], not knowing the arrangements that Mr. Brunel had made for him, told me that he was giving one hundred dollars per year, while Mr. Brunel, to show good faith, put in his book of arrangements that he was receiving only fifty dollars a year from Naudine, without even warning him about it."[28] She gave notice to Nodine and also to a Mr. Parsons, who was leasing their forty-acre lot on the west side of the Kingsbridge Road.[29]

It is not clear whether Brunel cheated Eliza and Stephen persistently or whether some of the problems were misunderstandings or the result of Eliza's eagerness to find someone to blame. The latter tendency is clear in a letter in which she mentions two ladies who were tenants in their downtown houses. They told me "they paid everything," she told Stephen, except for the quarter when there was a yellow-fever epidemic. They said "that Mr. Bernard had been to see them several times, showing [a] paper from Brunel that authorized him to receive those rents, and that they have several receipts from Bernard, who doubtless kept the money for his own use. But Mr. Brunel must be responsible," she concluded.[30] She presented herself to Stephen as the only person he could trust: "Thus you see that everyone betrays us, even those who have the reputation of having probity, so don't have confidence in anyone except"—here she switches from French into English—"your Eliza, who is and will be forever your true and faithfull [*sic*] and aff[ectionate] Wife."[31]

ALL ABOUT MONEY

*E*liza had the tenacity of a bulldog when anyone owed her money. "I have tormented Mr. Murry [*sic*] so much that he gave me a note payable in six months for 275 dollars," she wrote to Stephen, possibly referring to their neighbor John R. Murray. It wasn't all he owed them, but as Eliza informed Stephen, if she had insisted on having everything, she would have received nothing: "Mr. Hoffman even said to me that I couldn't claim anything, Murray having taken the *Act du bénéfice* [probably: filed for bankruptcy], but the rascals can't escape me."[1]

She worried that Stephen might be too lenient in her absence, as he pursued his creditors on the opposite side of the Atlantic: "You have not spoken about Mr. Rome. How is he? Is he still your friend or has he changed like the others; and have you taken another in his place? Don't fail to tell me frankly how your affairs are progressing and if you have collected the money people owe you. I hope that you have as much firmness and perseverance as I."[2]

Stephen was in fact having difficulty collecting on business debts. He offered to settle for 15 percent of what one creditor, Mr. Blanchard, owed him, but he had waited too long. "At present I can't get five," he wrote to Eliza. He wasn't going to pursue the debt, he explained, because it would cost him at least one hundred francs in legal fees, probably without any payoff in the end: "I judge that everything is lost."[3]

Nor was he making progress in collecting funds from Peter Pillero, a merchant who had long been his business contact in Havana. Although the consulate had named five arbiters to rule on their financial dispute, two had refused to serve. Then "Monsieur Pillero recused three of them," Stephen informed Eliza, "claiming that these gentlemen, being my friends, could only condemn him. Voilà: all that doesn't give me any money."[4]

To cut costs, Stephen sublet his and Eliza's apartment in the place Vendôme to a Madame Smith for six months. "They need four beds placed there for their family," he told Eliza. "As you know, there are five girls and a son. The last will sleep in the office; the mother in your bed with one girl; two other girls in my bedroom. I had to put another bed next to the dining room, where the general slept before we had the apartment. I am obliged to place a carpet in the salon at my expense. These are expenditures, but [they] are necessary in order to be able to rent it."[5]

Stephen hoped that he might be able to raise funds by reversing a sale made in New York in 1819 by Benjamin Desobry.[6] Back in 1813 Eliza and Stephen had transferred a plot of land on what is today the Upper West Side of Manhattan to St. Peter's Church for use as an Ursuline convent. The venture proved unsuccessful. The church never paid for the land, and the convent's nuns returned to Ireland in 1816. Desobry filed a lawsuit on Stephen's behalf in 1818, resulting in the foreclosure and sale of the land at auction, with the proceeds to be used to compensate Stephen.[7]

In the normal course of events, a foreclosed property would be purchased by a proxy of the owner and returned to him. At this auction, however, although Desobry was the high bidder at three thousand dollars, he didn't return the parcel to Stephen. Instead, he resold the land for seven thousand dollars, using three thousand to pay off a debt of his own and crediting the remaining four thousand to Stephen.[8] The transaction was questionable, at a minimum: he didn't own the land originally and had no business profiting from it. It was one more frustration for Stephen, and left him bitter at his former associate, who died penniless in October 1825.[9] "Please God that he may do penance in the other world for my money," Stephen wrote to Lesparre.[10]

Others he had helped in the past betrayed him also. Mr. Fenet of Bordeaux "owes me nearly $8000 of money loaned in New York to assist him in getting out of jail after he failed," Stephen told Lesparre. "He came to France and conveyed all his property to his wife. I cannot make a claim for I have not the books; they were in Desobry's hands as you know; he is dead; they have been sequestered; I have claimed them for more than a year; I cannot get them; I have only a statement of 1815."[11]

Stephen even found himself engaged in a lawsuit against the now-elderly Jean Pery, with whom he had done business cordially for so many years. The dispute, which he hoped they could settle in arbitration, concerned commissions Pery had collected on six of Stephen's ships that had picked up cargo in Bordeaux during the War of 1812.[12] Years had passed, but over two thousand dollars were at stake, and these days Stephen needed the money.

Family matters were not running smoothly either. Stephen was pursuing a claim for reparations from the government of Haiti (the country that was once Saint-Domingue) for the plantations that had been owned by his uncle Jacques Sonier. But the claim process was likely to drag on for years. To raise cash in the meantime, he hoped to sell a house in Mont-de-Marsan that he had purchased for his brother François in 1809. François, unsurprisingly, was not eager to give up something that was treated originally as a gift rather than a loan. Stephen took the matter to court and lost.[13]

It was unlike him to try to reverse something that he had done out of kindness and family affection. That he proceeded in the matter at all says something of the financial pressures he faced in 1826, but also reflects his growing exasperation with his brother, who possessed none of Stephen's determination and drive. As a young man in Saint-Domingue, François had fathered one or two children with slave women and was so lazy that his uncle had kicked him out of the house.[14] After the insurrection on the island, he was given a second chance. He won his aunt's gratitude by escorting her back to France and was rewarded with a property called Ages, near Mont-de-Marsan, which otherwise would have been the joint inheritance of him, Stephen, and their sister, Madelaine.[15] François did little with the gift, however, preferring instead to complain of his poverty and with his wife—a woman he had married after returning to France—hang on Stephen's sleeve. At a point when Stephen (briefly) considered appealing the verdict about the ownership of the Mont-de-Marsan house, he wrote in frustration to Lesparre:

> If I make my claim, it is on account of the badness of the wife of François Jumel, and for no other reason; only to put down that pride, which has full control over her; for but for me—and I mention it without criticism—they would be at Ages planting cabbages; but the sacks of coffee, the boxes of sugar, and even four thousand francs a year which I sent them! And still more, when he wrote me to send money to buy cows, sheep, and oxen, and that the armies in passing through your country had taken away all your cattle, and also to buy a farm, which being purchased, would increase the value of his place at Ages. But instead of increasing his prosperity, it has been reversed; he has sold one property, or part of one.[16]

"But all this does not amount to anything," he concluded. "I wish he may enjoy as good health as myself."[17] Even in his worst fits of exasperation, Stephen never held a grudge for long.

As he struggled with recalcitrant creditors in France, Stephen placed his faith in Eliza to collect money for him and improve the management of their lands in the United States. He seems to have assumed that after doing so she would return to France. In October 1826 he wrote to Lesparre about a desirable landholding not far from Mont-de-Marsan that he thought might make him and Eliza a pleasant home as they aged. He suspected that the property would be on the market soon—it included an old castle, a mill, a vineyard, and other dependencies—and in spite of his financial constraints, the prospect of buying it was tempting. It would be his wife's decision, he told Lesparre, but "as for myself, I would like to obtain from her a favorable answer. If her intention were to purchase it," he continued,

> I would spend the remainder of my days in the castle, enjoying some hunting parties with you, especially foxhunting; you would not miss them; since you are so skillful in shooting partridges, you could not fail to shoot foxes. It would also be a foothold for Texoeres [the husband of Stephen's niece Felicie]; he could sleep there when on his way to Mont-de-Marsan; but I fear it will not please Mrs. Jumel; three months hence [i.e., time for a letter to reach her and be answered] we will know something about it.[18]

Her reply to Stephen does not survive, but must have been negative; he speaks no more of the property. Eliza had begun to nudge Stephen to give up France for New York, just as she had done during her previous visit to the United States. As early as summer 1826, she wrote, "On reflection, I find that America offers more real happiness for our old age. Nevertheless I leave it to you to decide where we shall live after I have arranged our affairs."[19] Although her words suggested that she was leaving the decision to Stephen, soon she became more direct about her preferences. "Please let me know in your next if you believe I will have the happiness of having you here next spring, because I would wish that everything be in good order for your arrival," she wrote on September 21.[20] Here there is no more uncertainty about where "we" shall live, but rather an implication that the decision (at least hers) was made and only the exact time that Stephen would join her was in question. Her next sentence, however, reveals that she knew that he preferred to remain in France and that changing his mind would be difficult. "I beg you to quit that horrible country and come to the abode of happiness," she implored him, "where we can enjoy a peaceful and tranquil life, because our small income will suffice for our needs."[21]

Eliza did not explain how France had become "that horrible country" to her. Given her desire to socialize in fashionable circles and possess an aristocratic title, it is easy to imagine her brooding over slights and exclusions. The fact that she saved such trifles as three notes from the marquise de Vernon (wife of an associate of the marquis de Cubières)—each a polite refusal of an invitation—suggests both the value she placed on contacts with French aristocrats and the difficulty of building alliances with little social capital except wealth.[22] Although two letters to Eliza from the duchesse de Berry, written in Dieppe in 1825, imply that she achieved an introduction to this member of the royal family (daughter-in-law of the newly crowned Charles X), there is no indication that theirs was a close relationship.[23] In spite of her pleasure in boasting of ties to the high and mighty—for example, her claim in 1821 that her artworks had belonged to Cardinal Fesch—Eliza's social triumphs may have glittered more brightly in the retelling than in the uncomfortable reality.

Three months after her arrival in New York, Eliza had not sent Stephen any funds. She excused herself in a letter: "First of all, I have not yet received any rents," she informed him with regard to their houses downtown. "Mme Newport brought several accounts for the repairs, which ate up the rent, and the quarter that was in arrears, it was agreed between her and Mr. Brunel to give it to her because of the yellow fever."[24]

In addition, Eliza had decided to bring a family of farmers from Cherry Valley to work the Harlem Heights farms that Nodine and Parsons had rented previously. Since she wanted to put a herd of sheep, thirty cows, and a pair of horses on the lands, the plan would involve an outlay of funds rather than an immediate profit.[25]

Plus, she added, she would need to spend money on the mansion. The entryway was "falling into ruin," she reported. "The posts and columns are rotted and it will be absolutely necessary to replace them with new ones." The fences would have to be repaired as well. She had two hundred dollars on hand that she was trying "to save for these repairs," but "if you have great need of it," she told Stephen, "it is to you that it will be destined instead." It "being little in comparison with what you request is why I haven't sent it to you; but I will send it, if you prefer to have it, in place of it going for those repairs of Mᵗ Stephen. Be sure I will do everything that depends on me for your satisfaction and happiness."[26]

"For your satisfaction and happiness"—the words were easy to say, but Eliza's conduct did not fully support them. At the beginning of December, she told Stephen that the mansion's wallpaper was in shreds, and she would need to re-paper two rooms and the front hall. For the hall, would he send wallpaper decorated with gray columns and another printed with blue sky and clouds for the background? "For the other papers, I leave them to your choice, as they are cheaper in Paris than in New York."[27]

Given that the extensible purpose of Eliza's trip to the United States was to raise money for her husband, her desire to allocate funds for wallpaper rings off-key. In every letter she stressed her efforts to raise cash for him and her attachment to his interests, but she continued to spend rather than save.

By now Stephen needed five thousand dollars badly.[28] Eliza assured him on January 1, 1827, that she would do her utmost to provide the funds: "I quitted my bedchamber that I had not left for six weeks, sick as I was; I took myself to Monsieur Phillipon [*sic*] and employed all my eloquence so that he would help me procure the sum you ask of me."[29] Philippon tried to get a loan from Stephen's friend Mr. Salle, but without success. "Money is extremely rare here," Eliza told Stephen. "Everyone being in financial distress," even "friendship itself [is] set aside . . . And you can easily conceive that those who have money right now don't want to loan it at 7 percent," when companies in need of cash were offering 15.[30] The Panic of 1825 had taken its toll.

She thought that their agent James Morse might purchase their lands in Cherry Valley "at a 12 percent loss," but she was still waiting to hear from him. "And if I can obtain the money from him, it will be sent to you immediately," she assured Stephen, "because I am so tormented for that sum to send to you that I can't sleep at night. And I believe that if Capt. Macy [her trustee] was in New York right now, I would be capable of mortgaging the Broadway houses, even though I always promised myself not to do it, but if I do, what will we have to live on in our old age? Think carefully about that."[31] In fact, Stephen had already mortgaged the buildings for six thousand dollars in 1824.[32]

Eliza preferred to raise cash by selling forty shares of stock Stephen owned in the Hartford Bridge Company, a joint-stock corporation formed in 1809 to build a toll bridge over the Connecticut River.[33] Although the shares had paid a reliable quarterly dividend since 1811, Eliza had been eager to unload them ever since arriving in the United States. She had no personal stake in them and disposing of them was preferable to encumbering real estate she might have a claim on after Stephen's death.

Finalizing a sale proved problematic, however. In fall 1821 Stephen had transferred the stock to his nephew-in-law Lesparre.[34] The timing, only a few months after he had made a generous marriage settlement on his niece Felicie, suggests that he wanted to make a comparable gesture to Felicie's sister—Lesparre's wife, Rose.

The transfer stalled any potential sale. "Mr. Brunel absolutely refused to sell the Hartford Bridge stock," Eliza wrote, "without a letter of authorization from Mr. Lesparre, specifying that the money from the sale be delivered to Stephen Jumel as belonging to him."[35] She requested repeatedly that her husband obtain such a document. "You say nothing to me of Mr. Lesparre," she complained on December 1, 1826. Have him "send an order to sell or dispose of the Hartford Bridge shares as you would like, otherwise be sure we will lose them in the same way that we lost the house in Mont-de-Marsan. Don't trust anyone because we need everything that remains to us for ourselves."[36] The implication was clear: generosity to Stephen's family should not outweigh their own needs. She returned to the subject on New Year's Day: "Again I repeat to you to send the power of attorney and orders from Mr. Lesparre as soon as possible, because Mr. Lathrop, I believe, will buy or take the shares as mentioned above."[37]

Stephen left these demands from Eliza unanswered. Given how badly he needed money by 1827, his failure to facilitate a sale suggests that he intended the stock to be Lesparre and Rose's inheritance and would not go back on that decision. Rose's husband had become Stephen's confidant, a relative he treated in many ways like a son.

In February 1827 François Jumel's son Étienne (called Ulysses in the family), a hardworking young man who had a close relationship with his uncle Stephen, wrote to his father about the latter's troubles:

> My uncle is just now at Dieppe, where living is better *and cheaper than at Paris*. I know also that it is very necessary for him to economize, for when Mrs. Jumel sailed for the United States, like a good and confiding husband, he gave her full and complete power of attorney to collect all the income of his property. Since his chaste wife left, and it is nearly one year since she sailed, my poor uncle has not received one cent from her; on the contrary, after she had received all the back rents due by tenants, she obtained advances from them. She is spending the whole, leaving her husband in France in quite a critical position. Thus you perceive that want may be felt even with a large fortune.[38]

Ulysses and Eliza did not get along well, so any reading of this paragraph must take his biases into account.[39] Moreover, there is contemporary evidence that Eliza had not exaggerated the difficulty of wringing money from the Jumel farmlands in central New York. In February 1827 Morse had notified Eliza that most of her and Stephen's tenants were in arrears, and he had been unable to unload any of the property: "I have been to Albany, and have tried also to negotiate a sale with people here; but I find it impossible to sell the bonds and mortgages at the discount you propose or even at any other discount. People in the *city* will not at present advance money on bonds or mortgages in the *country*, and there is no one in the country that I can find has money at present to invest in this way."[40]

But with rental income coming in from the downtown houses, it seems that Eliza could have managed to send Stephen something. Instead she sent excuses: "I offered my diamonds for sale, but no one wanted to give me virtually anything for them."[41] She stressed her frugality: "I have neither horses nor cook, [we are] doing all the work ourselves [she and Mary]. Mr. Phillipon tells me that it is truly shameful to come into town on the diligence and run about on foot and offered to loan me enough to buy some horses, but I refused him, not wanting to be in debt to anyone."[42] She pressed again for the sale of the Hartford Bridge Company stock: "That will be a sacrifice but there is no other way to have the sum that you request."[43]

By fall Stephen had become frustrated with her evasions. Instead of one of his usual detailed letters, addressed to "my dear Eliza" and including a thoughtful inquiry about her health, a half-page letter dated October 14 opens with the unadorned salutation "Madame Jumel." To Stephen's displeasure, she had told Philippon that she was not able to supply the money her husband had requested. Stephen disagreed: "if you are economical, you don't need anyone's help to remit to me the sum that I need, of which I have received the larger part. I count on your economies to supply it and to remit me as promptly as possible four to five thousand francs [i.e., eight hundred to one thousand dollars], having the greatest need of it."[44]

If Eliza supplied the funds requested, there is no indication of it. On December 23 Stephen wrote her again, once more addressing her frigidly as Madame Jumel. He had just signed a note for four hundred dollars and required her help: "For the moment, I beg you, [if] you can, to send me double that amount. It would be to pull me out of a very great embarrassment, because I expected a decision from Havana a long time ago, in order to receive some funds. I count on your exactitude to remit the two thousand francs . . ."[45]

Their surviving correspondence from the period ends with this letter.

DECEPTION

*S*tephen spent the fall and winter of 1827 in the apartment in the place Vendôme. He shared it with his nephew Ulysses, who was working in a solicitor's office to gain legal experience after being admitted to the bar. Stephen's future plans were uncertain. "I pledged myself to Ulysses to keep him at my home until the fifteenth of April next when my lease expires," he told Lesparre in September. "After that I don't know what place I shall select, New York or the neighborhood of Toulouse. First without keeping house for the sake of my tranquility: a good table board, a little horse, a pointer, a country full of game. But I have not made up my mind about it. If I do go to New York, six thousand francs a year is enough to spend in the country."[1]

Eliza had continued to encourage her husband to return to the United States. "My dear Stephen," she wrote on May 1, in her last surviving letter from 1827, "come back and with economy we will live very well; there is absolutely nothing that can prevent you from returning."

> Capt. Skiddy's vessel is very excellent. He is the best captain and [has] the best packet that there is, so I beg of you, don't miss the earliest opportunity . . .

Think, my dear Stephen, you are no longer young. You need care that I will be able to give you as your wife. I will do all that depends on me to make you happy. The past will be forever forgotten and we will live one for the other.

The vines are in flower and it appears that we will have many grapes. Moreover we have six hundred vines. I have carefully cleaned and arranged them. You will have great pleasure in seeing them, and as for the garden, you will not be able to imagine how beautiful it is. The avenue and area around the house is so well kept that it seems a true paradise.[2]

Stephen was unconvinced. During Eliza's first visit to the United States, his loneliness and longing for her were clear. But during their second separation, there were no pleas for her return; no indications that he found life empty without her. Their relationship had grown colder. "The past will be forgotten," Eliza wrote; the implication was that there was something to regret.

Eliza had lived independently in New York between 1817 and 1821. She had been lady of the manor and made her own decisions. It would not have been surprising if she had found it difficult to subordinate her will to Stephen's afterward. Now that they were separated again, Stephen and even she may have found life more tranquil without each other.

In spring 1828 Stephen's lease had nearly expired, and he had yet to decide on his destination. "We are going to leave the place Vendôme, both I and your son," he wrote to François on April 10. "As for me, I do not know where I shall go."[3] Lesparre advised him to remain in France, but by the beginning of May, Stephen had concluded that he could not. "I will tell you that my inclination would lead me to do so," he wrote Lesparre, "but I must take another course. I gave my general power of attorney for the State of New York, where all my flowers are; that is the motive of my journey. It was to Mrs. Jumel. Revoke it and send it to anyone else in the country is what I shall not do . . . Men in the United States have changed very much; there is no longer this frankness as of old."[4] Stephen did not trust his fellow merchants to act for him anymore—and he suspected that he could not count on Eliza either.

━━━━━

Eliza Jumel betrayed her husband's confidence "by resorting to sham and fraudulent conveyances."[5] She perpetrated "gross frauds . . . upon him and his heirs."[6] That is how Stephen's relatives described her actions. If we might quarrel with the words they used, one fact was undeniable: between July 1827 and May 1828, Eliza transferred most of Stephen's property into her own hands.

The prospect of financial insecurity must have been terrifying to her. Indelibly marked by the poverty of her youth, she could not shrug off the periodic reversals of fortune that were part and parcel of a merchant's career. If we can imagine the specters that must have haunted her—cold, hunger, servitude, and the workhouse—it is easier to sympathize with her actions.

What she did was described by a lawyer named James Case, who investigated the matter in 1833 for François and Madelaine. According to Case, when Eliza arrived from France in 1826, "she represent[ed] with some show of reason that the industrious Jumel, the builder of a large fortune, the saving man, etc., etc., etc., ha[d] been the reverse of what he ha[d] been known to be in this country and that he [was] rushing headlong to the destruction of his wealth . . ."[7] This picture is not inconsistent with Washington Irving's 1824 statement that Eliza spoke about "Stephen Jumels [*sic*] being deranged."[8] From her perspective, Stephen was risking their future with unwise investments abroad.

She solicited advice from James Kent, "the most honest lawyer of the city."[9] Kent was the chief judge of New York's Court of Chancery and a man known to be sympathetic to women threatened by the missteps of their male relatives.[10] Case could not claim personal knowledge of Eliza's conversation with Chancellor Kent, but he could guess at it: "Most certainly she must have confessed to him the conduct of Jumel at Paris, her attachment for that misled man, and suggested that it was necessary to place beyond his reach some of the remains of their large estate for their common maintenance in the future. Who would not be caught, and who would not take an interest in a woman who speaks on the subject and especially who speaks well?"[11] Case added, "I know positively that it is with this language that she won over to her side Werckmeister," the tenant of the 150 Broadway store who would play a crucial role in this drama.[12]

With Kent's help, Eliza arranged matters so that Stephen would be unable to jeopardize their retirement by selling off their properties in the United States. What she did came down to six conveyances: deeds transferring parcels of real estate from one person to another. Acting in Stephen's name—using a power of attorney he had given her to manage his affairs in New York state—she "sold" Mary the two houses downtown, the uptown mansion, the thirty-six-acre homestead lot, and an additional sixty-eight acres of farmland on Harlem Heights, in return for supposed payments totaling $45,000. Mary, in turn, conveyed the properties to Werckmeister, to hold in trust for Eliza. As the only beneficiary of the trusts, Eliza was given the right to manage all of the lands for her sole use and benefit, independent of Stephen or any future husband. The trusts would end at her death and the properties would descend to her heirs free and clear—"in fee simple," in legal terminology.[13] Additionally, Eliza transferred 233½ acres of farmland in Otsego and Schoharie counties directly to Mary, making the young woman a landowner in her own right.[14]

From a twenty-first-century perspective, the conveyances Eliza made, with the exception of the one to Mary, seem unnecessarily complicated. Why place the real estate in trust for herself rather than putting it in her own name? The answer was straightforward: the arrangement was necessitated by the legal status of married women in early nineteenth-century America. In the common-law tradition the United States had inherited from England, a husband and wife were treated in legal matters as a single person. A married woman's property became her husband's automatically. If Eliza had transferred Stephen's real estate directly to herself, it would have remained his property, not hers. Creating a trust was the standard procedure used to permit a married woman to own assets separately from her husband.[15]

Because trusts could be used to hide property from creditors, they were scrutinized closely during bankruptcy proceedings and estate litigation.[16] Eliza tried to prevent suspicions from arising in the future by indicating that Mary had paid $45,000 for the Jumel real estate before settling it on Eliza. But because Mary had no money of her own, the "sales" were conducted on paper only. The illusory transactions had a single purpose: ensuring that Stephen's creditors and potential heirs would never be able to claim the lands. They were distanced from him through an outright (or apparently outright) sale, and then put in trust for Eliza (or, in the case of the last parcel, given permanently to Mary).

Eliza was never eager for her husband to spend money on his relatives, so her decision to disinherit them in favor of Mary and herself is unsurprising. "We need everything that remains to us for ourselves," she had written to sixty-one-year-old Stephen in 1826.[17] But it is disturbing that she made no provision for him, in case he happened to outlive her. Although Stephen was conscious of the need to protect their assets from creditors—in August 1826, he had even suggested that Eliza put the downtown houses in someone else's name in order to safeguard their interests in them—there is no indication that he envisioned or desired this wholesale transfer of his most valuable properties to his wife.[18] By the time he returned to the United States, he was left with nothing but farmland in Westchester County, some land in central New York, and around sixty-five acres on Harlem Heights. None of these lands yielded anything but very modest rents.

22

THE REUNION

$\mathcal{S}$tephen arrived in the United States in July 1828 after a stormy, seven-week voyage from Le Havre. "There were eight priests who brought bad luck to the ship," he told Lesparre. He had suffered as before from seasickness and only "went to the table four times to dine." But he could still sympathize with fellow travelers who were even less fortunate: "Then there were 150 steerage passengers inside doing their cooking. Those who were sick went without food, but thanks to the Supreme Being, we arrived all in good health."[1]

Stephen went immediately to the mansion on Harlem Heights: "Leaving the ship I jumped into a carriage, and one hour later I found an excellent dinner . . . You may think whether I reserved peaches and strawberries for my dessert."[2] Stephen said nothing to Lesparre about his reunion with Eliza, mentioning only that "Mrs. Jumel was in the city" when he reached New York. It is unclear whether she met the ship or if he discovered she was in Manhattan only when he arrived at their country home and found that he would be eating his first dinner on land without her.

His old friend, François Philippon, knew of the conveyances Eliza had made of Stephen's lands and encouraged him to contest them. "I advised him very often to do so," Philippon wrote in 1833; "he used always to promise me, but when it was necessary to take the proper steps, he always deferred it. At last I ceased speaking of it to him, assuming that he had some motive that he would not communicate to me."[3]

Stephen may have worried that creditors would claim the properties, if they were placed once again in his name. When Eliza had consulted James Kent after her return from France, one of the matters they had discussed was a past business dealing that might have placed Stephen in financial jeopardy. Kent considered the risk minimal, Eliza had reported to her husband: "He tells me that if all the papers were destroyed, there is no danger, and since the property was not seized, and it is such a long time since the affair, that is proof that no one believes it . . ."[4] She had followed this reassurance with advice that hinted at her own modus operandi for dealing with unpleasantness: "If you come back to New York and by chance anyone speaks to you about it, deny it flatly. Say that the whole yarn is false and an imposition: that you did not have any *profits* from the merchandise and that you only asked for the interest on your money, which you had lost as well as the capital, and that's the whole truth."[5] In Eliza's worldview, what you had done in the past mattered little; what mattered was what you could persuade people to believe.

In November 1828 she did make one change in what she had done, probably under Stephen's direction. Most of his real estate would remain under her control during her lifetime, but he would receive the lifetime use of the mansion, downtown houses, and Harlem Heights farmlands if she predeceased him, subject to an annuity of six hundred dollars to Mary. After his death, however, all the properties would go to Mary or her heirs, as Eliza desired, rather than being shared with Stephen's French relatives.[6]

Stephen may not have felt driven to battle with his wife for more. Philippon noted that, although he was "in very good health, he had not the same energy, the same moral faculties that I had known him possessed of in former years."[7] It may have been equally significant that he no longer needed money for mercantile investments. He had intended to go back into business after his return to the United States, but had become disillusioned. "There are so many swindlers," he wrote to Lesparre.[8] He had built his career in a world in which personal connections were all-important. Merchants had shared information for their mutual benefit. They had aided one another in difficult times and assisted newcomers to get a start. But times had changed and he had come to recognize that now it was each man for himself.[9] "If they fail, they go into bankruptcy to line their pockets to start again," he wrote. "That is the way in which business is conducted today . . . The more I look at it, the more disgusted I am; and therefore I am keeping quiet and living on my income, and unfortunately I am spending more than thirty thousand francs a year. I don't see anybody. Mrs. Jumel has her carriage."[10]

Four months after Stephen's return to the United States, Eliza used ill health as an excuse to spend the winter in the South.[11] In late November 1828, she sailed for Charleston on the ship *Lafayette*, accompanied by Mary and a few servants.[12] She would not return until the end of April. "She left on account of a cold," Stephen wrote to Lesparre in March 1829. "She wanted a warm climate; she has improved by it, but she is not quite cured."[13]

They wrote each other during their separation, as they had always done. One of Stephen's letters to Eliza is extant. Long and newsy, it suggests that the two had found a workable accommodation on the basis of shared household and agricultural concerns. "I see with pleasure that your health is getting better and better," Stephen wrote courteously. He described the new icehouse he was building to keep their meat fresh: it would be 11 feet square and 12 to 14 feet high, with 3-foot-thick walls. There were excavations in progress as well: several men were blasting the rocks from around the chestnuts of "Mademoiselle Mary's promenade," probably for use in building the icehouse. He and the workmen were well; "we all have good appetites," he reported to Eliza. They baked bread twice a week and cooked potatoes every day.

A small, peevish comment suggested that money was still a bone of contention in their relationship. Eliza had asked whether Stephen had gone sleighing, and he replied resentfully: "You know that I did not come back to the United States to take my pleasure. I am [at] Harlem Heights. When I have to go to New York to take my letters there, it is a great punishment for me to go there; I have testified it to you enough."

But he implied that they continued to manage their finances jointly, regardless of Eliza's legal authority over their income-producing properties. "I haven't been to see our tenant Mr Durand, not having any money to claim for the rent," Stephen wrote. "But I will have to pay him a visit." Significantly, he wrote "our tenant," not "your tenant."[14]

Now that he was retired from business and living at the mansion, he and Eliza's financial interests were essentially the same: to live on their income and manage their country property productively. As long as she could continue to live in the style to which she was accustomed—having her own carriage and using travel as an escape; as long as she need not fear that Stephen might sell their properties to repay creditors or assist his relatives, Eliza could trust him to manage their money and collect their rents, as he had always done.

The mansion with its surrounding acres functioned as a working farm. The population of the property fluctuated with the seasons, rising in the summer when Stephen hired men to work the land. Salaries were low, although not atypical for the region and time period. In 1831 Stephen paid farm laborers approximately $7.50 a month. The gardener, whose duties required more skill and background knowledge, received $8. An overseer, Gilbert Travis, hired in late March 1831, earned $150 per year. All of these men would have received room and board as well as their wages, a benefit that made the jobs more desirable. Nonresident laborers were employed as needed for a single day, a few days, or a specific project. Eliza handled the hiring of the female servants, as is indicated by a note in Stephen's hand:

"Madame Clark has made an arrangement with Madame Jumel at a rate of twelve shillings per week beginning Saturday the third in the morning. Madame Jumel has advanced her five dollars."[15]

Like many country landowners who had difficulty attracting household help, Eliza and Stephen turned to indentured servants from time to time. In February 1830 Stephen advertised for the return of two runaways: "a lad by the name of William Carr, about 16 years old, stout built, round and full face," who disappeared on December 19, and "a girl, Louise Pai, 8 years old," who absconded on January 30.[16] Whether William farmed under Stephen's supervision or did housework under Eliza's, Louise, given her age and gender, would have been under the care of the mistress of the house.

Was Eliza impatient with her or harsh? Later there were indications that she was a demanding employer, but she would not necessarily have been so to a young girl. Besides her fondness for children, she knew what it was like to be a frightened apprentice in a strange household. She had been only two years older than Louise when she was indentured as a servant herself. The girl may have been too young to thrive apart from her family. After being placed in another home, she ran away again.[17]

23

AN ARRANGED
MARRIAGE

*I*n July or August 1831, Eliza set off on another extended voyage with Mary.[1] They were headed for the Jumel properties in central New York to collect the rents and escape the heat of high summer. But the trip would prove profitable for nonmonetary reasons as well. During this journey, Eliza identified and secured a husband for thirty-year-old Mary.[2]

In 1880 Nelson Chase looked half a century into the past and described the circumstances of his initial acquaintance with his future wife. They met in the tiny hamlet of Worcester, New York, in Otsego County. He was a law student in Schuyler Crippen's office, he tells us, and "boarded in his family." Besides carrying on a legal practice and serving as the local postmaster, Crippen acted as the Jumels' agent, watching over their lands in the nearby town of Decatur and the neighboring county of Schoharie. Eliza called on Crippen, and Nelson was introduced to Mary.[3]

Eliza and Mary stayed for a time in the region, joining Nelson as boarders "in Mr. Crippen's family."[4] As the weeks passed, the young law student developed what he described as a "very intimate friendship" with Mary.[5] Then Eliza stepped in, as Nelson had explained more fully in 1873: "Madame Jumel said to me, I perceive there is a friendship between you and my niece Miss Mary; she added, if I and Mary could agree, she would be happy to have me for a son-in-law; that if we got married, she would expect us to come and live with herself and her husband on their place; she said that Mary was her adopted daughter and was to be her heir."[6]

The prospect of a wife with financial expectations was tempting to a youth with his way to make in the world. Nelson, born in Duanesburgh, in Schenectady County, New York, was the son of a builder, Ebenezer Chase, and Susannah Sheldon.[7] He worked initially as a clerk in a country store—probably from the time he was twelve or thirteen—first in the little village of Esperance on Schoharie Creek; then briefly in Troy; and finally for three or four years in Cooperstown. In 1830, aged nineteen, he moved to Worcester, where he began his legal studies.[8] Relocating to the New York City region could open up profitable opportunities for a budding lawyer, aside from what the Jumels might do for him and Mary.

For Mary, too, the marriage must have had its appeal. She had been educated as a gentlewoman, but her illegitimate birth and the gossip that swirled around her adoptive mother would have made it difficult to attract socially prominent suitors. She was still single at thirty—a telling indicator that Nelson might be her best (and perhaps only) option for matrimony. Although he was not a gentleman by birth, his profession would give him better-than-average financial prospects and entry into the upper-middle class.[9] As William Wirt, a future attorney general of the United States, wrote in 1803, "The bar in America is the road to honor."[10]

If Nelson had reservations about Mary's age—she was ten years his senior—Eliza knew how to overcome them.[11] When he was asked in 1837 if he received "any estate with [Mary] on marriage," he answered briefly, "I did." To the follow-up question, "What did you receive?" the answer was, bluntly, "Money."[12] The funds probably came from Eliza's sale of a farm that she and Stephen owned in central New York. Whether Stephen was aware of the January 2,

1832, transaction is an open question, but the deed was not registered until after his death.[13]

The marriage took place at Schuyler Crippen's home in Worcester on a Sunday evening in January 1832. "Mr. Crippen's family" was present, Nelson recalled, "some neighbors who had become acquainted with my wife, and the Rev. Mr. Bassett who performed the marriage ceremony." There was also the family of Seth Chase, "who lived a near neighbor of Mr. Crippen, and a variety of other persons whose names do not occur to me," Nelson said.[14] The occasion was recorded in the *Albany Argus*: "Married, at Worcester, Otsego County, on the evening of the 15th instant, by the Rev. Mr. Bassett. NELSON CHASE, Esq., to Miss Mary Jumel Bowne, adopted daughter of Stephen Jumel, Esq., of New-York."[15]

After the marriage, the young couple remained in Worcester for two months, continuing to lodge with Crippen. On February 29 they sold a 50½-acre farm in the town of Decatur, probably part of the real estate that Eliza had transferred to Mary when Stephen was in France.[16] Some years later, the Chases would sell a 110-acre farm in Worcester.[17] Thanks to Eliza's foresight, Mary was not a penniless bride.

In early March, Mary and Nelson left Worcester for Mount Stephen. Nelson described his first action on their arrival: "I handed Mr. Jumel a copy of the *Argus* [that contained the wedding announcement]. He read the notice. My wife and his wife were both present at the time."[18] If Nelson had been worried about his reception, Stephen's good-natured welcome dispelled any worries. He gave Nelson a "very slight pinch" on the cheek in "very friendly" fashion, and jokingly took to calling his new son-in-law "Governor."[19]

Nelson recalled much later that Stephen spoke English with "very good facility but with a marked accent." At sixty-six, he wore his years lightly: "he was very light of foot, though weighing a pretty heavy weight; I suppose he would have weighed in the neighborhood of two hundred pounds. He was as light on his feet as quite a good many younger men than he would be. He had fine spirits, in [*sic*] good health, regular appetite, was a good sound sleeper, and was cheerful and full of fun. As bright a man as I ever met with," Nelson added.[20]

According to Nelson, Stephen called his wife "Eliza," and "she called him 'Mr. Jumel'"—a mode of address that seems formal today, but was normal at the time, especially when a wife addressed her husband in the presence of others. In the European fashion, they had separate bedrooms, just as they had had in France.[21]

The Jumels knew how to hold household and entertained rarely; "they were very economical indeed," Nelson said. Nelson accompanied Stephen on visits to John M. Bradhurst and Dr. Samuel Watkins, both near neighbors, and Jacobus Dykeman, who lived farther away, near the northern tip of Manhattan Island.[22] Nelson also joined his father-in-law on his occasional trips into Manhattan. There Stephen would do the marketing, pick up letters, collect rent from his and Eliza's downtown retail tenant, Michael Werckmeister, and call on friends.[23]

The ladies of the house would have paid calls too, but Nelson mentions only one. About a week after his arrival in New York, he, his wife, and mother-in-law visited Maria Jones—at once Eliza's sister and Mary's mother. Nelson met Maria, her daughters Eliza and Louisa, and her younger son, Stephen. The older son, William Ballou Jones, he met later. There must have been regular intercourse with the Jones household, since Nelson would attend Louisa's wedding and was acquainted with Eliza Jones's husband, Charles John Tranchell.[24]

At home at the mansion, daily life centered around "the drawing room, on the first floor of the house, where the family used to meet together every day." Stephen would supervise work on the house, garden, and vineyard or, on inclement days, look through his papers.[25] With the help of Lesparre and Ulysses, he continued to pursue old business debts in France and his claim to a share in his late uncle's property in Saint-Domingue.[26]

Mary and Nelson would live with the Jumels for only two months. Eliza arranged for them to move to lodgings she rented for them in New Jersey—in Hoboken or Jersey City. The relocation probably took place May 1, still the traditional moving day in the region.[27] Neither city was much more than a country village at the time, but both had easy ferry access to New York, which would make it possible for Nelson to resume his legal studies. (Riding ten miles into Manhattan from Mount Stephen would have been impractical on a daily basis.) In after years, Nelson remembered the region in which he and Mary had set up household fondly: "Jersey was one of the most tranquil places then on the face of the globe almost."[28]

Less than a month after the newlyweds moved out, tragedy struck on Harlem Heights. Stephen was traveling north on the Kingsbridge Road in a one-horse wagon. The driver was unskilled, and Stephen was thrown from the vehicle. Ten or twelve days later, on the evening of May 22, 1832, he died at the mansion.[29] He had celebrated his sixty-seventh birthday only two weeks before.

Eliza, fifty-seven, was now a widow after twenty-eight years of marriage.

ENTER AARON BURR

aron Burr, onetime vice president of the United States, was a familiar figure in lower Manhattan. As the spring of 1832 warmed into summer, he might be seen entering his law office on Nassau Street or mounting the steps of city hall to plead a case in court. About five feet, six inches tall, he was not physically imposing. But few met him without being impressed. Although his voice was quiet and his demeanor restrained, Burr's mobile features and piercing hazel eyes gave him a magnetic presence. His upright posture and brisk walk belied his seventy-six years.[1]

In June 1832 a carriage stopped in front of 23 Nassau Street. Eliza Jumel stepped down and disappeared into Aaron Burr's office. "She wished to take legal advice respecting some real estate," according to James Parton, one of Burr's earliest biographers.[2] Probably Eliza consulted Burr on how to begin the process of settling her late husband's estate. Parton claimed that they parted on excellent terms: gallantly Burr handed his visitor into her carriage.[3]

It would take some months for the acquaintanceship to ripen. Almost immediately after her visit to Burr, Eliza, accompanied by Mary, Nelson, and a servant, left the city to escape a cholera epidemic that was spreading south from Canada. By the time the disease reached Manhattan on July 3, they were safe in Ulster County, enjoying the dramatic scenery of the Blue Mountains and Shawangunks. Later in the summer they moved east of the Hudson to Columbia County, enjoying rural tranquility at Hoffman's Gate (a stop on the post road between the villages of Claverack and Hillside) and then venturing further north to Lebanon Springs, a watering place close to the Massachusetts border.[4] There they could socialize, drive out, and bathe in the health-giving mineral spring, which remained at a comfortable 73 degrees winter and summer.[5] Mary's well-being may have been the impetus for the move to a watering place. By midsummer she must have known she was pregnant.

At the end of August, New York's Board of Health stopped issuing its daily cholera report.[6] The epidemic was contained—or so the doctors said. Eliza, returning to the city with the Chases in September, took the precaution of spending a night with them in Hoboken before crossing the Hudson to Manhattan. Beneath their window, they witnessed a shocking sight: "a person writhing in the agonies of death, dying with the cholera."[7] They fled north once more. This time they traveled beyond Albany, to the village of Saratoga Springs, which would become Eliza's second home.[8]

A summer resort like Lebanon Springs, Saratoga was considerably less developed than its older and more established competitor. But James Stuart, a visitor from Scotland, was impressed by the up-and-coming village. "It consists of a fine broad street, fringed with trees," he wrote, "having so many large and splendid hotels, that it appeared to me that there was more extensive accommodation of company than at Harrogate [an English town famed for its mineral waters]." Visitors thronged the hotels and boardinghouses at the height of the summer season. "Fifteen hundred people have been known to arrive in a week," he marveled, many traveling from as far south as New Orleans "to avoid the heat and unhealthy weather."[9]

There were fourteen mineral springs in the vicinity. The best known, on the grounds of the Congress Hall hotel, produced a sparkling water that was bottled and sold throughout the country, even on American packet boats. "The taste is very agreeable," Stuart commented, "and the briskness of the water at the fountain delightful. Three or four pint tumblers are generally taken in the morning before breakfast." Many people drank it at meals as well.[10]

Amusements included reading rooms, ballrooms, a library, a local newspaper, and four or five churches offering public services. From the gracefully colonnaded porticos of the hotels, vacationers could admire the passing scene and keep an eye peeled for celebrities, such as annual visitor Joseph Bonaparte. "The whole appearance of the place is cheerful," Stuart concluded with pleasure.[11]

When Eliza and her family arrived in fall 1832, the village was on the verge of a remarkable transformation made possible by a new invention, the railroad. Over the winter of 1831 to '32, hotel and boardinghouse owners had poured money into expanding and improving their facilities, anticipating the arrival of thousands of tourists on the "cars" from Albany and Schenectady.[12] No longer would visitors from the capital region have to endure a full day's carriage ride to reach Saratoga, lurching at a snail's pace over a rugged road and sinking into deep beds of sand.[13]

But in a disaster for a community whose economy depended on a three-month summer season, the promised visitors failed to arrive. Tourists were frightened of gathering in a busy resort on which the cholera might descend. Repeated assurances that no cases had been reported in the village were of no avail. Hotels were half empty, and their proprietors desperate for money.[14]

Shrewdly Eliza seized the opportunity. Arriving at Saratoga on the brand-new steam railroad—one of the first in the nation—she, Mary, and Nelson spent the night at the home of Mr. Benedict, the train conductor.[15] Venturing out in the morning in search of more convenient lodgings, they strolled down the flat, sandy length of Broadway, the main thoroughfare of the village.[16] Eliza noticed a handbill on a pump advertising a "French hotel" for sale, and she proposed viewing the structure, advantageously located at the corner of Broadway and Caroline Street.[17] Strictly speaking, the property was not a "French hotel"—the phrase Nelson used in describing it years later—but a "dwelling house." It was owned by a Cuban tight-rope walker cum acrobat, who had worked as a traveling performer with his equally talented wife and children.[18] Perhaps the family took in boarders, which could explain the hotel reference.

Besides the residence, the lot contained a small barn, yard, privy house, and—sure to appeal to Eliza—a theater.[19] Decisive as always, she acted quickly. In her first significant financial transaction as a widow, she arranged to buy the property.[20] It was the first in a string of purchases made over a twenty-year period that would make her one of Saratoga's leading landowners.

25

A CALCULATED
COURTSHIP

*I*n November the family returned to New York City. Nelson resumed his legal training. He entered the office of New York lawyer John Duer, but soon moved to the firm of Aaron Burr.[1] According to Burr's biographer Parton, the transfer grew from Eliza's June visit to the old lawyer. She had sent Nelson to pick up the resulting opinion, and Burr had cultivated Nelson's acquaintance. Soon he invited the young man to read law with him.[2]

After some months of study, Chase, appreciative of Burr's kindness, persuaded Eliza to ask the lawyer to dine at Mount Stephen. In Parton's telling, "It was a grand banquet, at which [Burr] displayed all the charms of his manner, and shone to conspicuous advantage." As Burr handed his hostess to the richly set table, he complimented her in his most courtly fashion, "I give you my hand, Madame; my heart has long been yours."[3]

After this agreeable prelude, Burr began to call on Eliza frequently.[4] She could not have failed to appreciate his polished manners or his ready wit and beguiling smile.[5] As one of his former law students reminisced, "He would laugh, too, sometimes, as if his heart was bubbling with joy, and its effect was irresistible."⁶ Even men prepared to dislike him found themselves succumbing unwittingly to his charm.

Eliza would have savored her visitor's attentiveness. As her family lawyer observed, "She was a lady of a great deal of vanity, and would tell me stories of personal vanities and attentions she had had from gentlemen in very high society, and all those sort of things."⁷ Burr, quick to guess what his auditor wanted to hear, would have flattered Eliza adroitly.⁸

Parton portrayed the old soldier as a determined campaigner. Eventually he proposed marriage—and was refused. But he treated the rebuff as a mere temporary setback. He continued to court Eliza until he received a less decisive refusal. "Improving his advantage on the instant, he said, in a jocular manner, that he should bring out a clergyman to Fort Washington on a certain date, and there he would once more solicit her hand."⁹

When Burr drove out to see Eliza, accompanied by the promised minister, "the lady was embarrassed, and still refused." But then she reconsidered, Parton wrote: "And, after all, why not? Her estate needed a vigilant guardian, and the old house was lonely. After much hesitation, she at length consented to be dressed and to receive her visitors." Then "she was married," the ceremony taking place immediately with Nelson and Mary in attendance.¹⁰

This colorful narrative needs to be considered with caution. It bears more than a passing resemblance to the fictional courtship of fortune hunter Captain Blifil and aging spinster Miss Bridget Allworthy in Henry Fielding's famous novel *Tom Jones* (1749). In Fielding's tale, the scene proceeds in much the same way:

> Blifil, the determined suitor, initiates the negotiations. He makes his addresses . . . and is rebuffed. However, he "perfectly well [understands] the Lady" and knows what the next move should be. "Very soon after," he repeats "his Application, with more Warmth and

Earnestness than before." Yet again he is, "according to due Form, rejected." But all is not lost. As "the Eagerness of his Desires" increases, "so the Lady, with the same Propriety, decrease[s] in the Violence of her Refusal." He continues to make "his Advances in Form," she defends "the Citadel . . . in Form." Finally, "at length, in proper Form," she surrenders "at Discretion."[11]

The ritualistic advance and retreat Fielding described in his novel was a stereotypical picture of eighteenth-century courtship. But it was believable because similar rituals were enacted in real life. It was a model that Parton could use to shape a scene he had not witnessed himself. At the time the biographer was writing, in the mid-1850s, Aaron Burr was long dead. Nelson Chase said that it was he who met with Parton to provide the details on Eliza's life with Burr.[12] Indeed it is difficult to imagine anyone besides Nelson or Eliza who could have had detailed knowledge of the courtship. Whether Eliza met with Parton personally or sent Nelson in her place, the story must reflect how she wanted to be seen, the narrative she wished future generations to remember. It represents her as a desirable bride, not initially eager for a second marriage, but persuaded by an ardent suitor.

In truth, both parties had practical reasons for the union. For Eliza, a second marriage would offer an entrance into polite society, giving her the status she lacked as a widow without family ties to New York's elite. Aaron Burr, from a prominent New Jersey family, was the grandson of renowned Calvinist cleric Jonathan Edwards, the son of the president of the College of New Jersey (now Princeton University), and a graduate of the college himself. He had served valiantly for five years in the War of Independence and later was always referred to by his military title, Colonel Burr, as was the common practice when addressing ex-soldiers of the Revolutionary generation. After leaving the army, he married happily, trained as a lawyer, and made his mark in New York politics. He was elected twice to the New York State Assembly, in 1784 and 1797; appointed New York's attorney general in 1789; and elected to the United States Senate in 1791, defeating Alexander Hamilton's father-in-law,

Judge Schuyler.[13] Only the death of his wife in 1794 shadowed these triumphs.

Had Burr's career continued as successfully as it had begun, a marriage with him might have been beyond Eliza's reach. But his reputation was not what it might have been, thanks to a series of reverses that had begun with the new century. In the presidential campaign of 1800, Thomas Jefferson, the Republican candidate, had asked Burr, also a Republican, to be his running mate. At the time, the Constitution mandated that each member of the electoral college vote for two contenders. The candidate with the most electoral votes became president and the runner-up vice president. To Jefferson's dismay, the election of 1800 ended in a tie, with seventy-three electoral votes each for Jefferson and Burr and sixty-five and fifty-four for their Federalist competitors, John Adams and Charles C. Pinckney, respectively.[14] The choice of president would have to be made by the House of Representatives.

Burr could have had the presidency.[15] In the House, he had considerable support across party lines, especially among New England Federalists who were unenthusiastic about Jefferson and his fellow Republicans from the South.[16] Nonetheless, he declined to put himself forward for the role, honoring an earlier pledge to Jefferson not to seek the presidency for himself. But he angered the Virginian by refusing to eliminate himself as a candidate, on the grounds that it would be his duty to serve if elected.[17]

Ultimately Jefferson was elected president on the House's thirty-sixth vote, and Burr became vice president. But Jefferson, wary of the respect in which Burr was held and the considerable political capital he wielded, marginalized his former running mate. He distanced him from important issues and made it clear that when he ran for a second term, Burr would have no place on the ticket.[18] Burr, therefore, pursued his political ambitions elsewhere. During his last year as vice president, he ran for governor of New York in the election of 1804. He was badly defeated, thanks to Jefferson's covert opposition and slurs about his character that had been disseminated for years by his fellow lawyer and political rival Alexander Hamilton.[19]

Burr had long borne Hamilton's enmity with equanimity. But smarting from his loss of the election and ostracism from national politics, his normal stoicism was shattered.[20] When he heard that Hamilton had vilified his character at a private dinner party, Burr challenged him to a duel. The parties met on July 11, 1804, on a dueling ground in Weehawken, New Jersey, across the Hudson River from New York City. There is still disagreement over who shot first, or whether Hamilton intended to shoot at all.[21] Only Burr's bullet found its mark, hitting Hamilton in the abdomen. The wound would prove fatal—to both Hamilton's life and Burr's reputation. General Alexander Hamilton, former soldier in the army of the republic, secretary of the treasury under President George Washington, and architect of the young nation's fiscal policy, would die the following morning. The popular press took Hamilton's side.[22] Burr would be reviled for the rest of his life for killing Hamilton.

The nadir of his career came three years later, just as Eliza's husband Stephen was reaching the peak of his success. In search of a way to recoup his fortunes, Burr had embarked on a career as a filibuster. The meaning of this word has changed since Burr's day. In the early nineteenth century, a "filibuster" was a man who raised a private army to seize land from a nation at war with his own.[23] Although George Washington had opposed this governmentally authorized form of piracy, Thomas Jefferson and Alexander Hamilton had encouraged filibusters since the 1790s, and soon James Madison would do so too.[24] Underlying the official tolerance, and even encouragement, of filibusters was the expectation that the settlers of lands newly freed from Spanish or French control would decide to join the United States, increasing the young country's size and population.

As early as 1804, Burr had floated plans to seize Mexico from Spain.[25] He acquired four hundred thousand acres of land in northeast Louisiana that he planned to settle with volunteers who could invade Texas and Mexico if a war with Spain began.[26] The outbreak of hostilities was not unlikely given tensions on the border between the Spanish colonies and the United States.

Rumors flew as Burr attempted to raise money to equip follow-ers. To tempt Spain and England, his intermediaries claimed that he would separate the states and territories west of the Appalachians from the United States—a story he was not beyond using himself to appeal to independence-minded Westerners—although it is unlikely he intended to divide the republic.[27] He was also happy to inform England—although not Spain—about his designs on Mexico.[28]

As word of his project leaked out, President Thomas Jefferson, now in his second term, saw an opportunity to crush Burr. On November 27, 1806, as Burr was traveling south to Louisiana with a small group of supporters, the president ordered the military and judiciary to stop what he termed an unauthorized military expedition against Spain.[29] Soon Jefferson had his former vice president charged with high treason for purportedly assembling an army to seize the restive city of New Orleans, instigate a rebellion in the adjoining territories, and divide the United States by splitting the eastern seaboard from the lands west of the Appalachian Mountains. He also had Burr prosecuted for high misdemeanor for launching a military campaign against a nation (Spain) with which the United States was at peace.[30]

When the case came to trial in Richmond, Virginia, in the summer of 1807, Burr was acquitted. His project hadn't garnered much active support—his "army" consisted of some sixty men—and he hadn't actually started a war against either the United States or Spain.[31] But with the Jefferson administration against him, further attempts at prosecution were likely. Burr took refuge in Europe. As late as 1812, when he returned to the United States, he had to slip into the country under a false name.[32]

Nevertheless, if Burr was still an outcast to many, he retained warm friendships and professional relationships with a number of prominent New Yorkers.[33] Contemporaries were beginning to reassess his reputation and question the treatment he had received from the Jefferson administration.[34] Despite the duel and the trial for treason, Eliza could anticipate that marrying a lawyer who had been a vice president of the United States would pry open social doors.

Burr had equally strong reasons to seek a marriage with Eliza. In spite of legal expertise that brought him a good income, he was chronically in debt. His warmhearted liberality was delightful to witness, but too often performed at the expense of others who had loaned him the money that he gave away. The many lawsuits filed against him testify to his longstanding practice of borrowing money and failing to repay it, and contracting for goods or services and not paying those who provided them.[35] To compound the matter, he had borrowed heavily to defend himself in court in 1807 and support his life in exile.[36] As early as 1812, the widowed Burr had contemplated remarriage as a way of discharging his debts and obtaining money to invest in speculations that he confidently expected would earn him riches. That year he wrote in his journal, penned for his daughter Theodosia, "I come now to sacrifice myself to you in every way; that of marriage is one."[37] He had even identified a suitable "fair object," whom he described optimistically as "a worthy lady some few years older than myself, with fortune enough, and I think good nature enough to make that appropriation of it."[38] Nothing came of the project; the fair object must have been insufficiently good-natured.

Twenty years later Burr still needed a fortune, if only to retire from the practice of law and enjoy a comfortable old age. The elderly lawyer's financial status was particularly precarious in the first half of 1833. In March Burr was turned down in his attempt to collect a federal pension for his military service during the Revolutionary War.[39] By May, if not earlier, he was in arrears on the rent of the home he occupied at 31 Reade Street (the street where both Stephen and Eliza had lived—only the spelling had changed).[40] He was also facing a lawsuit for an unpaid debt, which would result in a judgment against him on June 7.[41] (Irresponsibly generous as always, Burr had ordered a complete wardrobe as a New Year's gift for a young man who was his ward, but once the clothing was delivered, didn't pay for it.)[42] To improve his financial situation, he had been trying for months to collect legal fees for his work on a long-running case, although his once-grateful clients contended (almost certainly accurately) that he had received more than adequate compensation already.[43] How could

Burr *not* have considered pursuing Eliza to gain control of her late husband's fortune?

Eliza might even have placed the idea in his head, or at a minimum encouraged him to pursue it. She was undoubtedly aware that a union with Burr could raise her social status and that her wealth made her an attractive parti. Indeed Samuel H. Wandell and Meade Minnigerode, in a biography of Burr published in 1925, claimed that she proposed the match. Their source, they said, was William D. Craft, Burr's law partner during his final years.[44] John Stillwell, who also spoke with Craft, went further. Eliza "courted [Burr] assiduously and finally bagged him," he harrumphed. "Bagged is the only word for it."[45]

Although neither Wandell and Minnigerode nor Stillwell were sympathetic to Eliza, this claim deserves serious consideration. In arranging a marriage for Mary, Eliza had utilized marriage as a bond that could be dictated by financial and practical concerns. Years later she would use money again to secure a desirable suitor, this time for a child of Mary's. Why not arrange such a marriage for herself?

Certainly there was some horse trading going on. In spite of Parton's story, which has Nelson introducing Burr into the family after studying with him for "some months," Nelson himself stated that he did not begin training with the older lawyer until May 1833.[46] Until then they were scarcely acquainted.[47] Given the compressed time frame—the marriage would take place July 1—it is likely that either Eliza made Nelson's admission to Burr's office one of the criteria for the nuptials or, more probably, that Burr arranged the apprenticeship to gain closer access to Eliza.

There is indirect evidence that Eliza discussed money matters with Burr before their marriage, understanding that her financial assets would form part of her appeal. In a court filing in 1834, Burr testified that her personal estate amounted to fifteen thousand dollars, plus an income of five thousand dollars or more per year, not including the mansion house nor real estate held in trust for her that was valued at around two hundred thousand dollars.[48] This was probably information Eliza had shared with him before the marriage.

In addition, she had shown him a letter she had drafted to send to one of Stephen's relatives, in which she declared that her late husband had left only debts. Mailed just before or just after the wedding, the missive was written to ward off claims for money from Stephen's brother and sister.[49]

Ultimately both parties had practical reasons for the marriage: on Burr's side, money; on Eliza's, social acceptance—and probably also the utility of having a clever lawyer at her side to help her guard her assets. Eliza, then, was no passive victim of Burr's machinations, but a bride who expected to benefit from this union. It is a telling point that the couple's honeymoon would be a business trip to reclaim monies Eliza was owed under Stephen's estate. On balance, however, it was probably Burr rather than Eliza who was the aggressor in their alliance. Given his tangled finances, he needed Eliza more than she needed him.

AN OPTIMISTIC
BEGINNING

*T*he marriage of Madame Eliza Jumel, née Bowen, and Colonel Aaron Burr took place at the bride's house on Harlem Heights Monday evening, July 1, 1833.[1] The day was clear and a little sticky—seventy-two degrees at dawn, eighty by afternoon—presaging the dog days of the summer to come.[2] As evening fell, Nelson and Mary were in attendance. But no infant would interrupt the ceremony with a cry; on January 27, Mary's child had arrived stillborn.[3]

Burr, raised in the Dutch Reformed Church, had supplied the pastor, Reverend David Bogart.[4] As the bride and bridegroom stood in the southwest parlor of the mansion, waiting for the minister to begin the ceremony, did Eliza pause a moment to reflect on her first wedding, twenty-nine years before?[5] After the ups and downs of those decades with Stephen, what were her expectations for this marriage? Did she hope for love—and why wouldn't she; Burr could charm the birds from the trees—or simply a working relationship?

The sober opening of the Dutch Reformed marriage service hardly lent itself to optimism. "Married persons," Rev. Bogart would have intoned, "are generally, by reason of sin, subject to many troubles and afflictions." Although they could count on "the certain assistance of God," the Lord would "punish whoremongers and adulterers."[6]

As the ceremony continued, Burr and Eliza would have listened to Bogart describing the mutual respect they owed each other. The husband should honor, teach, comfort, and protect his wife; the wife should love, honor, and obey her husband. Given the occasional dissension in Eliza's first marriage, it wouldn't be surprising if she felt a moment's scorn when Bogart told her, "You should not exercise any dominion over your husband, but be silent: for Adam was first created and then Eve, to be a help to Adam."[7]

Whatever inner voices the couple heard, the two consented to the marriage: first seventy-seven-year-old Aaron, then fifty-eight-year-old Eliza. After solemnizing the union, Bogart would have stressed once more the sanctity of the marriage bond, warning against divorce. Finally he would have blessed the newly married couple: "The Lord our God replenish you with his grace, grant that ye may long live together in all godliness and holiness. Amen."[8]

A day or two after the marriage, Colonel and Mrs. Burr left for Hartford, Connecticut, on a trip that agreeably combined business and pleasure. In Hartford, they visited Burr's cousin, Henry Waggaman Edwards, a lawyer recently elected governor of Connecticut.[9] The meeting was a social coup that Eliza would have treasured. But the choice of destination was dictated by her need to settle Stephen's estate. Back in the mid-1820s, during the worst of their financial difficulties, Eliza had wanted to sell the forty shares of stock that Stephen had owned in the Hartford Bridge Company and put in Lesparre's name.[10] They had ended up retaining the shares, which faithfully yielded quarterly dividends. Now, however, as assets forming part of Stephen's estate, the stock would have to be sold.

The nuptial pair seem to have enjoyed their honeymoon. In July a Hartford newspaper reported that the "happy couple spent a few days of the 'first month,' in this city, apparently swallowed up in conjugal felicity . . . Mrs. Burr is a lady of fifty or fifty-five, rather comely, and we should think well fitted to sustain an old gentleman under the infirmities of age." However, the penman snarkily concluded, "We really hope she will prove an *Aaron's* rod, and not a rod to Aaron."[11] Had the journalist observed underlying tension between the two? Perhaps he was simply showing off a clever phrase.

While in Hartford Eliza and Burr met with the management of the Hartford Bridge Company. The sale of the stock was not entirely straightforward. Stephen had never registered the transfer of the shares to his nephew-in-law in the company's books.[12] But with the bulk of the paperwork showing Lesparre to be their owner, Eliza's claim to the shares as Stephen's widow was in question. Indeed, she and Nelson might have already visited Hartford after Stephen's death in an unsuccessful attempt to sell the stock.[13]

Whether or not they had done so, the present sally, at last, was successful. If Stephen had planned that the profits from the sale would go to Lesparre, as his refusal to sell the shares earlier had suggested, his intent would not be honored. On July 5, 1833, Eliza received the handsome sum of six thousand five hundred dollars for Stephen's forty shares.[14]

Of what happened next, we have only Parton's account. As with his story of the Jumel/Burr courtship, the details must have come directly from Eliza or through Nelson Chase. According to Parton, Eliza was offered the money, but ordered it paid to her husband instead. That done, Burr "had it sewed up in his pocket, a prodigious bulk, and brought it to New York, and deposited it in his own bank, to his own credit."[15] Regardless of the pocket that hid the money, the marriage gave Burr legal possession of all of Eliza's assets (except the real estate held in trust for her). This fact would soon trouble the tentative harmony between them.

After completing their business in Hartford, the couple returned to New York over the weekend. Monday, July 8, found Burr back at the legal grind, writing to an associate in Utica regarding the progress of a case.[16] But he was looking forward to retirement, which he hoped would come sooner rather than later. In early September, he wrote to his friend John Bigelow, a Bostonian, that he was still dealing with "vexatious concerns of business, which a determination to wind up [his] worldly affairs" had necessitated.[17] In this missive of September 8, he also thanked Bigelow for the latter's congratulations on his marriage. "Your letter of congratulation," he wrote, "amused me very much—I consider it as a sort of Epithalamium—but really my friend you did not consider that the parties who were the subject of congratulations were past their grand climacteric and it would therefore have been utterly impractical either by invocation of muses, or even by beat of drum, to have summoned the loves or graces to such a celebration."[18]

The amusement he felt at the idea of an ode to the marriage (or an "epithalamium," to use the terminology of English poetry that he had employed) is a damning admission that Burr never felt the kind of warmth or tenderness for which Eliza might have hoped, even if she had entered the alliance largely for practical purposes. Strictly speaking, only he and not Eliza was past the grand climacteric—the age of sixty-three, at which the physical powers were believed to undergo a marked decline. Evidence suggests that he remained attractive to, and attracted by, the fairer sex. In a codicil to his will, drawn up in 1835, he left his residuary assets to two natural daughters, one of whom was only two years old.[19]

Burr was also capable of deep loyalties and strong affections. When Luther Martin, one of the lawyers who defended him during his trial for treason, was an old, broken man, Burr gave him a home for the last year or two of his life.[20] In September 1833 he performed a similar action, welcoming John Pelletreau, a long-term client who was by then near death, into the mansion on Harlem Heights.[21]

But apparently his marriage to Eliza failed to touch Burr's heart. The lack of true affection, whether on his side or on both, would have made the inevitable stresses and strains of the early months of a marriage harder to weather with aplomb. Indeed the bonds knitted on July 1, 1833, would soon be ripped asunder. By October Aaron Burr had left Mount Stephen. By November he and Eliza had parted for good. On July 11, 1834—thirty years to the day of Burr's ruinous duel with Hamilton—Eliza filed for divorce.

THE UNRAVELING

On June 19, 1834, Eliza saluted an old acquaintance on the street. It was William Dunlap, the impresario of the Park Theatre, where she had trod the boards so many years before. If he had planned to pass her by in silence, she outfaced him by addressing him directly. "You don't know me, Mr. Dunlap?" she said.

"Oh yes, Mrs. Burr," he replied. "How does Colonel Burr do?"

"Oh, I don't see him anymore," Eliza replied brusquely. "He got thirteen thousand dollars of my property, and spent it all or gave it away and had [no] money to buy him a dinner. I had a new carriage and pair of horses cost me one thousand dollars; he took them and sold them for five hundred."

Dunlap was appalled at her frankness. "What confidence can be placed in the words of such a woman it is hard to say," he wrote in his diary, "but Burr's marrying her makes anything told of him credible."[1]

Bluntness shocked in nineteenth-century America when it came from a woman—especially when it was a commentary on her husband. Even a woman who managed her own lands and investments would be expected to show outward deference to her spouse.[2] But that was not Eliza's way.

If money had brought Eliza and Aaron together, it was also what tore them apart. Although Eliza knew that her money would attract Aaron, she cannot have suspected how fiscally irresponsible he was. Without contacts in the upper echelons of New York society, she lacked access to the informative gossip that circulated among the elite.[3]

The marriage barely celebrated, Burr began to lay claim to Eliza's money—now *his* money by virtue of the matrimonial laws of the day. In her bill of divorce, Eliza detailed his depredations. She had given him money (probably the proceeds of the shares in the Hartford Bridge Company) to pay down a mortgage on real estate held in trust for her. He had promised that he would do so, but kept the money for himself.[4] Eliza wouldn't be able to pay off the mortgage for another two years.[5]

Nor was that all. Burr's creditors had seized some personal property that Eliza had purchased since the marriage (including the carriage and horses she lamented to Dunlap, perhaps?). To save the items from being sold, she was forced to pay off her new husband's creditors herself.[6] Given Burr's usual state of chronic indebtedness, this tale rings sadly true.

Still more: Burr had been trying to obtain the rents and profits from real estate held in trust for her, and had even threatened to sell the property in Saratoga Springs that she had purchased shortly after Stephen's death.[7] This last was a particularly serious threat to Eliza. Burr would have had difficulty obtaining approval from her trustees to sell property in which Eliza held only a life estate, but as her husband the rest of her real estate was his.

In his answer to the bill of divorce, Burr admitted the truth of most of Eliza's charges, although he slanted the narrative to place his conduct in a more favorable light. He conceded that he had spent the money from the Hartford Bridge stock, but said he had paid out two thousand dollars of it on debts that Eliza had contracted before and after their marriage (although no records of any such debts can be found). Part of the rest went "for the support of himself and family," and the remainder he spent "for his own uses and purposes, as he had full and lawful authority to do." Moreover, he said, without his legal expertise, Eliza wouldn't have received the money for the stock at all.[8]

Nor, he stated, did he try to seize any of the profits on the real estate held in trust for her—although at the same time he conceded that he had forbade one of her trustees from paying her the rents without his own consent.[9] It is clear from Burr's words that he'd been exercising his rights as Eliza's husband to control her assets. Legal? Yes, except for meddling with the rents from the trust. Acceptable to Eliza? No.

To counter Eliza's claim that some of her property was seized by his creditors, forcing her to spend her own money to redeem it, Burr embellished his answer to the divorce bill with an implausible tale designed to make his wife look vindictive and unbalanced. Eliza, he claimed, had run up a bill before the marriage for repairs to her mansion; he and she were subsequently sued jointly for payment and lost.[10] Consequently the creditors were given the right to seize some of their possessions, including "two horses, one carriage, and harness" purchased with part of the money received for the Hartford Bridge Company stock. Eliza, Burr said, then made a secret agreement with the officer sent to carry out the seizure. She helped the official remove certain items from the house after they had been advertised for sale. These were taken to a place that "was difficult to access by persons inclined to purchase" to ensure that there would be no competing bids. She planned to have the possessions purchased cheaply by a confederate "to be clandestinely disposed of without [Burr's] knowledge so as to leave [him] personally liable for the residue of the amount due on the said execution." According to Burr, this ingenious plan failed because he had learned of it by chance and arranged for someone to attend the sale and purchase the items for a fair price. At that point Eliza, "discovering that her artifice was detected, forthwith directed one of the trustees of her real estate . . . to pay the amount due on said execution." But furious that her plan had been thwarted, she "then threatened to burn and destroy the carriage and shoot the horses which formed a part of the said personal property" that had been at risk from the execution.[11]

To further fix the image of his wife as an uncontrolled and irrational woman, Burr added a claim that Eliza, before their marriage, had defamed the character of a neighbor, Isabella Geagan. Isabella and her husband, he said, were now suing Aaron and Eliza for five thousand dollars in damages. But Burr himself had instigated the action for slander, Eliza said, and the suit was "discontinued by judgment as in case of nonsuit."[12] No record of any such legal action survives, suggesting that the case was indeed dismissed.

Strictly speaking, none of these charges and countercharges had any legal weight in a bill of divorce. In New York in 1834, the grounds for dissolving a marriage were few. An annulment could be granted if one or both parties were underage, mentally incompetent, married by force or fraud, physically incapable of consummating a marriage, or had a former spouse who was still alive.[13] Otherwise the only possibility of freeing oneself was divorce—permitted for but one reason: adultery.[14] That Burr was laying waste to Eliza's fortune was unfortunate but not illegal. That she had unleashed her temper against him was understandable, but irrelevant. Unless she could prove that he had committed adultery, Eliza was stuck with the marriage.

Luckily the details of Burr's private life provided the ammunition she needed to end their short-lived union. The smoking gun was a relationship Burr had enjoyed immediately before their marriage with a woman named Jane McManus. A dark-eyed beauty with a failed early marriage in her past, Jane Maria Eliza McManus was born in 1807 in Rensselaer City, New York. Married to a law student at eighteen, by 1832 she had moved to New York City and was raising a young son on her own.[15] McManus had become acquainted with Burr when they had both lived on Reade Street.[16] The acquaintanceship had ripened into friendship, if not more. Hannah Lewis, Burr's Reade Street landlady, testified during the divorce proceedings that McManus had called on Burr as often as four or five nights per week, beginning in October or November 1831. She had spent her visits alone with Burr in his rooms, staying until one or two o'clock in the morning.[17]

By fall 1832 McManus had obtained a position as bookkeeper at the New York offices of the Galveston Bay and Texas Land Company.[18] Probably Burr, whose friend Samuel Swartwout was an investor in the company, had suggested her for the position. The Galveston sold scrip to parcels of land in Spanish-ruled East Texas—papers that gave investors the right to settle in specific areas and claim the lands after occupying and surveying them.[19]

McManus and her brother Robert soon purchased or were given scrip for some of the company's holdings. In November 1832 they headed south to lay claim to their acres.[20] Burr wrote a glowing letter of recommendation to introduce McManus to an old friend, Judge James Workman, who was organizing immigration into Texas. Praising her courage and perseverance, Burr assured Workman "that she will be able to send out one or two hundred settlers in less time and with better selection than any man or half-a-dozen men who I this day know."[21]

By May 1833, as the marriage of Eliza Jumel and Aaron Burr approached, McManus was back in New York, signing up German immigrants to work her land in exchange for a meager salary and transportation to Texas.[22] But in late September she faced a setback. She had planned to share the costs of chartering a ship to Texas with another investor, but he withdrew from the arrangement at the last minute.[23] Desperate for funds, McManus reached out to Burr, asking him for an advance of two hundred and fifty dollars "for a year or even six months." She offered any quantity he demanded of her Texas lands as security. In the undated letter to him, sent to his and Eliza's home in upper Manhattan, Jane wrote breathlessly, "My plans are so far advanced that with that [the money] it seems I cannot fail of success – Heaven knows I have not spent a dollar of money or a moment of time for my own amusement – heart and soul has [*sic*] been devoted to this business – do not let me sink . . . I have delayed sailing until Wednesday morning[.] If you cannot lend me this money inform me let me know the worst — This suspense will drive me wild in three days more."

McManus closed the letter with an apology for her appeal: "Forgive me I entreat you for calling on you," she wrote, "but I feel I know your answer will give a color to the rest of my life — I shall expect your answer with the deepest anxiety — Farewell."[24]

Did Burr, now married, grant her request? Probably not. McManus's biographer, Linda S. Hudson, discovered that Jane sold five hundred acres of land in Texas to a purchaser in Troy, New York, on October 2, 1833—land that she had no title to sell. She received two hundred and fifty dollars from the risky transaction, the same sum she had requested from Burr.[25]

Although it is unlikely that Burr loaned McManus the sum for which she begged, her letter may have dealt a death blow to his relationship with his new wife. It survives among the Jumel papers at the New-York Historical Society in Manhattan. Whether at the time of its delivery—probably in the second half of September 1833—or in the months thereafter, it must have fallen into Eliza's hands. As the divorce filing makes clear, she and Aaron were already dueling over financial matters shortly after the marriage. By early fall, there was sufficient tension between them that Eliza was planning a solitary voyage as an escape, just as she had done when she was at odds with Stephen. On October 2, Nelson requested a passport for her from the State Department to travel from New York to France.[26]

Even if Burr refused to help McManus in September, the letter from her, if Eliza saw it at the time, could have increased tensions between the couple. Indeed, both parties stated in their divorce papers that Burr had left the mansion on Harlem Heights in "October or November" 1833—thus not long after the missive was received.[27] Burr's friend John Pelletreau was assisted into a carriage. Burr stepped in after him, followed by Maria Johnson, a servant of the colonel's who had been attending the sick man.[28] The three occupants of the carriage moved out of the mansion and into Burr's law office at 23 Nassau Street.[29]

The ambiguity over the precise dating of Eliza and Aaron's separation—"October or November"—is curious. The evidence suggests that Burr left Eliza, then returned temporarily to the mansion after suffering a disabling stroke, accounting for the absence of a single, specific departure date.

The medical crisis occurred in the autumn of 1833. Walking down Broadway with an acquaintance, Burr lost the ability to use one leg.[30] The exact timing of the event is not recorded, but a female acquaintance sent a letter to his office on November 1, 1833, to ask after the colonel's health, so the illness was probably a recent occurrence.[31] In a letter of October 18, she had made only a routine inquiry on how he did—nothing more than politeness demanded in correspondence with a friend.[32]

According to Parton, Eliza visited Burr after hearing of the stroke. She took him back to the mansion to recuperate and nursed him for the following month.[33] (Presumably her plans to travel to France were abandoned in the wake of this crisis.) Tending to confirm Parton's account, Burr, in his answer to Eliza's bill of divorce, claimed that she behaved "in a manner most undutiful, disobedient, and insulting, and particularly at a time when the defendant [Burr] was in a very low state of health and not expected to survive, which was in the month of October or November 1833, and that in consequence of such treatment this defendant did leave the house of the said complainant."[34] After this interlude in late fall 1833, Eliza and Aaron would not live together again.

Ultimately Eliza would use McManus's letter to Burr to build a case to divorce her husband for adultery. But for the moment, with Burr gone from the house and in uncertain health, she played a waiting game. Although there must have been a certain awkwardness in the situation, her nephew-in-law Nelson Chase, admitted to the New York bar as an attorney in October, was still working in her estranged husband's office.[35] In the winter of 1833 to '34, Burr, with Nelson's assistance, was again attempting to collect veteran's benefits for his army service during the Revolutionary War. By late December 1833 he had sent Nelson to Washington City, as the nation's capital was then known, to advocate for him and gather information on his behalf.[36] Letters to Nelson that Burr dictated to his secretary, John M. Lewis, show that the seventy-seven-year-old lawyer's mind was sharp in spite of his physical infirmities. Often he found it necessary to rebuke his junior for inattentiveness. On February 5, 1834, with Nelson still in Washington, Burr complained:

> No letter has been recieved [*sic*] since yours of the 31st. ult. which communicates nothing.
>
> That of the 30th informed me that you had made acquaintance with a gentleman of influence and consideration who was willing to assist you for a commission, the amount not named, but you are not pleased to give the name of that gentleman, nor any clue to, or indication of him.[37]

A week later Burr reproved Nelson for failing to provide any details on a Mr. Young and a Mr. Cox, nor even a progress report on the matters at hand.[38]

Nevertheless, Burr remained cordial to Nelson, typically closing his letters with "God bless you and speed you," and occasionally dropping in bits of family news. On January 5, 1834, he noted, "Your wife was here yesterday for a few minutes merely to inquire if I had heard from you and when your return might be expected to which inquiry I could give no reply."[39] It seems that Nelson could not be bothered to write to his wife of less than two years.

On January 20, 1834, Burr dropped a nugget of information about his own wife into the middle of a letter otherwise focused on business: "Madame, of the heights, has been here today. I had not the honor to see her, though She [*sic*] passed an hour in the office of Mr. C. [Burr's law partner, William D. Craft], who has not mentioned to me the visit, or the subject of it."[40] Had Eliza begun to consider the possibility of a divorce? Although she might have assumed—even hoped—in late 1833 that Burr's death would resolve the differences between them, by the new year the old soldier was on the mend. On February 10, 1834, John Lewis wrote to Nelson that "the health of Col. B is rapidly improving, and his manner quite changed since you last saw him."[41] By March he was up to a forty-five-hour stage-coach trip to Albany "with only one break for a meal," although the weather was cold enough that the coach was drawn on sleigh runners north of Peekskill and the wind whipped through the vehicle's torn curtains.[42]

On May 17 Burr wrote to Nelson from Albany regarding the progress of his claim for veterans' benefits, addressing him at their Nassau Street office.[43] (Burr would soon learn that he had been awarded an annual pension of six hundred dollars, payable retroactively from March 1831.)[44] He ended the letter with a courteous inquiry about his wife and Nelson's: "How is Madame, and la belle pite [petite]—are you in town or Country [*sic*]?—and where—?"[45]

If Burr hoped to maintain a polite status quo with regard to his unsuccessful marriage, he would soon be disillusioned. On July 11, 1833, Eliza filed her bill of divorce. In it she described Burr's financial depredations. She also accused him of adultery with Jane McManus. Date and place were carefully specified: the adultery occurred in Jersey City, New Jersey, in August 1833, a month after Eliza and Aaron's marriage. For good measure, Eliza claimed that since their marriage, Burr had been "in the habit of committing adultery at divers times with divers females," whose names Eliza did not know.[46] The phrasing was standard terminology in a divorce suit.

Even if only the charge involving Jane McManus were true, Burr had violated the civil laws governing marriage in New York state. He had breached the obligations of the "matrimonial contract," as Eliza wrote in her bill. The legal recourse for this breach of contract was divorce.

Eliza also requested—and received—an immediate injunction preventing Burr from selling, mortgaging, or otherwise disposing of any part of her personal property or real estate—a good indicator that her desire for divorce was driven by her need to protect the fortune built during her twenty-eight-year marriage to Stephen. In addition, she asked for alimony from the chronically broke Burr, raising the distasteful possibility that she had waited to file until his pension claim was decided in order to claim a share in that asset.[47] But it is more likely that she and her lawyers simply followed the usual practice: asking for more than they could expect to get in order to maximize the eventual award.

Once the divorce proceedings commenced, Nelson Chase threw in his lot with Eliza. On July 10, a day before the bill of divorce was filed, he sued Burr for three hundred dollars in law books that Nelson owned, but Burr had kept in his own possession.[48] To his mentor, Nelson's defection must have felt like a betrayal.

THE DUEL

"*He* is credibly informed and believes it to be true"—
Aaron Burr framed his sentences in the third person—"that the Complainant" (Eliza) had, since their marriage, "committed adultery without the connivance or consent of this defendant with one or more persons whose name or names is and are at present unknown to this defendant, but whose names, when discovered, this defendant prays may be inserted herein."[1]

Aging and desperate for financial security, Burr contested the divorce proceedings strenuously. Eliza would collect half of Stephen's assets, once her late husband's estate was settled. If Burr remained her husband, all the money would be his. In common law man and wife were one person, and that person was the husband.[2]

To try to save the marriage, Burr accused Eliza of adultery. Pointing a finger at the other party was a standard tactic used by defendants in divorce actions, because a divorce petition would be dismissed if the complainant had been unfaithful.[3] In 1835 Burr worked up a list of eight men who were supposedly Eliza's lovers.[4]

Her lawyers demolished the straw men speedily. Robert Coveny, for example, one of Eliza's purported bedmates, had worked for her as a laborer until dismissed for drunkenness and then lost a lawsuit against her for back wages.[5] In autumn 1834 he had visited a neighbor of hers and offered to pay him "liberally" if he "would procure any person who would state that [Eliza] had committed adultery with any person."[6] In January or February 1835 he had bragged that he was intimately acquainted with Burr and "fared well" whenever he visited him.[7]

Charles Perry, another of Eliza's alleged amours, was "a very great liar," according to Eliza's neighbors.[8] He had illegally changed his name from Boothe and deserted a wife and two children.[9] Like Coveny, he would perjure himself to order.

Then there was Patrick Delahanty, Eliza's former coachman, named by Burr for no other reason than propinquity. Delahanty swore that he had never seen or heard anything that would lead him to suspect his employer of unchastity.[10]

And so it went.

On July 11, 1835—again acting on the anniversary of Burr's duel with Hamilton—Eliza countered her husband's libels by swearing to a devastating affidavit. Burr had tried to get her to agree to a settlement, she revealed: he would admit to adultery and let the divorce proceed if she would pay him an annuity of three hundred dollars a year. It was only after she "declined paying the sum of money so proposed by said Burr as the wages of his depraved and immoral conduct," that he "and his agents commenced fabricating false and scandalous reports against" her.[11] Indeed, at no point after her marriage to Stephen did rumor suggest that Eliza had engaged in affairs or even the most trifling dalliances. Only her conduct before her first marriage had been the subject of whispers.

However contrived Burr's charges were, gossip must have been flying as the investigations advanced. If Eliza had hoped that her marriage to Burr would bring her invitations and visitors, the divorce proceedings had put an end to such dreams. As the suit wound its way through the Court of Chancery, the New York State court that handled divorces, she lived in the old mansion alone but for the servants. One of them, Margaret Mulhollen—probably a housekeeper or maid—said that Eliza "lived a retired life," and didn't receive "the company or visits of any person or persons whatsoever, except the visits from [her] niece and nephew" (i.e., Mary and Nelson Chase).[12] John Hopwood, probably also a servant, confirmed "that her habits of life were reserved and retired—that she was not in the habit of receiving the visits or company of any person or persons except the visits of her relatives."[13]

With few options remaining, Burr compromised, signing an agreement with Eliza two days before Christmas. He would not contest the adultery charge nor claim a right to her money, but would not be obliged to pay alimony or cover her legal costs either.[14]

In accepting the arrangement, Eliza wasn't giving up anything. Where would the feckless Burr have found money for support payments or legal fees? Instead the agreement gave her the hope of having the divorce finalized at last—although Burr's willingness to let the charges in the bill of divorce be taken *pro confesso* (as confessed) would not result in an immediate divorce, as both he and Eliza knew. An investigation was still required by state law to make sure that the spouses weren't colluding to obtain a divorce by having one of them admit to an adulterous relationship. The case would be referred to a master in chancery—the improbably named Philo T. Ruggles—who would collect evidence to determine whether the charge of adultery was credible, before the vice chancellor ruled on whether to grant a divorce.[15]

The records of the master's investigation offer a glimpse into Burr's life at the time of his marriage to Eliza. After the union Burr lived at least part time in a house in Jersey City, New Jersey.[16] This pied-à-terre, less than twenty minutes from lower Manhattan by ferry, would have offered quicker access to his office on Nassau Street than Eliza's mansion, nearly ten miles north of New York City.[17] Burr's servant Maria Johnson testified that her employer used the lodging from July 1 until mid-August. Nelson Chase shared the house; "he came over there shortly after we removed there," Johnson said.[18]

But another interpretation is more probable: that Eliza herself had rented the lodging for Nelson and Mary—they were living in nearby Hoboken, New Jersey, by 1837—and Burr was the one who shared it. The timing is suggestive. Leases in the region typically began on May 1; on May 2, 1833, Burr had been evicted from his Reade Street house for nonpayment of rent.[19] His close acquaintance with Nelson is said to have begun in "May 1833"; perhaps it started with an exchange of a place to live for legal training. Burr didn't return to Jersey City after his marriage broke up, making it unlikely that it was he who held the lease there.[20]

The sleeping arrangements were consistent with Nelson being the primary occupant of the house. The parlor floor had a front and back room separated by folding doors. Burr slept in the back room on a settee that was made up with bedclothes at night. Nelson, however, had a bed, probably upstairs, as did a Mrs. Price, presumably the landlady. Also living in the house were Mrs. Price's child; Burr's black servant Maria Johnson; Maria's son, around seventeen or eighteen years old; another woman servant; and one of Burr's wards (probably yet another illegitimate child), Henry Oscar Taylor, aged about fifteen.[21] If Mary Chase lived in the house, in all probability she shared Nelson's room. She is not mentioned—possibly an intentional omission to keep her name out of an unsavory affair. Alternately, she may have spent the summer living at Mount Stephen with Eliza, with Nelson joining her on Harlem Heights on Saturday and Sunday nights, but staying in their Jersey City home on weekdays to be near Burr's Manhattan office.

The servant Maria Johnson would become the key witness in the Jumel/Burr divorce. Eliza arranged for her to give evidence, calling on her twice, accompanied by Mary Chase.[22] According to Johnson's testimony before the master, Burr's adulterous episode with Jane McManus took place in the crowded Jersey City house at the end of the first week of August 1833. McManus arrived around four o'clock in the afternoon on Friday. That evening Johnson came up from the kitchen carrying a jug of steaming water for Burr. Passing quietly through the front room, she pushed open the folding doors into the back chamber. A lamp in the corner of the room spread a pool of light, exposing Burr and McManus entangled on the settee. "Colonel

Burr had his trousers all down" and his hands beneath McManus's clothing. Johnson "saw her nakedness."[23]

The next day, Johnson said, she spied on the pair. Climbing onto the roof of a shed adjacent to the back stoop, she was able to reach one of the windows of the back parlor. Rotating a slat of the blinds, she peered in. McManus and Burr were "about as close as they could set together" on the settee. Johnson, three times married, knew what she was seeing. She "looked at them till they got through with their mean act and looked at them when they sat on the settee." But there would be no more to see that day. About 2:00 PM McManus left to return to New York City, escorted by Nelson Chase.[24]

Burr's counsel cross-examined Johnson. Would she swear that sexual intercourse took place? Johnson stood her ground. "Yes sir," she said firmly, adding that she had seen Burr and McManus similarly engaged "several times before." Further questioning revealed that the prior sightings had not been in the New Jersey City house, but rather in Burr's former lodging on Reade Street. Before McManus left New York in November 1832, she had called on Burr there "almost every other day," staying until ten or eleven at night, and sometimes as late as two o'clock in the morning. Pressed to state whether she had actually seen the two in a compromising position, Johnson described what had happened one Sunday. Just as she was ready to leave for church, the bell in Burr's room rang. She hurried to answer it. Burr, it seems, had rung the bell by accident without realizing what he'd done; it was "right over the settee close by his head." When Johnson entered, she "saw Jane McManus with her clothes all up & Colonel Burr with his hands under them and his pantaloons down." The pair were flustered by the servant's unexpected entrance. Jane exclaimed, "Oh, la! Mary saw us." Quickly Burr sent Johnson away on an errand: she should go get oysters (then considered an aphrodisiac) at Bear Market for McManus's dinner. Later he gave Johnson "a new pair of shoes not to tell."[25]

This story, although colorful, was not strictly relevant. The alleged events didn't constitute adultery since they had occurred before Aaron and Eliza were married. Therefore Eliza's counsel was denied permission to question Maria about any other "irregularities" that might have been committed in the Reade Street house.[26]

But the testimony she had given already was enough. Although Burr had managed to stall the case by obtaining fifteen adjournments and petitioning for an extension, the marriage was dissolved on July 8, 1836.[27] Eliza, innocent of infidelity, would be free to remarry. Burr, the adulterous spouse, would not be permitted to do so unless Eliza predeceased him.

From Eliza's point of view, the most important clause in the decision was at the end: "And it is further adjudged and decreed that the said complainant be entitled to retain possession, have, hold, use, and enjoy all her real and personal property and estate, of what nature or kind soever, free from any interference of any kind whatever by or from the said Aaron Burr."[28] The remainder of the Jumel fortune was safe, and the specter of poverty that Burr's improvidence had summoned was held once more at bay.

Although from this point onward Eliza had little to fear, the divorce decree did not quite end the story of the marriage. Failing in health, maintained through the kindness of friends in a small hotel on Staten Island, Burr fought to the end.[29] He and McManus charged that Maria Johnson had committed perjury when she claimed to have witnessed adultery between them, and Burr petitioned New York's chancellor for a rehearing of the divorce suit.[30] He argued that the evidence of adultery was unconvincing; the vice chancellor had refused to hear his opposing evidence; and his age at the time of the "pretended adultery" rendered "the committing of the said offense according to the laws of nature impossible."[31] But this skirmish was over almost before it began. On September 14, 1836, at approximately two o'clock in the afternoon, Aaron Burr died in his lodgings on Staten Island.[32] Eliza would not marry again.

All in all, she had stage-managed her case shrewdly. Only once did her chosen witness, Maria Johnson, slip up. The servant claimed to have peered through the window of the Jersey City house by rotating a slat in the blinds, but later said that the windows were closed.[33] How then could she have moved the slat? Nevertheless, the probable liaison between Burr and McManus before the colonel's marriage to Eliza made Johnson's evidence more convincing than that offered in most divorce suits, in which perjury and collusion were commonplace.[34] Burr's tarnished reputation would have worked to Eliza's benefit as well.[35] He had dueled fatally with Alexander Hamilton and faced charges of high treason against his country. Former chancellor James Kent was far from alone in considering him "a miserable monument of perverted talents and licentious principles."[36]

At the time of the divorce, Burr was facing yet another lawsuit, an accusation that he had defrauded the heirs of his friend Pelletreau by persuading the dying man to sign a dubious contract.[37] The deal was suspiciously favorable to Burr, and the dispute over its legality cannot have helped his standing among his peers.[38] Burr's reckless behavior with Eliza's money would have been another black mark against him, along with his richly deserved reputation as an incorrigible debtor. As the cashier of the Manhattan Company—the bank Burr himself had founded—said bluntly, "I would not trust him five dollars without security."[39]

What did Eliza think of Burr, once her divorce was secure? According to Parton, she "cherished no ill will toward him and shed tears at his death."[40] It's hard to believe that she was so forgiving immediately after the divorce—consider her comments to her former employer Dunlap in 1834—but she left us no written records of her emotional state. What remain, then, are the bare facts: Eliza not only triumphed in court over Aaron Burr—one of the cleverest lawyers in New York—but would one day transmute the brief and troubled marriage into an instrument to enhance her own reputation. For the moment, however, she had other priorities. She was enmeshed in a new legal battle in which she would employ tactics worthy of Burr himself. The issue—once again—was money.

FINANCIAL
SHENANIGANS

*I*n early nineteenth-century French vaudeville plays, there is a stock character referred to as the *oncle d'Amérique* (American uncle). This personage is typically a younger son who leaves France in early adulthood, before the play opens. Decades later he returns home with a fortune, which he uses to resolve family financial dilemmas. Often a poor nephew or niece becomes the object of his bounty. The favored recipient, newly wealthy, is able to marry the object of his or her affections.[1]

Stephen Jumel was a real-life *oncle d'Amérique*. Returning to France twenty years after his departure, he had showered gifts on his delighted family. He had made allowances to his brother and sister, helped younger members of the family complete their educations, and enabled his niece Felicie's marriage by promising her a large sum of money to be inherited after his death.[2] But the curtain had not fallen after this happy ending. Stephen's family had grown to depend on his largess and their demands had strained his purse.[3] Eliza had resented the money he spent on them, and they had begrudged her claims on his support.[4] When Eliza had put Stephen's real estate in trust for herself in 1827 and '28, she must have acted, at least in part, to shield his property from his relatives.

Her husband's passing increased the need for caution. Under New York State law, Stephen's relatives were entitled to half of his estate, if his assets exceeded four thousand dollars.[5] When Eliza took out letters of administration—the documents that would allow her to wind up Stephen's affairs—she stated that his estate was worth less than the crucial sum and his only surviving relatives were a brother and nephew (i.e., François and Ulysses).[6] She hid the existence of Madelaine and her daughters, Felicie and Rose; did not inform Stephen's family of his death; and did not pay Felicie and her husband the fifteen thousand francs that Stephen had promised them. She protected herself further by not submitting an inventory of the estate to the surrogate (the official in charge of probate and inheritance).[7]

Eliza was not unique in hiding resources after the death of a spouse. Delaying submission of an inventory in order to withhold or deplete assets was so common that some states passed legislation against the practice.[8] Because needy widows might be forced to move in with relatives or resort to an almshouse, women tried to secure as much money and property as possible after a spouse's passing.[9] Other potential heirs would fight back. Eliza had to battle Stephen's family for his fortune.

The fight was slow to heat up. Rumors of Stephen's death did not reach France until six months after his burial. Family members reached out to his former business connections for confirmation.[10] Was he dead? How much money had he left? How much of it could be claimed by his heirs? After confirming Stephen's decease, Lesparre wrote a condolence letter to Eliza and offered her his hospitality, should she desire to revisit France.

In a letter dated June 30, 1833, she thanked her "dear nephew" for his missive: "It is in the highest degree grateful to me to hear eulogies on my dear departed husband, especially from one who had such peculiar opportunities of estimating his character and virtues. The desolation occasioned in my heart by the sudden loss of my dear friend and husband has disqualified me for the accustomed enjoyments of life."[11] She did not mention that she would be embarking on a second marriage the next day.

Mary's recent union was worthy of note, however. Nelson was still a half-trained law student, but Eliza inflated his stature when she described him to Lesparre: "My dear Niece Mary, of whom you have the goodness to inquire, was married about a year and a half since to a gentleman who is a lawyer by profession, and whose residence is in New York. And I have great comfort and relief in the society of my niece and her husband, who is a gentleman of eminent talents."[12]

Eliza's need to exaggerate Nelson's accomplishments seems sad. She was an intelligent and accomplished woman. She read, wrote, and spoke two languages and was knowledgeable about the fine arts. She knew how to run a household, care for a garden, and manage a landed property. From a deprived childhood, she had risen to become a woman of means. Yet in spite of the haughty exterior she presented to the world, she remained uncertain enough of her worth that she craved borrowed glory.

Finally she addressed Lesparre's underlying concern. There was nothing to inherit, she told him:

> In reply to the inquiries which you have the goodness to make respecting the affairs of Mr Jumel, I might refer to your recollection of the circumstances under which he left Europe; since that period nothing has happened to improve his fortune or to redeem the errors suffered in France, which so tended [*sic*] so greatly to impoverish him. The value of his whole property is appraised under the direction of the public authorities of the city, amounting to only four thousand dollars—and the debts which he owed in this country amounted to upwards of fifty thousand francs [ten thousand dollars], although the whole amount of them has not yet been ascertained. In this is not included a debt which he owed to Doctor Berger of Paris of thirty thousand francs. Under the circumstances I have been compelled to relinquish many of the comforts of life to which I had been accustomed. I have therefore no prospect of visiting France.[13]

The letter was deceptive. Stephen owed only trifling sums in America at the time of his death, and his debt to Dr. Eloi Berger—a six-thousand-dollar mortgage on the downtown properties—was not chargeable to the estate. Paying off the mortgage to Berger (an old friend of Stephen's) was Eliza's personal obligation under the terms of the conveyance that gave her control of the buildings.[14]

Eliza concluded her piece of creative fiction politely:

> I thank you nevertheless for your very civil offers of hospitality as well as for the very great interest manifested in your letter for my welfare, which I assure you is most sincerely reciprocated by your most affectionate aunt.
>
> Eliza Jumel
>
> P.S. Mary and her husband join me in most affectionate salutations, to yourself, Madam [i.e., Lesparre's wife, Rose], and her cousins your dear children.[15]

The letter was a lie and Stephen's relations knew it, thanks to financial details gleaned from Stephen's former business associates.[16] Acting from abroad, Madelaine and François hired New York lawyers who forced Eliza to produce inventories and accounts of the estate.[17]

Hidden assets emerged. Eliza had collected cash from Stephen's account in the Manhattan Company's bank. She was owed large sums from two marine insurance companies. She had received compensation from the French government for the loss of the ship *Prosper*, seized in San Sebastián twenty years before. Even the Hartford Bridge Company stock that she had sold after her marriage to Burr had belonged to Stephen's estate.[18] On the debit side of the equation, she had used funds from the estate to pay off the mortgage held by Berger (and later would be forced to reimburse the money to the estate with interest).[19]

Suspicious that Eliza was still hiding funds, Stephen's siblings forced her to submit to an examination before the surrogate. The hearing, on December 17, 1836, began with questions about some of Stephen's minor investments: stock in a turnpike in New Jersey and a textile mill on the Hudson River. As Eliza stated accurately, both initiatives had long since failed.[20] Next she was asked how she became acquainted with Stephen's relatives. "I visited his native town and province," Eliza said, "and I was introduced to his relations or to those who were called so."[21]

Then she dropped a bombshell: "But my husband said that they were no relations of his as he was changed at the nurse . . . I don't know whether he was in joke or earnest when he talked of being changed at the nurse, but he often spoke of it."[22] Under further questioning, she explained what she meant: when the real Stephen Jumel was an infant, he was sent to be breast-fed by a wet nurse. But when it came time for him to return to his family, another child—Eliza's Stephen—was sent back in his place.

The examiner was properly incredulous: "Did your husband say that he was changed at nurse in the presence and hearing of all those persons who were called his relatives?"

"Not to my recollection," Eliza answered prudently.

"Did not Mr. Jumel, whenever he spoke to them or of them in their presence, call them his relatives?" the examiner continued.

At this, Eliza's resentment of Madelaine came to the fore: "He called the woman an old witch," she claimed. As for François, she acknowledged that Stephen called him his brother, but intimated that she had never actually been introduced to him as such: "I believe there was no introduction, I don't recollect that there was any, he came to Bordeaux when we first arrived, and he came and dined with us. Mr. Jumel perhaps did not mention who he was and I asked Mr. Jumel why he had this dirty man at table."[23]

The germ of Eliza's story could have been folktales in which fairies stole an infant and replaced it with another, or a play in which children were swapped at birth.[24] Alternately, she may have been inspired by long-standing rumors that the sixth Duke of Devonshire (1790–1858) was a changeling.[25] It is improbable that she expected her account to be believed. It was an improvisation, deployed as a delaying action. If she were going to be forced to share her late husband's estate, she would not pay out a penny sooner than she must. Walter Skidmore, a lawyer who represented Stephen's siblings, told them that "Mrs. Jumel tells people who converse with her on the subject, that as she is the widow of Stephen Jumel, deceased, she ought in justice to have the whole personal estate, and that his relations, whom she says are so remote, ought not to have anything, and therefore she feels justified in contesting their claims as far as possible."[26] The particular narrative she chose in mounting her defense—a child stolen away at nurse—hints at her emotions. In spite of her differences with Stephen, she saw him as hers and hers alone. In trying to claim what had belonged to him, his brother and sister were stealing bits of him away.

Unlikely as Eliza's story was, it would have to be tested. If Stephen wasn't really a Jumel, then François and Madelaine had no claim on his estate. The next act in the drama took place in southwest France on April 22, 1837. At 10:00 AM, as church bells cacophonously marked the hour, a parade of elderly residents of Mont-de-Marsan made their way slowly through the arched doorway of the Palais de Justice. Jacques Laborde, justice of the peace, probably recognized most of the lined faces before him. Mont-de-Marsan was not a big place.

Six witnesses, ranging in age from sixty to ninety years, swore to having known Stephen's parents and the three children born of the marriage, having "been personally acquainted with them since their births." Stephen had treated François and Madelaine as his siblings, "as well before his departure [from France] as during his absence and after his return from the United States of America and further . . . these facts [were] of public notoriety." François and Madelaine, in their seventies, looked on.[27]

The testimony completed, a copy of the paperwork began its travels, collecting signatures and seals as it went. From the tribunal of Mont-de-Marsan to the ministry of justice in Paris. From the ministry of justice to the ministry of foreign affairs. From the ministry of foreign affairs to the U.S. consul in Paris. From there to the coast and onto a ship to New York. From the bustling wharves to the desk of the surrogate.[28]

Eliza would have to share the estate.

→ 30 ←

THE WIDOW'S MITE

*E*liza would hardly be penniless after paying Madelaine and
François their dues. She was entitled to not only half the
estate's assets but also the income from the downtown properties
and Harlem Heights farmlands. Protected by the trust she had set up
for herself, these holdings were not part of her late husband's estate.

In addition, she had a modest inheritance that Stephen's French
relatives could not claim. A widow was entitled to a one-third share—
known as her dower—in the income from any real estate owned
by her husband during their marriage.[1] Paid quarterly or annually
by whoever owned the real estate that had at one time belonged to
the deceased spouse, dower functioned much as an annuity would,
ensuring that a widow would not be left destitute.

In Eliza's case, dower would come not from the properties in the
trust (all of the income from these was hers already), but rather from
the real estate remaining in Stephen's hands at the time of his death.
In 1837 Eliza launched fifteen lawsuits to claim her dower in lands
he had owned in Westchester and central New York.[2] With Nelson's
assistance, she sued the farmers who were working the lands, and
then renounced her dower rights in return for lump-sum payments.[3]

She won all fifteen suits, but lost a sixteenth, on a property at 57 Pearl Street in Manhattan. This was a house that Stephen and Benjamin Desobry had owned jointly and then sold.[4] (A widow retained dower rights in any property her husband had ever owned, unless she had renounced them at the time of the sale.)[5] The occupants of the building hired Charles O'Conor, a brilliant young lawyer, to handle their defense. He argued that Eliza was ineligible to collect dower payments because Stephen's transfer of the Broadway and Liberty Street properties to her in 1826 was designed to provide a settlement for her in lieu of dower.[6]

This was a clever line of reasoning, taking advantage of a gap in the law. If a man willed property to his wife in lieu of dower, his widow could claim either the property or her dower rights, but not both.[7] But no statutes indicated whether a woman who received a settlement from her husband *during* his lifetime would have to choose between it and dower. The matter would have to be adjudicated in New York's Court of Chancery.

Wisely Eliza opted against pursuing the case. If the chancellor decided that the 1826 settlement had been made in lieu of dower, she might have had to give up dower payments received already. She withdrew her demand for dower rights on 57 Pearl.[8]

In the meantime her tussle with Stephen's relatives went on. Thanks to continued stalling on her part, including an unsuccessful appeal of the decision that barred her from discharging the mortgage held by Berger using monies from the estate, it was not until October 1839— more than seven years after Stephen's death—that Eliza paid half of his net assets to François and Madelaine. Each received just over five thousand dollars, a sum roughly equivalent to $129,000 today.[9]

Strictly speaking, the inheritance arrived too late for François, who had died in April. His share went to his son, Ulysses, who, with Madelaine, continued to fight for more. The two launched an attempt to claim the Jumel lands that Eliza had put in trust for herself.[10] Taking aim at the questionable conveyances used to establish the trust,

The home Eliza and Stephen purchased in 1810, today a museum.

COL. ROGER MORRIS' HOUSE,
Washingtons Head Quarters Sep.r 1776
now known as Madame Jumel Res.ce

The Jumel Mansion in 1854, with its sweeping view of the Harlem River.

The entrance to the mansion, ca. 1875. The colonnade terminated in a gatehouse at each end.

In the early 1820s, Eliza and Stephen lived at 16, Place Vendôme, just to the left of center on the right side of the square (hidden by the building in the right foreground).

Eliza's painting of a girl with a dog by Jean-Frédéric Schall was either this picture or one similar to it.

This Jean-Marc Nattier portrait of a youth dressed as the wine god, Bacchus—the sitter was once thought to be the young Louis XV—is almost certainly the painting of *Louis XV in the Dress of Bacchus* that Eliza owned.

King David Playing the Harp by Simon Vouet, once in Eliza's collection.

Hagar, the Angel, and Ishmael in the Desert, another painting Eliza acquired in Paris.

A mourning miniature, traditionally said to be of Eliza, dating from around the time of Stephen's death. The goldfinch symbolizes both the resurrection and the soul.

Eliza's second husband, Aaron Burr, about six months after their marriage.

Eliza had her silhouette taken in Saratoga Springs, the resort where she summered for twenty-seven years.

Eliza's faithful nephew-in-law Nelson Chase (far right). The artist, Augustin Édouart, pasted his file copies of Eliza and Nelson's silhouettes side-by-side in his album

LEFT: The lithograph Eliza commissioned in Paris in 1852.

BELOW: Eliza with her great-niece and great-nephew in Rome, painted by Alcide Ercole (detail).

Eliza's summer home in Saratoga Springs.

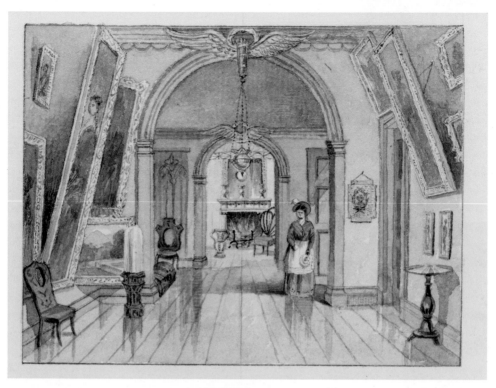

The front hall of the Jumel Mansion.

Eliza, seated at right, with family and friends at the Jumel Mansion, ca. 1860.

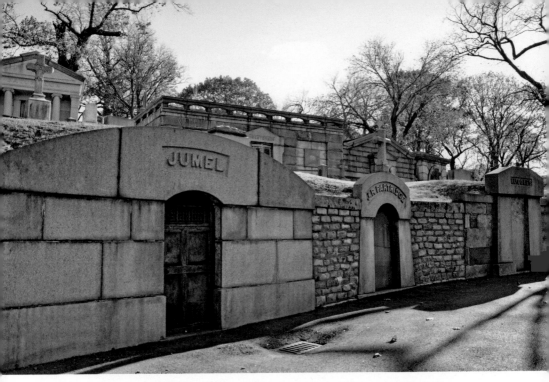

The Jumel crypt at Trinity Cemetery & Mausoleum in Upper Manhattan.

The Count Johannes, failed actor turned advocate, performed as histrionically in court as on the stage.

Lawyer Charles O'Conor, famed for his involvement in the Jumel will case.

George Washington Bowen, the most determined claimant to Eliza's fortune.

they argued that she had defrauded Stephen and his heirs. Her husband had failed to challenge her, they claimed, only because intemperance and "weakness and imbecility of mind" had overcome him "during the latter part of his residence in France."[11] Their suit failed, however. There was insufficient evidence of fraud.[12]

At the same time Eliza was sued by Felicie and her husband, Joseph Benjamin Texoeres, for the fifteen thousand francs (three thousand dollars) that Stephen had promised them in their marriage contract.[13] The money should have been paid within a year of his death, but Eliza had ignored the obligation. Once more she triumphed. Most of the money in the estate had been distributed by the time the couple made their claim. Madelaine and Ulysses would be obliged to pay 50 percent of the sum out of their share of the estate, and Eliza negotiated a clever compromise for her half. She would leave Felicie the sum in her will.[14]

Eliza's most colorful legal battle of the period resulted from a claim by a Parisian woman, Mademoiselle Marie-Antoinette-Ambroisine Guendet. In 1823 Stephen had agreed to pay Guendet an annuity of 1,200 francs a year for life (the reason for his generosity was not stated). But the promised payments had not been made since he left France, and Guendet sued in 1840 to claim the money from his estate.[15]

Shrewdly Eliza delayed the resolution of the case by refusing to be served with a summons. When lawyer Walter Skidmore called at Mount Stephen in September 1840, Eliza was there, but declined to receive him. Skidmore gave the subpoena to a servant, instructing him to deliver it to Madame Jumel, "which the said servant promised to do." But Eliza failed to show up in court.[16]

A man named Edward Cavanagh, probably a summons server, fared no better in January 1842. He went to Eliza's residence, but she had gone into the city, and he, like Skidmore, had to leave the subpoena with a servant. But Cavanagh had a stroke of luck a week later—or so it appeared initially. "On the 29th of January last," he testified, "he saw the defendant Eliza B. Jumel in John Street, opposite the office of Nelson Chase Esq." He

> was in the act of handing a copy of said subpoena to said Eliza B. Jumel when the said Chase took it out of [his] hand and looked at it and said he would attend to it. The said Eliza B. Jumel said to Chase, "Let me see it." The said Chase then assisted her to get in the carriage which was standing near her and whispered something to her which appeared to satisfy her as to the nature of the paper. And the carriage was then driven off without the said subpoena being served; and [the] deponent was prevented from making personal service of the said writ of subpoena by reason of the interference of the said Nelson Chase Esq.[17]

Ultimately Guendet collected—but only because Eliza valued spiting Madelaine more than resisting Guendet. Since late 1839, when Madelaine had received her quarter share of Stephen's estate, Eliza had collected additional funds that the estate was due. However, she hadn't given Stephen's sister her cut, according to a petition Madelaine addressed to the chancellor in September 1840. Eliza managed to stall this newest demand for nearly two years, before finding a cunning way to deny it. Possibly she concocted the solution in collaboration with her former adversary, Charles O'Conor, whom she hired as her counsel. First Eliza settled with Guendet for $2,100. Then she announced that she had collected an additional $1,542.35 due to the estate, but had spent it all on the settlement with Guendet.[18] Madelaine, disappointed, died in 1844.[19] Eliza's battle with Stephen's family ended with her.

As late as 1846, however, Eliza was still pursuing her late husband's assets in the United States. Presenting herself as an impecunious widow, she asked for payment for silver and church vestments that Stephen had purchased for Saint Patrick's Cathedral thirty years before.[20] Bishop Fenwick of Boston, who had served in New York early in his career and remembered the items Stephen had sent from Paris, supported Eliza's quest for reimbursement. "Madame Jumel is now a widow, and it appears she stands greatly in need of the money—surely under the circumstances not a moments [*sic*] further delay ought to be suffered," he wrote to Bishop Hughes of New York.[21]

It is hard to believe that Eliza was cash-strapped. In 1839 the City of New York had taken a strip of land running through her acreage on Harlem Heights for the building of the Croton Aqueduct, which would supply clean water to Manhattan. She was paid $11,524, which has the purchasing power of $298,000 today.[22] But by the mid-1840s she had new demands on her purse—personified by two young children.

A SECOND FAMILY

*I*t took time for Mary and Nelson to build their family. After a year of marriage, there had been the stillborn child: in the frost of winter, in the dark year after Stephen's death, a tiny shoot of new life had withered away. Another child slipped out of the world too, so quietly and unobtrusively that only the barest mention of its existence remains.[1]

But to Eliza's joy, two infants arrived and thrived. Her namesake, Eliza Jumel Chase, entered the world on March 25, 1836. She was born, it was said, at the Jumel mansion.[2] A brother, William Inglis Chase, joined the family on August 17, 1840, when Mary was nearly thirty-nine years old.[3]

The young family lived in rented quarters in New York in the mid-1830s and then in Hoboken from 1837.[4] According to Nelson, Eliza lived with them some of the time and other times, chiefly "in winter, when the ice made it difficult to cross the river," occupied furnished lodgings in Manhattan.[5] She rented out the mansion, returning to it whenever tenants departed.

Leases and legal papers help us reconstruct the financial dealings that allowed her to support herself and assist Nelson and Mary in the years after her divorce from Aaron Burr. Although the female businesswoman is virtually absent from nineteenth-century American literature—perhaps because pecuniary pursuits would have seemed unfeminine—throughout the era women of all classes were deeply involved in the capitalist economy. Mostly barred by their gender from active involvement in the stock market, manufacturing, or shipping, and professions such as law and medicine, women found investment opportunities as mortgage holders and moneylenders, collecting interest payments that provided a regular income. They were prominent among the ranks of the landlords as well, renting out rooms in homes or boardinghouses they occupied or leasing out commercial properties or residences they owned. Female investors—Eliza among them—proved to be as quick as their male peers to foreclose or prosecute if rent, mortgage, or loan payments were not made.[6]

The majority of Eliza's income came from renting out the buildings on the lot at the corner of Broadway and Liberty Street that she and Stephen had purchased in 1812. In 1835 she had the three-story Liberty Street house torn down and replaced with two attached, five-story buildings, 71 and 73 Liberty Street.[7] She replaced the three-story building at 150 Broadway with a five-story structure as well.[8] Given the timing of the rebuilding campaign—just before Eliza was forced to begin settling Stephen's estate—there may have been cash reserves in the mansion at the time of his death that she wanted to spend before an inventory was taken.

The rents from the properties in lower Manhattan totaled approximately $5,500 per year by the mid-century point.[9] An observation made by Sidney George Fisher of Philadelphia helps put the buying power of this sum in perspective. In 1842 he found that his annual income of under $3,000 was adequate to supply him with "a comfortable house—servants, a good table—wine—of course—books—'country quarters,'—a plentiful wardrobe—[and] the ability to exercise hospitality."[10] At the other end of the spectrum, $600 was an adequate annual budget for a working-class family of four in New York City as late as 1853, with $100 allocated for the year's rent and $273 for groceries.[11] In such an economy, Eliza's rental income from the downtown properties made her a wealthy woman.

Her real estate in northern Manhattan was less consistently profitable. A Mr. Pell occupied the mansion and homestead lot for a year or two in the second half of the 1830s.[12] Then Eliza leased out the property in April 1838 for one thousand dollars a year, but evicted the tenant within a year for nonpayment of rent.[13] By April 1842 the best deal that she could arrange was a profit-sharing agreement with a farmer. He received the use of the mansion, garden, and fruit trees in return for half of the money he could earn selling the produce. The agreement specified that Eliza was allowed to retain fruit and vegetables for her family.[14] When she and the Chases were not living at the mansion, they had fresh vegetables and firewood sent to them from Harlem Heights. This would have been a substantive contribution to the household economy in an era when food could consume a quarter or more of an average family's budget.[15]

In addition to the 36-acre homestead lot, Eliza owned 136 acres of farmland, also in upper Manhattan. Although the lands were rocky and not very fertile, she found ways to profit from them nevertheless. The history of a forty-acre parcel extending between the Kingsbridge Road and the Hudson River is instructive in this regard. The Jumels had sold it to their neighbor John R. Murray for $5,495 before leaving for France.[16] When Murray failed to make the required payments, they foreclosed and reclaimed the land.[17] In May 1835 Eliza sold it again, this time for nearly four times the sum negotiated with Murray. Two New York City merchants agreed to pay five thousand dollars upfront, another five thousand within a year, and an additional ten thousand within two years. When the buyers did not produce the second installment of the purchase price, Eliza foreclosed. She made five thousand dollars on the transaction, since she had the right to retain the down payment.[18]

She continued to derive income from the repossessed lot. In 1847 she gave the Hudson River Railroad Company the right to run its tracks through the western edge of the acreage for a payment of eight hundred dollars.[19] Then in 1850 she sold the parcel to Ambrose C. Kingsland, a wealthy merchant and future mayor of New York. She demanded the same twenty thousand dollars she had asked in

1835.[20] With the neighborhood, now served by the railroad, ripe for development, the forty acres constituted a good investment for Kingsland. This time the property did not return to her hands.

In contrast to the forty-acre parcel, a ninety-six-acre lot north of the mansion yielded little but trouble and aggravation.[21] Some years Eliza did not collect any rent; instead, she would give the use of the land to a tenant who would be responsible for maintaining the fences and giving her half the profits from any livestock pastured on the plot.[22]

She went to court more than once to pursue tenants who failed to fulfill their side of the bargain.[23] A lease she negotiated in 1838 with a farmer, Philip A. Levy, came to a particularly dramatic end. Levy rented the property—which included a house, cider mill, apple trees, meadows, and arable land—for a modest two hundred dollars per year. Eliza loaned him some of her cattle—probably he was permitted to sell milk and butter in exchange for pasturing them—and he agreed to keep the fences and buildings in good repair.[24]

The situation soured quickly. In 1840 Eliza filed suit against Levy for failing to return the animals when she asked for them: "four English milch cows and four calves . . . property of the said plaintiff of great value, to wit, of the value of two hundred dollars."[25] Levy sued Eliza in return. He had been leasing a barn from her and claimed she hadn't paid him for storing her carriage in it. She owed him some fifty dollars, he said, at the agreed-upon rate of two dollars per month.[26]

At that point Eliza unleashed a defense that, on the face of it, seems truly bizarre. The suit should be dismissed, she argued, because the plaintiff, Levy, was a married woman rather than a man, and a married woman couldn't file a lawsuit in her own name. Odd as it seems, this argument was actually a variant on a legal tactic used by men wanting to weasel out of agreements with women. In common law a wife did not exist legally apart from her husband and could not contract with anyone. Therefore, if a married woman negotiating an agreement did not have her husband act for her or have a power of attorney designating her as his agent, a man could claim that the provisions of the resulting compact were unenforceable. For example, in 1858, when a male New Yorker was sued for failing to pay rent to a woman, he didn't dispute the fact that the money was due, but argued that their contract was invalid because of her married status.[27]

Eliza, then, was not unusual in making gender a bar to a lawsuit, but the way in which she did it—claiming that an apparently male plaintiff was female—was unprecedented. Even more remarkably, she produced a respectable witness to testify for her: the Rev. John Power, vicar general of the Roman Catholic Church of the Diocese of New York.[28]

On July 3, 1840, Power stood in a Manhattan courtroom. How long had he known Levy? he was asked. He had been acquainted with her for about twelve years, the priest replied. Initially Levy had come to his house requesting to be married to a man named Anthony Bolla. "Levy gave her name as Jane or Jean," Power testified, "which [one], he did not recollect," but "said Levy was dressed in men's apparel." Nevertheless, "he accordingly married them [and] has seen said Levy frequently since." Eliza's lawyer testified that Levy and Bolla "reside[d] together."

On cross-examination, Power admitted "that he did not put down the marriage in his register" and did not know for sure whether Levy was a man or a woman. There his statement ended.[29]

What are we to make of this curious testimony? Was Levy a cross-dresser, a woman who dressed as a man? Or was he a man, perhaps with androgynous features? The court records are silent. Nelson Chase claimed years later that "the gender of this person was a great deal in doubt in the neighborhood. She dressed as a man, but in fact was a woman. Madame Jumel, in speaking of her, always called her 'it.'"[30]

If Nelson was telling the truth, neighborhood gossip about Levy—with respect to his/her gender or relationship with Bolla—could have inspired the unlikely defense Eliza chose. That said, Nelson is not always a reliable witness. At the time he spoke these lines, he was involved in litigation in which it would have been beneficial to portray Eliza as perfectly rational until the last six years of her life.

Admitting that she had trumped up an outlandish story years earlier would hardly have supported his case.

The question of Nelson's veracity aside, the whole affair is reminiscent of the defense Eliza concocted during the fight over Stephen's estate. There is the same tinge of melodrama—this time with a cross-dressing protagonist rather than a changeling—and the same readiness to contest a case by whatever means possible. When Eliza thought she was justified, she would adjust the facts to suit herself and fight even the most unpromising lawsuit to the end.

In all events, her attempt to have the case dismissed on gender grounds failed: Levy's lawyer pointed out that she had referred to his client as a man in her previous lawsuit against him. Then the suit over the storage fees was tried before a jury, which decided in Levy's favor. Eliza appealed—probably to delay payment of the judgment—but failed to show up or send a lawyer to represent her when the case was reheard. She must have known that her chances of winning were slim. Levy won a judgment of $98.95 against her—just under the $99.38 she had been awarded in her suit against him.[31]

Eliza was not unique among businesswomen in resorting to the legal system to pursue money she was owed. A female litigant was involved in approximately 15 percent of the cases brought before New York State Supreme Court in Manhattan between 1845 and 1875.[32] Virtually all of those suits were clashes over money.[33] Nevertheless, the sheer number of lawsuits in which Eliza was involved suggests that she could be a difficult employer and landlord. For example, she was sued by a laborer named Antoine Soili, who claimed that she owed him eight months' unpaid wages at a rate of eight dollars per month. He demanded sixty-four dollars plus his legal costs, but agreed to take thirty dollars in settlement of the suit.[34] The fact that the normally combative Eliza offered a settlement suggests that there was some truth to his claim.

In a more disturbing case, a youth named John Rogers, who probably had worked for her as a house servant or farm laborer, accused her of beating him. In the ritualized words of the complaint, she "with force and arms, to wit with swords, staves, ropes, hands and feet, made an assault upon the said John Rogers and did then and there beat, wound and ill treat him so that his life was greatly despaired of." Through his "next friend" (the term refers to a person who represents a minor in legal proceedings), Rogers demanded damages of one hundred dollars.[35]

Exactly what Eliza did to him—whipped him? beat him with a cane?—is unexplained. She was protective of her public image and vulnerable to any perceived loss of dignity. If Rogers had spoken to her insolently, or she had seen him mocking her to a fellow servant, it is possible to imagine her reacting with violence.

She was nearly sixty-nine years old at the time of the incident, and he must have exceeded her in physical strength. But it is easy to understand why he did not respond to the attack with force. If he had fought back and injured her, the consequences could have been severe. Because of the age difference—and the probable difference in social class as well—it would have been difficult for him to convince a jury that he was the injured party. It was safer to pursue his assailant through the courts.

Eliza pleaded not guilty, but then withdrew the plea and agreed to pay thirty dollars to Rogers in damages.[36] The concession suggests that she was at least partially at fault.

Although Eliza could be a difficult woman, she was deeply devoted to the members of her family, especially Mary and young Eliza and William Chase. Tragically, she would outlive her adopted daughter. Mary suffered from consumption—tuberculosis, as we would call it today—and by 1843 her condition was grave. On May 1, the Chases moved from Hoboken to Manhattan's West Nineteenth Street to be closer to Francis Berger, the family physician.[37] They had barely arrived when the end came. Mary died on May 5, 1843, her husband and her half sister Eliza Jones Tranchell at her bedside.[38] She was only forty-two years old.

Eliza did not attend the funeral ceremony. "She had a constitutional difficulty in going to funerals," Nelson said; she "didn't like them." But he offered a further explanation as well: "She was overborne with grief at the loss of my wife." She "took to her bed and remained there for one week, if not longer. I went to her house and saw her when in that condition and knew the reason; that was the reason she didn't come to the funeral."[39]

It's hard to imagine that Eliza did not grieve profoundly. Mary had been a daughter to her; had called her "Mama," while Maria Jones was simply "Mother."[40] She had grown from childhood to maturity under Eliza's eye. She had been her constant companion whenever Eliza traveled, at least until her marriage, which Eliza had arranged. More often than not, the two had shared a home, even after Nelson had entered the family. She was the person that Eliza had designated as her heir: her niece and at the same time her dearly loved daughter.

Mary was buried at fashionable Green-Wood Cemetery in Brooklyn.[41] Because the inscription on the flat top of the sarcophagus has worn away, how Eliza and Nelson memorialized her is lost to time. But Eliza's actions proved her devotion. At the age of sixty-eight she took on the responsibility of raising Mary's two young children.

According to Nelson, Eliza welcomed seven-year-old Eliza Chase into the Jumel mansion first. She "had charge of her and supported and maintained and educated her until her marriage."[42] William, not quite three when his mother died, soon joined the household as well: "My son, who was a little bit of an infant at the time of the death of his mother, after some little short time was also taken by Madam and she kept him until the year 1859 in her charge; reared him up, sent him to school, maintained and supported him as she had done my daughter."[43] Nelson visited his children once or twice a week but lived in downtown Manhattan to be near his office until 1848.[44] Even after he moved uptown to the mansion, it was Eliza who saw to their upbringing.

She sent young Eliza to "Mrs. Haines'"—probably a dame school in the neighborhood—and then, when the girl was older, to the Convent of the Sacred Heart, a girls' school in upper Manhattan.[45] The details of William's early education are lost, but he was attending a boarding school by the time he was eleven.[46] Both children accompanied Eliza to Saratoga each summer.[47] Technically they were her great-niece and great-nephew, but she treated them as her grandchildren.

MADAME JUMEL

During much of the year, Eliza and the children led a quiet life at the mansion. But she arranged periodically for a change of scene. First with Mary and Nelson, and then with Nelson and the children, she spent part of every summer in Saratoga Springs.

The resort offered occupations for every taste. Eliza and her family could learn about temperance, phrenology, "the inutility of animal food," and even "the destructiveness of tight lacing."[1] They could marvel at demonstrations of "animal magnetism" (i.e., hypnotism); propel themselves in hand-cranked cars on a circular railway; and enjoy pleasure-boat rides on Saratoga Lake.[2] On Sundays they could compare the sermons at half a dozen churches (after watching a conjurer evoke the supernatural on Saturday night—in an old chapel, no less!).[3] They might even have their silhouettes cut by a traveling artist, as Eliza and Nelson did in 1843.

During Eliza's early years in the village, the theater on her property at Broadway and Caroline Street contributed to the cultural life of Saratoga. In the summer of 1833, managers Barrabino and La Burriss kept the playhouse open six nights a week "with an efficient company and a good orchestra."[4] Two years later a performance by "the great magician, Adrien," launched the high season with a bang.[5]

The artist John Vanderlyn's *Panoramic View of the Palace and Gardens of Versailles* hung in the theater in the summer of 1839, while the usual gallery in which Vanderlyn displayed it was being rebuilt.[6] The 360-degree view of the landscape and château featured Louis XVIII on a balcony overlooking the gardens. The sovereigns and generals who had restored him to the throne strolled on the greensward below.

It is not clear if the immense canvas was used as a backdrop for performances or the theater served merely as an alternative exhibition space. But the choice of this particular panorama, rather than Vanderlyn's views of Geneva or Amsterdam, accorded with Eliza's revised self-presentation after her visits to France. As early as her first return to New York in 1817, she had begun to reinvent herself as an habitué of Parisian high society. By the late 1820s she was using the French form of her name in the United States—"Madame Jumel" rather than "Mrs. Jumel."[7] After her divorce from Aaron Burr, she readopted the French sobriquet, passing the remainder of her life as Madame Jumel, "widow" of the former vice president (with occasional, strategic reversions to "Mrs. Burr"). The members of her family addressed her affectionately as "Madam."[8]

As a major landowner in Saratoga, Eliza was a personality at the resort. Although she sold her Broadway and Caroline Street lot in 1841 (for two and a half times the price she had paid for it), she retained 217½ acres of farmland acquired in 1836.[9] Her extensive property holdings allowed her to enjoy a prestige in Saratoga denied her by the Manhattan elite. An Englishman who visited the village in 1838 commented on the permeability of class barriers in the village:

> Hundreds who in their own towns could not find admission into the circles of fashionable society there—for the rich and leading families of America are quite as exclusive in their coteries as the

aristocracy of England—come to Saratoga, where, at Congress Hall
or the United States [Hotel], by the moderate payment of two dollars a day, they may be seated at the same table, and often side by
side, with the first families of the country; promenade in the same
piazza, lounge on the sofas in the same drawing-room, and dance
in the same quadrille with the most fashionable beaux and belles of
the land: and thus, for the week or month they may stay at Saratoga,
they enjoy all the advantages which their position would make inaccessible to them at home.[10]

Eliza and her family stayed at the United States, which was
favored by "the rich mercantile classes"—and by Joseph Bonaparte
as well.[11] At night the hotel hosted balls and hops, where as many as
"three cotillions, of twelve couple [*sic*] each, [were] danced at the
same time."[12] Clerics and invalids favored the respectable Union
Hall, while the Congress Hall hosted visitors who prided themselves
on birth rather than money.[13] Striving clerks and upwardly mobile
grocers headed for the Pavilion, "more miscellaneous in its company." Innumerable boardinghouses welcomed travelers of modest
means.[14]

Social tensions were never far beneath the surface in Saratoga,
in spite of—or perhaps because of—the mixing of classes in public spaces. A visiting Swede remarked that he had heard "on various occasions, individuals boarding at the fashionable Congress
Hall speak of those who had taken up their quarters at the Union,
or United States Hotel, in a way which clearly indicated their own
presumed superiority in point of rank."[15] Visitors who challenged
class distinctions risked derision, as an incident that involved Eliza
illustrates.

The event took place in 1846. In August she had arrived in Saratoga with an unusually elegant equipage: "a turn out consisting of
four grey horses and a barouche with a seat behind." She had ridden
out several times "with her footman seated behind the carriage,"
and "no one . . . took any notice of it." But on August 26 she had
the coach await her in front of the United States Hotel for an hour.

A black footman was seated in the jump seat and two postilions, also black, were mounted on the left-hand horses to guide the vehicle. They were "dressed in livery with broad gold band[s] around their hats."[16]

A "dense crowd had collected" before she exited the hotel for "an afternoon excursion," accompanied by ten-year-old Eliza Chase and six-year-old William.[17] The reason for onlookers' excitement became clear almost immediately, as the *Alexandria* (Virginia) *Gazette* reported. "She had no sooner started off in her carriage, and at the very instant she passed the corner of the hotel, than she encountered another turn out exactly like her own, with the exception that it had white postilions and footmen"—dressed "in a ragged livery," according to another observer.[18] The horses "were a shade lighter" than hers, the *Gazette* reported, and the carriage's occupant "a shade darker, he being nothing more nor less than the Negro Tom Campbell, and away they both went in gallant style amid a deafening cheer from the assembled multitude."[19]

The two dueling carriages raced down the street:

> On reaching Congress Spring, the Negro's carriage had distanced the Madam's. At this point Madam Jumell's [*sic*] carriage turned around, and up she came again. But Black Tom was not to be outgeneraled in that manner. His postilions wheeled his carriage around in a masterly style, and away he went up Broadway again . . . standing erect in his open carriage, displaying a shining rope of ivory from ear to ear, and as he passed the different hotels, gracefully acknowledging cheers he received by bowing to the assembled multitude, or holding his beaver [hat] in one hand, while with a white handkerchief in the other he saluted the bystanders on the sidewalks. In this manner they drove up Broadway, and turned down Church Street. About one hour afterwards they were seen coming down Congress Street, the horses attached to both carriages neck and neck. Turning the corner they both came up side [by] side to the hotel; Black Tom's postilions having managed to get their carriage on the inside, Madam Jumell was compelled to drive around to the side door.[20]

The affair "created a great excitement" in town.[21] Eliza's supporters called the incident "a flagrant insult" to her, a "disgraceful scene," and an "outrage to an aged and unprotected Female."[22] She is "a harmless person," the *Springfield* (Massachusetts) *Gazette* declared, "and had done nothing to provoke such an insult."[23]

Her critics held "to a very different opinion."[24] A Saratogian, writing in 1881, said that Eliza "had offended some persons who had worked on her property, and they got up this burlesque to ridicule her in revenge."[25] The explanation is plausible, given her history of conflicts with tenants and employees, as well as the identity of one of the participants in the charade. Thomas Campbell, the passenger in the "phantastic Vehicle which was driven after" her, worked for Jacobus Baryhyte, whose land was adjacent to one of Eliza's farms.[26] Campbell could have labored on Eliza's property as well. Possibly he hatched the plot or, alternatively, acted on someone else's behalf, as was suggested by the *Alexandria Gazette*: "Several gentlemen have been employed by Madam Jumell [*sic*] to ferret out the persons who furnished the Negro with the money to hire the horses, and paid him and his postilions for their services."[27] The latter scenario does not rule out the possibility that Campbell was among those offended by the original insult.

An anonymous contributor to the *Bellows Falls* (Vermont) *Gazette* explained the episode not as the outgrowth of a private quarrel but as an expression of working-class outrage against Eliza. "The B-hoys"—the term referred to gangs of rowdy young men, often recent immigrants from Ireland—"had some fine sport here with Madame Jumel," the correspondent wrote. "She came to Saratoga, took rooms at the United States Hotel, and paraded the streets in 'coach and four,' attended by three servants in livery. The feelings of the people were outraged at such an impudent exhibition of this paragon of corruption, and they manifested their indignation by getting up a counter establishment, with a Negro inside, which followed her carriage about the streets."[28] The writer implied that Eliza was no better than a prostitute and that she was affecting airs unbecoming to her station. The *Alexandria Gazette* had hinted at similar themes, discernible in the double meaning of the phrase "the Negro's carriage had distanced the Madam's," and the light manner in which the cruel behavior was treated.[29]

The reading of Eliza as a woman who had made a living on her back was made explicit in the second paragraph of the story in the *Bellows Falls Gazette*, in which she was described as "the widow of the notorious Aaron Burr." The author claimed that she

> married Jumel, after living with him in a state of concubinage; but a quarrel arising between them, they separated, dividing Jumel's large fortune between them. She afterwards went through the same course of profligacy with Aaron Burr, and at his decease was the wife of that vicious but talented man. Jumel lost his property in France, and returned to this country penniless. He sought out his former wife, who took him into her family, and supported him through life, as a sort of 'upper servant.' At the decease of Burr, she assumed the name of Jumel, and is now living upon the fortune acquired by her first marriage.[30]

Factually, there is little to praise in this summary. The chronology is jumbled; Eliza's relationship with Stephen is distorted; and she is turned into Burr's mistress, his reputation tainting hers. But it gives a sense for what must have been whispered salaciously behind her back. The only bright spot was that the writer swallowed Eliza's ongoing fib of being Burr's widow rather than his divorced wife.

Eliza's four-horse carriage and servants in livery would have been a flashpoint even if her character had not been in question. The gulf between the rich and the poor was widening in the mid-nineteenth century, and increasingly the lower classes resented the elite.[31] In 1849 the *Home Journal* cautioned readers that "wealth, in a republic, should be mindful where its luxuries offend."[32] Although most middle-class families had a young servant or two to help with the manual labor of running a home in an era before the advent of modern appliances, liveried black servants were employed rarely by the 1840s.[33] In New York they were utilized only by wealthy residents or visiting plantation owners from the South.[34] Their purpose was to "emphasize the social position of employers."[35]

With her use of a liveried footman and postilions rather than a simply dressed coachman, Eliza was aping the modes of a class to which she was not born—a class that was facing mounting hostility for its excesses. Many appreciated her comeuppance. At one and the same time, she had infuriated the elites who disdained social climbers and the disadvantaged who hated the affectations of the elite.

Eliza stood up to her hecklers. She rode out again the next day, "drawn by her four greys with their mounted postilions" and "provide[d] . . . with a six-barreled revolving pistol."[36] Or so said the *Alexandria Gazette*. But undoubtedly the firearm was a journalistic flourish. Eliza outfaced her critics through strength of character, refusing to be driven away by detractors.

Over the years, she continued to embellish her image through canny self-presentation, adjusting facts as necessary. In 1850 she or a family member slipped a writer for the *Saratoga Whig* a scintillating description of a costume she planned to wear to a ball at the United States Hotel:

> Mad[ame] Jumel will, on this occasion, personate the Duchess of Orléans—dress white lace—diadem of diamonds—headdress of diamonds, the same owned and used by Josephine, the wife of Napoleon Bonaparte, bequeathed to her niece, and sold to Mons[ieur] Jumel for $25,000. Her watch is the same that was purchased after the Duchess de Berry had offered $2,000 for it. Besides these, her dress will be spangled with diamonds to the amount of upward of $3,000.[37]

Eliza being Eliza, she had inflated the value of the jewels—her diamonds were valued at $5,500 dollars, not $25,000, in 1872.[38] Almost certainly she had invented their distinguished provenance as well.[39]

A pleasing puff piece, also focused on her attendance at the ball, gives us a sense for how she presented herself to others at the age of seventy-five. After signaling out Madame Jumel among "the distinguished individuals arrived for the Fancy Dress Ball," the anonymous author commenced with compliments:

> A fashionable acquaintance of good authority and most familiar with the history of this distinguished lady, informs us that neither lapse of time, nor a multiplicity of cares attended upon administering her immense estate, impairs in the least her strong mental vigor and extraordinary [*sic*] charming conversational powers . . . For nine years she was the only lady admitted at the Court of France, except the nobility, and none in France except these, during that time, could excel her in the value and magnificence of her apparel.[40]

"As much as ever determined not to be outshone," she would be costumed in white lace in her personification of the Duchess of Orléans, while "Miss Eliza, her niece," remarked last season "as a pretty, happy, sprightly, and fawnlike lass," would dress as a flower girl "in plain white muslin, with tucks—ornamented with roses—a gypsy hat with roses—apron decorated with pink—a little basket of flowers upon her arm."[41]

"Duchess" and "flower girl" attended the event, but Eliza could never escape malicious tongues entirely. In early October, nearly two months after the masquerade, an agricultural journal in Massachusetts noted briefly: "At the late Saratoga Ball, Madame Jumel, in the character of the Duchess d'Orléans, wore $25,000 worth of diamonds, it is stated. 'This,' says a croaker, 'rendered the lady the biggest toad in the puddle!'"[42]

ELIZA BURR ABROAD

*J*n Europe, where few knew her, Eliza could reinvent herself more fully. After Stephen's death, she returned to France three or four times, traveling as Mrs. Eliza Burr. She reveled in the prestige of being the "widow" of a vice president. According to Eliza Chase, she said often, "You know I can take that name if I choose."[1] With a new identity to give her status, "that horrible country"—as she had once called France—felt more welcoming.

Her first overseas voyage as a widow may have taken place in 1841. On October 9 she applied for a passport, "being about to proceed to Europe." The document, duly granted two days later to "Mrs. Eliza Burr," informs us that she was still a brunette at sixty-six—perhaps she had recourse to the dye pot—and looked young enough that her age was given as fifty years.[2] Whether she utilized the passport is unknown, but in early October she was staying at Astor House, New York's most luxurious hotel, possibly in preparation for departure.[3] There she achieved an introduction to the prince de Joinville, third son of King Louis-Philippe, France's reigning monarch.[4]

In the winter of 1850, she was surely abroad, although the surviving documentation is meager. A two-page letter from her that surfaced in 1922 contained the following lines: "You would take me to be a scarecrow. I long to return to America to find tranquility. My life is almost worn out."[5] The dealer offering the document provided no other details of its contents, but the little information provided is consistent with Eliza's habits. She traveled when she was ill, whether physically or emotionally, returning home refreshed in spirit.

Eliza took great enjoyment in an eight-month trip to England, France, Italy, and Scotland in the winter of 1851 to '52, in spite of a "severe illness" that marred part of the journey.[6] Her fifteen-year-old great-niece accompanied her. "Alas!" she informed Nelson in a letter, "I shall have to spend money very freely for Eliza—court dresses will be very costly." But she did not truly regret the expense: they expected to enjoy themselves more in Paris "than in all the other cities" they planned to visit, including Naples, Venice, and Rome.[7] Indeed, in Paris "Prince Louis"—probably Louis-Napoléon Bonaparte, France's elected "Prince-President," who would soon mount the throne as Napoleon III—obtained tickets for them to attend the splendid ceremony of the Distribution of the Eagles to the Army.[8] The event attracted tens of thousands of spectators to the Champs de Mars, as Eliza Chase reported to her father.[9] Also in Paris, Mrs. Burr sat for a portrait drawing.[10] She had it lithographed, adding a suitable caption: "MADAM WIDOW OF THE LATE AARON BURR, VICE PRESIDENT OF THE UNITED STATES, FORMERLY MADAM JUMEL."[11] Her name was given typographical parity with Burr's.[12] Other highlights of the trip included, in Italy, attendance at the balls of Prince Alessandro Torlonia, the so-called Roman Rothschild; and in Edinburgh, visits to Holyrood Palace and the monument to Sir Walter Scott.[13]

Eliza took pleasure in smaller matters as well. She told Nelson proudly of a stratagem she had employed to secure a comfortable journey from southern France to Nice:

When we arrived in Marseilles, we went to take our passage before the steamship sailed, when to my great surprise, they informed me that all the berths were taken, and not another person could be accommodated, but that we could wait till the next day and get a

berth to ourselves. I told them I must go in this steamer, if I have
[*sic*] to sleep on the planks; his answer was, "Do as you please, for
we have no accommodation." Eliza strove to dissuade me, but to no
purpose. I paid my money and on board we went. The first thing
I did was to call on the captain, and in a very low tone I addressed
him: "Sir, I have been looking for a berth; you would permit a President's wife to sleep on the planks?"[14]

Eliza's self-elevation in rank served its purpose. "O[h], no, my
good lady," the captain replied, "I will go down and procure you a
good berth." Then "he descended and ordered the best, telling the
ladies they were taken. So the poor ladies had to go into the gentlemen's room, and we enjoyed the good things with the rest."[15]

Eliza's manipulations may have saved her life. "I have no doubt
that you have read in the papers of the disastrous event which took
place in the steamer the day after," she wrote to Nelson, "and I have
no doubt we should have been lost had we waited."[16] Probably they
had escaped one of the boiler explosions that were tragically common in the early days of steam.[17]

Eliza closed her letter with kind words for eleven-year-old William, too young to join his sister on the European venture: "Give
my love to Will, and tell him I often think of him, and was pleased
to learn so good an account of him." Then with "grateful thanks" to
Nelson for the "affectionate letter" she had received from him, she
signed herself "your true friend, Eliza Burr."[18]

In 1853 to '54 "Mrs. Burr" took another trip abroad, this time accompanied not only by Eliza, now seventeen, but also by thirteen-year-
old William. With her great-niece approaching marriageable age,
Eliza stopped strategically in Bordeaux on the way to Italy. In the
"port of the moon," they called on Jean Edouard Pery, nephew of
Stephen's decades-long business associate Jean Pery. The couple's
twenty-year-old son Paul received Eliza and her young relatives.
Paul and Eliza Chase were given a chance to become acquainted.[19]

From there, Eliza and her great-niece and nephew traveled on to Malta, Sicily, and Rome. In the latter city, they sat for a grand portrait that would be shipped back to the United States.[20] Eliza, in dark green brocade, trimmed amply with lace, sits straight-backed and alert between her great-niece and great-nephew. The triangular composition recalls Italian Renaissance images of the Holy Family, with Eliza in the center as the benevolent Holy Mother.

When the trio reached Paris, Eliza took pleasure in reencountering Louis-Napoléon, now emperor of France. Their meeting, reported in the French press, was considered worthy of note by the *Kenosha* (Wisconsin) *Democrat*:

> The Paris *Patrie* of a late date says that "at the last Tuileries ball, the brilliant toilette of a stranger, with an incredible number of diamonds, attracted the attention of all present. In a moment the attention was changed to the most intense curiosity, when Louis-Napoléon was observed to accost the lady, and remain some moments in conversation. The enigma was soon solved. The lady was the widow of Aaron Burr, formerly vice president of the United States, with whom Louis-Napoléon was on terms of intimacy whilst in that country, and at the end of fifteen years he recognized the widow as his old American friend."[21]

The *Democrat* credited Eliza with (illusory) estates on the island of Malta, but blew the whistle on her marital status, noting that she was the divorced wife rather than widow of Burr.[22]

Eliza looked up two other old acquaintances while in France. Either on this European tour or perhaps the prior one—Eliza Chase did not specify which—she and her great-niece called on Adèle and Henriette de Cubières, who were living in retirement outside Paris. According to Eliza Chase, her great-aunt's old friends spoke with fond nostalgia of their childhood, "in the fresh and blooming country" that is now Manhattan's Upper West Side.[23]

Eliza knitted new French connections as well. A second visit to Bordeaux had resulted in a growing intimacy between Eliza Chase and Paul Pery. The notion of a marriage was floated, although it is unclear who suggested it. Asked later if Mrs. Burr had put forward the match to him, Paul denied it. "I did my own love-making," he said, "and proposed in *propria persona*, as every plucky young man should do."[24] But the union was not approved by the young people's elders until its financial aspects were negotiated. In nineteenth-century France, marriage remained as much an economic as a romantic transaction. Thus in 1827 Stephen had cautioned Lesparre: "We must think of marrying Ulysses, but he wants a large sum of money."[25] Jean Edouard Pery was a prosperous notary and Paul was his and his wife's only child. They could insist on a young woman with a handsome dowry for their son.

Shrewdly Mrs. Burr negotiated with Paul's father. The majority of her fortune was destined to Eliza and William Chase, she assured him in a letter from Paris. "This fortune can be estimated at two million dollars," she wrote, "which corresponds to about ten million francs."[26] (Considering the probable value of her real estate in 1854, she was doubling, if not tripling, her net worth.) Next she made a carefully calculated offer: "If my niece should marry your son, I would assure her an income of five thousand francs [i.e., one thousand dollars]. I cannot go beyond that because I have no present intention of touching my capital."[27]

She declined Pery's request to guarantee the promised income by placing a principal of one hundred thousand francs in an interest-bearing investment. All her fortune was in real estate that she was not "disposed to sell [or] mortgage." Besides, she added, it wasn't an American custom to give women dowries when they married. Mrs. Burr proposed that she guarantee the income herself instead— she would sign any contract Pery wished—"and the obstacle will be overcome." She closed the letter by promising that Eliza Chase would be remembered in her will: "My niece having lost her mother in early childhood, it is I who raised her; she has not quitted me and I have a veritable affection for her. Without appointing the share that she may have in my estate today, that share may be considerable and by my testamentary dispositions . . . will be assured to her."[28]

Paul's parents agreed to the union, essentially on Eliza's terms. In the marriage contract she promised her great-niece one hundred thousand francs—twenty thousand dollars—but specified that the sum would not be paid until after her own death. The Perys named Paul their heir. In addition, they agreed to take the young couple into their household and pay all their living expenses, unless the bride and groom preferred to reside elsewhere.[29] To match this generosity, Eliza promised to provide her great-niece with one thousand dollars annually, the income she had suggested previously.[30] With this relatively modest upfront outlay, she had secured an affluent husband for her namesake. It was a bravura performance.

With Nelson's consent, obtained by mail from New York, the nuptial rite (or rather, rites) took place in Bordeaux in early July. Paul and his bride were married no fewer than three times "to guard against trouble on account of the peculiarities of the French law."[31] They had a civil ceremony performed by the mayor of Bordeaux, a second wedding celebrated in the Roman Catholic church (Paul was Catholic), and a third solemnized in the Episcopal Church (Eliza Chase was Episcopalian).[32] "The ordeal lasted two days," and "when it was over," Paul "felt not only considerably fatigued, but quite sure that he 'had been very much married.'"[33]

The young couple set up housekeeping in the household of the groom's parents. Mrs. Eliza Burr and Master William Chase left for home by way of Liverpool. They crossed the Atlantic incongruously on the *Pacific*, one of the record-breaking steamships of the Collins Line.[34] When they reached New York, Eliza, or someone acting for her, slipped one of the journalists meeting the arriving ship a so-called "letter from Bordeaux, dated June 25." Its unnamed author claimed to have had a visit "from the widow of Aaron Burr," whose business in Bordeaux was "the marriage of a niece to a gentleman of this place . . . She gives $100,000 as a marriage gift"—Eliza quintupled her contribution for the public record—"and Mr. Perry [*sic*], the father of the young man, gives the same amount"—a complete invention. Creative license extended to the disposition of the funds that Mrs. Burr had kept safely in her own hands: "Mr. Bowen, the

United States consul, has been requested to be the trustee of the money." The letter, showing Eliza's gift for self-promotion at its best, concluded with a flattering reference to her: "Mrs. Burr is the American lady who created such a sensation at the balls in Paris last winter."[35] She, and not her newly married great-niece, played the starring role in this drama.

→ 34 ←

A ROMANTIC WIDOW

*L*ess than two weeks after their marriage, Paul and his new wife set out on an extended visit to the United States.[1] They spent most of the time with Eliza, who was touched by the young couple's affection for each other.[2] When Jean Edouard Pery wrote to thank her for welcoming Paul into her family, she expressed her joy in their children's marriage: "I am no less fortunate than you, Monsieur, in all the circumstances that have contributed to their blessed union, and I see in it the decrees of divine Providence, which has thus liberally bestowed its gifts on you, on me, and on our children."[3] She addressed Paul himself with the familiar *tu* (you) rather than its formal counterpart, *vous*, when she thanked him for a letter sent from Boston, before he and his wife reembarked for France. "I reread often, with sweet satisfaction and ineffable happiness, the lines you wrote to me before your departure: A filial love breathes in all that you say to me, and my heart is devoted to you with a truly maternal love."[4]

Eliza's deepest affection was reserved for Paul's wife. She responded fulsomely to a letter the young woman wrote her from Boston: "So much esteem and respect for me, so nobly expressed, inspire me with a legitimate pride and pleasure, natural to a person who sees her work successfully achieved. I am assured that my efforts to form your mind on the solid basis of religion and virtue are by no means wasted; and duty will dictate to you a constant love and eternal gratitude toward me." If she seems in these lines to treat her great-niece as her creation—the Galatea to her Pygmalion—the genuine warmth of her feelings shines through in other passages: "All my joy, all my contentment, will be to learn that you are living in happiness and prosperity: You understand that you are still the dearest object of my attention and thoughts, and that you can always count on me as on a mother and true friend . . . Formerly your worthy late mother possessed my love and tenderness, and since she is no more, you have naturally become the center of my affections."[5]

In a letter sent a few weeks later, Eliza expressed pleasure in a coincidence; Paul and her great-niece had written to her on the same day that she had written to them: "I see with pleasure that, although we are separated, our hearts are still united . . . They felt at the same time the need to converse with each other: The day that I wrote, you were writing to me; I received your letter and without doubt you received mine of January 21 last. We read together, we think together, we remember each other together; what charming, happy, and admirable harmony!!! It is that of nature."[6]

She described how she, Nelson, and William consoled themselves "more or less" for Eliza's absence: "In the evening we retire into the large drawing room, where you know that the famous family portrait faces the scene; and there our imagination in ecstasy permits us to enjoy her presence. Then the young lady in court dress is the principal personage here; she attracts our regards, the attentions of the whole family, and each fancies himself conversing with her in person. This painting is indeed a source of happiness for us, since one person of this little group is settled on foreign soil."[7]

The missing member of the party was soon to be present in the flesh. In the summer of 1855, young Mrs. Pery paid another visit.[8] But her temporary presence was not enough for her great-aunt. By the following spring, "Madame Burr" had determined that her great-niece and Paul should live permanently in the United States.[9]

She made the economy, which was beginning to soften, the excuse. Nelson wrote to John Edouard Pery on March 22, 1856, enclosing a bill of exchange for 2,050 francs "for our dear children Paul and Eliza" and a letter "proving to them the necessity that exists, in the present state of their affairs here, that the money we are sending by this present must not be employed for any other purposes [than to] furnish them with the means to make certain of their return voyage to this country."[10] In April the young couple left France for New York, accompanied by an eighteen-year-old female servant and the newest member of their little family: a twelve-month-old daughter, Mathilde.[11] Eliza would have her closest relatives gathered about her again.

By the second half of the 1850s, the old slurs that had tarnished Eliza's reputation had been mostly forgotten. In 1855 a New York correspondent for the *Albany Express* offered readers a deferential picture of her and her domain. Her estate was "surrounded by forests and dells," its grounds "beautifully improved," and its "gardens laid out with taste." Inside her home, "costly paintings (and among them a genuine Rubens), articles of vertu, presents from noble and distinguished persons, autographs, and everything that is rare and costly and curious" could be seen "in lavish profusion."[12]

A watercolor of the hallway gives an idea of the setting, showing the remnants of the Jumel collection mingled with objets d'art that Eliza had brought back from her later visits to Europe. In the left middle ground, Napoleon I's traveling chest—the one she claimed to have received from the emperor as a gift—occupies a prominent place.

Eliza herself, "from having mingled so much in the best kind of society," had "all the courtly graces and blandness of manner which distinguished *les dames d'honneur*" of the eighteenth century. She bore "herself very haughtily, forbidding anything like approaches to familiarity"—truly "as much of a despot in her own dominions as any monarch who sways a scepter." Perhaps inspired by her house's history as George Washington's military headquarters, she had a gun fired each evening to deter potential intruders.[13]

Each summer Eliza emerged from her self-imposed isolation in upper Manhattan to pay her annual visit to Saratoga Springs. In 1851 she had purchased a house on Circular Street to serve as her summer home.[14] With its massive square columns supporting a brooding triangular pediment, it is akin to, if less graceful than, her New York mansion. As if in compensation, she gave it the delicate name Rose Cottage and replaced the back piazza with an elegant dining room, lit by four large windows.[15]

Once or twice in the early 1850s, she took advantage of having her own lodging in Saratoga to welcome members of her sister's family. Maria Jones had died in 1850, but Eliza hosted her sister's oldest surviving daughter, Eliza Jones Tranchell, and Emily Maddox, child of the younger Jones daughter, Louisa.[16] In 1853 the women stayed for four months in order to attend the state fair, which was held on farmland Eliza owned a mile east of Saratoga (no doubt she charged a rental fee for use of the property).[17] Although that year "she was sick almost all the time" and "didn't receive much company," she was in better form a few years later.[18] In 1857 she gave an evening entertainment for the Utica Citizens Corps, presenting the company with a "modest but beautiful" white satin banner, decorated with gold fringe and the image of the goddess of Liberty.[19] Her guests received the gift following the "Army regulations for reception of colors," and "gave her a lively serenade" before they left.[20] When she departed Saratoga for New York on September 30, the local newspaper paid her an amiable compliment: "What with her presents to and entertainment of the Corps, and their attentions in return, her residence has been the scene of much that was gay and imposing."[21]

The year 1858 brought Eliza renewed attention with the publication of James Parton's *Life and Times of Aaron Burr*. In this wildly popular biography (it went through fourteen editions by 1861), she was treated sympathetically as "a daughter of New England" who was "as remarkable for energy and talent as [Burr] himself."[22] According to Parton, Eliza was "a favored frequenter" of the French court during the "many years" she resided in Paris with Stephen—by now the legends had become the reality. After her return to New York, she had undertaken "with native energy the task of restoring her husband's broken fortunes."[23] Stephen was given a vivid back story: supposedly he had emigrated to Saint-Domingue as a young man and watched his coffee plantations burn at the time of the rebellion, but escaped the massacre thanks to (1) a faithful slave and (2) a passing boat that deposited him on Saint Helena—the island where Napoleon I would live in exile years later. From there Stephen made his way to New York.[24] Surely it was Eliza who reassigned the Saint-Domingue getaway from François to his brother, heightening the drama by inserting a loyal slave and a mythical layover in Saint Helena. With Napoleon III on the throne of France, her tales had taken on a Bonapartist tinge.

Parton treated the divorce from Burr with tact, protecting both Eliza's and McManus's reputations: "The accusation [i.e., that Burr had committed adultery] is now known to have been groundless; nor, indeed, at the time was it seriously believed."[25] Burr had been losing Eliza's money in unwise investments, Parton explained, and the charge "was used merely as the most convenient legal mode of depriving him of control over her property."[26] Eliza's claim of being Burr's widow rather than his wife was accepted. Their union, Parton wrote, "was, in effect, though never in law, dissolved."[27]

Had she truly never been divorced from Burr? The investigation of that matter formed a curious sequel to her relationship with that complex and enigmatic man. In 1863 Nelson Chase arranged with a Washington lawyer, Samuel A. Pugh, to claim Burr's military pension for the former vice president's surviving "spouse."[28] Potentially Eliza could receive six hundred dollars for every year since Burr's death in 1836. Pugh agreed to pursue the claim in exchange for two-fifths of any arrears awarded, while Nelson would receive five hundred dollars of Pugh's cut.[29]

The case rested on a copy of a document that proved (supposedly) that there had not been a divorce at all.[30] At a guess, the item may have borne the date that the papers relating to the divorce suit were enrolled (i.e., legally registered).[31] Because Burr's appeal of the divorce was in progress when he died, the records of the case were not filed away until his death—an event that terminated the appeal. As a result, the vice chancellor's final signature on the documents was dated September 14, 1836, inspiring the poetic but inaccurate story still circulating today that the divorce was handed down on the day of Burr's death.[32] The dating of the signature could have prompted Nelson and Eliza to claim that Burr had died before the divorce could be concluded.

Unfortunately for their attempt to revise history, the marriage had been dissolved on July 8, 1836, in spite of the subsequent appeal.[33] Eliza had even identified herself occasionally in legal matters as the divorced wife of Aaron Burr.[34] Trying to change her status on a technicality—a possible delay in the enrollment of the decree—was a losing battle, Pugh realized, after putting in a year of uncompensated efforts. This "has been the most vexacious [*sic*] case I ever had," he wrote with frustration in 1863.[35] He would earn nothing for his trouble, and Eliza would not get the pension she had claimed. To the federal government, she was, and would remain, the divorced wife and not the widow of Burr.

THE END OF AN ERA

*I*n 1859 the *Saratoga Sentinel* reported that "Madame Jumel, once the wife and now the widow of the celebrated Aaron Burr," continued to visit Saratoga annually:

> She comes here ostensibly to look after an estate which she owns, located near our village, but, like all other ladies, she mingles with, and seems to enjoy, the festivities of this gay watering place with as much delight as if she was the reigning belle of the season.
>   . . . Although she has outlived most of her contemporaries, having attained upwards of eighty years, she seems to be just as full of life and vivacity as she was forty years ago, and apparently possessing all her faculties unimpaired.[1]

The 1859 visit to Saratoga would be Eliza's last. A photograph that must date from around 1860 reveals unmistakable signs of age.[2] Posed with her family outside her home, she allowed herself to be portrayed without hair dye or wig, white hair drawn back beneath one of the delicate lace head coverings she had favored for twenty-five years. Although she sat rather than stood for the long exposure, she had the strength to support in her lap an unidentified child, seemingly about twelve months old.

Mathilde is seated on the steps of the mansion and her mother in a chair with a book in her lap. The man whose left arm is hidden by a column may be Paul. Nelson is nearby, hat in hand. William, hands behind his back and coat buttoned up to the neck, stands at a short distance from the family group on the porch. He and Eliza, posed on either side of their relatives and friends, seem slightly isolated from the others.[3]

The photograph, faded from exposure to light, is tantalizing but unsatisfying. The tiny faces, examined through a loupe, fade into the background instead of moving into sharper focus. The expression on Eliza's face cannot be read. Cannily she retains her secrets.

In spite of her frailty—she stopped sallying out to Sunday church services in 1859—Eliza remained active as a businesswoman into her mid-eighties.[4] In late 1859 she filed suit against a man who had leased her troublesome ninety-six-acre lot and then defaulted on the three-hundred-dollar rent. The proceeding became a family affair. Nelson acted as her attorney, as he typically did, and William served the summons on the defendant. Eliza's signature on the complaint is tremulous, but clearly legible. She won her case.[5]

A year and a half later, persons interested in purchasing or leasing her "two very valuable farms" in the village of Saratoga Springs were advised to call on Nelson Chase at his office, 46 Exchange Place, or on Eliza B. Jumel, at Washington Heights (as Harlem Heights had been renamed in honor of the first president).[6] As late as 1863, when she was eighty-eight years old, Eliza's attention to her property remained keen. Concerned "that an adjoining owner [in upper Manhattan] had encroached upon her premises, so as to take from her two acres of land on the northern bounds," she hired a surveyor to map her farm and then refused to pay him when he did a negligent job. He attempted to collect his $375 fee in court, but abandoned the case after the quality of his work was questioned by experts.[7]

While Eliza remained alert to what was going on around her, there are hints that she became more difficult to live with in the late 1850s and early '60s. The Perys resided with her at the mansion after moving to New York from France in 1856, but either at the end of 1857 or in the spring of 1858, they relocated to a house purchased by Eliza at Seventh Avenue and Forty-First Street.[8] A year later, they were on West Forty-Fifth Street near Fifth Avenue, and by fall 1862, at 143 East Sixty-Fifth Street.[9] William, now twenty, was living with them by the summer of 1860.[10]

Nelson remained with Eliza most of the time, commuting downtown to his law practice. However, in September 1862 he left the mansion, lodging with his son, daughter, and son-in-law on Sixty-Fifth Street; then returned uptown in May.[11] The reason for his temporary departure remains unexplained, but Eliza appears to have become distrustful of the members of her family. In the summer of 1862, she was in contact with Rev. John Howard Smith, rector of the Church of the Intercession (the Episcopal church in Washington Heights that she had attended in her later years).[12] By 1864 or early 1865 she had given her bank book into his charge, but subsequently her suspicions extended to him as well.[13] She insisted that six thousand dollars was missing from her account and asked Smith to account for the discrepancy. He did so twice in Nelson Chase's presence.[14]

Although Eliza remained rational on many subjects, her fictions became increasingly real to her as she aged, shifting from creative exaggerations to near delusions. In December 1861 she addressed a letter to the prince de Joinville—then visiting the United States—whom she had met at Astor House twenty years before. Would he call on her at the mansion, she asked? They could converse about "his noble father," the late King Louis-Philippe of France, whom she had known at the court of Charles X when Louis-Philippe was still the duc d'Orléans. "It was because of me or my encouragement that he much later mounted the throne," she claimed in her letter.[15]

It was at a grand ball of the court; the ladies-in-waiting and the gentlemen of the king's house surrounded the throne, waiting for the arrival of his Majesty. Although foreign, I had the honor to be with the ladies-in-waiting of the duchesse de Berry. The king arrived, saluting and smiling with his usual grace, but when he mounted his throne, his hat fell; that is when your noble father, the duc d'Orléans, approached, caught it, mounted several steps of the throne and presented it to the king. As if inspired, like one who sees everything and knows the future, I cried: "Good Omen, Good Omen, the duc d'Orléans will be king." They came forward to lead me out and perhaps throw me in prison, when the good King Charles made a sign and seemed to say to me with regret, "It is true."[16]

Eliza concluded her tale on a modest note: "The events that followed have proven your humble servant was right [Charles X was forced to abdicate in 1830], but I don't like to flatter myself; I was only an instrument of a Superior Being that made me interpret and encourage your father to hasten the execution of his plans."[17]

What the prince made of this implausible story remains a mystery. Sadly there is no indication that he paid Eliza a visit.

Eliza put off one crucial duty as she advanced in age. From 1859 onward, she spoke several times to her family lawyer, William Wetmore, about drawing up a will, but could never make up her mind to do so.[18] Instead, Wetmore said, "She generally, when I went to see her conversed about Mr. Jumel, and how she got the property, and about her friends in Europe, and about her visiting the various courts of Europe . . . My visits to her most always were four or five hours long."[19]

In the summer and early fall of 1862, she consulted Rev. Smith instead. According to his description of their meetings, she asked him to call on her. When he did, she broached the possibility of bequeathing money to construct a new building for the Church of the Intercession. In addition, she asked him to draw up a list of charities that would be suitable objects of her bounty (she had requested and received a similar list from Wetmore). She suggested leaving Smith a personal legacy also. But again she failed to act.[20]

The turning point came in March 1863. While suffering from a severe illness, Eliza agreed to the rector's suggestion to ask an architect, Mr. Mold, to bring some church designs for her to consider. She went over the plans with Smith and Eliza Pery, expressing a preference for a structure with "a very beautiful façade" that Mold estimated could be built for sixty thousand dollars.[21] Then, again at Smith's prompting, she called in Wetmore to prepare a will. Although the lawyer could not persuade her to finalize anything, he left a draft containing the provisions he had discussed with her.[22] A few weeks later, Smith modified the draft under Eliza's direction. On April 15, she signed the document at last.[23]

The details of Eliza's last years are hazy. The Civil War roiling the country barely touched her life. Its only recorded impact on her was financial. She, Nelson, and Paul were subject to the first federal income tax, imposed to cover the costs of the conflict. In 1865 Eliza reported $7,739 in income in addition to a watch and three carriages.[24]

By 1863 she is said to have been afflicted with gastric trouble and kidney disease.[25] Then in June or early July 1865, she suffered a fall.[26] The accident marked the beginning of the end. Eliza, born two weeks before the Revolutionary War began, died two months after the Civil War ended. She took her last breath on Sunday morning, July 16, at home in the Jumel mansion.[27] She was ninety years old.

By the end of her life, Eliza had become, in the eyes of many, a survival of the grand old years when the republic was young. In an impressively inaccurate obituary, the *New York Times* identified her as the daughter of an Englishwoman, Mrs. Capet (the surname of the French royal family before the Revolution), and placed her at the 1774 opening of Congress in Philadelphia and the 1789 inauguration of George Washington in New York.[28] The *World*, reporting on her funeral, commented that her passing made "one less to the now small number of those who lived in those memorable days."[29] As a serial weaver of romances herself, Eliza would have appreciated not only these inventive tributes but also a small and unwitting fiction: on her death certificate, attending physician Dr. Alonzo Clarke gave her place of birth as France. The disease causing her passing was identified as "old age."[30]

During the first forty-eight hours after Eliza's death, her body lay in a "splendid rosewood coffin" in one of the parlors of her mansion.[31] At one o'clock Tuesday afternoon, the casket was closed and removed to the Church of the Intercession.[32] As it rested on trestles in front of the chancel, Rev. Smith read the Episcopal burial service and the lesson from I Corinthians: "But now is Christ risen from the dead."[33] Then the choir chanted the anthem from the thirty-ninth Psalm: "Lord, make me to know mine end, and the measure of my days."[34] Finally, six prominent men from the neighborhood—among them Sheriff James Lynch; John E. Develin, Corporation Counsel of the City of New York; and Richard F. Carman, a large landowner in Washington Heights—served as pallbearers as the body was returned to the hearse.[35]

Eliza's last journey, to Trinity Church's tranquil uptown cemetery, was short. Her body was laid to rest in a stone mausoleum set into a hillside overlooking the Hudson River.[36] Today birds chirp in the trees shading the crypt and flashes of sunlight play over the sloping lawn. But if Eliza's bones were at peace, her legacy was not. A line of the psalm sung at the church proved prophetic: "He heapeth up riches, and knoweth not who shall gather them." The Jumel fortune would have many claimants. They would keep Eliza's name alive, but indelibly smear her legacy.

A DISPUTED
INHERITANCE

*W*ithin two days of Eliza's funeral, a reporter for the *New York Observer and Chronicle* had scented scandal. "It is understood that nearly one-half of [her] property has been left for benevolent purposes, and if the will is unbroken, some of the institutions in the neighborhood of Washington Heights may be enriched by her death."[1] The innocent little phrase—"if the will is unbroken"—cleverly suggested that the reverse might occur.

Eliza had left a bequest of five thousand dollars to Rev. Smith of the Church of the Intercession, seventy thousand dollars for a new church and rectory, and a plot of land to build them on. Nine charitable institutions—ranging from the Society for the Relief of the Destitute Children of Seamen to the Association for the Relief of Respectable Aged Indigent Females—would receive legacies of five hundred to five thousand dollars each.[2]

Eliza's family, in contrast, was partially disinherited. William would get nothing. Nelson, for over thirty years her loyal son-in-law (or strictly speaking, nephew-in-law), would receive the interest on a principal of ten thousand dollars—an income of about seven hundred dollars per year.[3] His daughter, Eliza Pery, would receive the same, instead of the twenty-thousand-dollar legacy she had been promised in her marriage contract. However, she would share the residuary estate (what remains of an estate after specific legacies are paid) with the charities.[4] The residuary estate contained about 90 percent of the Jumel fortune. The estate as a whole was worth approximately one million dollars—equivalent in purchasing power to nearly fifteen million dollars today.[5]

The will was a bitter blow to Nelson and his children—particularly William. In an earlier testament drafted in 1851, most of Eliza's property had been left to her great-nephew.[6] He would have received the farms in Saratoga Springs outright and the income from the downtown properties, mansion, and homestead lot. In addition, he and his sister, Eliza, would have shared sixty acres of Washington Heights farmland. His sister would presumably have a husband to support her as well (she was a girl at the time that document was written), plus any marriage settlement that might be made in the future. Although Nelson would have been guaranteed only five hundred dollars per year, he could have anticipated support from his son, who would have been a very wealthy man. With the 1863 testament, everything had changed. William was left penniless and most of Eliza's estate would go to charity.

The Chases decided to challenge the will. Nelson proved himself a worthy successor to Eliza in the shrewdness with which he managed the litigation. He made an agreement with his children to oversee the legal proceedings in exchange for one-third of what they would receive from the estate.[7] Although not a blood relative of Eliza, with this maneuver he secured a claim on a third of her enormous fortune.

In addition, Nelson negotiated a crucial deal with the four surviving children of Eliza's sister, Maria Jones. If the will were to be overturned, by New York State law the estate would be divided among Eliza's nearest relatives: the four Jones children (her nieces and nephews). Nelson bought out the Joneses' claims for forty thousand dollars, so that William and Eliza, her great-niece and great-nephew, would become their great aunt's only heirs.[8]

Quiet consultations with the charities named in the will followed. Nelson promised to pay each organization the bequest it had been promised if it did not obstruct his attempts to overturn the will or demand its cut in the residuary estate.[9] As much as it must have grated on him, he agreed to pay Smith's five-thousand-dollar legacy and a portion of the money promised to the Church of the Intercession as well.[10]

Nelson neglected to contact one of the will's beneficiaries. During the battle over Stephen's estate, Eliza had agreed to pay her half share of the three thousand dollars her husband had promised his niece Felicie, but not until after her own death. The bequest was listed in her will, but Nelson ignored it.[11] Felicie was on the other side of the Atlantic and unlikely to hear of Eliza's death.

The next move was to arrange a court hearing: a jury would have to be convinced to set the will aside. Nelson and his children hired Charles O'Conor, the most celebrated member of the New York bar, to serve as lead counsel.[12] Thirty years before, O'Conor had served on Aaron Burr's legal team, helping Burr to defend himself against Eliza's bill of divorce.[13] Then he had driven Eliza to a draw in one of her dower rights cases, but represented her in a later tussle over Stephen's estate.[14] In the 1850s he had become famous for his defense of Catherine Sinclair Forrest, accused of adultery by her actor husband, Edwin Forrest.[15] More recently he had been in the news for agreeing to defend Jefferson Davis, former president of the Confederacy, against charges of treason.[16] He was acquainted with Nelson, who had assisted him in handling the Forrest case.[17]

The offense O'Conor and Nelson designed was two-pronged. They claimed that Smith had exerted undue influence on Eliza to convince her to make bequests to him and his church.[18] Concurrently they put forth the complementary argument that Eliza had suffered from dementia during her last years, making her incapable of comprehending her duty to her family and preparing a valid will.[19]

When the case came up for trial in New York State Supreme Court on November 13, 1866, the testimony of Eliza's loving family members was riveting. They drew a picture of a woman who had become increasingly irrational over the last six years of her life. In response to carefully calibrated questions from O'Conor, Nelson dated her decline to her last visit to Saratoga, in 1859. One evening at dinner, she had felt a transient shock, followed by persistent headache. Later, homeward bound on the train from Saratoga to Schenectady, she was disturbed by some boisterous travelers. The first clear manifestation of her insanity followed. In Nelson's telling, she jumped up, put her face close to theirs, and, startlingly, "gave a most powerful screech."[20]

After her return to New York City, she developed strange delusions: "She charged some very respectable gentlemen, neighbors of hers, with robbing her or trying to rob her of her property" and "persisted in that charge for three or four years before her death." On other occasions, "she used to tell that she had been in heaven, and she insisted upon it; and when told she must have been in a trance or a dream, she would insist upon it that it was a reality; she said she had seen the angels of heaven fluttering about her, and that she had seen the winding sheets of the dead and bright new pins which had come out of their grave clothes in very large piles." In 1860 and '61 she had become convinced that British loyalists had buried valuables on the grounds of the mansion for safekeeping during the American Revolution. She hired men to dig and blast rocks in search of the treasure.[21]

Most disturbingly, Nelson said, Eliza had become convinced that he and his children were trying to kill her: "I used to get my breakfast very early, and she would reserve her tea and would not touch it at all until I got back, under the idea that it had been poisoned, and I had on my return to buy and convince her to take the tea and drink it myself in her presence; I did so many times; she also charged me and my daughter with attempting to poison her food, her beef tea, and her medicine." Often he would have to drink a little of the medicine before she would take it herself.[22]

Eliza Pery seconded her father's narrative: "She gave manifestations of craziness; she accused us all of poisoning her; she said my father put the bed-bug poison in her tea—(laughter)—and put tacks in her shoes when she got out of bed, so that it would kill her." She accused her great-niece of trying to poison her too: "She said I carried arsenic in my pocket to sprinkle in her tea and over her beefsteak; afterwards she would turn around and kiss me very affectionately, and say, 'how much I love you!'"[23]

William testified that Eliza had changed toward him too, beginning in 1859:

> I was still at the supper table, when she came down from [her] room in a furious passion, and said that I intended to kill her. I said, "How is that?" She said, "Oh, you know," and further, "You have been in my rooms and unscrewed the top of my wardrobe to kill me." I said "That is outrageous." I then brought her up into the room and showed her that there was nothing the matter with the wardrobe; she would not believe it; I said I better leave the house, then. I left and afterwards met my sister, and she wanted me to call on her and see her, which I did. She received me very kindly, but in going away she always repeated the charge that I intended to kill her and asked if I was not sorry and wanted me to confess it. I said I would not confess a thing of that kind that I was not guilty of.[24]

After that 1859 incident, she put a patch over the image of his face in the portrait painted in Rome—or so William said.[25] The canvas shows no indication of damage today.

Regardless of whether the picture drawn of Eliza in court was an accurate representation of her mental state, the tactic used to challenge the will—arguing that the testator was insane at the time she made it—was widely employed in estate litigation by the 1860s.[26] This approach had become possible after medical practitioners in the late eighteenth century began to differentiate among degrees of insanity, arguing that an individual could be irrational in certain domains, but competent in others.[27] For example, a woman like Eliza might be capable of conducting business, but "morally insane"—emotionally and ethically unbalanced.

A will with provisions that cut off a child or other "natural" heir could be presented as evidence that the testator was of unsound mind when it was made. As early as 1811, Philadelphia physician Benjamin Rush had opined that a man who left most of his estate "to a church, or any other public institution, or to a stranger, to the injury of a family of children who had never offended him, and whose necessities, or rank in life, as well as their blood, intitled [*sic*] them to be his heirs . . . should be considered as morally deranged; and his will should be set aside as promptly as if he had disposed of his estate in a paroxysm of intellectual derangement."[28]

More often than not, charges of undue influence by a person acting against the testator's best interests accompanied moral insanity claims in estate litigation.[29] Smith was assigned the unsavory role of the influencer in the Jumel case, accused of having taken advantage of Eliza's derangement to persuade her to benefit him and his church. He was questioned aggressively about his meetings with her.

The picture that could be pieced together from his answers was far from black and white. His claim that Eliza had asked him to visit her in 1862 was suspect, since she had not seen him for three years previously. Her decision to give him a personal legacy raised the possibility of undue influence as well. On the other hand, most of the provisions of the will that Eliza had signed under his supervision did not differ greatly from those drafted by her family attorney, Wetmore. Even many of the charities that he and Smith had suggested were the same.

Nelson had fared the worst from the revisions Smith had superintended. In Wetmore's draft, he was to receive the interest on thirty thousand dollars. According to the clergyman, Eliza had said that "it must be put down at ten thousand dollars." She had insisted that Eliza Pery's share be reduced also: her great-niece should receive the interest on ten thousand rather than on twenty thousand dollars. The reverend had tried to dissuade her, he claimed: "I said, 'Madame, I have one request to make of you, and that is that you will not put down Mrs. Pery.' She said that she must do so, as it was too much;

that Mrs. Pery was vain and frivolous and would waste it all in folly. 'But Madame,' said I, 'remember that this is your last act.'" After further persuasion on his part, Eliza said, "Perhaps we had better split it; put it down at fifteen thousand dollars." But when Smith read the revised will back to her, "she declared 'that she could not allow it to stand at fifteen thousand dollars, that it was too much, and that she must put it at ten thousand dollars.'"³⁰

The narrative is not implausible. Wetmore himself had tried unsuccessfully to persuade his client to increase her bequest to her great-niece when he prepared the draft will. "I want you to give to Eliza twenty thousand dollars more," he had said. But she wouldn't discuss the matter. "I suggested, after all, that she should give Eliza another sum," Wetmore said, "but I could not bring her mind to comprehend it; she would talk always of persons trying to kill her; her mind was vague." Indeed, he was unable to get her to specify the disposal of more than about one hundred thousand dollars of her estate.³¹ "When he could not persuade her to make any other bequests, he said, 'Shall I put down that the rest shall be divided evenly among these people?'" In the end he did so, leaving her with the draft.³² Wetmore, therefore, was largely responsible for the way in which the residuary estate was handled.³³

Was Eliza insane when she made the 1863 will? Its provisions were certainly different from those she had envisioned twelve years before. In the interim, she had become strongly resistant to drawing up a testament and developed mixed feelings about her family. But it is unclear whether she was as delusional as they painted her to be. In the early 1860s she was still involved in business transactions, in spite of the family's later efforts to represent her as divorced from reality. The statement made by Nelson that she had "charged some very respectable gentlemen, neighbors of hers, with robbing her or trying to rob her of her property" may have been made to explain away her sharp-witted 1863 investigation of the individuals she suspected of encroaching on her lands. Her suit against the surveyor hired to determine the property lines might otherwise have been used as evidence that she had remained competent to manage her affairs.

Other stories the family had told in court could have been opportunistic distortions of actual events as well. For example, the contention that she had men digging and blasting on her property in search of buried treasure may have been inspired by blasting operations she had ordered in 1857 for the digging of a new well near the mansion.[34] Another startling tale Nelson had offered from the witness stand had riffed off Eliza's habit of having a gun fired from her grounds each evening (recounted in the profile of her published in 1855). Building on this minor eccentricity, Nelson had claimed that from December 1854 through May or June 1855, she had "got up a military company which she called her French legion, and uniformed them in a very fantastical manner, and had them march about the house." At night, "a guard was set and a countersign agreed upon and given; guns were fired and guards were relieved from time to time . . . and there was a pretty general disturbance of all rest."[35] Supposedly William had been given a uniform and served as their commander, a detail that may have been suggested to Nelson by Charles Dickens's *Great Expectations* (1861), in which the boy Pip, commanded to amuse the unstable Miss Havisham, claimed that he, she, and her niece had "played with flags" and then "all waved [their] swords and hurrahed."[36]

During the attempt to overturn the will, no explanation was offered for why William had been cut off entirely when his sister and Nelson weren't. In truth, Eliza had grounds for being upset with her great-nephew, although they were not revealed in court. Sometime in the late 1850s or early 1860s, he had had an affair, of which Eliza was aware.[37] Then he had secretly married Isabella A. Nolston, a woman a year his junior who was said to have been a servant.[38] He must have known that his family would not approve, because he had left it to his sister to break the news.[39]

No record of the marriage has been located and its date remains obscure. Reportedly William was asked in 1866 whether he was married, but said he couldn't answer the question, because two women claimed him as husband.[40] This anecdote may have been a scurrilous invention, but a curious fact remains: William fathered two children born within the space of a year—and there is no indication that they were twins. A son, Leslie, arrived in either the second half of 1864 or the first half of 1865, and a daughter, Louisa, entered the world within the same time period.[41] Unlike Leslie, she was not listed as living with her father and Isabella in 1870, but had joined them by 1880, raising the possibility that she was born of William's earlier relationship and brought into the household belatedly.[42]

Although Eliza's will was made before the worst of William's amatory entanglements surfaced, she might have been upset not only by his earlier affair but also his reluctance to settle into a profession. He had begun working in his father's law office in 1856, shortly before his sixteenth birthday, but was listed at the firm's address for only a year.[43] Two years later Eliza had set him up in the grocery business, a venture that lasted twelve months at most, from May 1859 to spring 1860.[44] There is a hint that he may have treated the business as a cash cow rather than a professional opportunity. Nelson was asked in 1873 whether Eliza had accused William of robbing her in connection with it. Although Nelson said Eliza made no such charge, the posing of the question raises the possibility that the allegation had a basis in fact.[45]

After the short-lived grocery closed, Nelson had written to a fellow lawyer in search of job opportunities for his son.[46] But no business or professional addresses were listed for William in the New York City directories during the last five years of Eliza's life.

Whether or not she was justified in cutting him off, her decision would not stand. After only a few minutes of deliberation, the jury ruled "that Madame Jumel was of unsound mind" when she made her 1863 will. Eliza would be considered to have died intestate—that is, without a will. Her property would be divided among her blood relatives, as dictated by state law.

Thanks to Nelson's foresight in buying out the Joneses' claims, his two children were Eliza's sole known heirs—and they had agreed to share one-third of her fortune with him. But within a year the three presumed inheritors would face unanticipated claims on the estate.

PROLIFERATING
PRETENDERS

*A*s soon as Eliza's will was overturned, aspirants to her estate sprouted like skunk cabbage in the spring. Her brother, John, assumed to have died without issue more than half a century before, was resurrected in the form of four hopeful siblings who said that they were his children.[1] These young pretenders, easily vanquished, were replaced by the Jones siblings, regretful of having sold their claim to a million-dollar estate for forty thousand dollars. Their lawyer, the count Johannes—a failed actor bearing a noble title suspected of having been self-bestowed—offered up extravagant courtroom theatrics in what had become by then a cause célèbre.[2]

Sporting corkscrew curls and velvet-collared coat, he began by declaiming the bill of complaint, "a document of preternatural legal length requiring two hours to read."[3] Charles O'Conor, representing Nelson and his children, thought it unnecessary to read aloud his answer to the bill, so the count did it for him, "consuming nearly another hour."[4] Next the tireless count embarked on his argument, in which he charged Nelson with having defrauded the Joneses by offering them less than the Jumel estate was worth. His opening, reported the *New York Herald*,

> was biographical, historic, eulogistic, poetic, impassioned, and rhapsodic—in fact, going through all the alternating changes of the most diverse schools of oratory, with skilled specimens of his peculiar power of mimicry thrown in as pleasing interludes. The biographic embraced a sketch of the family histories of Madame Jumel and that portion of the Jones family whose names appear as plaintiffs in the case; the historic ran all the way through from antediluvian times; the eulogistic was when he compared the judge to Paul of Tarsus at Caesarea; the poetic gleamed like sabers flashing in the sunlight; the impassioned was when bathos and pathos struggled for the mastery; and the rhapsodic the peroration, wherein he grew greatly and almost tearfully agonizing over the divine attributes of justice. His mimic representations included the litigants on both sides and the opposing counsel, who smiled at them or at the count, it was impossible to tell which, as heartily as the rest.[5]

Through this torrent of oratory, the presiding judge "kept himself busy whittling."[6]

The case was adjourned until late the next morning to allow the count to produce witnesses to the value of the estate. Instead he returned unaccompanied, and to the open glee of the spectators in the crowded courtroom, called opposing counsel O'Conor, who owned land in Washington Heights, "to testify as to the value of property there."[7] Later in the proceedings, he informed his auditors that "he never wrote out a line of his speeches, but relied on the Holy Spirit to tell him what he should say." When laughter rippled across the room, "he turned about on the assembled throng and pitched into them for scoffing at the Scriptures."[8]

The drama ended with the judge's measured decision that no proof of fraud had been presented: "The plaintiffs, not having been mentioned in the will, were no parties to the suit to set [it] aside." The money "paid them was not, under the circumstances, an inadequate consideration."[9] Nelson "was warmly congratulated by a large host of friends," while the Joneses were nowhere to be seen, having failed to attend the trial prosecuted on their behalf.[10] Even before it opened, they may have come to share an exasperated lawyer's opinion that the count Johannes was "a public pest and a disgrace to the profession."[11] Alternately, the count may have been correct in claiming that Nelson had bribed at least one of them to stay away.[12]

A more worrisome set of claimants pursued a case against Nelson and his children that meandered on expensively for more than three years. The thirty-three plaintiffs were descendants of a man named James Bowen, who had lived and died in Rehoboth, Massachusetts, about eleven miles northeast of Providence. The Bowen clan claimed that Eliza, née Betsy Bowen, had been James's youngest child, making them her relatives and entitled to share in her estate.

In their depositions, recorded by commissioners crisscrossing Rhode Island and Massachusetts, James's descendants painted a new picture of Eliza. In their telling, she was a farmer's daughter; a girl who visited Providence with her father to peddle huckleberries.[13] She worked out as a servant from about the age of twelve, sometimes in Rehoboth and other times in Providence.[14] When she was around eighteen, an older brother traveling to western New York left her in New York City so that she could attend school.[15] Subsequently she met and married Stephen Jumel. But she maintained contact with her favorite sister, Elizabeth ("Lizzie") Thatcher, née Bowen, and sometimes sent her money.[16]

The Bowens claimed that Eliza and Stephen paid a visit to Lizzie in Rehoboth sometime between 1808 and 1812. Lizzie's daughter, Selva, and Selva's husband, John Bullock, were visiting at the same time, bringing tea and sugar because Lizzie was ill. As described in 1868 by ninety-eight-year-old John Bullock, the two couples spent the night in Lizzie's house in case her condition worsened.[17] Later Eliza sent money to pay for Lizzie's gravestone.[18] Around 1821 she visited Rehoboth again to attend the funeral of a distant cousin by marriage.[19]

Holes and inconsistencies appeared in the story as the deponents were cross-examined. Eliza was claimed first to be an illegitimate daughter of James Bowen's daughter Patience and then a daughter of James himself.[20] Her supposed relatives were unable to describe her beyond saying that she "was richly dressed" and "a handsome woman."[21] They had trouble accounting for the existence of her sister Maria Jones, sometimes identifying her with Patience Bowen and sometimes claiming her as an illegitimate child of Patience.[22] To explain why she and Eliza had referred to their mother as Phebe, they averred that James Bowen's wife, Abigail, had changed her name to Phebe Hannah after her marriage.[23]

It was hoped that an examination of eighty-nine-year-old Elizabeth Salisbury, who knew the Bowen family history down to her fingertips, would clarify these discrepancies. Although she was half-deaf, almost blind, and unable to walk, mentally she was still as sharp as a tack. Interviewed in her two-room house in Warren, Rhode Island, she reeled off genealogical data with ease: "Did I know Uncle James Bowen? I guess I did. Lived not more'n half a mile from him all the days of my life as long as he lived . . . He was a fine old man, too." Martin Bowen? Of course she knew him: "He was Uncle James Bowen's son. Living? No, bless your soul and body, he's been dead these twenty years."[24]

Under questioning, Salisbury detailed several generations of the family with impressive clarity. But just as the crucial cross-examination that would focus on Eliza began, she put her hand to her head and complained of pain. Assisted to her bed, she moaned, trembled, and fell into convulsions. The paperwork recording her deposition terminates with a brief, sad note: "The commissioners are of the opinion that the witness is entirely unfit and unable to testify unless there be hereafter an improvement in her condition."[25] She never recovered sufficiently to be reexamined.

A jury verdict against the Bowens in late April 1871 ended the matter at last.[26] But Nelson and his children had no time to celebrate. A more threatening claimant—both to the Jumel fortune and to Eliza's reputation—had advanced fully armed for battle from the wings.

ENTER GEORGE
WASHINGTON

*E*liza's newest relative, a man in his seventies, bore the patriotic name of George Washington Bowen. This prosperous grocer and resident of Providence announced himself to be Madame Jumel's illegitimate child. He had been born during her youth in Rhode Island, he said—fathered by none other than the first president of the United States!

Bowen's claim was simultaneously startling and ominous. His backers said that he was born in October 1794, a perplexingly undocumented period of Eliza's life.[1] Of her young adulthood—the years that spanned the mid-1790s—almost anything could be posited and even believed. Worse yet for Nelson and his children, if Bowen was indeed Eliza's son—whether by George Washington or anyone else—he would receive the entire Jumel fortune. When a woman died without a will in New York State, her children's claims superseded any others—and bastardy was no bar. Thanks to a New York law enacted in 1855, illegitimate children could inherit from their mother "as if legitimate."[2]

To support his case, Bowen produced Anne Eliza Vandervoort, born in Providence but resident in New York since childhood.[3] She too, it appeared, was related to Eliza Jumel. Her mother, Lavinia, had been Eliza's sister, she claimed. Maria Jones, previously thought to be Eliza's sibling, instead had been the fruit of the first marriage of Jonathan Clark, Phebe Bowen's second husband. In other words, she had been Eliza's stepsister rather than sister.[4] If this newly revealed genealogy was valid, then *none* of Maria's descendants were blood relatives of Eliza—not William Chase, not Eliza Pery, and not the four children of Maria and William Jones, whose claims Nelson had purchased. Nelson and his children would lose their title to the Jumel estate.

Crucially Vandervoort possessed a precious family document that recorded the maternity of George Washington Bowen. Handed down to her by her mother, it was a slender volume, barely more than a pamphlet, containing a history of the first part of the reign of King Henry IV of England. Although published in 1599, it carried a more recent inscription on the back of the title page: "George Washington Bowen born of Eliza Bowen at my house in Toun [*sic*] Providence R. I. October 9, 1794." The inscription was signed "Reuben Ballou."[5]

The name Ballou was a blast from the past. Reuben, born in 1747, belonged to the same Ballou clan in Cumberland, Rhode Island, as William B. Ballou, the boy Eliza had raised. (William's father, David, was Reuben's second cousin.)[6] Reuben had worked as a butcher in Cumberland, raised a family, been widowed, and then remarried. With his second wife, Freelove, and two young children, he had moved from Cumberland to Providence in 1792. There the Ballous began to have run-ins with the law.[7] Reuben was jailed briefly in December for debt.[8] In mid-1794 the town officers attempted to eject him and his family from Providence, but Cumberland's officials didn't want them either.[9] They stayed in Providence and by 1799 were taking in poor transients as lodgers.[10]

At some point their domicile became notorious. In 1802 Freelove was charged with selling "spirituous liquors" without a license.[11] A year later she, Reuben, and a woman named Luthanea Leland were

accused of being "persons of bad fame and evil conversation, keep-
ers of disorderly and bawdy houses."[12] Eliza, it was said, joined the
questionable Ballou household as a servant.[13] From there, according to Bowen's supporters, matters proceeded as follows: Reuben
was injured in a fall from a horse during the time Eliza had lived
with his family. He was, or had been, an express rider for General George Washington, and the commander in chief paid him a
few visits after the accident.[14] The brief calls had lasting results.
Washington "became enamored of the beautiful servant girl, Betsy
Bowen."[15] They had a liaison that produced the infant George Washington Bowen, named after his illustrious father. On the night of the
baby's birth, Reuben recorded the event in an old book he had lying
about—the very book that Eliza's sister Lavinia had preserved and
passed down to her daughter Anne Vandervoort.[16]

Eighty-three-year-old Daniel Hull of Providence testified to
the presence of Eliza and an infant in the Ballou's home. As a child
he had lived in the house of a baker named George Wheeden, who
would send him "with a hand-basket with biscuits to Mrs. Newell's
and Mrs. Ballou's" every morning. One day, he said, Eliza "called
me into her bedroom and wanted to show me her good fat boy, as
she called it; afterwards she gave me some coppers to buy candy."
The baby "was about three or four days old," he estimated, and Eliza
somewhere between fifteen and eighteen years of age. He continued
to "see her pretty often," because there was a monkey at the Ballous'
house that he "used to go up to see." Between four and eight months
later, Eliza and her sister Lavinia moved to New York, leaving the
baby in Freelove Ballou's care. Years later she returned to Providence and delivered a lecture about her life in France from the porch
of a tavern, Hull said. But "the boys made such a hooting at her, hal-
low, and hissing that [he] couldn't hear half she said."[17]

Elderly witnesses who claimed to have known Eliza when they
were children described her as a girl likely to have had an illegitimate
child. In a deposition read to the jury, Reuben's eighty-one-year-
old daughter-in-law Sally Ballou spoke of seeing the future Madame
Jumel "walking the streets of Providence."[18] Eighty-three-year-old

Catherine Williams tottered to the stand in person to say that Eliza had passed her house in Providence "in the company of disreputable persons."[19] Nelson provided unwitting ammunition to those attacking Eliza's character. During the 1866 battle to overturn her will, he had hinted that his wife, Mary, was Eliza's illegitimate daughter, fathered by Stephen before he and Eliza had married.[20] The slur, designed to strengthen his children's claim to the Jumel estate, came back to haunt him. Bowen's lawyers used it as evidence that it would have been in character for Eliza to have had an illegitimate child.[21]

Bowen supplemented his case by producing witnesses who swore that Eliza had mentioned to them that she had a son. It appeared that she had spoken of the matter to a remarkable number of people: the wife of a dentist who had treated her; a woman who had worked as the caretaker of her Saratoga home; long-ago servants who were children at the time.[22] A fire marshal who had met with Eliza after a conflagration in her barn testified that she had told him that "she had a son who would one day return and drive away the people who were around her."[23]

Eliza's apparent openness about her child's existence raised the question of why she had not reached out to him during her years in New York. In fact, she had done so after her marriage, Vandervoort said, but Freelove Ballou had refused to give up young Bowen.[24] Later Nelson, who "had made the pursuit of Madame Jumel's wealth the business of his lifetime," had cut her off from the world.[25] He had denied her the opportunity "to send to Providence for her son, even if she had desired to do so."[26] The latter contention, at least, was hardly convincing. As Nelson observed, "Madame Jumel was the most determined spirit he had ever met with, either in life or in history, and, so far as he knew, she could at any time have gone to Rhode Island until she became so infirm as not to be able to travel."[27]

As the suit advanced, progressing from depositions taken in Rhode Island to an eight-week trial in federal circuit court in New York, cracks and holes appeared in Bowen's case. In spite of his mild likeness to the first president—"the assertion of his counsel that he [bore] a striking resemblance to the Father of his Country [was] not altogether fanciful"—the story of his distinguished paternity disintegrated quickly.[28] As Charles O'Conor pointed out, if Reuben Ballou had been injured during his military service, George Washington's visit to him and concurrent affair with Eliza "could not, as a matter of history, have been later than 1782 . . . and all that time [she] must have been carrying that child until Hull saw him, some twelve years after, a fine, fat baby."[29] Perhaps the incident had occurred after the war instead—but Washington's last visit to Rhode Island had taken place in 1790.[30] Anticipating this difficulty, Bowen's counsel had already adjusted the narrative to make Reuben Ballou rather than George Washington his client's father.[31] In support of this genealogy, Reuben's granddaughter Maria Cook testified that her grandfather had begotten an illegitimate son, with Eliza being the child's mother.[32] Catherine Williams said she had known Bowen when he was a boy living in the Ballou family and that he bore a striking resemblance to Eliza.[33]

Although this revision of the narrative did the plaintiff no great harm, other weaknesses in his case were identified. The authenticity of the inscription in the so-called King Henry book identifying him as Eliza's child was challenged. Ballou's purported signature did not resemble other signatures of his that survived on authenticated documents.[34]

There was a charge of perjury to deal with as well. Witness Joseph F. Perry, who claimed he had lived in Providence and had been aware that Reuben "had an illegitimate child by [Eliza]," was proven never to have resided in Providence at all.[35] Vandervoort's reliability was questioned too. Not only had she promulgated the George Washington story (before backpedaling and claiming it to be a joke told by her mother), she had offered multiple accounts of Bowen's maternity, supposedly identifying him at different times as Maria Jones's son, Eliza's son, and even the son of her own mother, Lavinia.[36] It came out that Bowen had promised her half of anything he received in return for supporting his case.[37]

Bowen himself had changed his tune. He had denied being related to Eliza in 1866, when inquiries were made to identify any possible relatives before her will was overturned.[38] It was only later that he had claimed Eliza as his mother. This inconvenient fact was discounted by one of his lawyers, who explained that his client had been told that his mother was Betsy Bowen and didn't know that she had become Madame Jumel.[39]

If the credibility of Bowen and his supporters was shaken, Eliza's reputation took a beating as well. Details of her youth and parentage, hidden discreetly throughout her adult life, were dragged out into the light of day. Now all the world knew that she had lived with her mother in two brothels and spent time in a workhouse, and that her mother had been jailed and warned out of Providence.[40] These details made it easier for auditors to believe that she could have had an illegitimate child. The defense's inability to document exactly where Eliza had been in 1794 didn't help. The gap in the record made it possible to conclude that she had been in Providence giving birth to Bowen.

Those chosen to weigh the rights and wrongs of the affair were unable to untangle the knotty strands. At 11:10 PM on March 17, 1872, the jurors returned to the courtroom after more than eight hours of deliberation. When the deputy clerk "asked them if they had agreed upon a verdict," the foreman answered, "we have not." The trial ended with a hung jury.[41]

By the time the suit was reheard during the winter of 1872 to '73, Bowen had gathered additional witnesses to support his case. The deposition of "Henry Nodine, an ancient person," was particularly dramatic.[42] When he was a teenager, Nodine said, he had worked at the Jumels' mansion for two or three years, before Eliza and Stephen went to France. One day he was called up from the kitchen. When he entered the hallway, his employers were arguing. Stephen, in fractured English, referred to himself in the third person. "My Eliza," Stephen said, "You never tell Mr. Jumel you have one little boy, or else Mr. Jumel won't marry you; then you tell Mr. Jumel you very sick and going to die; then you want to die one married woman; you go straight to Heaven you sure; the doctor tell Mr. Jumel marry you, you die before morning; the doctor tell Mr. Jumel one story too; Mr. Jumel marry you—two days [later] you ride around town in carriage."[43] This narrative was cooked up from the story John Pintard had told years before about Eliza tricking Stephen into marriage. Now Bowen had been stirred into the mix.

Nodine added that Eliza would curse Stephen occasionally, calling him "'a damned old French son of a bitch,' and all such names." Then she would threaten him with a pistol and chase him out of the house.[44] This last piquant detail may have been inspired by the six-barreled pistol (almost certainly imaginary) that Eliza was said to have purchased after being mocked in Saratoga.[45]

Nelson's lawyers attacked Nodine's credibility: he had claimed to have served in the militia during the War of 1812, yet had been too young to participate.[46] They could have made an even stronger case against him had they realized that Eliza had evicted a "Mr. Naudine" from one of the Jumel farms, and Stephen had sued Lewis and Peter Nodine—probably Henry's older brothers— over an unpaid debt.[47] But few outsiders could have known that the Nodines had reason to be vengeful against Eliza or that Henry's account had been fabricated from repurposed bits and pieces. Details of his deposition, reported in the newspapers, further tarnished Madame Jumel's reputation.[48]

It was stained blacker yet as a parade of witnesses, recycled from the earlier trial, trooped in and out of the courthouse. Each claimed that Eliza had mentioned having a son—or rather, was barred from saying so. At the beginning of the trial, the judge had ruled that testimony on what Eliza might have said to others about having a child in Providence was inadmissible hearsay. Bowen's lawyers got around this by introducing the witnesses one by one, questioning each about his or her relationship with Eliza, and then telling the judge that they would like to use the witness to prove that Eliza said she had a son. Although the judge refused every time, the repeated use of the strategy gave listeners the impression that Eliza had spoken of Bowen frequently.[49]

Vandervoort was not called to testify—Bowen's lawyers must have concluded that her credibility was ruined—but Daniel Hull reappeared and fared badly. Cross-examination revealed that he had been an infant at most in 1794, the year in which he was supposed to have seen Eliza with the newborn Bowen.[50] The stories of other elderly witnesses were challenged too, as a correspondent for the *Boston Journal* reported:

> Old and decrepit people have been placed in the stand to tell of conversations held in their presence when they were four and five years old. One person gave a circumstantial conversation she had held with Madame Jumel, which detailed the disgrace of the madame. On cross-examination the party admitted that she was only five years old at the time. A damaging witness was cornered on cross-examination by fixing dates, by which it appeared that his wife, when he married her, was only eight years old. There is a good deal of bad blood in the case, and O'Conor, usually cold as an iceberg, denounced the opposing counsel as a liar.[51]

A note of humor was introduced by former U.S. attorney general Ebenezer R. Hoar, one of Bowen's lawyers. After seating his client in front of the jury, he held up an impression of the lithographed self-portrait Eliza had commissioned in 1852, using it to detail the "very striking" resemblances between Bowen's features and hers, from the length of the ear flap to the placement of the eyelid crease. Next he requested his client "to look at the foreman of the jury and laugh." This novel instruction "excited general laughter, in which Mr. Bowen joined." Taking advantage of the moment, Hoar pointed out to the jury "that when Mr. Bowen smiled he had a dimple in his left cheek which did not appear in the other," just like his putative mother. Getting in a dig at Nelson's lawyers, who had implied that he and his colleagues had manufactured evidence, Hoar said sarcastically that the "dimple had doubtless been put there by Mr. Tucker [Hoar's fellow counsel], having been gotten up because Madame Jumel had a similar peculiarity."[52]

It is only fair to say that Nelson and his lawyers adjusted facts too, if not as spectacularly as their opponents did. They cleaned up Eliza's family history by suggesting that Mary was born legitimately of a marriage between Maria and "some worthless fellow who had deserted her" and pushing back the date of Maria's union with William Jones so that her oldest son arrived sixteen rather than four months later.[53]

In a dramatic change in strategy from the initial trial, they produced the conveyances Eliza had implemented in the 1820s that gave her the downtown and Harlem Heights properties, with reversion to Mary or Mary's heirs after her death. The significance of these deeds is hard to overstate. As O'Conor explained, they showed that Eliza had never owned the real estate that made up the bulk of the Jumel fortune. The properties were only in trust for her during her lifetime—so Bowen couldn't inherit them even if he proved to be her son.[54] The real estate would have to go to Mary's heirs, not Eliza's. O'Conor glossed over the irregularities that had accompanied the formation of the trusts, such as the purported sales of the lands to Mary. Just in case anyone questioned their validity, however, he and Nelson produced a carefully coached witness, who testified to having worked at the Jumel mansion as a boy and hearing Stephen say that he was content to have the property go to Mary.[55]

The judge understood the importance of the trusts and made that clear in his instructions to the jurors. They were to decide whether Bowen was Eliza's son. But whatever that verdict might be, he also directed them to find "the special fact 'that Eliza B. Jumel, at the time of her death, had no estate or interest in the lands claimed which was descendible to her heirs.'"[56]

After an hour and a half of deliberation, the jury returned to the courtroom. As instructed, its members found "the special fact" that Eliza's title to the Jumel estate could not be inherited. They delivered their verdict on the plaintiff's parentage as well. "We find for the defendant," the foreman said. George Washington Bowen was not Eliza's son.[57]

One week later Bowen appealed the case to the United States Supreme Court.[58]

ON THE HOME FRONT

*O*utside the courtroom, life continued for the Chases. On August 12, 1868, fifty-seven-year-old Nelson married twenty-two-year-old Hattie Dunning, daughter of a prosperous lumber merchant in upper Manhattan.[1] They had a child, Jumel, who died in infancy in 1869, but a second son, Raymond, born in 1874 or '75, survived the epidemic diseases of the era.[2] His name was a thoughtful tribute to Nelson's son-in-law, just as the choice of Jumel for his older brother had honored Stephen and Eliza. Raymond was a traditional name in the Pery family and one of Paul's middle names.

Nelson and Hattie lived at the Jumel mansion, sharing the house with the Perys and the William Chases. By 1870 the homestead housed not only the three adult couples but four children as well—the Perys' fifteen-year-old daughter Mathilde, William and Isabella's infant daughter, Ella, and their sons, William and Leslie, aged three and five.[3] Five female domestics and a gardener and coachman served the trio of families.[4]

The stress of the endless litigation began to tell on the occupants of the mansion. The legal bills were colossal, and money was tight. Much of the Jumel fortune could not be touched until the litigation over its ownership ended. Nelson had been administering the estate since Eliza's death. In spite of some substantial influxes of cash—including $24,000 for the sale of two lots Eliza had owned at Seventh Avenue and Forty-Third Street and $170,000 for land taken by the city for public improvements—he had had to take out a $25,000 mortgage as security for payment of a legal bill and borrow $75,000 from lead counsel O'Conor.[5] Unpaid invoices accumulated alarmingly: $2,236 for horse feed and groceries; $12,604 for renovations at 150 Broadway; $306.50 for coal.[6]

William resented having to depend on his father for money. In 1873 he sued Nelson to force him to give an accounting of his stewardship of the estate and share the available funds.[7] A settlement was negotiated that allowed the children to control some of the money the estate generated.[8] William and his family moved to Suffolk County, Long Island, and took up farming.[9] Eliza Pery, with her husband and daughter, remained at the mansion with Nelson and Hattie.

Paul Pery would not live to see the end of the fight over the Jumel fortune. He died of tuberculosis on February 27, 1875, and his bones were laid to rest in the Jumel crypt.[10] He was only forty-two years old.[11] Six months later, his widow took their twenty-year-old daughter Mathilde to Europe, probably to visit his relatives.[12] In 1878 Mathilde made a French marriage, just as her mother had done. The bridegroom was Louis-Antoine Gourreau of Bordeaux.[13]

Eliza Pery remarried in 1876, choosing a prosperous merchant, Julius Henry Caryl.[14] They set up housekeeping at the mansion, where Eliza had lived with Paul. As with her first marriage, family connections were at work. When her father, Nelson, had lived in Worcester as a young man, he had studied law with Schuyler Crippen. Caryl, born in Worcester, was Crippen's nephew.[15]

As a backdrop to the marriages, births, and deaths, Bowen's appeal to the Supreme Court moved up on the court calendar. In a document weighing in at more than eleven hundred pages, he argued that the circuit court had erred in its handling of the suit against Nelson, chiefly in the admission and exclusion of evidence.[16] The judge had allowed hearsay regarding the identity of Mary Jumel, but had stopped witnesses from testifying that Madame Jumel had spoken of a son.[17] In addition, Bowen contended that the judge had misinterpreted the laws governing trusts when he had instructed the jury that Eliza had no heritable interest in the Jumel estate.[18]

Nelson and his children, proving worthy opponents, appealed to the Supreme Court too. They asked the court to bar Bowen from pursuing further suits to obtain the Jumel estate (including his appeal to the Supreme Court itself).[19] Their suit was heard first, in October 1876. The justices upheld the final conveyance Eliza had made in November 1828, by which the downtown properties and uptown real estate would go to Mary or Mary's heirs after she and Stephen were dead. Bowen would not be allowed to enter into more litigation to claim the lands described in the deed.[20] However, he was permitted to continue his appeal with regard to a sixty-five-acre tract in Washington Heights that was not mentioned in the 1828 document.[21] This parcel (probably omitted from the conveyance inadvertently) was the only portion of Jumel real estate in Washington Heights that Eliza had not transferred to herself, although she had managed it later as if it were hers.

The concession did Bowen little good when the Supreme Court took up his appeal in 1878. In spite of some ambiguity regarding the status of the sixty-five acres, the justices ruled that Eliza had no interest in it that could be inherited, regardless of whether Bowen was her son. The other components of his appeal—mainly objections to the admission or exclusion of testimony—were dismissed as irrelevant, since Eliza had no property for him to receive.[22] Exit George Washington Bowen—at long last.

In truth, Bowen never moved entirely offstage. In spite of the weakness of his case and the jury verdict that denied his claim to be Eliza's son, history, marching on, gave him the mother he had claimed. His story, blazoned across the newspapers for years, became fact by virtue of repetition. To this day, the received wisdom is that George

Washington Bowen was Eliza's illegitimate son.[23] The depiction of her as a streetwalker became part of her persona as well—to the point that a historian termed her in 1992 "the leading prostitute in post-Revolutionary America."[24]

The lies might have been exploded if any facts had been available about Eliza's life circa 1794. But none were. Through all the years of litigation, no one ever determined what she had been doing during her early adulthood, other than not giving birth to Bowen.[25]

As it turns out, it was as well for her family that she could not be tracked. Records of a previously unremarked lawsuit dating from the crucial time period would have raised uncomfortable questions about her character. The neatly folded documents, preserved in the Judicial Records Center in Pawtucket, Rhode Island, place Eliza in Providence in 1795.[26] On January 21, she visited the shop of Samuel W. Greene, where candles, soap, crockery, and glassware crowded broadcloth, firkins of butter, and bags of tea.[27] At Greene's emporium, Eliza purchased materials for an expensive dress: ten yards of green lutestring (a glossy silk), three yards of Irish linen, a pair of tapes (used to fasten skirts at the waist), and several skeins of thread.[28] On September 16 she returned to the shop for a pair of shoes, a skein of silk, and five yards of ribbon.[29]

These elegant threads were at risk of unraveling. All the purchases had been made on credit, and as of mid-November, the bill was unpaid. Greene filed suit in Providence's Court of Common Pleas against "Betsey Bowen," a single woman of Providence, "for the recovery of the sum of six pounds two shillings—equal to twenty dollars and thirty-three and one-third cents—due to the plaintiff from the said Betsey."[30]

Eliza was arrested on December 1 and spent seven days in the county jail. She owed her liberation to David Ballou, who paid four dollars in bail and forty-one and two-thirds cents in fees. He did not settle Greene's bill, however. Execution, meaning that the local sheriff could seize and sell Eliza's possessions to cover what she owed, was granted on March 28, 1796, for $23.01 (the amount of the debt plus $2.68 in costs).[31]

The reason for Ballou's intervention remains a mystery. Perhaps Eliza was working for him in 1795, and Greene had extended credit under the assumption that her employer would pay the sum expended. Maybe Ballou had even promised Eliza a new outfit as wages, but ran into financial problems and left the bill unpaid. Alternately, if she had worked in the Ballou family as an adolescent, her former master might have been someone to call on in an emergency. Was her later care for his son William a way of paying back the debt?

There is at least one other possibility that could account for Ballou's involvement. He and Eliza might have had an affair, resulting in William, born in December 1790. Although this last explanation is not impossible, it is unlikely nevertheless. The boy would have been conceived when Eliza was only fourteen and Ballou a married man with a household of young children. Eliza's failure to have children later is another argument against her having been William's mother, although possibly Stephen was infertile. The question of the boy's ancestry remains unresolved.

Whether or not William was Eliza's son, certainly George Washington Bowen wasn't. The papers detailing the 1795 lawsuit offer further evidence, if any were needed, that Bowen had fabricated his case. The inscription indicating that he had been born of "Eliza Bowen" in Reuben Ballou's house on October 9, 1794—supposedly written on the night of his birth—referred to his alleged mother by a first name that she had yet to adopt. As the record of Greene's lawsuit proves, she was still going by Betsy in 1795. In addition, the suit demonstrates that she was in Providence throughout that year. In contrast, Bowen's witness Daniel Hull had contended that she had left the city in the spring or summer of 1795.[32] Whether she continued to reside in Providence in the second half of the nineties or accompanied her mother and stepfather south in 1797 is unknown.

Bowen's dethronement must have been a sad disappointment to American journalists, who had filled many a column with his claims. But the Jumel estate, which had "already provided material that would serve for a three-volume novel," had not exhausted "its capacity in this respect." A fresh troop of claimants had stepped up with "allegations respecting the family history" that promised to "furnish an entirely new chapter for the dénouement."[33]

MURDER MOST FOUL?

"*H*istory tells us that Troy, although it held out for ten years, was at length taken and destroyed. Such may be the case with the famous Nelson Chase," speculated a reporter for the *Cincinnati Daily Gazette* in 1876. "The danger which now threatens Mr. Chase is one which he least expected. It rises suddenly before him like Banquo's ghost. Who would have dreamed that Stephen Jumel ever had heirs in France? Why, he had been dead a half century, and never an heir appeared, until suddenly at this late hour, the suit is brought in the United States Court by these very heirs."[1]

Banquo's ghost had risen indeed. The grandchildren and great-grandchildren of Stephen's long-dead brother and sister had decided to make a bid for the Jumel fortune. They claimed that Eliza's conveyances of the Jumel properties in the 1820s, particularly those with purported payments from Mary, had been illegal transactions designed to defraud Stephen and his heirs. This argument was not new—Madelaine and Ulysses had tried to overturn the deeds on the same grounds after Stephen's death—but this time it was bolstered by vigorous attempts to besmirch Eliza's reputation. The "French heirs," as they came to be called, asserted that Eliza had abandoned Stephen callously after he returned to the United States. First she went south with Mary (a reference to the 1828 trip to Charleston) and then "into the interior of New York" (where Mary had met Nelson). The latter trip was assigned an ominous purpose. It was not "to find cool weather, as they [Eliza and Mary had] alleged," but rather to consult with Schuyler Crippen "as to the most effectual mode of defrauding the said Stephen Jumel out of his property." In this retelling, Nelson joined the conspiracy after Eliza promised to leave Stephen's estate to him and Mary.[2]

Eliza was said to have cemented her betrayal of Stephen by isolating him from his friends. The French heirs claimed that he was "in a condition of absolute physical and social duress" from the time of Nelson and Mary's marriage, and "as he became more infirm, he was the closer watched and confined." It was only in "the early part of the year 1832, [that] he, for the first time, acquired any knowledge of the gross frauds that had been perpetrated upon him and his heirs." He "had declared his purpose of taking legal steps to annul the whole of the said fraudulent deeds and conveyances," but was prevented from doing so by "his feeble condition and advanced age." Eliza and Mary treated him "in the most cruel manner" during this time period, until he died suddenly "from the effects of an alleged fall from a load of hay, whereby he broke his leg and soon expired, without any of his personal friends or acquaintances having been permitted to see or speak to him previous to his death."[3]

The French heirs asked uncomfortable questions. Why had the details of Stephen's decease been kept secret, "other than it was said to have been very sudden, and the result of a fall"?[4] Why had there not been any "information or reason given why a man of his advanced age should be riding on a load of hay, even if it were customary for hay to be harvested as early as the 22d of May in the latitude of New York"?[5] The implication was that the death had been suspicious and Eliza had been involved. The French heirs did not fail to note that "her bridal couch was already spread for Aaron Burr" at the very moment she had declared herself "disqualified for the accustomed enjoyments of life" due to "the sudden loss of her dear friend and husband."[6]

Once more depositions were taken, evidence was trumped up, and family secrets were divulged. John G. Caryl, a cousin of Eliza Pery's second husband, Julius Caryl, was brought in to bolster the validity of the conveyances of the estate. He had worked at the Jumels' mansion as a boy, he said, and witnessed Mary making payments to Madame in "large bank bills . . . [t]he idea was conveyed that property was being sold to Mary."[7] The point of this testimony was to suggest that the transactions challenged by the French heirs had not been fraudulent, because Mary had paid for the lands before putting them in trust for Eliza.

Caryl added that Stephen had been aware of the conveyances well before his death and had come to an agreement with Eliza about them: "Mr. Jumel talked about the property being sold and about Madame selling him out, and that he had compromised the matter with her and had an arrangement, by which, as I understood, the Madame and he should enjoy the property while they lived, and after their death it was to go to the girl—to that effect."[8]

None of this testimony was terribly convincing, especially after Caryl, unnerved by a cross-examination, retreated from his assertions that Mary had paid for the disputed lands.[9] Although Nelson was less easily rattled, he fared badly too, particularly in attempts to whitewash tensions between Eliza and Stephen. For example, he indicated that Eliza had spent most of the fall and winter of 1831 to '32 in Washington Heights with Stephen. However, deeds that Eliza had executed while in central New York with Mary were used to prove that he lied.[10] Eliza's gift to Mary of some of Stephen's lands in New York State was exposed as well.[11] Nelson's sale of 50½ acres of the Jumel lands in Otsego County, six weeks after he and Mary had wed, added color to the French heirs' contention that he had conspired with her and Eliza to defraud Stephen.[12]

As the litigation dragged on, family tensions reached the breaking point yet again. William, who wanted the Jumel lands auctioned in order to have his share of the money, broke with his father and sister and settled with Stephen's relatives in 1880. He agreed to give them half of his one-third share in the Jumel fortune.[13] Then he filed suit against all the interested parties, including his father and sister, to force a partition or sale of the estate.[14] He won his case, a sale was ordered, and Nelson, too, decided to compromise.[15] He managed to obtain a better deal than William, however. He promised the French heirs half of his one-third share in the Washington Heights properties, but retained his full third in the valuable downtown lots. In addition, they agreed to pay him twenty thousand dollars.[16] Eliza held out longest, not settling until 1883.[17] All told, the French heirs would receive a little under one-sixth of the estate.[18]

If William had not settled with the claimants, probably Nelson could have held out and defeated them in court. Letters that the French heirs themselves submitted as evidence revealed that Stephen knew at least four years before his death of the conveyances that Eliza had made of his lands, yet did not act to overturn them.[19] Even the Supreme Court had upheld the trust documents in favor of Mary and her heirs, making the likelihood of nullifying them slim.[20] Nor was there any evidence that Eliza had treated Stephen cruelly and kept him from contacting his friends and relatives. This line of argument appears to have been inspired by a single sentence in a letter written by Stephen's acquaintance François Philippon in 1833: "The death of Mr. Jumel in consequence of a fall was, so to say, sudden, at least for his friends, since no one saw him after that unfortunate event; before he enjoyed very excellent health and could expect to live many years."[21] This statement of fact was far from a charge that Stephen was isolated intentionally. Indeed, within a year of filing their lawsuit, the French heirs had abandoned the story that he had fallen from a hay cart and had stopped hinting that his demise was suspicious.[22]

But the Chases already owed their lawyers nearly two hundred thousand dollars—equivalent to approximately $4.7 million today.[23] If they continued to fight the French heirs in court, they risked seeing the entire estate eaten up in legal costs—or not living long enough to enjoy the proceeds of an eventual victory. It was better to move on with their lives. Stephen's relatives replaced the Chase family as the main protagonists of the never-ending Jumel case. The French heirs fought their own lawyers over the legal fees (which exceeded the amount recovered for them) for another seven years, and ultimately they too appealed to the United States Supreme Court.[24] Wisdom prevailed and they settled in 1890 before the case was heard.[25] Their lawyers fought among themselves into the 1890s over the apportionment of the fees.[26]

Eliza's reputation did not escape unscathed from the last rounds of the battle over the Jumel estate. Although the French heirs had abandoned their charge that she was complicit in Stephen's death, the slur persisted in the court of public opinion. By the early twentieth century, she was said to have unwrapped bandages placed on Stephen's arm after bloodletting, causing him to bleed to death.[27] In 1965 an even worse story was floated during a séance at her former residence, by then a museum. Supposedly a boy had pushed Stephen from a hay cart so that he fell on a pitchfork, and Eliza, complicit, had arranged for her husband to be buried alive.[28]

In fairness to Eliza, it is worth taking the time to deconstruct the origin of these legends. They started with the account that the French heirs had picked up about Stephen falling from a load of hay. By 1876, when they were building their case, there could have been few neighbors who remembered the details of the accident. Because Stephen was known to have been thrown from a wagon—the fact had been stated in Parton's 1858 biography of Aaron Burr—an agricultural use of the vehicle may have been assumed.[29] But in the early nineteenth century, it was common for country dwellers to use one-horse wagons for transportation as well as farm work.[30] Stephen followed this practice unless he was traveling into the city. He "had a stool, being the lower part of a chair, a common Windsor chair with the back off," that he used when riding in his one-horse wagon.[31]

The improvised seat bore part of the blame for his death. As Nelson described the accident in a deposition, Stephen was being driven up the Kingsbridge Road to the ninety-six-acre lot by "rather a poor driver, a Frenchman who did not know how to drive, and through some mismanagement this stool was pitched out, and he fell out and struck [*sic*] on his breast and injured himself very much."[32] A physician who lived in Harlem, which was then "quite a rural place and little settled," came to bleed him—a standard treatment for serious injuries at the time.[33] The procedure was mismanaged. The doctor "touched an artery and the arm filled from the wrist to the shoulder."[34] Here, no doubt, is the seed of the tale that Stephen bled to death—a charge that was not made by the French heirs. Much later it was grafted onto the muddled story of the wagon they had filled mistakenly with hay and from there grew the extravagant fiction that Stephen had fallen on a pitchfork.

In actual fact, after the bloodletting was botched, he was treated by two highly competent doctors for "some ten or twelve days," before "he succumbed to this injury."[35] Could Eliza have interfered with her husband's care after the doctors had gone home? Perhaps, but why would she? She and Stephen were living comfortably in the United States, the location she preferred. Her husband was supervising the farms, improving the property, maximizing their income, and making it possible for her to travel. She had no motivation to wish him dead, nor is there any indication that she was suspected of harming him at the time. The doctor who provided the bulk of Stephen's care was Francis Berger, at once his family physician and the son of his old friend Eloi Berger—a man unlikely to have remained silent if he had suspected foul play.[36] Berger did not request an inquest—or at least none was performed—an indicator that he did not consider the death suspicious.[37]

According to the death certificate, Stephen's demise was caused by "inflammation of the lungs," or pneumonia, as we would call it today.[38] The diagnosis is believable. Even now pneumonia remains a threat to people immobilized from injuries. The risk is especially high when breathing is impaired, as Stephen's might have been from the fall "on his breast."

During the years that Eliza's reputation was blighted, first by George Washington Bowen and then by the French heirs, her family fought back by romanticizing her life as vividly as she had done herself. By the early 1870s, Nelson and his daughter, Eliza Pery, were disseminating the tale that Stephen had offered Napoleon I a ship on which to escape to America.[39] They endowed the old Jumel mansion with distinguished guests as well. Charles-Maurice de Talleyrand, the marquis de Lafayette, and King Louis-Philippe (before ascending the throne) were among the notables who, in their telling, had stepped within its gates.[40] The legend that Eliza and Stephen had socialized with French émigrés during the early years of their marriage originated with Nelson and his daughter too.[41]

Eliza's furnishings were given distinguished, if imaginary, histories. "A silver tea service, which once graced the table of Marie Antoinette, and a bit of tapestry wrought by the fingers of the Empress Josephine" were displayed in the Octagon Parlor of the mansion near vases, tables, and a chandelier allegedly owned by General Moreau.[42] Other treasures of the mansion included Eliza's bed, said to have belonged to Napoleon I when he was First Consul, and a sofa purportedly from the palace of Charles X.[43] In the hallway was a chess table "at which Louis Napoleon [Napoleon III] liked to play with Madame Jumel."[44]

In anticipation of the moment when the Jumel lands could be sold, Nelson bolstered the value of the estate by leaking information to the newspapers about ostensibly interested purchasers. Supposedly Napoleon III had been negotiating for the Jumel estate during the Franco-Prussian War "to use for a residence in case of his being dethroned."[45] He was forced into exile in 1870, after the Battle of Sedan, but "the loss of much of his wealth by the war forced him to look for a retreat of more moderate dimensions."[46] Subsequently ex–Queen Christina of Spain began bargaining for the property, or so the story went.[47] None of these reports had a basis in fact, any more than the stories told about Eliza's home furnishings.

The settlements with the French heirs ended much of the drama. The Jumel estate was sold off in well-attended auctions in 1882, 1886, and 1888.[48] Nelson and his daughter bought the mansion and the homestead lot. They and their spouses and young Raymond Chase went on sharing the premises until 1887.[49] Hattie's sister, Lizzie Dunning, lived with them until her marriage in 1886.[50] Although the French heirs continued to fight with their lawyers, the Chases and Caryls, free from the shadow of the courthouse, settled into quiet retirement.

EPILOGUE

"For it is a peculiarity of these long-winded cases that they
are as nearly immortal as anything mortal can be."
—"The Jumel jumble," *New-York Tribune*, April 4, 1877

*I*n 1887 the Chases and the Caryls sold the Jumel mansion
and the remaining acreage surrounding it.[1] Eliza and Julius
moved to Yonkers. They spent their summers in Saratoga Springs,
occupying Madame Jumel's former home.[2]

Nelson, Hattie, and Raymond relocated to Ridgewood, New Jersey, where Nelson died in 1890.[3] Raymond fell into bad company.
One of his friends was James Tynan, whose father claimed to have
been complicit in the politically motivated assassinations of Lord
Frederick Cavendish and Thomas Henry Burke, the British secretary
and undersecretary for Ireland.[4] At seventeen, Raymond accused his
widowed mother, Hattie, of adultery with his uncle, Lizzie's husband, and claimed that his uncle had withheld Raymond's share of
the Jumel fortune.[5] Two years later, Raymond died of Pott's disease,
a complication of tuberculosis.[6]

Eliza Caryl lived to be eighty years old, guarding her great-aunt's relics and reputation until her own death in 1915.[7] Her husband predeceased her, dying in 1911. He left all of his property to her—although one of his nephews challenged the will.[8]

Two years before Eliza Caryl's death, her granddaughter Agnes Gourreau, one of four children born to Mathilde, came from Bordeaux to tend her.[9] Eleven months after her grandmother's decease, Agnes married Dr. J. Wade Hampton, the scion of a wealthy southern family.[10]

Jane McManus, Aaron Burr's alleged lover in the Jumel divorce case, found her reputation permanently stained. In 1837 she was named the respondent in yet another divorce action.[11] Her ill repute made her an easy target, but she was probably blameless in that particular case. Subsequently she became a journalist and author. In an 1845 article advocating the annexation of Texas to the United States, she coined the now-famous phrase "manifest destiny." The fact that she was the first to use the term was only rediscovered at the end of the twentieth century.[12]

George Washington Bowen died in 1885 at the age of ninety.[13] He assigned his claim to the Jumel fortune to John R. Vandervoort, a relative of the Anne Vandervoort who had borne witness for him.[14] This newest aspirant to the fabled millions donated land from the estate to several philanthropic institutions in order to promote his supposed acquisition. But the coordinates of the plots proved difficult to pinpoint. Although they were located "in a part of the city where land is worth almost as much as good gold ore," whether they were "below the ground, or . . . raised some two feet in the air," the donor failed to say.[15]

Shortly before Vandervoort died in 1903, he sold his claim to James Wallace Tygard of Netherwood, New Jersey.[16] Politely Tygard notified the mayor of New York City of his "title" to the Jumel property—including as-yet-unearthed Napoleonic relics that he claimed Eliza had buried on her lands.[17] Six months later he and a friend were arrested in a sting operation, after contracting to sell a lot that was once part of the Jumel estate. It was already owned by someone else.[18]

Eliza's old home became a museum in 1907.[19] Today it is known as the Morris-Jumel Mansion, commemorating Roger and Mary Morris, the couple who built it, and Eliza Jumel, its most famous occupant. Eliza Caryl preserved the furnishings that her great-aunt and Stephen had purchased for the house. After she died in 1915, the most important pieces were acquired for the museum.[20] They can be admired at the Morris-Jumel Mansion to this day.

Eliza's reputation is not as well preserved as her furniture. The lies told by those who sought her fortune turned her into a prostitute, the mother of an illegitimate son, a cruel wife, even the murderer of her husband. She deserves better. Although Eliza was in some ways a difficult woman, her determination, intelligence, and strength of character were what allowed her to survive and thrive in spite of the disadvantages of her youth. The affection of her niece and great-niece testify to her ability to form loving bonds.

Her contemporaries would have been less disturbed by her ascent into the upper middle class had she been a more conventional "womanly" woman—a lady who hid her emotions and ambitions beneath a veneer of delicacy, gentleness, and charm. That was not a façade Eliza could maintain for long. But on her own terms, she achieved much: financial security, a certain social status, a landed estate, an elegant home staffed with servants. She rose far above the social class to which she was born, attaining the upward mobility thought to exemplify the American experience, but in reality so hard to achieve. The stories told about her are less dramatic in the end than the life she composed and acted for herself.

ACKNOWLEDGMENTS

I am deeply grateful to the staff of the many archives, libraries, and museums where I conducted my research for accommodating my endless requests for manuscripts and books. I would like to single out for special mention the New-York Historical Society, the New York Public Library, and the Division of Old Records of the New York County Clerk's Office. I spent many months delving into the collections of each of these institutions.

Without the following people, who offered special assistance in many and various ways, I could not have completed this project: Bruce Abrams, Archivist (retired), Division of Old Records, New York County Clerk's Office; Cherry Fletcher Bamberg, FASG; Jessica Becker, Public Services, Manuscripts and Archives, Yale University Library; Teri Blasko, Local History Librarian, Saratoga Springs Public Library; Paul Campbell, City Archivist, Providence City Hall; Ken Carlson, Reference Archivist, Rhode Island State Archives; Sofie Church, Junior Cataloguer, Sotheby's Old Master Paintings, London; Tracy L. Croce, Local Government Records Analyst, Rhode Island State Archives; Robert Delap, Assistant, Department of Rights and Reproductions, New-York Historical Society; Lindsey Felice, Special Collections and Preservation Assistant, Oberlin College Library; Christine Filippelli, Head of Adult Services, Troy Public Library; Peter Flass; Françoise Hack, Assistant Director Collections, John and Mable Ringling Museum of Art; Agnes Hamberger, Saratoga Springs History Museum; Tammy Kiter, Manuscript Reference Librarian, New-York Historical Society Museum and Library; Colette Lamothe; Thomas Lannon, Assistant Curator, Manuscripts and Archives Division, New York Public Library; Joseph Lapinski, Assistant Archivist, Trinity Wall Street Archives; Daniel Legatino, Trinity Cemetery and Mausoleum; Laura K. O'Keefe, Head of Cataloging and Special Collections, New York Society Library; Brigitte Pallas, Médiatrice culturelle et agent de traitement des fonds, Archives départementales, Conseil général des Landes; Anne Petrimoulx, Archivist, Trinity Wall Street Archives; Erin Schreiner, Special Collections Librarian, New York Society Library; Barbara Sicko, Registrar, Bob Jones University Museum & Gallery; Andrew Smith, Administrative Assistant, Rhode Island Supreme Court Judicial Records Center; Matthew Spady; Gabriel Swift, Reference Librarian, Department of Rare Books and Special Collections, Princeton University Library; Joseph Van Nostrand, Archivist in Charge, Division of Old Records, New York County Clerk's Office; Suzanne Wray; Liz Zanis, Collections Management Assistant, Department of Drawings and Prints, Metropolitan Museum of Art.

Databases rarely receive special credit in acknowledgments, but I must tip a hat to Readex's *America's Historical Newspapers* database. Without the full-text access that it provides to eighteenth- and nineteenth-century American newspapers, the research for this book would have been vastly more time-consuming. I also made good use of *ProQuest Historical Newspapers*.

I owe a considerable debt to two prior biographers of Eliza Jumel. William H. Shelton, Civil War veteran and original curator of the Morris-Jumel Mansion, offered the first extended biographical treatment of Eliza within a book devoted to the mansion's history.[1] He knew a good story when he heard one, and the narrative he fashioned of Eliza's life—legends and all—remains the dominant version today. Constance M. Greiff produced the first modern, scholarly analysis of Eliza, as part of a report she prepared for the Morris-Jumel Mansion.[2] Her study provided my first introduction to the real Eliza and the cornerstone for my research.

I sincerely appreciate the support of the Morris-Jumel Mansion staff, including director Carol S. Ward, curator Jasmine Helm, archivist Emilie Lauren Gruchow, and former director Ken Moss. They permitted me to spend many happy hours rooting about in the mansion's archives; provided access to objects in the collection; and supplied a rich selection of images for this book. In addition, Emilie supplied a crucial need by photographing Eliza's hands from the Jumel family portrait—the handsome detail that appears on the book's cover. Trish Mayo, also at the Morris-Jumel Mansion, not only shared her own photographs of the family portrait, but also braved unseasonably cold weather to shoot a beautiful selection of images of the Jumel crypt.

Barbara Breen has my eternal gratitude for being kind enough to read the entire manuscript as I was racing to finish it. She gave me excellent feedback and welcome encouragement during those last, agonizing stages of the project. Michelle Williams, Developmental Editor at Chicago Review Press, kept the production process running smoothly, despite the challenges posed by a manuscript heavily freighted with sixty-plus pages of endnotes.

My special thanks to agent Malaga Baldi for finding the book a home, and to Lisa Reardon, Senior Editor at Chicago Review Press, for seeing the promise in a working manuscript that was in far from finished form.

A NOTE ON THE SOURCES

*T*his book makes heavy use of eighteenth- and nine-teenth-century newspapers and manuscript material. I have slightly modernized the original punctuation for easier reading. Dashes used to terminate sentences (an accepted practice well into the nineteenth century) are replaced by periods, and the placement of commas and semicolons has been adjusted to follow modern American usage. Translations from French are mine unless otherwise indicated.

I made silent corrections of typographical errors in newspaper articles and of misspelled words in handwritten depositions. If necessary punctuation was missing, I added it. In quoting from legal testimony reported in the newspapers, if a witness's words were run together with sentences separated by semicolons, I used periods to divide them instead. Throughout the book, estimates of what a given sum of money would be worth today were generated using the simple purchasing power calculator available at MeasuringWorth.com (www.measuringworth.com/ppowerus).

When translating excerpts from Eliza's and Stephen's original letters in French, I did not attempt to reproduce their mistakes in spelling or grammar. Eliza made frequent errors when writing in French, but most were minor: "rich" instead of "riche" for "wealthy"; "mouttons" rather than "moutons" for "sheep"; "collons" instead of "colonnes" for "columns." Occasionally a misspelling hints at a mispronunciation: "beaucoup" becomes "beaucoupe," suggesting that she may have pronounced the final, silent p. Other mistakes are evident only because she was writing rather than speaking. For instance, Eliza wrote "je ferais" (I was doing) when she meant "je ferai" (I will do), but the two verb forms are pronounced identically (the final s of "ferais" is silent). Often she omitted accent marks— but native speakers, including Stephen, were not meticulous about including them either. Every so often a common construction was scrambled. "I have been in Cherry Valley for three weeks" became "Me voici il y a trois semaines à Cherry Vally [*sic*]" (I have been three weeks ago in Cherry Valley). "Il même" replaces "lui-même" for "himself." On occasion, a specialized French term escaped her, and she adapted an American one—for example, "une morgage" rather than "une hypothèque" for "a mortgage."[1] The end results, easy to interpret for a native English speaker with a working knowledge of French, would be more confusing for a Francophone reader. Yet it is impressive that she turned out three- and four-page letters in a language that she did not acquire until adulthood.

Stephen had his own quirks as a writer. Generally he completed the infinitive forms of regular verbs ending in *er* with the letters és instead: for example, "loués" rather than "louer" (to rent); "depansés" rather than "dépenser" (to spend); "menagés" rather than "ménager" (to economize on or use sparingly). He made other minor spelling errors—"j'ai" (I have) became "je" (which he must have pronounced "jé"); "quartier" (quarter) became "cartier." In these and similar cases, he was writing phonetically. The sound of the words would have remained the same, in spite of the altered spelling. The biggest challenge in reading Stephen's letters is his handwriting, sometimes nearly illegible. He could write neatly, but often didn't take the time to do so.[2]

A few of the letters Eliza wrote in French were available to me only in later translations. If more than one translation existed, I used the wording that seemed to best reflect her typical writing style. Also used in translation were more than forty-five letters relating to Stephen, including letters between him and his French relatives, among his relatives, and between his relatives and others. Used as exhibits in the 1876 lawsuit filed by the French heirs, they were published in English, together with the bill of complaint, by a legal printer for use during the litigation.[3] I did not have access to the French originals, which would have been returned to their owners, but the translations provided crucial information on Stephen's life in France between 1815 and 1828 and his relatives' fights over his estate (first after his death and then after Eliza's).

Much of the information in this book comes from testimony and depositions given by witnesses in lawsuits. Some of these individuals lied outright, some shaded the truth, and almost all made inadvertent errors in recounting long-past events. The depositions of Nelson Chase in the lawsuits over the Jumel estate offer particularly rich detail on Eliza, but also hidden pitfalls. Nelson shaped his testimony to strengthen his and his children's claims to Eliza's fortune. In this worthy endeavor, he was not beyond telling fibs. Skeptical questions posed in cross-examinations helped me to identify at least some of his and others' evasions and lies. In drawing on depositions and other testimony, I have prioritized information that I could cross-check.

NOTES

ABBREVIATIONS

STATE AND LOCAL COURT RECORDS

I drew heavily on manuscript records of court cases, especially those stored in the Department of Old Records of the New York County Clerk's Office. A given file may contain anything from a one-page judgment record to a rich history of a case, including bills of complaint, exhibits, and depositions. The abbreviations used in the endnotes referring to these records are as follows:

N.Y. Com. Pl., New York Court of Common Pleas
N.Y. Ct. Ch., New York Court of Chancery
N.Y. Mayor's Ct., New York Mayor's Court
N.Y. Sup. Ct., New York Supreme Court
N.Y. Super. Ct., New York Superior Court

Unless otherwise indicated, citations in this book using the foregoing abbreviations refer to courts located in New York County. Frequently cited cases are abbreviated as follows:

BM 710-J   N.Y. Ct. Ch., Eliza B. Jumel, Administratrix, vs. François Jumel, BM 710-J.

Liber 368   Copies of Equity Judgments, Liber 368.

FEDERAL COURT RECORDS

Most of the federal circuit court records used in researching this book make part of the collections of the National Archives and Records Administration—Northeast Region (New York City). They may be found in Record Group 21, Records of District Courts of the United States. A given box may contain hundreds of pages of documents. I have tried wherever possible to provide information that will help future researchers locate specific material within boxes. For example, some lengthy bills of complaint and answers to bills of complaint were published by legal printers for the convenience of the court. When I refer to such a document, I provide not only the box number that contains it, but also the title and publication data of the printed document. Frequently cited cases are abbreviated as follows:

3-312   United States Circuit Court for the Southern District of New York. Champlain Bowen vs. Nelson Chase. Law case files, 3-312, 1869.

3-466   United States Circuit Court. Second Circuit of the Southern District of New York. George W. Bowen vs. Nelson Chase. Law case files, 3-466, 1871.

B-779   United States Circuit Court. Second Circuit of the Southern District of New York. François Henry Jumel et al. vs. Nelson Chase et al. Equity cases, vol. B-779, 1878.

ABBREVIATIONS FOR OTHER FREQUENTLY USED SOURCES

1873 Transcript of Record   Transcript of record. Supreme Court of the United States, no. 312. George W. Bowen, plaintiff in error, vs. Nelson Chase. In error to the Circuit Court of the United States for the Southern District of New York. Filed November 1, 1873. Photocopy available at the Morris-Jumel Mansion, New York, NY.

1876 Bill of Complaint   United States Circuit Court for the Southern District of New York. *François Henry Jumel, Louise C. L. Jumel Plante, Marie R. M. Jumel, Madeline R. Texoeres Marrast, Marie C. F. Lesparre Tauẕiede vs. Nelson Chase. Bill of complaint and exhibits.* New York: Benjamin H. Tyrrel, Law Printer, 1876. Available at the New-York Historical Society, New York, NY.

ADG   Bordeaux, Archives départementales de la Gironde.

ADL   Mont-de-Marsan, Archives départementales des Landes.

Greatorex   Eliza Greatorex. *Old New York from the Battery to Bloomingdale.* Text by M. Despard. New York: G. P. Putnam's Sons, 1875.

MJM   Morris-Jumel Mansion, New York, NY. Archives.

NARA-NY-RG21   Records of District Courts of the United States, Record Group 21. National Archives and Records Administration—Northeast Region (New York City).

NYHS-AHMC   American Historical Manuscripts Collections. New-York Historical Society. New York, NY.

NYHS-BV Jumel   BV Jumel, Stephen, MS 1647. New-York Historical Society. New York, NY.

NYHS-JP   Stephen Jumel Papers, MS 336. New-York Historical Society. New York, NY.

NYPL   New York Public Library. New York, NY.

NYPL-Letter Book   MssCol 1610. Jumel and Desobry records, 1808–1810. New York Public Library. New York, NY.

Parton   J[ames] Parton. *The Life and Times of Aaron Burr*. New York: Mason Brothers, 1858.

PTP   Providence Town Papers, Rhode Island Historical Society, Providence.

PUL Fuller   Fuller Collection of Aaron Burr (C0081), Manuscripts Division, Department of Rare Books and Special Collections, Princeton University Library.

Shelton   William Henry Shelton. *The Jumel Mansion: being a full history of the house on Harlem Heights built by Roger Morris before the revolution; together with some account of its more notable occupants*. Boston and New York: Houghton Mifflin Co., 1916.

TCMR   Town Council Meeting Records, Providence, Rhode Island, City Archives.

PROLOGUE

1. "Jumel," *Commercial Advertiser*, February 8, 1873, 2.

2. Greatorex, 243; "A personal sketch of Madame Jumel, wife of Aaron Burr," *Pioneer and Democrat* [Washington Territory], November 14, 1856, [1]; Parton, 661.

3. *New York Herald*, articles on the Jumel will case appearing between January 26 and March 17, 1872, especially February 8, 1872, 8 (for Eliza walking the streets of Providence as a girl) and March 16, 1872, 11 (summing up the claim that she had an illegitimate son); 1873 Transcript of Record, esp. 16–17; 1876 Bill of Complaint, 9–27.

4. The widow of Aaron Burr," *New York Observer and Chronicle*, July 20, 1865, 230.

5. Richard Weiss, *The American myth of success: From Horatio Alger to Norman Vincent Peale* (1969; repr., Illini Books, 1988), 29.

6. Stephan Thernstrom, *Property and progress: Social mobility in a nineteenth century city* (Cambridge, MA: Harvard University Press, 1964), 103–104, 107, 113; Edward Pessen, *Riches, class, and power before the Civil War* (Lexington, MA: D. C. Heath and Company, 1973), 52–58, 64–66; Jackson T. Main, "Social mobility in Revolutionary America," in

Three centuries of social mobility in America, ed. and with an introduction by Edward Pessen (Lexington, MA: D. C. Heath and Company, 1974), 50–51, 54.

7. Elaine Foreman Crane, *Ebb tide in New England: Women, seaports, and social change 1630–1800* (Boston: Northeastern University Press, 1998), 106–107, 134; Ruth Wallis Herndon, "'Proper' magistrates and masters: Binding out poor children in southern New England, 1720–1820," in *Children bound to labor: The pauper apprentice system in early America*, ed. Ruth Wallis Herndon and John E. Murray (Ithaca: Cornell University Press, 2009), 51.

Chapter 1: Beginnings

1. TCMR 5:215.
2. PTP, Mss 214, Sg. 1, ser. 1, vol. 6, item 2746.
3. "New-York, October 19," *Weekly Museum*, October 19, 1793, [3].
4. Ibid.
5. "An airing!" *New-York Journal, & Patriotic Register*, October 16, 1793, [3].
6. "New-York, October 19."
7. "New-York. Wednesday, October 16," *Daily Advertiser*, October 16, 1793, [2]; PTP, Mss 214, Sg. 1, ser. 1, vol. 6, item 2746.
8. Pauline Maier, *From resistance to revolution: Colonial radicals and the development of American opposition to Britain, 1765–1776* (New York: Alfred A. Knopf, 1972), 4–5; Timothy J. Gilfoyle, *City of Eros: New York City, prostitution, and the commercialization of sex, 1790–1920* (New York and London: W. W. Norton & Company, 1992), 77–78.
9. Gertrude Selwyn Kimball, ed., *Pictures of Rhode Island in the past 1642–1833 by travelers and observers* (Providence, RI: Preston and Rounds Co., 1900), 55–56 (from Rev. Jacob Bailey's journal).
10. Ibid.
11. Lynne Withey, *Urban growth in colonial Rhode Island: Newport and Providence in the eighteenth century* (Albany: State University of New York Press, 1984), 78.
12. Kimball, *Pictures of Rhode Island*, 104.
13. Ibid., 82.
14. Ruth Wallis Herndon, *Unwelcome Americans: Living on the margin in early New England* (Philadelphia: University of Pennsylvania Press, 2001), 14, 19.
15. Ibid., 19, 178–79.
16. PTP, Mss 214, Sg. 1, ser. 1, vol. 7, item 2916.
17. TCMR 5:169–71.
18. PTP, Mss 214, Sg. 1, ser. 1, vol. 6, item 2746.
19. PTP, Mss 214, Sg. 1, ser. 1, vol. 6, item 2745.
20. Ibid. My description of Elizabeth Gardner is based on Ruth Wallis Herndon's description of Sarah Gardner (*Unwelcome Americans*, 62–65, 146), who was almost certainly the person that the issuers of the warrant intended to summon, although they wrote Elizabeth instead of Sarah.
21. PTP, Mss 214, Sg. 1, ser. 1, vol. 6, item 2745.
22. Ibid.

23. TCMR 5:215.

24. The four prostitutes who had lived in the house in 1780 were women of color also (ibid., 169–71).

25. Withey, *Urban growth*, 72–73.

26. TCMR 4:295, 5:409.

27. Sharon Braslaw Sundue, *Industrious in their stations: Young people and work in urban America, 1720–1810* (Charlottesville and London: University of Virginia Press, 2009), 42–43.

28. Female slaves were frequently hired out by their masters in this way, as described by John J. Zaborney in *For hire: Renting enslaved laborers in antebellum Virginia* (Louisiana State University Press, 2012), 4 and chapter 2.

29. TCMR 4:295.

30. She signed her testimony with an X and continued to do so during later brushes with the town authorities. It remains possible that she was able to read, because reading was taught before writing at the time. See E. Jennifer Monaghan, *Learning to read and write in colonial America* (Amherst and Boston: University of Massachusetts Press, 2005), 344.

31. Herndon, *Unwelcome Americans*, 5 (see chap. 1, n. 14).

32. Ibid., 2, 5–10.

33. James N. Arnold, *Vital records of Rhode Island 1836–1850: First series; Births, marriages and deaths; A family register for the people*, vol. 10 (Providence, RI: Narragansett Historical Publishing Company, 1898), 157.

34. His origins are unclear (he might have gained local status by apprenticeship rather than by birth). However, he would be buried some years later at the expense of the town of Providence, an expenditure the municipality would not have approved had there been any question about his residency (PTP, Mss 214, Sg. 1, ser. 1, vol. 10, item 4077, and vol. 11, item 4563).

35. No record of John Thomas's birth has survived, but Phebe gave his age as seventeen on January 1, 1787, which implies that he was born in 1769 (TCMR 5:409). Since her pregnancy appears to have led to her examination by the town council on September 29, 1769, John Thomas must have been born between that date and the end of the year.

36. Probably she should be identified with the Mary Bowen who was born on June 28, 1772; see Arnold, *Vital records of Rhode Island 1836–1850: First series; Births, marriages and deaths; A family register for the people*, vol. 2 (Providence, RI: Narragansett Historical Publishing Company, 1892), 5. She later told her husband she was born on December 19, 1775 (1873 Transcript of Record, 305). While it remains possible that the month and day are correct, she must have adjusted the year to make herself no older than her husband, who was born June 17, 1775.

37. PTP, Mss 214, Sg. 1, ser. 1, vol. 7, items 3077, 3119, 3140 (for references to her as Elizabeth); NYHS-AHMC, Mauer, Charles Arthur: untitled notes, 10 (for her date of birth); "The courts," *New York Herald*, February 27, 1872, 5 (for the quotation).

CHAPTER 2: A HOUSE OF BAD FAME

1. Robert W. Kenny, *Town and gown in wartime: A brief account of the College of Rhode Island, now Brown University, and the Providence community during the American Revo-*

    lution (Providence, RI: The University Relations Officer of Brown University, 1976), 24–25.

2. Sharon Braslaw Sundue, *Industrious in their stations: Young people and work in urban America, 1720–1810* (Charlottesville and London: University of Virginia Press, 2009), 104; Gloria L. Main, "Women on the edge: Life at street level in the early republic," *Journal of the Early Republic* 32 (Fall 2012): 337.

3. Sundue, *Industrious in their stations*, 25.

4. Ibid., 24–25, 42.

5. PTP, Mss 214, Sg. 1, ser. 1, vol. 7, items 3077, 3119, 3140.

6. Stephanie Grauman Wolf, *As various as their land: The everyday lives of eighteenth-century Americans* (New York: HarperCollins, 1993), 119.

7. Heli Meltsner, *The poor houses of Massachusetts: A cultural and architectural history* (Jefferson, NC: McFarland & Company, 2012), 15–16, 19–20.

8. State of Rhode Island, &c. In General Assembly, October Session, A.D. 1796, "An act of better ordering of the police of the town of Providence and regulating the work-house in the said town," *Early American Imprints*, Series 1, no. 49438 (digital supplement).

9. Ruth Wallis Herndon, "'Who died an expense to this town': Poor relief in eighteenth-century Rhode Island," in: *Down and out in early America*, ed. Billy G. Smith (University Park, PA: The Pennsylvania State University, 2004), 140, 151. There are numerous references to the cage in the Providence Town Papers at the Rhode Island Historical Society, e.g., Mss 214, Sg. 1, ser. 1, vol. 6, item 6406.

10. Providence, Rhode Island, City Archives, Providence Town Meetings 4:67.

11. For example: PTP, Mss 214, Sg. 1, ser. 1, vol. 7, items 3077, 3102, 3119, 3140, 3163, 3185, 3202; vol. 8, item 3474 (verso).

12. TCMR 5:317–18; *Providence Journal, and Town and Country Advertiser*, May 29, 1799, [2] (for Ingraham's age).

13. TCMR 5:213.

14. TCMR 5:207, 213, 320.

15. Ingraham had two other sons under fourteen years of age, William and Joseph (ibid.), but they seem to have been living away from home as apprentices before the Bowens moved in.

16. PTP, Mss 214, Sg. 1, ser. 1, vol. 8, items 3483, 3484 (two nearly identical copies of the inventory).

17. Although there is no distinction in the inventory between upstairs and downstairs, the furnishings described here are listed first on the inventory. Logically they would be found in an upper story or attic, suggesting that the upper part of the house was inventoried first. Items that would be less likely to be kept upstairs, such as three flatirons and a gridiron, follow.

18. For the layout of seventeenth- and eighteenth-century New England homes, see Abbott Lowell Cummings, ed., *Rural household inventories: Establishing the names, uses and furnishings of rooms in the colonial New England home 1675–1775* (Boston, MA: The Society for the Preservation of New England Antiquities, 1964), xiv–xxv.

19. PTP, Mss 214, Sg. 1, ser. 1, vol. 8, item 3484.

20. TCMR 5:317.

21. Ibid., 318.

22. Ibid.

23. Ibid.

24. PTP, Mss 214, Sg. 1, ser. 1, vol. 8, item 3474 (verso).

25. Ibid.

26. TCMR 5:320.

27. Herndon, "'Proper' magistrates and masters," 40–41, 44 (see prologue, n. 7); Robert E. Cray Jr., *Paupers and poor relief in New York City and its rural environs, 1700–1830* (Philadelphia: Temple University Press, 1988), 81; Wolf, *As various as their land*, 119–20.

28. Eric Nellis and Anne Decker Cecere, eds., *The eighteenth-century records of the Boston Overseers of the Poor* (Boston: The Colonial Society of Massachusetts, 2007), 971; James Flint, *Letters from America, containing observations on the climate and agriculture of the western states, the manners of the people, the prospects of immigrants, &c. &c.* (Edinburgh: Printed for W. & C. Tait, 1822), 98.

29. E.g., Vincent Di Girolamo, "'Though the means were scanty': Excerpts from Joseph T. Buckingham's *Memoirs and recollections of editorial life*, in *Children and youth in a new nation*, ed. James Martin (New York: New York University Press, 2009), 239, 236; *The diary of Elizabeth Drinker*, eds. Elaine Forman Crane et al. (Boston: Northeastern University Press, 1991), 2:1527 (June 27, 1802), 3:1963 (September 7, 1806), 3:2039 (May 25, 1807).

30. Sundue, *Industrious in their stations*, 33–34.

31. TCMR 5:409.

32. Ibid., 5:375.

33. Ibid., 5:409.

34. John E. Sterling, *North Burial Ground: Providence, Rhode Island; Old section 1700–1848* (Greenville, RI: Rhode Island Genealogical Society, 2000), 14, 146 (for their ages). Although indenture documents have never been found for the Bowen girls, genealogical records identify no other Samuel Allen family in Providence at this time, making it reasonable to assume that this was the couple with whom Betsy was placed.

35. Joseph Jencks Smith, *Civil and military list of Rhode Island 1800–1850* . . . (Providence, RI: Preston and Rounds Co., 1901), 710.

36. U.S. Works Progress Administration, Rhode Island, *Ship registers and enrollments of Providence, Rhode Island: 1773–1939* (Providence, RI: The National Archives Project, 1941), 1:459, no. 1446; 1:648, no. 2034; 1:770–71, no. 2436.

37. *The diaries of Julia Cowles: A Connecticut record, 1797–1803*, ed. Laura Hadley Moseley (New Haven: Yale University Press, 1931), 36, 37, 41 (for washing on Monday and ironing on Tuesday). See *Diary of Elizabeth Drinker* for other typical household activities.

38. Elizabeth Drinker mentions making jelly and candles, although she does not indicate whether she was helped by a servant; see *Diary of Elizabeth Drinker*, 1:102 (July 12 and 13, 1763), 1:343 (April 5, 1779). For dairy work by an indentured servant, see Herman Mann, *The female review* (1916; repr., Bedford, MA: Applewood Books, 2009), 44–45.

39. Betty Ring, *Let virtue be a guide to thee: Needlework in the education of Rhode Island women, 1730–1830* (Providence, RI: Rhode Island Historical Society, 1983), 53, 94. The girls sheltered in New York's House of Refuge in the nineteenth century were expected to do the sewing and mending for the boys who lived there; see *Documents of the Assembly of*

the State of New-York, Seventy-third Session, 1850, vol. 6 (Albany: Weed, Parsons & Co., 1850), no. 172:7.

40. For example, by the age of twelve, Boston schoolgirl Anna Green Winslow was adept at spinning flax; see *Diary of Anna Green Winslow: A Boston school girl of 1771,* ed. Alice Morse Earle (Boston and New York: Houghton, Mifflin and Company, 1899), 34.

41. For a bound-out girl going along to carry a child when the mistress of the house was visiting friends or taking a walk, see *Diary of Elizabeth Drinker,* 1:588 (September 1, 1794); 1:592 (September 11, 1794); 1:597 (September 22, 1794).

42. *A season in New York 1801: Letters of Harriet and Maria Trumbull,* ed. Helen M. Morgan (University of Pittsburgh Press, 1969), 96.

43. E.g., *Diary of Elizabeth Drinker,* 1:584 (August 20, 1794).

44. Ibid., 1:586 (August 28, 1794).

45. Ibid., 3:1963 (September 7, 1806).

CHAPTER 3: A DEATH IN THE FAMILY

1. "General and field-officers of the Militia, appointed at the last session of the Assembly," *Providence Gazette and Country Journal,* May 20, 1786, [3]. The sentence relating to John Bowen appears at the end of this otherwise unrelated article.

2. PTP, Mss 214, Sg. 1, ser. 1, vol. 11, item 4563; PTP, Mss 214, Sg. 1, ser. 1, vol. 10, item 4077.

3. PTP, Mss 214, Sg. 1, ser. 1, vol. 10, item 4077.

4. TCMR 6:108.

5. Ibid., 6:116.

6. Ibid.; 1873 Transcript of Record, 304.

7. TCMR 6:116.

8. Ibid.

9. Herndon, *Unwelcome Americans,* 89, fig. 3 (see chap. 1, n. 14).

10. TCMR, No. 6: 1787–1794, 164; PTP, Mss 214, Sg. 1, ser. 1, vol. 15, items 6395, 6406.

11. Arnold, *Vital records of Rhode Island,* vol. 10, 135, 137 (see chap. 1, n. 33).

12. William Cary Duncan, *The amazing Madame Jumel* (New York: Frederick A. Stokes Company, 1935), 29–35, 39–40; 1873 Transcript of Record, 304.

13. Although it has been suggested that the girls traveled with the Clarks, no documentation indicates that they did.

14. Duncan, *The amazing Madame Jumel,* 41, 43.

15. Ibid., 43.

16. 1873 Transcript of Record, 304.

17. Duncan, *The amazing Madame Jumel,* 44.

18. Ibid., 44; B-779, box 112, deposition of Nelson Chase.

19. "Madame Jumel's estate," *New York Herald,* November 13, 1866, 4; Nelson Chase, "The Jumel estate—card from Mr. Nelson Chase," *New York Times,* February 1, 1868. In 1880 Nelson said that Eliza had told him that John had died of a fever in New Orleans (B-779, box 112, deposition of Nelson Chase). However, no other information places John in Louisiana.

CHAPTER 4: THE MAKING OF A MERCHANT

1. Louis et Michel Papy, *Histoire de Mont-de-Marsan: Tome 1; Des origines à 1800* (Mont-de-Marsan: Editions InterUniversitaires, 1994), 258–60.

2. Ibid., 251–52, 257, 263, 265, 268.

3. The address is given in his sister Madelaine's marriage contract of November 9, 1790. ADL, 3 E 13 / 46.

4. Vincent Lagadère, *Le commerce fluvial à Mont-de-Marsan du XVIIe au XVIIIe siècle* (Paris: L'Harmattan, 2012), 261–62.

5. Ibid., 262–63.

6. Dominique Jumel is listed as a *marchand droguiste* in the May 13, 1762, record of Madelaine Jumel's birth and baptism (ADL, E dépôt 192 / GG 56), and the Jumels' shop is mentioned in Madelaine's marriage contract (ADL, 3 E 13 / 46).

7. [Eustache-Marie-Pierre-Marc-Antoine] Courtin, *Encyclopédie moderne, ou, Dictionnaire abrégé des sciences, des lettres et des arts* . . . (Paris: Au bureau de l'Encyclopédie, 1828), 12:5; *Trésor de la langue française: Dictionnaire de la langue du XIXe et du XXe siècle (1789–1960)*, ed. Paul Imbs, vol. 7 (Paris: Éditions du Centre Nationale de la Recherche Scientifique, 1979), 508, 511.

8. For the products sold in *drogueries* described in this and the next paragraph, I drew on the following sources: *Encyclopédie methodique, ou par ordre de matières; par une société de gens de lettres, de savans et d'artistes. Commerce*, vol. 2 (Paris: Chez Pankouke , 1783), especially the entry titled "Droguerie"; [Nicolas] Lemery, *Dictionnaire universel des drogues simples, contenant leurs noms, origine, choix, principes, vertus, etimologies* . . . , nouvelle édition (Paris: Chez d'Houry, 1760); *Nouveau dictionnaire général des drogues simples et composées, de Lemery; révu, corrigé, et considérablement augmenté par Simon Morelot* (Paris: Rémont, 1807).

9. A separate address is not given for the shop in Stephen's sister Madelaine's marriage contract (ADL, 3 E 13 / 46), which sets out a plan to expand the *droguerie* with the help of an investment from her future husband. The young couple was to share the house at 16, rue du Bourg with the Jumels and run the business with them as equal partners.

10. ADL, E dépôt 192 / GG 56 (124). The maiden name of Stephen's mother is spelled in a variety of ways, including Sonier, Sonnier, Sonié, and Sounier. I have chosen Sonier, the form she used in signing her name to a contract (ADL, 3E 4 172 / 75).

11. ADL, E dépôt 192 / GG 56 (for all three births).

12. A note in a legal document prepared in France in 1824 testifies to his consistent use of the name Stephen. The notary preparing the document observed that he had been "improperly named Étienne Stephen Jumel instead of Stephen Jumel, which is his only first name" in a record drawn up four years earlier. See ADL, 4 Q 1/10, no. 487.

13. Papy, *Histoire de Mont-de-Marsan*, 296.

14. Ibid.

15. Lagadère, *Le commerce fluvial*, 263.

16. 1876 Bill of Complaint, letters 6, 7, 11, 24.

17. [Nicolas] Lemery, *Dictionnaire universel des drogues simples, contenant leurs noms, origine, choix, principes, vertus, etimologies* . . . , nouvelle édition (Paris: Chez d'Houry, 1760), vii;

Jaques Savary, *Le parfait négociant, ou, Instruction générale pour ce qui regarde le commerce des marchandises de France, & des pays étrangers, nouvelle édition, revûe et corrigie . . . par Philémon-Louis Savary* (Genève: Chez les Frères Cramer & Cl. Philibert, 1752), vol. 1, preface (n.p.) and 1:4.

18. Amitiés Généalogigues Bordelaises, *Passagers pour les iles embarqués à Bordeaux de 1713 à 1787: depouillements des registres appartenant au fonds de l'amiraute de Guyanne* (Mont-de-Marsan, 1993), n.p.

19. Mats Lundahl, "The Haitian dilemma reexamined: Lessons from the past in the light of some new economic theory," in *Haiti renewed: Political and economic prospects*, ed. Robert I. Rotberg (Washington, DC: Brookings Institution Press; Cambridge, MA: World Peace Foundation, 1997), 62; Laurent Dubois, *Avengers of the New World: The story of the Haitian revolution* (Cambridge, MA and London: The Belknap Press of Harvard University Press, 2004), 21; Alexandre-Stanislas de Wimpffen, *Haiti au XVIIIe siècle: Richesse et esclavage dans une colonie française*, ed. Pierre Pluchon (Paris: Édition Karthala, 1993), 295; Jeremy D. Popkin, *A concise history of the Haitian revolution* (Wiley-Blackwell, 2012), 20.

20. Dubois, *Avengers of the New World*, 35.

21. Jacques de Cauna, *L'Eldorado des Aquitains: gascons, basques, et béarnais aux îles d'Amérique (XVIIIe-XVIIIe) siècles* (Biarritz: Éditions Atlantica, 1999), 183; 1876 Bill of Complaint, letter 13.

22. One of the plantations owned by Jacques Sonier and Angelique Sterlin measured only 6 to 7 *carreaux* in size—that is, up to 9.1 hectares—producing eight thousand pounds of coffee per year. Similarly, Angelique's sister Mrs. Blanchard had only twelve *carreaux* (15.6 hectares), yielding twelve thousand to eighteen thousand pounds of coffee (1876 Bill of Complaint, letter 28). Although yield numbers for both of these properties fall within the norms (fully cultivated land typically produced about one thousand pounds of coffee per hectare), the plantation sizes are modest (Wimpffen, *Haiti au XVIIIe siècle*, 78n2). The average cultivated area on a Saint-Domingue coffee plantation at this era has been estimated at 27 hectares (David P. Geggus, "Sugar and coffee cultivation in Saint Domingue and the shaping of the slave labor force," in *Cultivation and culture: labor and the shaping of slave life in the Americas*, ed. Ira Berlin and Philip D. Morgan [Charlottesville: University Press of Virginia, 1993], 76–77).

23. Anne-Marie Cocula, "Contrats d'apprentissage autour de Langon dans la seconde moitié du XVIIIe siècle," *Revue historique de Bordeaux de la Gironde* 20, nouvelle série (1971), 115, 115n20.

24. Stendhal, *Mémoires d'un touriste* (Paris: Calmann-Lévy, 1891), 2:365.

25. Paul Butel, *Les dynasties bordelaises de Colbert à Chaban* (Paris: Librairie Académique Perren, 1991), 16; Meudre de Lapouyade, "Impressions d'une allemande à Bordeaux en 1785," *Revue Historique de Bordeaux et du Département de la Gironde* 4, no. 3 (May–June 1911): 172, 177–78.

26. Alan Forrest, *Society and politics in revolutionary Bordeaux* (London: Oxford University Press, 1975), 11.

27. NYHS-JP, box 1, folder 11, business notebook of Stephen Jumel.

28. Alan Forrest, *The Revolution in provincial France: Aquitaine 1789–1799* (Oxford and New York: Oxford University Press, 1996), 64–65.

29. ADL, 3 U 1/293, fol.77 verso; ADL, 3 E 51 16.

30. Stephen Auerbach, "Politics, protest, and violence in revolutionary Bordeaux, 1789–1794," *Proceedings of the Western Society of French History* 37 (2009): 160.

31. Anne de Mathan, *Mémoires de Terreur: L'an II à Bordeaux* (Pessac: Presses Universitaires de Bordeaux, 2002), 33.

32. Auerbach, "Politics, protest, and violence," 160.

33. Mathan, *Mémoires de Terreur*, 33–34.

34. ADL, 3 E 13 / 46 (marriage contract of November 9, 1790); E dépôt 192 / GG 58 (record of the marriage).

Chapter 5: Transitions

1. Mrs. Felton, *American life. A narrative of two years' city and country residence in the United States* (London: Simkin, Marshall, and Co., 1842), 54.

2. Flint, *Letters from America*, 10 (see chap. 2, n. 28).

3. William Duncan, *The New-York directory and register for the year 1795* (New York: Printed for the editor by T. and J. Swords, 1795), 115.

4. Graham Russell Hodges, *New York City cartmen, 1667–1850* (New York and London: New York University Press, 1986), 2–3, 49, 132.

5. See Duncan, *New-York directory and register for the year 1795*.

6. William Duncan, *The New-York directory and register for the year 1794* (New York: Printed for the editor by T. and J. Swords, 1794), 146; Duncan, *New-York directory and register for the year 1795*, 115, 128, 168.

7. Sylvia Marzagalli, "The failure of a transatlantic alliance? Franco-American trade, 1783–1815," *History of European Ideas* 34, no. 4 (December 2008): 457–59.

8. Robert Greenhalgh Albion, "Maritime adventures of New York in the Napoleonic era," in *Essays in modern English history in honor of Walter Cortez Abbott* (Cambridge, MA: Harvard University Press, 1941), 317.

9. The court's proceedings on May 29, 1797, are recorded in NYPL, MssCol 3094, Proceedings of the United States District Court, New York, 1796–1798.

Chapter 6: Reinvention

1. *A guide to the city of New York; containing an alphabetical list of streets, &c. accompanied by a correct map* (New York: J. Disturnell, 1837), 12.

2. "Longworth's New-York register and city-directory," *Daily Advertiser*, July 2, 1803, [3].

3. *Daily Advertiser*, July 7, 1803, [3] (an advertisement for Longworth's directory).

4. *Longworth's American almanac, New-York register, city directory for the twenty-eighth year of American independence* (New York: David Longworth, 1803), 98.

5. Daniel Defoe, *Roxana: The fortunate mistress*, ed. John Mullan (New York: Oxford University Press, 1996; Oxford World's Classics Paperback, 1998), xvi–xix.

6. In 1802 Elizabeth Drinker commented that her granddaughter Elizabeth's parents called the baby Betsy, "which is now old-fashioned" (*Diary of Elizabeth Drinker*, 3:1509 [April 20, 1802]).

7. *The female marine and related works: Narratives of cross-dressing and urban vice in America's early republic*, ed. Daniel A. Cohen (Amherst: University of Massachusetts Press, 1997), 70.

8. Like Eliza, the Brinckerhoffs are listed at 87 Reed in *Longworth's American almanac*, 1803, 96.

9. New York County, Land and Property Records, Conveyances, Liber 53:154–55; Liber 60:315–19; Liber 65:211–13; Liber 71:71–72.

10. *The family of Joris Dircksen Brinckerhoff, 1638* (New York: Richard Brinckerhoff, 1887), 89–91.

11. Brooks McNamara, *The American playhouse in the eighteenth century* (Cambridge, MA: Harvard University Press, 1969), 132.

12. Ibid., 133–34, 137–38.

13. *Diary of William Dunlap (1766–1839): The memoirs of a dramatist, theatrical manager, painter, critic, novelist, and historian* (New York: Printed for the New-York Historical Society, 1930), 3:796.

14. [Joseph Haslewood], *The secret history of the green-room: Containing authentic and enterprising memoirs of the actors and actresses in the three Theatres Royal* (London: Printed for J. Owen, 1795), 2:199.

15. William Dunlap, *A history of the American theater* (New York: J. & J. Harper, 1832), 158.

16. H. N. D. [Joseph Norton Ireland], *Fifty years of a play-goers journal or, annals of the New York stage, from A.D. 1798 to A.D. 1848* (New York: Samuel French, Publisher, 1860), 13–14, 17–19, 25.

17. Her height is given as 5'4" on a passport issued in 1841 and 5'5" on a passport issued in 1833; see Ancestry.com, *U.S. Passport Applications, 1795–1925* [database online] (Provo, UT: Ancestry.com Operations, Inc., 2007). I have used the 1841 figure, because Eliza appeared in person before the notary who wrote out the description. In 1833 the passport was requested by her nephew-in-law, who supplied a brief description of her.

18. [Tom Ford], *A peep behind the curtain, by a supernumerary* (Boston: Redding & Co., 1850), 10.

19. Claudia D. Johnson, "That guilty third tier: Prostitution in nineteenth-century American theaters," in *Victorian America*, ed. Daniel Walker Howe (University of Pennsylvania press, 1976), 111–13; Dunlap, *History of the American theater*, 211, 277; *The American Chesterfield, or way to wealth, honor, and distinction* (Philadelphia: John Grigg, 1828), 203.

20. For example, only about five performances at the Park Theatre required female supernumeraries between November 14, 1803, when the fall season opened, and the end of December 1803. (Advertisements were placed in the New York City newspapers for each performance, making it possible to identify the dates and program for each.) For salaries, see [Ford], *A peep behind the curtain*, 9–10.

21. Adin Ballou, *An elaborate history and genealogy of the Ballous in America* (Providence: Arial Ballou and Latimer W. Ballou, 1988), v.

22. Ibid., 202–203.

23. Ibid., 203. It is not clear where David Ballou went after his wife's death. Adin Ballou writes that he moved to New York and lived there many years, but this seems implausible; David's name doesn't appear in any of New York's city directories between 1800 and 1840. He may have gone west, as in 1832, according to Adin Ballou, he was settled in Union County, Ohio (ibid., 203).

24. Ballou, *Elaborate history*, 203, 463.

25. *United States Chronicle: Political, Commercial and Historical*, September 24, 1789, [3]; Sterling, *North Burial Ground*, 146.

26. Herndon, "'Proper' magistrates and masters," 46 (see prologue, n. 7).

CHAPTER 7: MARRIAGE

1. [Haslewood], *Secret history of the green-room*, 2:193 (see chapter 6, n. 14).

2. Stephen had business premises for a time on Upper Reed Street (the part of the street east of Broadway), even after moving from the lodging at 44 Reed he had occupied in 1795.

3. NYHS-BV Jumel, entry for February 7, 1804.

4. Ibid., entry for November 7, 1808.

5. Ibid., entry for February 1, 1804.

6. Ibid., entries for June 10 and June 13, 1804. William's tutor received payment directly from Stephen, whereas "Miss Brown" handed over the money for her own lessons. However, as the transactions appear in Stephen's receipt book, it was probably his money that paid both bills.

7. NYPL, MssColl 318, Elizabeth De Hart Bleecker Diary 1799–1806, entry for April 9, 1804 (for the weather).

8. Morris-Jumel Mansion Archives, 26.13 (English translation of the certificate).

9. *Letters from John Pintard to his daughter Eliza Noel Pintard Davidson 1816–1833. Vol. II: 1821–1827* (New York: Printed by the New-York Historical Society, 1940), 31.

10. New York County, Land and Property Records, Deeds, Liber 96:330–33; N.Y. Ct. Ch., Stephen Jumel vs. the Ursuline Convent of the City of New York and the Trustees of St. Patrick's Cathedral, CL-161, 184–251.

11. For the significance of gossip, see Edith B. Gelles, "Gossip: an eighteenth-century case," *Journal of Social History* 22, no. 4 (Summer 1989): 667–68, 676.

12. *Letters from John Pintard to his daughter Eliza Noel Pintard Davidson 1816–1833. Vol. IV: 1832–1833* (New York: Printed by the New-York Historical Society, 1941), 170.

13. Their marriage does not appear in the register of marriages performed at the Church of Saint Peter the Apostle (NYPL, Records of St. Peter's Church, New York City).

14. Ellen K. Rothman, *Hands and hearts: A history of courtship in America* (New York: Basic Books, 1984), 78.

15. Ibid., 78–81.

16. A search of Ancestry.com for the last name "Lapeyre" or "Lepeyre" returns no hits with any even vaguely similar first names for the period 1790 through 1830.

17. NYHS-BV Jumel, entry for June 13, 1804.
18. Herbert Ross Brown, *The sentimental novel in America 1789–1860* (1970; repr., Freeport, NY: Books of Libraries Press, 1970), 19n73; Eliza Haywood, *The History of Miss Betsy Thoughtless*, ed. Christine Blouch (Peterborough, Ontario, Canada: Broadview Press, 1988), 421–26.
19. Herndon, "'Proper' magistrates and masters," 51 (see prologue, n. 7).
20. Sharon V. Salinger, *'To serve well and faithfully': Labor and indentured servants in Pennsylvania 1682–1800* (Westminster, MD: Heritage Books, 2000), 118–19; 127–28.
21. Ibid., 116.
22. *Diary of Elizabeth Drinker*, 3:1683 (September 12, 1803); 3:1941 (June 24, 1806) (see chap. 2, n. 29).
23. John van der Zee, *Bound over: Indentured servitude and American conscience* (New York: Simon and Schuster, 1985), 99.
24. Linda L. Mathew, "Gleanings from Rhode Island town records: Providence Town Council records, 1789–1801," *Rhode Island Roots*, Special Bonus Issue 2007 (April 2007): 113–14, 118.
25. For Sampson, see Herman Mann, *The female review* (1916; repr., Bedford, MA: Applewood Books, [2009]) and Alfred A. Young, *Masquerade: The life and times of Deborah Sampson, Continental soldier* (New York: Alfred A. Knopf, 2004), 5, 11, 179, 249, 190, 197–200, 271.

CHAPTER 8: MRS. JUMEL

1. NYHS-BV Jumel, entry for June 14, 1804. The gig was "guaranteed for one year from the 6th instant," which pinpoints June 6 as the date of purchase.
2. *New-York Evening Post*, April 5, 1802, [3] (advertisement placed by Sebring & Van Wyck).
3. *Moreau de St. Méry's American journey 1793-1798*, trans. Kenneth and Anna M. Roberts (Garden City, NY: Doubleday and Company, 1947), 334.
4. Suggested by a payment "for varnishing the carriage" and other sums expended for a coachman's boots and wages (NYHS-BV Jumel, entries for November 28, 1809; May 26, 1812; and March 7, 1815).
5. *New-York Evening Post*, January 4, 1810, [3].
6. James D. Davidson and Ralph E. Pyle, *Ranking faiths: Religious stratification in America* (Plymouth, UK: Rowman & Littlefield, 2011), 10.
7. Ibid., 13, table 1.2; 71, table 4.1; 8, table 1.1.
8. Felton, *American life*, 39 (see chap. 5, n. 1).
9. Baptismal records of Eliza Jumel and William Ballow [*sic*], October 25, 1807, in the Register of the Parish of Trinity Church [online], available at http://registers.trinitywallstreet.org/files/history/registers/registry.php; accessed March 28, 2013. Strictly speaking, the records do not indicate at which church in Trinity Parish the two baptisms took place. But the minister who officiated performed marriages only at the parish's main church, Trinity, and presumably performed baptisms at the same place.

10. John C. Goodbody, *One peppercorne: A popular history of Trinity Church* (New York: The Parish of Trinity Church, 1982), 41, 43.

11. 1873 Transcript of record, 305.

12. NYHS-BV Jumel, entries for June 15, 1805, and February 3, 1806; NYPL-Letter Book, June 21, 1808, to Samuel Ward.

13. NYPL-Letter Book, March 28, 1810, to Batard, Sampson & Sharp.

14. 1873 Transcript of record, 303, 305; B-779, box 112, deposition of Nelson Chase.

15. "Law reports," *New York Times*, October 22, 1870, 3; "The Jumel will," *New-York Tribune*, October 22, 1870, 2.

16. Leonard B. Chapman, *Monograph on the Southgate family of Scarborough: Their ancestors and descendants* (Portland, ME: Hubbard W. Bryant, 1907), 14–17.

17. Ibid., 17 (for the date of the marriage).

18. Marriage record of William Jones and Maria Bowne, December 19, 1805, and baptismal record of William [B.] Jones, September 20, 1810 (with notation of the date of birth), in the registers of the Parish of Trinity Church [online] (see n. 9, above).

19. Baptismal record of Eliza Jumel Jones, September 20, 1810, in the registers of the Parish of Trinity Church [online] (see n. 9, above).

20. NYHS-BV Jumel, entry for May 5, 1809.

21. Baptismal records of William Jones, Eliza Jumel Jones, and Louisa Jones, September 20, 1810, in the registers of the Parish of Trinity Church [online] (see n. 9, above).

22. *Elliot's Improved New-York Double Directory* (New-York: Printed and sold by William Elliot, 1812), 162. This was the only year in which William Jones was listed as running a boardinghouse.

23. NYHS-BV Jumel, entry for August 18, 1810; also see the entry for "William B. Ballow" at 34 Cedar St. in the 1810 edition of *Longworth's American almanac, New-York register, and city directory* (New York: David Longworth, 1810), 98.

24. William's wife, née Eliza Wiggins, worked for a woman named Margaret Brett who did some dressmaking for Eliza. William could have met Wiggins when she accompanied Brett to the house or when she stopped at Stephen's office to pick up ten dollars Brett was owed. See NYHS-BV Jumel, entry for March 31, 1808.

25. Ibid., entry for April 7, 1813.

CHAPTER 9: BLOOMINGDALE

1. Hopper Striker Mott, *The New York of yesterday: A descriptive narrative of old Bloomingdale* (New York and London: G. P. Putnam's Sons, 1908), 87.

2. Ibid., 88–89.

3. Ibid., 87–89.

4. Ibid., 89.

5. J. Fr. Michaud, *Biographie universelle ancienne et moderne*, vol. 9 (Graz, Austria: Akademische Druck- u. Verlagsanstalt, 1966; reprint Paris: C. Desplaces and M. Michaud, 1854), 542–44.

6. "Reminiscences of New-York," *Talisman*, January 1, 1829: 310.

7. Henriette Luce Dillon, marquise de La Tour du Pin Gouvernet, *Journal d'une femme de cinquante ans, 1788–1815*, ed. Aymar de Liedekerke-Beaufort (Paris: Librairie Chapelot, 1913), 2:105.

8. "Reminiscences of New-York," 310.

9. David Lawday, *Napoleon's master: A life of Prince Talleyrand* (London: Jonathan Cape, 2006), 73, 75–76, 87.

10. Charles-Maurice de Talleyrand-Périgord, prince de Bénévent, *Mémoires I: 1754–1807*, ed. Paul-Louis Couchoud and Jean-Paul Couchoud (Paris: Librairie Plon, 1957), 1:243–250; Gouvernet, *Journal d'une femme*, 2:104; Michel Poniatowski, *Tallyrand aux États-Unis 1794–1796* (Paris: Presses de la Cité, 1967), 328–29.

11. *Diary of my travels in America: Louis-Philippe, King of France, 1830–1848*, trans. Stephen Becker (New York: Delacorte Press, 1977), 10, 153, 125, 165; *New York Gazette*, October 10, 1797, [3] (notice of their arrival in New York). For political reasons, the brothers made a convoluted return to Europe in 1799 by way of Havana, the Bahamas, Halifax, and New York, but there is no indication that they remained in the latter city longer than was necessary to board a packet boat to England (*Mémoires de Louis-Philippe, duc d'Orléans, ecrits par lui-même* [Librairie Plon, 1973], 2:440–43).

12. Greatorex, 189.

13. T. E. B. Howarth, *Citizen-king: The life of Louis-Philippe, king of the French* (London: Eyre & Spottiswoode, 1961), 89–90.

14. NYPL, MssCol 717: D'Auliffe [Olive] family letters, 1800–1801. See in particular no. 5:182–83 for the identification of the writer and his wife as the Olives.

15. Edith Pilcher, *Castorland: French refugees in the western Adirondacks 1793–1814* (Harrison, New York: Harbor Hill Books, 1985), 13, 53; Gouvernet, *Journal d'une femme*, 2:83–84, 103–104; François-Alexandre-Frédéric, duc de La Rochefoucault-Liancourt, *Travels through the United States of North America, the country of the Iroquois, and Upper Canada, in the years 1795, 1796, and 1797; with an authentic account of Lower Canada* (London: Printed for R. Phillips, 1799), 2:465.

16. Ancestry.com, *Paris, France & vicinity marriages, 1700–1907* [database online] (Provo, UT: Ancestry.com Operations, Inc., 2008).

17. New York County, Land and Property Records, Deeds, Liber 96:330–33; N.Y. Ct. Ch., Stephen Jumel vs. the Ursuline Convent of the City of New York and the Trustees of St. Patrick's Cathedral, CL-161, 184–251.

18. NYHS-BV Jumel, entries for May 26, 1812, and March 7, 1815.

19. Ibid., entry for May 27, 1809.

20. Ibid., entries for March 31, 1808, and February 4, 1813; *A season in New York 1801: letters of Harriet and Maria Trumbull*, ed. Helen M. Morgan (University of Pittsburgh Press, 1969): 96.

21. NYHS-BV Jumel, entry for February 6, 1812.

22. MJM 4.2, Eliza Jumel to Paul and Eliza Pery, August 27, 1855.

23. Donald Fraser, *A compendium of the history of all nations . . .* (New York: Printed by Henry C. Southwick, 1807).

24. Donald Fraser, *The mental flower garden: or, An instructive and entertaining companion for the fair sex* (New-York: Printed by Southwick & Hardcastle, 1807).

25. NYHS-BV Jumel, entry for July 22, 1813; John McVickar, *The professional years of John Henry Hobart, D.D. being a sequel to his early years* (New York: Protestant Episcopal Press, 1836), 177; *An abridgment of the Book of Martyrs* (New-York: Printed and sold by Samuel Wood, 1810).

26. Geoffrey O'Brien, *The fall of the house of Walworth: A tale of madness and murder in Gilded Age America* (New York: St. Martin's Griffin, 2010), 94.

27. NYHS-BV Jumel, entries for April 7, 1813; July 20, 1813; October 18, 1813; October 25, 1814.

28. Ibid., entries for July 19, 1814, and April 19, 1815.

29. Ibid., entry for April 28, 1815.

30. NYHS-JP, box 1, folder 3, Stephen Jumel to Eliza Jumel, February 5, 1819.

CHAPTER 10: THE FORTUNES OF WAR

1. *Daily Advertiser*, March 22, 1804, [3]; *Spectator*, May 23, 1804, [3].

2. *New-York Gazette*, May 28, 1804, [1] (for her berth on the Old Slip); John Lambert, *Travels through Canada and the United States of North America, in the years 1806, 1807, & 1808*, 2nd ed. (London: Printed for C. Cradock and W. Joy, 1814), 2:62–64 (for the description of the port).

3. *Daily Advertiser*, March 22, 1804, [3].

4. Ibid.

5. Robert P. Watson, *America's first crisis: The War of 1812* (Albany: State University of New York Press, 2014), 12–15.

6. Ibid., 15.

7. *New-York Gazette & General Advertiser*, January 12, 1805, [3] (announcement). BM 710-J, second inventory, filed December 17, 1836, reveals that Desobry had a one-third share in the business and Stephen retained two-thirds.

8. Silvia Marzagalli, "Guerre et création d'un réseau commercial entre Bordeaux et les États-Unis, 1776–1815. L'impossible économie du politique," in *Guerre et économie dans l'espace atlantique du XVIe au XXe siècle*, eds. Silvia Marzagalli and Bruno Marnot, Actes du colloque international du Bordeaux, October 3–4, 2003 (Pessac: Presses Universitaires de Bordeaux, 2006), 385.

9. The most common alternative port that he used was San Sebastián, in Spain. My assessment of the scope of his trading activities is based primarily on a careful reading of shipping reports that appeared in American newspapers between 1799 and 1814. These reports are accessible through the *America's Historical Newspapers* database (Readex).

10. See, for example, purchases listed in NYHS-BV Jumel, as well as NYHS-JP, box 4, folder [6], certificate of goods delivered to Pedro Queheille by the brig *Sally Tracy*, which departed New York for San Sebastián on November 28, 1808. For the use of American beeswax in Europe to make candles, see "American beeswax," *Albany Argus*, December 13, 1869, [2].

11. See, for example, the certificate of goods delivered to Pedro Queheille and a certificate of May 2, 1811, listing goods to be shipped to Bordeaux by Stephen Jumel on the schooner *Maria Louisa* (both in NYHS-JP, box 4, folder [6]).

12. My summary of Stephen's imports is based on dozens of shipping reports printed in New York newspapers between 1799 and 1814 that detail the cargoes he received.

13. Silvia Marzagalli, "The failure of a transatlantic alliance? Franco-American trade, 1783–1815," *History of European Ideas* 34, no. 4 (December 2008), 463.

14. *New York Gazette and General Advertiser*, September 17, 1805, [2]; *New York Gazette and General Advertiser*, August 2, 1805, [2].

15. NYPL-Letter Book, July 6, 1808, to Batard, Sampson, & Sharp; August 23, 1808, to Samuel Ward.

16. NYPL-Letter Book, August 4, 1808, to John Perry [*sic*]; August 4, 1808, to Batard, Sampson, & Sharp; *North American and Mercantile Daily Advertiser*, June 2, 1808, [3] (the latter article notes the exoneration of the cargo, but states that the brig was carried into Portsmouth rather than Plymouth).

17. NYPL-Letter Book, August 4, 1808, to John Perry [*sic*].

18. "An act laying an embargo on all ships and vessels in the ports and harbors of the United States," *New-York Evening Post*, December 26, 1807, [2].

19. New York City Works Progress Administration Writers' Program, *A maritime history of New York*. (1941; repr., Brooklyn, NY: Going Coastal, 2004), 87.

20. NYPL-Letter Book, October 26 and December 5, 1808, to F. Philippon Jr.

21. NYPL-Letter Book, December 5, 1808, to Captain Berry.

22. *New-York Gazette and General Advertiser*, February 11, 1809, [3]; "Government look out," *Augusta* [GA] *Chronicle*, March 11, 1809, 2 (reprinting information from the *New York Public Advertiser*).

23. Heaton, "Non-importation," 185.

24. Ibid., 192.

25. *New-York Commercial Advertiser*, August 3, 1809, [3].

26. NYPL-Letter Book, April 14, 1810, to Gordon S. Mumford.

27. Ibid.; Heaton, "Non-importation," 193.

28. *Commercial Advertiser*, February 1, 1811, [3]; *Poulson's American Daily Advertiser*, February 14, 1811, [3].

29. NYHS-JP, box 4, folder [2], James Berry to Jumel & Desobry, January 19, 1811.

30. *New-Hampshire Gazette*, April 3, 1811, [3].

31. *Repertory*, July 30, 1811, [3].

32. Mary Elizabeth Ruwell, *Eighteenth-century capitalism: The formation of American marine insurance companies* (New York and London: Garland Publishing, Inc., 1993), 99.

33. *New-York Gazette & General Advertiser*, May 7, 1803, [3]; *New-York Gazette & General Advertiser*, May 14, 1811, [1].

34. NYPL-Letter Book, August 3, 1809, to Skiddy.

35. NYPL-Letter Book, August 17, 1809, to Skiddy.

36. NYPL-Letter Book, January 17 and February 16, 1810, to Skiddy.

37. NYPL-Letter Book, June 21, 1810, to Batard, Sampson, & Sharp.

38. NYPL-Letter Book, August 18, 1810, to Batard, Sampson, & Sharp.

39. E.g., Philippon Jr. and Baron Jr. in New Orleans, Mr. Coquillon in Savannah, François Depau in Charleston, Soulage V. André in Norfolk, J. Bujac in Philadelphia, Martin Foäche in Havana. These names were gleaned from NYPL-Letter Book and Jeanne Chase, "War on trade and trade in war: Stephen Jumel and New York maritime com-

merce (1793–1815)," *Bulletin du Centre d'Histoire des Espaces Atlantiques*, nouvelle série, no. 4 (1988), 128.

40. See the NYPL-Letter Book for many letters to Pery. There his name is spelled "John Perry," but I have used the French form of the name throughout for the sake of consistency.

41. E.g., a letter of September 15, 1820, to Monsieur Perry [*sic*] fils ainé, in NYHS-JP, box 1, folder 6, letter book of Stephen Jumel.

42. NYPL-Letter Book, August 4 and September 12, 1808, to John Perry [*sic*].

43. NYPL-Letter Book, October 7, 1809, to John Ducasse, October 9, 1810, to Charles Wright.

44. NYPL-Letter Book, April 16, 1810, to Walter Bowne and John Delafield; November 15, 1810, to Walter Bowne, the Colombian Insurance Company, and John Delafield.

45. "Further disasters by the late storm," *Connecticut Courant*, January 8, 1812, 3; NYHS-AHMC, Jumel, Stephen, wardens' certificate recording a sale of damaged goods from the *Maria Louisa*, January 23, 1812.

46. NYHS-JP, box 4, folder [5], Pedro Quehuille to Jumel and Desobry, February 7, 1813, with added note of April 30, 1813.

47. BM 710-J, examination of Eliza B. Burr, December 17, 1836; NYPL-Letter Book, November 21 and 24, 1808, to John Phelan; August 18 and September 5, 1808, to Thomas B. Cook; Connecticut Historical Society, Hartford Bridge Company Record Book, 1809–1850, Ms 32203, vol. 1.

48. New York County, Land and Property Deeds, Liber 297:86–88; Liber 94:206–8; Liber 96:330–33, and Liber 89:435–41; B-779, box 112, deposition of Nelson Chase.

CHAPTER 11: MOUNT STEPHEN

1. Advertisement for the New York and Albany Mail Stage, in *American Citizen*, January 4, 1810, [1].

2. *Moreau de St. Méry's American journey*, 96 (see chap. 8, n. 3).

3. 1876 Bill of Complaint, letter 24.

4. Shelton, 3–4, 17.

5. Ibid., chapters 3 and 6.

6. Ibid., 128–31.

7. Ibid., 134.

8. Ibid., 135–36.

9. New York County, Land and Property Records, Liber 88:79-86; NYHS-BV Jumel, entry for March 13, 1810. They purchased lots five, seven, and nine through fifteen.

10. New York County, Land and Property Records, Liber 88:86–92.

11. For the property lines as described in this paragraph, see J. B. Holmes, *Map of the Jumel, Murray, Burrill, Dickey and other estates showing the farm lines as they existed 100 years ago and the present streets, drives and boulevards*, 1887 [NYPL, NYC Farm Map 44]; C. J. Hunt, *Map of property in Harlem formally belonging to the Bowers, Smedes, Benson, Bussing, and other estates, showing the topography [sic] old roads, lanes &c. as they existed 100 years ago and the present streets, boulevards, drives &c.*, March 1887 [NYPL, NYC Farm Map 46].

12. *New-York Daily Gazette*, March 24, 1792, [4].

13. Ibid. (for all quotations in this paragraph).

14. "Rambles in the environs. Fort Washington," *The New-Yorker*, June 1, 1839, 167.

15. NYHS-BV Jumel, entries for January 13, 1813; November 1813 (sometime between November 2 and November 5, but the exact date is not recorded); and November 27, 1813.

16. *Mercantile Advertiser*, December 7, 1814, [4].

17. Ibid.

18. *New-York Gazette & General Advertiser*, October 8, 1810, [2].

19. *Mercantile Advertiser*, December 7, 1814, [4] (for all details in this paragraph).

CHAPTER 12: FRANCE BECKONS

1. [Anne Newport Royall], *Sketches of History, Life, and Manners, in the United States* (1826; repr. New York: Johnson Reprint Corporation, 1970), 242 (for all quotations in the paragraph).

2. New York County, Lands and Property Records, Deeds, Liber 97:394–97.

3. *Minutes of the Common Counsel of the City of New York 1784–1831*, vol. 7 (New York: The City of New York, 1917), 136.

4. *New-York Gazette & General Advertiser*, August 18, 1814, [2] (advertisement).

5. Although referred to as "new" in 1814, the only references to it in Stephen's receipt books (NYHS-BV Jumel, entries for April 25 and September 8, 1814) are suggestive of upgrades rather than a major building campaign: payments for painting, installing windows, and ironwork.

6. For a business venture he engaged in with Stephen in 1808, see NYPL-Letter Book, James B. Durand to Jumel & Desobry, December 6, 1808. For his inventory a few years before he moved to 150 Broadway, see *New-York Commercial Advertiser*, February 24, 1807, [2] (advertisement). 150 Broadway is identified as his home address in the city directories from 1818/19 to 1820/21. Thereafter his home address is not provided, but a letter from Stephen to Eliza indicates that he was still their tenant in 1829 (MJM 98.12, Stephen Jumel to Eliza Jumel, January 22, 1829).

7. *New-York Gazette & General Advertiser*, August 18, 1814, [2] (advertisement for the property). His business is listed at 150 Broadway in the city directories from 1813/14 through 1816/17.

8. Stephen paid the Manhattan Company $8.75 for a year's worth of water deliveries beginning May 1, 1814. See NYHS-BV Jumel, entry for January 21, 1815.

9. Stephen's intention not to return to the United States is clear from comments in later letters, e.g., NYHS-JP, box 1, folder 3, Stephen Jumel to Eliza Jumel, June 6 and November 9, 1818.

10. The information in the subsequent paragraphs on the books Eliza checked out comes from the following source: New York Society Library, Circulation Ledger, 1814–1815. Where the specific edition Eliza read could be identified, I have cited it. Most of the identifications were made using the 1813 catalogue of the library's collections (*A catalogue of the books belonging to the New-York Society Library; together with the charter and by-laws of the same* [New-York: Printed by C. S. Van Winkle, 1813]). For Eliza's membership in the library, see New York Society Library, Shareholder Payments, 1807–1814.

11. *Alf Von Duelman* [*sic*]; *Or, the History of the Emperor Philip and his daughters*, translated from the German by Ms. A. E. Booth (London, 1794). Although the book is not listed in the 1813 catalogue of the library, other readers, including Jane Schermerhorn and Anna Maria Schieffelin, checked it out in 1814 and 1815.

12. Patrick Bridgwater, *The German gothic novel in Anglo-German perspective* (Amsterdam and New York: Editions Rodopi, 2013).

13. *Pliny the Younger's letters, from the Latin, with observations*, by the Earl of Orrery (London, 1752); *Pliny the Younger's letters, with occasional remarks*, by W. Melmoth (London, 1786).

14. Joseph F. Kett and Patricia A. McClung, "Book culture in post-revolutionary Virginia," *Proceedings of the American Antiquarian Society* 94, no. 1 (Jan 1, 1984):123, 128, and table 5.0.

15. The circulation ledger refers to "Racine 2d" [i.e., second] rather than "2ème" [i.e., *deux-ième*], implying that she checked out volume 2 of an English rather than French set, but this may have been the fault of a clerk unfamiliar with French numbering. The 1813 catalogue of the library's collection contains only a French and not an English edition of Racine's plays: the three-volume *Oeuvres de J[ean] Racine* (Paris, 1755). The library owned *Racine's Letters to his Son* as well, but this was a single volume, not a multivolume set.

16. *Mercantile Advertiser*, Dec. 30, 1814, [2] (advertisement). The work, titled *Paul and Virginia*, was probably the eponymous three-act opera by Joseph Mazzinghi and William Reeve, which opened at Covent Garden in 1794.

17. Charles Drelincourt, *The Christian's consolations against the fears of death* . . . (Edinburgh: Printed by A. Murray & J. Cochran, 1771).

18. *Ana, ou, Collections de bons mots, contes, pensées détachées, traits d'histoire et anecdotes des hommes célèbres, depuis la renaissance des lettres jusqu'à nos jours* . . . (Amsterdam: Chez Belin, an VII [1799]).

19. B-779, box 112, deposition of Nelson Chase.

20. [George Anderson], *An estimate of the profit and loss of religion* . . . (Edinburgh, 1753).

21. *New-York Gazette & General Advertiser*, January 4, 1811, [2].

22. NYHS-JP, box 1, folder 6, letter book of Stephen Jumel.

23. Ibid., e.g., Stephen Jumel to G. Vespre, August 30, 1820; Stephen Jumel to Benjamin Desobry n.d. [August 30, 31, or September 1, 1820]; Stephen Jumel to Vaillat père et fils, August 27, 1820.

24. N.Y. Sup. Ct., Nelson Chase against William Inglis Chase et al., 1880 C-3, exhibit C, no. 1.

25. *Mercantile Advertiser*, December 7, 1814, [4].

26. Ibid.; *New-York Gazette & General Advertiser*, August 18, 1814, [2].

27. Sale, New York, Swann Galleries, February 1, 1996 (sale 1714), no. 160.

28. Although the Jumels left no records of the name of the ship, shipping reports published in American newspapers show that the *Maria Theresa* was the only vessel that left New York for Bordeaux between May 31 and June 19, 1815. That their port of entry was Bordeaux is made clear in NYHS-JP, box 1, folder 3, Stephen Jumel to Eliza Jumel, June 6, 1818. For the ship's ownership, see *New-York Evening Post*, October 7, 1815, [2].

29. *New-York Gazette & General Advertiser*, May 31, 1815.

30. Mrs. Felton, *American life*, 7 (see chap. 5, n. 1).

31. NYHS-JP, box 1, folder 3, Stephen Jumel to Eliza Jumel, June 6, 1818.

CHAPTER 13: AN IMPERIAL INTERLUDE

1. Greatorex, 243.
2. Ibid.
3. Shelton, 154.
4. Ibid.
5. *Mechanics' Gazette, and Merchants' Daily Advertiser* [Baltimore], August 16, 1815, [3].
6. Stephen Coote, *Napoleon and the Hundred Days* (Da Capo Press, 2004), 262.
7. *New-York Evening Post*, October 7, 1815, [2] (for the ownership of the *Maria Theresa*).
8. Alan Schom, *Napoleon Bonaparte* (New York: HarperCollins Publishers, 1997), 762–64; Frank McLynn, *Napoleon: A biography* (New York: Arcade Publishing, 2002), 630–33.
9. McLynn, *Napoleon: A biography*, 631.
10. *American Beacon and Commercial Diary*, August 22, 1815, [2].
11. Ibid.
12. Schom, *Napoleon Bonaparte*, 765; McLynn, *Napoleon: A biography*, 633–34.

CHAPTER 14: PARIS

1. BM 710-J, examination of Eliza B. Burr, formerly Jumel.
2. NYHS-JP, box 1, Stephen Jumel to Mary Jumel, August 19, 1815.
3. Lady [Sydney] Morgan, *France in 1816*, with appendices by Sir T[homas] C[harles] Morgan (Paris, 1817), pt. 2:50, 52, 56.
4. Ibid., pt. 2:2–3.
5. Ibid., pt. 2:56.
6. NYHS-AHMC, Jumel, Mme. Stephen, unknown to Eliza Jumel, "Mardi [Tuesday]," otherwise n.d., but postmarked April 27, 182[final digit missing].
7. On the basis of correspondence addressed to them, they were at 13, rue de la Paix on January 24, 1816 (NYPL, Jumel, Stephon [*sic*] - Miscellaneous File, Death notice for Count Henri Tascher de la Pagerie); and at the Hôtel de Breteuil (a furnished hotel offering lodgings and meals) in the rue de Rivoli in June 1816 (NYHS-AHMC, Jumel, Mme. Stephen, Adèle Olive to Eliza Jumel, "ce Dimanche au seis [this Sunday in sixteen, i.e., 1816]," with internal reference to the June 1816 Paris exhibition of the trousseau of the Duchess of Berry). Another letter from Adèle (NYHS-AHMC, Jumel, Mme. Stephen), "ce Vendredi au seis [this Friday in sixteen]"), is addressed to Eliza at the Hôtel de Londres, rue Traversière, and probably dates from sometime between the two previously mentioned letters. The earliest datable letter carrying the 40, rue de Cléry address (NYHS-AHMC, Jumel, Mme. Stephen) is an 1816 communication from Adèle, which from internal evidence probably dates from just after the writer's birthday, August 18.
8. NYHS-AHMC, Jumel, Mme. Stephen, Marie-Françoise de Cubières to Eliza Jumel.
9. NYHS-AHMC, Jumel, Mme. Stephen, Adèle Olive to Eliza Jumel, "ce Dimanche au seis [this Sunday in sixteen]."
10. NYHS-AHMC, Jumel, Mme. Stephen, Henriette Olive to Mary Jumel, "jeudi matin [Thursday morning]."

11. Michaud, *Biographie universelle*, 542–44 (see chap. 9, n. 5); *Nouvelle biographie générale depuis les temps plus reculés jusqu'à nos jours*, vol. 11 (1855; repr., Copenhagen: Rosenkilde et Bagger, 1965), 576–77.

12. Ibid. The quotation is from the title of Cubières's treatise, *Discours sur les services rendus à l'agriculture par les femmes* [Paris: Huzard, 1809].

13. Gouvernet, *Journal d'une femme*, 2:83 (see chap. 9, n.7).

14. NYPL, MssCol 717, D'Auliffe [Olive] family letters, no. 3:138.

15. Philip Mansel, *The court of France 1789–1830* (Cambridge: Cambridge University Press, 1988), 19, 98.

16. NYHS-AHMC, Jumel, Mme. Stephen, English transcript of an 1823 letter from the compte d'Abzac to Eliza Jumel; [Jean Baptiste Pierre Julien de] Courcelles, *Histoire généalogique et héraldique des pairs de France, des grands dignitaires de la Couronne, des principales familles nobles de royaume . . .*, vol. 9 (Paris: De l'imprimérie de Plassin, 1828), 81–82 (for the comte d'Abzac) and page 87 for the vicomte d'Abzac, Cubières's associate.

17. NYPL, Jumel, Stephon [*sic*] - Miscellaneous File, Death notice for Count Henri Tascher de la Pagerie; Shelton, 154–55. The count died at the age of thirty in January 1816. The story that his widow lived with the Jumels in Paris for nine years (Shelton, 155) has no foundation.

18. Testu, *Almanach royal, pour les années M. DCCC. XIV et M. DCCC. XV* (Paris: Chez Testu, n.d.), 434.

19. NYHS-AHMC, Jumel, Mme. Stephen, A. Noël to Eliza Jumel (English transcript); J. D***, *Almanach de 25,000 adresses de Paris, pour l'année 1816* (Paris: C. L. F. Panckoucke, January 1816), 428.

20. Ralph Gibson, *A social history of French Catholicism* (London and New York: Routledge, 1989), 189.

21. Yale University Library, Manuscripts and Archives, Samuel Waldron Lambert Papers, Ms 938, Adèle de Cubières to Eliza Jumel, "ce Dimanche matin [this Sunday morning]," asking Eliza to "come see us this morning as you leave the mass." The phrasing suggests that Eliza would be nearby, presumably at the Royal Chapel.

22. *An American lady in Paris 1828–1829: The diary of Mrs. John Mayo*, ed. Mary Mayo Crenshaw (Boston and New York: Houghton Mifflin Company, 1927), 79.

23. Ibid., 37; NYHS-AHMC, Jumel, Mme. Stephen, marquise de la Suze to Eliza Jumel, December 13, 1822.

24. NYHS-AHMC, Jumel, Mme. Stephen, marquise de la Suze to Eliza Jumel, October 27, [1816].

25. NYHS-AHMC, Jumel, Mme. Stephen, marquise de la Suze to Eliza Jumel, January 6, [1817].

26. F.V. Goblet, *Paris, sa banlieue, et itinéraire des administrations, édifices, ministères, monumens, rues de la capital . . .*, 4ème ed. (Paris: Chez Anselin et Pouchard, 1825), 7, 11.

27. *Galignani's Paris guide; or, Stranger's companion through the French metropolis . . .*, 10th ed. (Paris: A. and W. Galignani, 1822), cxxii.

28. NYHS-AHMC, Jumel, Mary E., Anna Selena Hooke to Mary Jumel, May 23, 1818.

29. Shelton, 156.

30. Ibid.

CHAPTER 15: THE COLLECTOR

1. NYHS-AHMC, Jumel, Mme. Stephen, Adèle Olive to Eliza Jumel, dated "ce Vendredi au seis [this Friday in sixteen, i.e., 1816]."

2. NYHS-AHMC, Jumel, Mme. Stephen, Adèle Olive to Eliza Jumel, dated "ce Dimanche au seis [this Sunday in sixteen]."

3. C[laude] G. Fontaine, *Catalogue of original paintings, from Italian, Dutch, Flemish and French masters of the ancient and modern times, selected by the best judges from eminent galleries in Europe, and intended for a private gallery in America* (New York, 1821).

4. Henry Milton, *Letters on the fine arts, written from Paris in the year 1815* (London: Printed for Longman, Hurst, Rees, Orme, and Brown, 1816), 26.

5. Ibid., 195–96.

6. Ibid., 76, 89.

7. Philip Mansel, *Paris between empires: Monarchy and revolution 1814–1852* (New York: Saint Martin's Press, 2001), 154.

8. Sale, Paris, April 23–24, 1816, no. 56; Sale, Paris, June 15, 1816 [Streicker and Barbier collections], no. 4; Sale, Paris, October 7, 1816 [Streicker collection], no. 1 (sold for 24 francs 10 centimes per the Getty Provenance Index sales catalogues database).

9. Thomas Jefferson, one of the greatest eighteenth-century American collectors, owned approximately forty-one paintings, of which the majority were copies (and were knowingly purchased as such). See Seymour Howard, "Thomas Jefferson's art gallery for Monticello," *Art Bulletin* 59, no. 4 (December 1977): 597–600.

10. Sale, Paris, October 17–19, 1816 (Collection of François-Andre Vincent), no. 10; price supplied in the Getty Provenance Index (sale catalogues database). It disappears subsequently from the Parisian art market.

11. "Fine arts," *National Advocate*, September 16, 1817, [2].

12. Mary Bartlett Cowdrey, *American Academy of Fine Arts and American Art Union exhibition record 1816–1852* (New York: New-York Historical Society, 1953), 323, no. 51 (as by "Scholl" [*sic*]); "Fine arts. Review—continued," *National Advocate*, September 20, 1817, [2].

13. *Catalogue d'une belle collection de tableaux des écoles hollandaise et flamande, pierres gravées, mozaïque, miniature, ivoire, bronzes, curiosité ancienne et moderne. Rapportés des voyages d'Italie et de Hollande, par J. A. L. B*** [Barbier]* (Paris, 1816), no. 50 (sold for seventy francs, per an annotation in a copy in the Frick Art Reference Library); *Notice de tableaux des trois écoles composant le cabinet de M*** [Rolland]* (Paris, 1816), no. 45 (sold for sixty francs, per an annotation in a copy in the Rijksbureau voor Kunsthistorische Documentatie, available through the Art Sales Catalogues Online database).

14. *Louis XV in the Dress of Bacchus* is probably identifiable with a Nattier *Portrait of an Aristocratic Youth (possibly the Duc de Chaulnes) as Bacchus* in The John and Mable Ringling Museum of Art in Sarasota, Florida, today. As late as 1949, the picture in the Ringling collection was referred to as a *Presumed Portrait of Louis XV, King of France* by Nattier (William E. Suida, *Catalogue of Paintings in the John & Mable Ringling Museum of Art* [John and Mable Ringling Museum of Art, 1949], no. 380). The donor, John Ringling,

acquired it from a New York collection, that of Edgar Mills, in 1930; see *Catalogue of paintings and portraits to close the estate of Edgar Mills, deceased* (New York: The Alexander Press, [1930]), no. 185, as *Bacchus*, "French school, 18th century." Before that the painting may have been for a time in the collection of the Hon. Thomas B. Carroll, a resident of Troy and Albany, New York (Troy, New York, Young Men's Association, *Catalogue of the Loan Exhibition, being one hundred and forty ancient and modern oil paintings, loaned by the Hon. Thomas B. Carroll for the benefit of the Association* [Troy, NY: Daily Press Steam Printing House, 1878], no. 26, *Louis XIV, as Bacchus*, by Fran. Sneyders [*sic*]).

15. *The diary of James Gallatin: Secretary to Albert Gallatin; A great peace maker 1813–1827,* ed. Count Gallatin (New York: Charles Scribner's Sons, 1916), 100.

16. Mansel, *Paris between empires,* 154–55.

CHAPTER 16: SEPARATE LIVES

1. "Ship news. Port of New-York," *National Advocate,* May 15, 1817, [2].

2. NYHS-JP, box 1, folder 3, Stephen Jumel to Eliza Jumel, April 16, 1817.

3. NYHS-JP, box 1, folder 3, Stephen Jumel to Eliza Jumel, April 18, 1817.

4. NYHS-JP, box 1, folder 3, Stephen Jumel to Eliza Jumel, May 5, 1816 [*sic*] (actually written on May 5, 1817].

5. Ibid.

6. Sean Michael Scanlan, *Narrating nostalgia: Modern literary homesickness in New York narratives, 1809–1925,* PhD diss., University of Iowa (Ann Arbor: ProQuest/UMI, May 2008, UMI Number 3323465), 27, 39; Susan J. Matt, *Homesickness: An American history* (New York: Oxford University Press, 2011), 5–6.

7. NYHS-JP, box 1, folder 3, Stephen Jumel to Eliza Jumel, May 5, 1816 [*sic*] (actually written on May 5, 1817].

8. NYHS-JP, box 1, folder 3, Stephen Jumel to Eliza Jumel, April 16, 1817.

9. Ibid.

10. NYHS-JP, box 1, folder 3, Stephen Jumel to Eliza Jumel, letters of March 6 and June 6, 1818.

11. NYHS-JP, box 1, folder 3, Stephen Jumel to Eliza Jumel, May 12, 1817.

12. 1876 Bill of Complaint, letter 2.

13. NYHS-JP, box 1, folder 3, Stephen Jumel to Eliza Jumel, May 12, 1817. In this letter, he speaks of the expense of paying for the education and maintenance of three young children, most likely referring to the Jones children. In 1866 Eliza Jones (by then Eliza Tranchell) said that Eliza Jumel sent her, her sister, Louisa, and her brother, Stephen, to school in Connecticut in 1817, but it would have been Stephen who paid their tuition.

14. NYHS-JP, box 1, folder 3, Stephen Jumel to Eliza Jumel, May 5, 1816 [*sic*] (actually written on May 5, 1817].

15. Shelton, 156.

16. Ibid., 156–57.

17. Ibid., 157.

18. NYHS-JP, box 1, folder 3, Stephen Jumel to Eliza Jumel, April 16, 1817.

19. NYHS-JP, box 1, folder 3, Stephen Jumel to Eliza Jumel, letters of May 5, 12, and 28, 1817.

20. NYHS-JP, box 1, folder 3, Stephen Jumel to Eliza Jumel, June 6, 1818; NYHS-JP, box 2, folder E, Eliza Jumel to "Mr. Banard" [sic], October 6, 1817.

21. Lillian B. Miller, *Patrons and patriotism: The encouragement of the fine arts in the United States 1790–1860* (Chicago: University of Chicago Press, 1966), 147.

22. Carrie Rebora, "The American Academy of Fine Arts, New York 1802–1842" (PhD diss., City University of New York, 1990), 3, 35–36.

23. NYHS, American Academy of the Fine Arts, Minutes, 25 (October 4, 1817).

24. Ibid., 26, and NYHS, American Academy of the Fine Arts, Correspondence 1: no. 37.

25. NYHS, American Academy of the Fine Arts, Correspondence 1: no. 37.

26. *Commercial Advertiser*, September 1, 1817, [3] (advertisement).

27. "Communication," *New-York Evening Post*, September 2, 1817, [2].

28. "Communicated," *New-York Columbian*, September 3, 1817, [2].

29. The exception was the *Battle of Cavalry*.

30. NYHS, American Academy of the Fine Arts, Correspondence 1: no. 37; "Communication," *New-York Daily Advertiser*, September 3, 1817, [2]; NYHS, American Academy of the Fine Arts, Minutes, December 6, 1817:33.

31. Wayne Craven, "Introduction: Patronage and collecting in America, 1800–1835," in *Mr. Luman Reed's picture gallery: A pioneer collection of American art*, by Ella M. Foshay (Harry N. Abrams, Inc., in association with the New-York Historical Society, 1990), 12–13.

32. Henry Johnson, *Descriptive catalogue of the art collections of Bowdoin College*, 3rd ed. (Brunswick, ME: The Record Press, 1906), 5, 43–44.

33. Jessica Lanier, "Martha Coffin Derby's Grand Tour: 'It's impossible to travel without improvement,'" *Women's Art Journal* 28, no. 1 (Spring–Summer 2007), 41–42.

34. Craven, "Introduction: Patronage and collecting," 14–15.

35. Maurie D. McInnis, "'Picture mania': Collectors and collecting in Charleston," in *In pursuit of refinement: Charlestonians abroad 1740–1860*, exh. cat. by Maurie D. McInnis, in collaboration with Angela D. Mack, with essays by J. Thomas Savage, Robert A. Leath, and Susan Ricci Stebbins (Columbia, SC: University of South Carolina Press, 1999), 44–46.

36. Craven, "Introduction: Patronage and collecting," 17; Rebora, "The American Academy of Fine Arts," 36, 341–42, 347.

37. Craven, "Introduction: Patronage and collecting," 17–18, 11.

38. With the term "private citizen," I exclude art dealers, most notably Michael Paff in New York and the firm of Blake and Cunningham in Boston. The number of paintings they imported is unknown. Joseph Allen Smith might have offered competition to Eliza, but of thirteen cases of paintings he assembled in Italy in the 1790s, most were seized during the French occupation of the Italian peninsula before he could ship them home (McInnis, "'Picture mania': Collectors and collecting in Charleston," 46). Gilmor, another potential rival, had only forty-five paintings in 1817, although he would purchase some

fifty more during a trip to Europe in 1817 to '18 and by 1828 would possess approximately 230 paintings (a mix of American and European works) (Lance Lee Humphries, "Robert Gilmor, Jr. (1774–1848): Baltimore collector and American art patron" [PhD diss., University of Virginia, 1998], 1:183, 185, 318). During the eighteenth century, the largest groups of European paintings reaching the future United States appear to have been collections that practicing artists brought with them. Robert Edge Pine, an English artist, brought along one hundred or more historical paintings, portraits, and prints to Philadelphia in 1782, although it is not clear whether the pictures were painted by him or others. See Peter Benes, "'A few monstrous great Snakes': Daniel Bowen and the Columbian Museum, 1789–1816," *New England collectors and collections*, ed. Peter Benes (Boston: Boston University Scholarly Publications, 2006), 27. Among eighteenth-century American private collectors, the largest collection may have been Thomas Jefferson's, with approximately forty-one paintings and a rich selection of prints, watercolors, and stone and plaster busts (Howard, "Thomas Jefferson's art gallery," 597–600 [see chap. 15, n. 9]). The collections of James Hamilton and his nephew William Hamilton are less well documented, but are unlikely to have exceeded Jefferson's in size. For the Hamiltons, see James A. Jacobs, "William Hamilton and Woodlands: A construction of refinement in Philadelphia," *Pennsylvania Magazine of History and Biography* 130, no. 2 (April 2006): 203–207.

39. Dianne Sachko Macleod, "Eliza Bowen Jumel: Collecting and cultural politics in early America," *Journal of the History of Collections* 13, no. 1 (2001), 68.

40. "Fine arts. Review—continued," *National Advocate*, September 27, 1817, [2].

41. "Review," *National Advocate*, September 12, 1817, [2].

42. "Fine arts. Review—continued," *National Advocate*, October 2, 1817, [2].

43. "Fine arts review—continued," *National Advocate*, September 18, 1817, [2].

44. "Review—continued," *National Advocate*, September 30, 1817, [2]. In addition, Smith complained that the perspective in the painting was inversed: "the head being thrown back, in the act of singing, would naturally *foreshorten* the face—but in this the features are *elongated*." Smith's description matches *King David Playing the Harp*, by Simon Vouet, today in the collection of the Bob Jones University Museum and Gallery.

45. "Fine arts," *National Advocate*, September 16, 1817, [2].

46. "Fine arts. Review—continued," *National Advocate*, September 27, 1817, [2] (for the first three quotations in this paragraph); "Fine arts review—continued," *National Advocate*, September 18, 1817, [2].

47. "Fine arts review—continued," *National Advocate*, September 18, 1817, [2].

48. "Fine arts. Review—continued," *National Advocate*, September 20, 1817, [2].

49. NYHS, American Academy of the Fine Arts, Minutes, November 8, 1817: n.p. (between pages 27 and 28).

50. NYHS, American Academy of the Fine Arts, Minutes, December 6, 1817:33, and Correspondence 1: no. 37 verso.

51. NYHS-JP, box 1, folder 3, Stephen Jumel to Eliza Jumel, March 6, 1818.

52. NYHS-JP, box 1, folder 3, Stephen Jumel to Eliza Jumel, June 6, 1818.

53. Ibid.

54. Ibid.
55. Ibid.

CHAPTER 17: INDECISION

1. "Daily Advertiser Marine List. Port of New-York," *New-York Daily Advertiser*, August 21, 1818, [2].
2. NYHS-JP, box 1, folder 3, Stephen Jumel to Eliza Jumel, July 16, 1818. That he still occupied the rue de Cléry address is clear from a letter book he used during this time period (NYHS-JP, box 1, folder 6, letter book of Stephen Jumel; see, for example, the letter from Stephen Jumel to a Monsieur Laveau, September 5, 1820).
3. NYHS-JP, box 1, folder 3, Stephen Jumel to Eliza Jumel, November 9, 1818.
4. NYHS-JP, box 1, folder 3, Stephen Jumel to Eliza Jumel, July 27, 1819.
5. NYHS-JP, box 1, folder 3, Stephen Jumel to Eliza Jumel, January 20, 1819.
6. NYHS-JP, box 1, folder 3, Stephen Jumel to Eliza Jumel, January 23, 1819.
7. NYHS-JP, box 1, folder 3, Stephen Jumel to Eliza Jumel, February 5, 1819.
8. Ibid.
9. NYHS-JP, box 1, folder 3, Stephen Jumel to Eliza Jumel, March 23, 1819.
10. Ibid.
11. *Mercantile Advertiser*, March 1, 1819, [2] (advertisement for a coachman and housemaid).
12. NYHS-JP, box 1, folder 3, Stephen Jumel to Eliza Jumel, March 23, 1819.
13. Clyde A. Haulman, "The Panic of 1819: America's first great depression," *Financial History* (Winter 2010): 22.
14. Ibid., 20–22.
15. Samuel Resneck, "The depression of 1819, a social history," *American Historical Review* 39, no. 1 (October 1933), 42.
16. Ibid.
17. NYHS-JP, box 1, folder 3, Stephen Jumel to Eliza Jumel, July 27, 1819.
18. Ibid. (for all of the quotations in this paragraph).
19. NYHS-JP, box 1, folder 3, Stephen Jumel to Eliza Jumel, September 1, 1819; NYHS-JP, box 1, folder 6, letter book of Stephen Jumel, letter to James B. Durand, July 30, 1820, and letter to Monsieur Labat, September 5, 1820.
20. NYHS-JP, box 1, folder 3, Stephen Jumel to Eliza Jumel, September 1, 1819; NYHS-JP, box 1, folder 6, letter book of Stephen Jumel, Stephen Jumel to James B. Durand, July 30, 1820.
21. NYHS-JP, box 1, folder 3, Stephen Jumel to Eliza Jumel, September 1, 1819.
22. Ibid.
23. NYHS-JP, box 1, folder 6, letter book of Stephen Jumel, Stephen Jumel to Monsieur Fouache et Fils, August 27, 1820.
24. Clarence Edward Macartney and Gordon Dorrance, *The Bonapartes in America* (Philadelphia: Dorrance and Company, 1939), 86–90.
25. New York, Silo's Fifth Avenue Art Galleries, *Catalogue of the Jumel Collection of Napoleonics [sic] relics and other historical articles removed from the famous Jumel Mansion* (1916), no. 131.

26. NYHS-AHMC, Jumel, Madame Stephen, typewritten English transcript of a letter from Joseph Bonaparte to Eliza Jumel.

27. *Mercantile Advertiser*, April 28, 1820, [2] (the advertisement appeared six more times through May 18, 1820); *New-York Evening Post*, February 20, 1821, [4].

28. *New-York Evening Post*, March 19, 1821, [3] (advertisement for the auction).

29. Fontaine, *Catalogue of original paintings* (see chap. 15, n. 3).

30. *Letters from John Pintard . . . II: 1821–1827*, 30–32 (see chap. 7, n. 9).

31. Resneck, "The depression of 1819," 33.

32. *Letters from John Pintard . . . II: 1821–1827*, 31.

33. Ibid.

34. For the sale of Fesch's paintings, which took place in June 1816, see *Catalogue de tableaux des trois écoles . . .* (Paris: Chez Thiesson et al., [1816]). No. 47 in the Fesch catalogue is probably identifiable with Eliza's *Tap room or tabagia* by Thomas van Apshoven (Fontaine, *Catalogue of original paintings*, no. 208), and it is possible that no. 127 could be her *St. Marguerite* by Parmeggiano (Fontaine, *Catalogue of original paintings*, no. 182). Fesch also owned a portrait of Madame de Montespan by Pierre Mignard (no. 87). While it is tempting to identify this with Eliza's *Miss De Montaspan* [*sic*] by Mignard (Fontaine, *Catalogue of original paintings*, no. 194), the descriptions of the latter provided by reviewers of the 1817 exhibition ("Review," *American Monthly Magazine and Critical Review* 1, no. 6 (October 1817), 456; "Review," *National Advocate*, September 12, 1817, [2]) do not match the description of Fesch's painting provided in the 1816 sale catalogue, making it clear that her portrait of Montespan was not the one owned by the cardinal.

35. *New-York Evening Post*, June 13, 1821, [3] (advertisement placed by M. Ward & Co.).

36. *National Advocate*, June 14, 1821, [3] (advertisement placed by M. Ward & Co.).

37. Silo's Fifth Avenue Art Galleries, *Catalogue of the Jumel Collection*, nos. 308, 313, 314, 318, 319, 320, 321, 323, 328, 330, and possibly 315 and 316, identifiable with, respectively, Fontaine, *Catalogue of original paintings*, nos. 91, 89, 137, 16, 110, 90, 76, 7, 46, 148, 136, and 80. A nineteenth-century French cut-glass chandelier today in the parlor of the mansion could have been the one offered for purchase at the Park Hall Auction Room. In addition, a set of ten mahogany chairs at the mansion might have been part of the group of three dozen chairs offered for sale.

38. *New-York Evening Post*, June 16, 1821, [2].

CHAPTER 18: PLACE VENDÔME

1. NYHS-JP, box 1, folder 6, letter book of Stephen Jumel.

2. 1876 Bill of Complaint, letter 9.

3. 1876 Bill of Complaint, letters 2, 2a, 3, 5–7, etc.

4. ADL, 4 Q 1 445 (May 22, 1821).

5. *Galignani's Paris guide*, 241–44, 246. (see chap. 14, n. 27)

6. Jacques Hillairet, *Dictionnaire historique des rues de Paris* (Paris: Les Éditions de Minuit, 1997), 616.

7. Ibid.

8. Michaud, *Biographie universelle*, 543 (see chap. 9, n. 5).

9. NYHS-AHMC, Jumel, Mme. Stephen, Adèle Olive to Eliza Jumel, headed "à Larue ce Mardi matin [at Larue this Tuesday morning]."

10. NYHS-AHMC, Jumel, Mme. Stephen, Madame Butler to Eliza Jumel, "Samedi le 4 [Saturday the 4th]."

11. Shelton, 161.

12. Mansel, *The court of France*, 123, 127–28 (see chap. 14, n. 15).

13. Shelton, 162–63.

14. Mansel, *The court of France*, 124, 127–28, 159.

15. NYHS-JP, box 3, folder 3, Dᵉⁱ d'Egvilly to Eliza Jumel; *Almanach royal, pour l'an M DCCC XXVI* (Paris: Chez A. Guyot et Scribe, 1826), 53.

16. Shelton, 163–64.

17. 1876 Bill of Complaint, letter 3.

18. Ibid.

19. NYHS-AHMC, Jumel, Mary E., Mary Jumel to Maria Jones, n.d.

20. 1876 Bill of Complaint, letter 3.

21. Ibid.

22. Ibid.

23. Ibid.

24. Ibid.

25. Washington Irving, *Journals and notebooks: Volume III, 1819–1827*, ed. Walter A. Reichart (Madison: University of Wisconsin Press, 1970), 430.

26. BM 710-J.

CHAPTER 19: THE PANIC OF 1825

1. Larry Neal, "The financial crisis of 1825 and the restructuring of the British financial system," *Federal Reserve Bank of St. Louis Review* 80, no. 3 (May/June 1998): 64–65; Michael D. Bordo, "Commentary," *Federal Reserve Bank of St. Louis Review* 80, no. 3 (May/June 1998): 79.

2. Bordo, "Commentary," 78; Neal, "The financial crisis of 1825," 64.

3. "Money," *Niles' Weekly Register*, September 10, 1825, 23.

4. "Cotton—its supply and demand," *Niles' Weekly Register*, September 24, 1825, 52.

5. "Money—stocks—banks," *Niles' Weekly Register*, December 3, 1825, 210.

6. "Foreign news. From London papers of December 8," *Niles' Weekly Register*, January 21, 1826, 327; Carlos Marichal, *A century of debt crises in Latin America: From independence to the Great Depression, 1820–1930* (Princeton: Princeton University Press, 1989), 44; Neal, "The financial crisis of 1825," 65.

7. "Foreign news," *Niles' Weekly Register*, January 21, 1826, 327.

8. "Latest news. By an arrival at New York, with London papers to the 3rd January," *Niles' Weekly Register*, February 18, 1826, 404; Neal, "Financial crisis of 1825," 65.

9. 1876 Bill of Complaint, letter 5.

10. Marichal, *Century of debt crises*, 46.

11. "Later foreign news," *Niles' Weekly Register*, April 15, 1826, 117.

12. "Foreign news," *Niles' Weekly Register*, August 26, 1826, 449.

13. Marichal, *Century of debt crises*, 47–49.

14. Ibid., 51, 53–54, 59.

15. 1876 Bill of Complaint, letter 8.

16. Shelton, 165–66.

17. NYHS-JP, box 1, folder 1, Eliza Jumel to Stephen Jumel, received October 4, 1826.

18. N.Y. Sup. Ct., Nelson Chase vs. William Inglis Chase et al., 1880 C-3 (1880), exhibit C, no. 9 (this is a duplicate of exhibit C, no. 2, which is misdated January 13, 1824).

19. N.Y. Sup. Ct., Nelson Chase vs. William Inglis Chase et al., 1880 C-3 (1880), exhibit C, no. 4.

20. PUL Fuller, box 2, folder 83, Eliza Jumel to Stephen Jumel, December 1, 1826.

21. Ibid.

22. PUL Fuller, box 2, folder 83, Eliza Jumel to Stephen Jumel, September 21, 1826.

23. Ibid.

24. Ibid.

25. NYHS-JP, box 1, folder 1, Eliza Jumel to Stephen Jumel, January 1, 1827.

26. NYHS-JP, box 1, folder 1, Eliza Jumel to Stephen Jumel, received October 4, 1826.

27. PUL Fuller, box 2, folder 83, Eliza Jumel to Stephen Jumel, December 1, 1826.

28. Ibid.

29. NYHS-JP, box 1, folder 1, Eliza Jumel to Stephen Jumel, received October 4, 1826.

30. NYHS-JP, box 1, folder 1, Eliza Jumel to Stephen Jumel, November 5, 1826.

31. NYHS-JP, box 1, folder 1, Eliza Jumel to Stephen Jumel, December 5, 1826.

CHAPTER 20: ALL ABOUT MONEY

1. PUL Fuller, box 2, folder 83, Eliza Jumel to Stephen Jumel, December 1, 1826.

2. PUL Fuller, box 2, folder 84, Eliza Jumel to Stephen Jumel, September 21, 1826.

3. NYHS-JP, box 1, folder 3, Stephen Jumel to Eliza Jumel, October 14, 1826.

4. Ibid.

5. Ibid.

6. Ibid.

7. N.Y. Ct. Ch., Stephen Jumel vs. the Ursuline Convent of the City of New York and the Trustees of Saint Patrick's Cathedral, CL-161. The original deal for the land was with Saint Peter's Church, but Saint Patrick's was dragged into the proceeding because it was incorporated briefly with Saint Peter's (between 1813 and 1817).

8. Ibid.; NYHS-JP, box 1, folder 3, Stephen Jumel to Eliza Jumel, October 14, 1826.

9. Ancestry.com, *Paris, France & Vicinity Deaths, 1707–1907* [database online] (Provo, UT: Ancestry.com Operations, Inc., 2008), reconstituted death certificate for Victor Prosper [Benjamin] Desobry; 1876 Bill of Complaint, letter 20.

10. 1876 Bill of Complaint, letter 20.

11. Ibid.

12. Ibid.

13. 1876 Bill of Complaint, letter 13; ADL, 3 U1 / 293, no. 3259.

14. 1876 Bill of Complaint, letter 11.

15. ADL, 3 U1 / 293, fol. 77–78.

16. 1876 Bill of Complaint, letter 11.

17. Ibid.

18. Ibid.

19. MJM 4.7, two English translations of an undated letter from Eliza Jumel to Stephen Jumel.

20. PUL Fuller, box 2, folder 84, Eliza Jumel to Stephen Jumel, September 21, 1826.

21. Ibid.

22. Shelton, 162.

23. Silo's Fifth Avenue Art Galleries, *Catalogue of the Jumel Collection*, nos. 99, 130 (see chap. 17, n. 25). Unfortunately the content of the two letters is not recorded.

24. PUL Fuller, box 2, folder 84, Eliza Jumel to Stephen Jumel, September 21, 1826.

25. Ibid.

26. Ibid.

27. PUL Fuller, box 2, folder 83, Eliza Jumel to Stephen Jumel, December 1, 1826.

28. NYHS-JP, box 1, folder 1, Eliza Jumel to Stephen Jumel, February 15, 1827.

29. NYHS-JP, box 1, folder 1, Eliza Jumel to Stephen Jumel, January 1, 1827.

30. Ibid.

31. Ibid.

32. BM 710-J. The mortgage agreement was drawn up in Paris on September 16, 1824.

33. Connecticut Historical Society, Hartford Bridge Company Record Book (see chap. 10, n. 47).

34. The company's record book shows that Stephen was paid quarterly dividends on forty shares from the issuance of the first dividend on July 2, 1811, but beginning with the quarterly payment of October 1, 1821, the block of shares is listed as belonging to Lesparre.

35. NYHS-JP, box 1, folder 1, Eliza Jumel to Stephen Jumel, November 5, 1826.

36. PUL Fuller, box 2, folder 83, Eliza Jumel to Stephen Jumel, December 1, 1826.

37. NYHS-JP, box 1, folder 1, Eliza Jumel to Stephen Jumel, January 1, 1827.

38. 1876 Bill of Complaint, letter 28.

39. 1876 Bill of Complaint, letter 24.

40. NYHS-JP, box 2, folder A, James A. Morse to Eliza Jumel, February 14, 1827.

41. NYHS-JP, box 1, folder 1, Eliza Jumel to Stephen Jumel, February 15, 1827.

42. NYHS-JP, box 1, folder 1, Eliza Jumel to Stephen Jumel, May 1, 1827.

43. Ibid.

44. PUL Fuller, box 2, folder 86, Stephen Jumel to Eliza Jumel, October 14, 1827.

45. PUL Fuller, box 2, folder 87, Stephen Jumel to Eliza Jumel, December 23, 1827.

CHAPTER 21: DECEPTION

1. 1876 Bill of Complaint, letter 15.

2. NYHS-JP, box 1, folder 1, Eliza Jumel to Stephen Jumel, May 1, 1827.

3. 1876 Bill of Complaint, letter 19.

4. 1876 Bill of Complaint, letter 20.

5. 1876 Bill of Complaint, 14.

6. Ibid., 26.

7. 1876 Bill of Complaint, letter 37.

8. Irving, *Journals and notebooks*, 430 (see chap. 18, n. 25).

9. 1876 Bill of Complaint, letter 37.

10. Norma Basch, *In the eyes of the law: Women, marriage, and property in nineteenth-century New York* (Ithaca: Cornell University Press, 1982), 63, 78–79; Hendrik Hartog, *Man and wife in America: A history* (Cambridge, MA: Harvard University Press, 2000), 170–72.

11. 1876 Bill of Complaint, letter 37.

12. Ibid.

13. N.Y. Sup. Ct., Nelson Chase vs. William Inglis Chase et al., 1880 C-3 (1880), exhibit C, nos. 5, 6, 7, 8, 10, 11 (identical copy of 8).

14. B-779, box 112, deposition of Nelson Chase.

15. Basch, *In the eyes of the law*, 16–17, 75, 89.

16. Ibid., 89.

17. PUL Fuller, box 2, folder 83, Eliza Jumel to Stephen Jumel, December 1, 1826.

18. NYHS-JP, box 1 folder 3, Stephen Jumel to Eliza Jumel, August 19, 1826.

Chapter 22: The Reunion

1. *New-York Spectator*, July 29, 1828, [1]; 1876 Bill of Complaint, letter 24. According to the *Spectator*, there were only eighty-four passengers in steerage.

2. 1876 Bill of Complaint, letter 24.

3. 1876 Bill of Complaint, letter 34.

4. MJM, 4.7, two English translations of an undated letter from Eliza Jumel to Stephen Jumel.

5. Ibid.

6. N.Y. Sup. Ct., Nelson Chase vs. William Inglis Chase et al., 1880 C-3 (1880), exhibit C, no. 19.

7. 1876 Bill of Complaint, letter 35.

8. 1876 Bill of Complaint, letter 25.

9. Jennifer L. Goloboy, "Business friendships and individualism in a mercantile class of citizens in Charleston," in *Class matters: Early North America and the Atlantic world*, eds. Simon Middleton and Billy G. Smith (Philadelphia: University of Pennsylvania Press, 2008), 109–111, 118–19.

10. 1876 Bill of Complaint, letter 25.

11. 1876 Bill of Complaint, letter 24.

12. NYHS-JP, box 2, folder B, receipt of passage to Charleston, November 27, 1828; NYHS-JP, box 3, folder E, receipt for a month's rent, Charleston, January 30, 1829.

13. 1876 Bill of Complaint, letter 24.

14. MJM 98.12, Stephen Jumel to Eliza Jumel, January 22, 1829 (for the details and quotations in this and the prior two paragraphs).

15. This quotation and the other details on hiring and pay in this paragraph are found in NYHS-JP, box 1, folder 11, business notebook of Stephen Jumel.
16. *New-York Evening Post*, February 13, 1830, [3].
17. *New-York Evening Post*, October 12, 1830, [1].

CHAPTER 23: AN ARRANGED MARRIAGE

1. B-779, box 112, deposition of Nelson Chase.
2. B-779, box 112, deposition of Nelson Chase (for the date of Mary's birth). Mary turned thirty on September 6, 1831.
3. B-779, box 112, deposition of Nelson Chase (for the details and quotation in this paragraph).
4. Ibid.
5. Ibid.
6. 1873 Transcript of Record, 306.
7. FamilySearch.org (record of the marriage of Nelson Chase and Hattie Crombie Dunning, August 12, 1868) (for the names of his parents); B-779, box 112, deposition of Nelson Chase.
8. B-779, box 112, deposition of Nelson Chase.
9. Gary B. Nash, "The social origins of antebellum lawyers," in *Three centuries of social mobility*, ed. Pessen, 94 (see prologue, n. 6); Samuel Haber, *The quest for authority and honor in the American professions, 1750–1900* (Chicago and London: University of Chicago Press, 1991), 87.
10. Haber, *Quest for authority*, 87.
11. He was born on November 11, 1811 (1873 Transcript of Record, 305).
12. BM 710-J, examination of Nelson Chase, November 21, 1837.
13. B-779, box 112, deposition of Nelson Chase.
14. B-779, box 112, deposition of Nelson Chase. Whether Seth Chase was related to Nelson is unknown.
15. *Daily Albany Argus*, January 19, 1832, [2].
16. B-779, box 112, deposition of Nelson Chase.
17. Ibid.
18. 1873 Transcript of Record, 305–306.
19. B-779, box 112, deposition of Nelson Chase.
20. Ibid.
21. Ibid.
22. Ibid.
23. Ibid.
24. Ibid.
25. Ibid.
26. 1876 Bill of Complaint, letters 25 and 26; NYHS-AHMC, Jumel, Stephen, Étienne, called Ulysses, Jumel to Stephen Jumel, July 12, 1829, and August 1, 1830.
27. On a trip to the Hudson Highlands with the Chases in late June 1832, Eliza traveled south into Manhattan and across the Hudson on the Hoboken ferry (B-779, box 112, deposition of Nelson Chase). The only reason to structure the trip that way, instead of traveling

straight north, was if she were picking up the Chases in New Jersey. Although Nelson claimed that they all began the trip at the mansion (ibid.), his statement was made many years later when he was trying to show that he and his wife had been very close to Eliza. He would not have been eager to admit that they had moved from the mansion to lodgings in New Jersey soon after their marriage.

28. B-779, box 112, deposition of Nelson Chase.

29. Ibid.; *New-York Spectator*, May 25, 1832, [3] (death notice).

CHAPTER 24: ENTER AARON BURR

1. For these details of Burr's appearance and demeanor, see Matthew L. Davis, *Memoirs of Aaron Burr. With miscellaneous selections from his correspondence* (New York: Harper & Brothers, 1837), 1:181–82; Samuel L. Knapp, *The life of Aaron Burr* (New York: Wiley & Long, 1835), 64; Charles Burr Todd, *Life of Colonel Aaron Burr, Vice President of the United States* (New York: S. W. Green, Printer, 1879), 116; *Newburyport* [Massachusetts] *Herald*, July 19, 1833, 5.

2. Parton, 661-62.

3. Ibid., 662.

4. B-779, box 112, deposition of Nelson Chase; *History of Columbia County, New York: With illustrations and biographical sketches of some of its prominent men and pioneers* (Philadelphia: Everts & Ensign, 1878): 305–306.

5. James Stuart, *Three years in North America* (New York: J. & J. Harper, 1833), 1:190.

6. Charles E. Rosenberg, *The cholera years: The United States in 1832, 1849, and 1866* (Chicago: University of Chicago Press, 1987), 35.

7. B-779, box 112, deposition of Nelson Chase.

8. "The Jumel estate case," *Providence Evening Press*, February 1, 1873, [3]. In this much later testimony during the Jumel estate case, Nelson Chase indicated that the move to Saratoga occurred in August, but it is likely that he misremembered. The family would not have returned to the New York region before the announcement of the abatement of the epidemic at the end of August, and the trip to Saratoga was subsequent to the initial return. Also see note 20 below for a transaction that took place on September 13, which Eliza is said to have made immediately after her arrival in Saratoga.

9. Stuart, *Three years in North America*, 1:129.

10. Ibid., 1:129–30.

11. Ibid., 1:131–32.

12. "Preparations at Saratoga," *American Traveler*, March 20, 1832, [2].

13. "Rail road from Albany to Saratoga Springs," *Commercial Advertiser*, July 9, 1832, [2].

14. *Independence* [Poughkeepsie, New York], July 11, 1832, [4]; "The springs," *Saratoga Sentinel*, July 31, 1832, [2]; *New-York Evening Post*, August 23, 1832, [2].

15. B-779, box 112, deposition of Nelson Chase.

16. Ibid.; Stuart, *Three Years in North America*, 1:132.

17. B-779, box 112, deposition of Nelson Chase.

18. Saratoga County Clerk, Civil Court Files, 1825–1900, box A 35, Eliza Jumel vs. Jonathan Hall and John Hall. For the previous owner, Jose Villalave, see, for example, advertisements in: *Boston Gazette*, May 2, 1814, [3]; *Boston Daily Advertiser*, May 5,

1814, [3]; *New-York Evening Post*, May 24, 1814, [2]. By 1826, he had adopted the French honorific "monsieur" rather than the Spanish "signor" (i.e., señor) or "don"; compare the advertisements in the *Evening Post* and *Boston Daily Advertiser* with these later examples: *National Advocate*, December 18, 1826, [3]; *Saratoga Sentinel*, June 25, 1833, 3.

19. Eliza Jumel vs. Jonathan Hall and John Hall.
20. B-779, box 112, deposition of Nelson Chase; B-779, box 113, deposition of Nelson Chase; Saratoga County Clerk, Deeds Book 10, 138–40 (September 13, 1832).

CHAPTER 25: A CALCULATED COURTSHIP

1. "The Jumel estate case," *New York Herald*, January 30, 1873, 8; B-779, box 112, deposition of Nelson Chase.
2. Parton, 662.
3. Parton, 663 (for both quotations).
4. Ibid.
5. John E. Stillwell, *The history of the Burr portraits: Their origin, their dispersal and their reassemblage* (1928), 1–2; Davis, *Memoirs of Aaron Burr*, 1:182; Todd, *Life of Colonel Aaron Burr*, 124 (see chap. 24, n. 1); Milton Lomask, *Aaron Burr: The conspiracy and years of exile 1805–1836* (New York: Farrar, Straus and Giroux, 1982), 373; Todd, *Life of Colonel Aaron Burr*, 116, 119.
6. Todd, *Life of Colonel Aaron Burr*, 119 (see chap. 24, n. 1).
7. "Madame Jumel's estate," *New York Herald*, November 13, 1866, 5.
8. For Burr's striking ability to read others and imply what they wished to hear, see David O. Stewart, *American emperor: Aaron Burr's challenge to Jefferson's America* (New York: Simon & Schuster, 2011), 297; Joseph Wheelan, *Jefferson's vendetta: The pursuit of Aaron Burr and the judiciary* (New York: Carroll & Graff Publishers, 2005), 84.
9. Parton, 663.
10. Parton, 663 (for all quotations in this paragraph).
11. Henry Fielding, *The history of Tom Jones, a foundling*, ed. Thomas Keymer and Alice Wakely (Penguin Books, 2005), 66.
12. "The Jumel case—the defendant's cross examination continued," *New York Times*, Feb. 1, 1873, 8.
13. Milton Lomask, *Aaron Burr: The years from Princeton to vice president 1756–1805* (New York: Farrar, Straus and Giroux, 1979), 3–4, 39–42, 48–50, 53–56, 61–63, 73–75, 119, 134–35, 141–44, 200.
14. Samuel L. Knapp, *Life of Aaron Burr*, 84–85 (see chap. 24, n. 1).
15. Ibid., 85; Wheelan, *Jefferson's vendetta*, 62–63.
16. Wheelan, *Jefferson's vendetta*, 59, 62–63.
17. Stewart, *American emperor*, 18–19, 25.
18. Ron Chernow, *Alexander Hamilton* (New York: Penguin Press, 2004), 644–45; Wheelan, *Jefferson's vendetta*, 77–79, 82.

19. Wheelan, *Jefferson's vendetta*, 35–37, 84–86. It has been rumored that Burr and Hamilton had been rivals over the favors of Eliza Jumel before her marriage to Stephen, but these slurs, which don't appear in print until the twentieth century, have no grounding in fact. Eliza's marriage to Burr, added to the long-standing rumors about her virtue before her first marriage, probably prompted the imaginative to see her retrospectively as one cause of the two politicians' enmity.

20. Roger G. Kennedy, *Burr, Hamilton, and Jefferson: A study in character* (New York: Oxford University Press, 2000), 80–81.

21. Nancy Isenberg, *Fallen Founder: The Life of Aaron Burr* (New York: Viking, 2007), 256–57.

22. Knapp, *Life of Aaron Burr*, 89.

23. Kennedy, *Burr, Hamilton, and Jefferson*, 111.

24. Ibid., 112, 128–29, 184.

25. Wheelan, *Jefferson's vendetta*, 120. He appears to have considered Spanish-owned East Florida (approximately today's state of Florida) as a target also (Kennedy, *Burr, Hamilton, and Jefferson*, 183–84). That prospect, however, would have seemed less tempting after the Jefferson administration began quiet negotiations to purchase East and West Florida (the latter now the southern portions of Louisiana, Mississippi, and Alabama) in November 1805, although perhaps of interest again after the talks collapsed in early 1806 (Wheelan, *Jefferson's vendetta*, 129, 134).

26. Wheelan, *Jefferson's vendetta*, 132.

27. Ibid., 120. Stewart believes that Burr did seriously consider setting up a separate republic west of the Appalachians, but realized by 1805 that there weren't enough Westerners who favored the move, given that the United States had acquired New Orleans, which provided an outlet for trade down the Mississippi, a burning economic issue in the West (Stewart, *American emperor*, 114–15, 141). However, Kennedy points out that Burr swore to respected contemporaries, including William Henry Harrison, Henry Clay, and Andrew Jackson, that he didn't intend secession, and French intelligence agents indicated that Burr himself had never expressed any desire to break up the United States (Kennedy, *Burr, Hamilton, and Jefferson*, 143–44).

28. Wheelan, *Jefferson's vendetta*, 120, 132.

29. Ibid., 148.

30. Knapp, *Life of Aaron Burr*, 111.

31. Wheelan, *Jefferson's vendetta*, 151, 237, 246.

32. Aaron Burr, *The private journal of Aaron Burr reprinted in full from the original manuscript in the library of Mr. William K. Bixby, of St. Louis, Mo. with an introduction, explanatory notes, and a glossary* (Rochester, NY, 1903): 2:434–36.

33. Lomask, *Aaron Burr: Conspiracy*, 392.

34. For example, see Knapp's *Life of Aaron Burr*, published in 1835, for a sympathetic treatment of Burr's career. Davis, in his *Memoirs of Aaron Burr*, published two years later (a year after Burr's death), takes Burr's side in the treason trial and conflict with Jefferson, e.g., 2:138–39.

35. E.g., N.Y. Mayor's Ct., Joshua D. Waterman and Ralph Wells vs. Aaron Burr, 1820-#1002; N.Y. Mayor's Ct., Patrick Denn vs. Aaron Burr, 1820-#258; N.Y. Com. Pl., William L. Vandevoort and John S. Van Winkle vs. Aaron Burr, 1823-#908; N.Y. Com. Pl., Francis J. Berier vs. Aaron Burr, 1825-#48; N.Y. Com. Pl., Robert A. Caldcleugh vs. Aaron Burr, 1826-#242; N.Y. Super. Ct., Thomas C. Morton and James Paton vs. Aaron Burr, 1831-#294; N.Y. Super. Ct., Thomas McKie vs. Aaron Burr, 1832-#86; N.Y. Super. Ct., Anne C. Cannon vs. Aaron Burr, 1833-#114; N.Y. Com. Pl., Hickson Sarles vs. Aaron Burr, 1835-#1022.

36. Parton, 604–605.

37. Burr, *Private journal*, 450.

38. Ibid., 448.

39. Aaron Burr, *Political correspondence and public papers of Aaron Burr*, ed. Mary-Jo Kline et al. (Princeton, NJ: Princeton University Press, 1983), 2:1217.

40. N.Y. Com. Pl., Helen M. Catlin and others vs. Aaron Burr, 1834-#282.

41. N.Y. Super. Ct., Anne C. Cannon vs. Aaron Burr, 1833-#114.

42. Ibid. The young man in question, Charles Burdett, was probably one of Burr's illegitimate children; see Burr, *Political correspondence*, 2:1196–97.

43. N.Y. Ct. Ch., Aaron Burr vs. John Pelletreau and others, BM 2759B, with additional details in the bill of complaint of a subsequent suit, N.Y. Ct. Ch., Aaron Burr vs. Benjamin Waldron and Sally his wife, John L. Wilson and Rebecca his wife, BM 2758B.

44. Samuel H. Wandell and Mead Minnigerode, *Aaron Burr: A biography compiled from rare, and in many cases unpublished, sources* (New York and London: G. P. Putnam's Sons, 1925), 324.

45. Stillwell, *History of the Burr portraits*, 64 (see chap. 25, n. 5).

46. B-779, box 112, deposition of Nelson Chase. Although this statement was made in 1880, it is consistent with a declaration made decades earlier that he did not become intimately acquainted with Aaron Burr until "the spring of 1833"; see N.Y. Ct. Ch., Alexander L. Botts vs. Aaron Burr, BM 1710B, Part 2, deposition of Nelson Chase, March 30, 1836. There was no reason for Chase to lie in the 1836 deposition, since no legal point turned on the date of his acquaintance with Burr.

47. N.Y. Ct. Ch., Alexander L. Botts vs. Aaron Burr, BM 1710B, Part 2, deposition of Nelson Chase, March 30, 1836.

48. Liber 368:310.

49. This letter survives in two versions. One, dated June 30, seems to be a copy that Eliza kept for herself (NYHS-AHMC, Jumel, Madame Stephen, Eliza Jumel to Lesparre Sante [*sic*], June 30, 1833). The other is an English transcription of the version received by Lesparre. If the transcription is correct, the letter Lesparre received was dated June 28 (1876 Bill of Complaint, letter 38). Although the writer signed herself "Eliza Jumel," her name until July 1, and Burr said she showed him the letter before the marriage (Liber 368:307), it could also have been written just after the marriage and intentionally misdated, whether to June 30 or June 28. The circumstances surrounding the letter's composition are described more fully in chapter 29.

CHAPTER 26: AN OPTIMISTIC BEGINNING

1. *New-York Spectator*, July 8, 1833, [1].
2. Dunlap, *Diary*, 3:718 (see chap. 6, n. 13).
3. 1873 Transcript of Record, 306.
4. Parton, 663; *New-York Spectator*, July 8, 1833, [1].
5. Greatorex, 244 (for the location of the wedding, but wrongly stating that Aaron and Eliza were married by the same clergyman who had performed Burr's first marriage).
6. John D. Livingston, *Hymns, with the catechism, confession of faith, and liturgy of the Reformed Dutch Church in America* (Philadelphia: GW Mentz, 1829), 603–607.
7. Ibid.
8. Ibid.
9. Parton, 664.
10. NYHS-JP, box 1, folder 1, Eliza Jumel to Stephen Jumel, letters of November 5, 1826; January 1, 1827; and May 1, 1827.
11. *Newburyport* [Massachusetts] *Herald*, July 19, 1833, 5, reprinted from the "Hartford Review" (presumably either the *New-England Daily Review* or *New-England Weekly Review*, both published in Hartford; I have been unable to locate surviving issues for the time period).
12. 1876 Bill of Complaint, letter 34.
13. Liber 368:308.
14. BM 710-J, first account of the administratrix, filed January 22, 1836.
15. Parton, 664.
16. Aaron Burr, *The papers of Aaron Burr* [microform], eds. Mary-Jo Kline and Joanne Wood Ryan (Glen Rock, NJ: Microfilming Corp. of America, 1977), reel 2, Cty:3516/Burr.
17. Burr, *Papers of Aaron Burr*, reel 2, MH:2271.
18. Ibid.
19. Burr, *Political correspondence*, 1228 (see chap. 25, n. 39).
20. "Hon. Luther Martin," *Christian Watchman*, August 11, 1826, 148.
21. N.Y. Ct. Ch., Alexander L. Botts vs. Aaron Burr, BM 1710B, Part 2, depositions of Nelson Chase, March 30, 1836, and Maria Johnson, March 5, 1836.

CHAPTER 27: THE UNRAVELING

1. The quotations in this and the preceding three paragraphs are from Dunlap, *Diary*, 3:796 (see chap. 6, n. 13).
2. Lisa Wilson, *Life after death: Widows in Pennsylvania 1750–1850* (Philadelphia: Temple University Press, 1992), 3, 5, for what one woman said as distinct from what she did.
3. Edith B. Gelles, "Gossip: An eighteenth-century case," *Journal of Social History* 22, no. 4 (Summer 1989): 667–68.
4. Liber 368:301–302.
5. BM 710-J, first account of the administratrix, filed January 22, 1836. Although Eliza does not identify the mortgage in her bill of complaint, it must have been the six-thousand-

dollar mortgage on 150 Broadway, which Stephen had taken out on September 16, 1824, and Eliza ultimately paid off on November 25, 1835.

6. Liber 368:302.

7. Ibid.

8. Ibid., 308–10.

9. Ibid., 312.

10. No record of any such lawsuit exists.

11. Liber 368:310–11.

12. Ibid., 312–13, 332.

13. Oliver L. Barbour, *A treatise on the practice of the Court of Chancery, with an appendix of precedents* (Albany: Wm. & A. Gould & Co., 1844), 2:245–46.

14. Barbour, *Treatise*, 2:245.

15. Linda S. Hudson, *Mistress of manifest destiny: A biography of Jane McManus Storm Cazneau, 1807–1878* (Austin: Texas State Historical Association, 2001), 7, 15–16.

16. Liber 368:375.

17. NYHS-JP, box 1, folder 13, testimony of Hannah Lewis, May 30, 1836.

18. Hudson, *Mistress of manifest destiny*, 15.

19. Ibid., 17.

20. Ibid., 17–18.

21. Burr, *Papers of Aaron Burr*, reel 2, TxU:2352/Bryan (see chap. 26, n. 16).

22. Hudson, *Mistress of manifest destiny*, 27–28. She may have tried to raise money by selling other real estate in Texas, whether acting as an agent for others or hawking property she or her family members owned. An advertisement offering investors fifty thousand acres of land in East Texas appeared in the *Albany Argus* on August 27 and September 10 ("Lands in Texas," *Albany Argus*, October 27, 1833, 4). Although the owner of the land was not stated, potential buyers were advised to apply to Nelson Chase at 23 Nassau Street in New York City. McManus could have been involved, given that Nelson was acting as agent and the address was that of Aaron Burr's law office. Perhaps she had applied to Burr for assistance in advertising and selling the parcel.

23. Hudson, *Mistress of manifest destiny*, 29.

24. NYHS-JP, box 1, folder 13.

25. Hudson, *Mistress of manifest destiny*, 30.

26. Ancestry.com, *U.S. Passport Applications, 1795–1925* (see chap. 6, n. 17).

27. Liber 368:301, 306–7.

28. N.Y. Ct. Ch., Alexander L. Botts vs. Aaron Burr, BM 1710B, Part 2, deposition of Maria Johnson, March 5, 1836.

29. Ibid.

30. Parton, 667.

31. Burr, *Papers of Aaron Burr*, reel 2, NHi:1685/Burr (see chap. 26, n. 16). On November 23, 1833, *Atkinson's Saturday Evening Post* noted that Burr "lately had a paralytic attack, from which he has not yet recovered."

32. Burr, *Papers of Aaron Burr*, reel 2, NHi:1754/Burr.

33. Parton, 667.

34. Liber 368:306–307.
35. *Commercial Advertiser*, November 2, 1833, 2.
36. Burr, *Political correspondence*, 1218 (see chap. 25, n. 39).
37. Ibid., 1220.
38. Ibid., 1221n3.
39. Burr, *Papers of Aaron Burr*, reel 2, NjP:3088.
40. Burr, *Political correspondence*, 1218.
41. NYHS-JP, box 1, folder 13, John Lewis to Nelson Chase, February 10, 1834.
42. Davis, *Memoirs of Aaron Burr*, 2:25 (see ch. 25, n. 5).
43. Aaron Burr, *Political correspondence*, 1227.
44. Ibid., 1227n2.
45. Ibid., 1227.
46. Liber 368:301.
47. Ibid., 302–303.
48. NYHS-JP, box 2, folder J, N.Y. Sup. Ct., Nelson Chase vs. Aaron Burr, Copy of narr. in replevin and notice of rule to plead.

CHAPTER 28: THE DUEL

1. Liber 368:306.
2. Basch, *In the eyes of the law*, 17 (see chap. 21, n. 13).
3. Barbour, *Treatise*, 2:253 (see chap. 27, n. 16).
4. Liber 368:322–23, 325–26.
5. Ibid., 331.
6. Ibid., 342–43.
7. Ibid., 343.
8. Ibid., 338, 41.
9. Ibid., 338–40.
10. Ibid., 333–34.
11. Ibid., 332.
12. Ibid., 336.
13. Ibid., 334–35.
14. NYHS-JP, box 1, folder 13, agreement of December 23, 1835.
15. Barbour, *Treatise*, 2:257–58.
16. Liber 368.
17. Brian J Cudahy, *Over and back: The history of ferryboats in New York Harbor* (New York: Fordham University Press, 1990), 20–22.
18. Liber 368:376.
19. Mrs. Felton, *American life. The narrative of two years' city and country residence in the United States* (London: Simkin, Marshall, & Co., 1842), 54; N.Y. Com. Pl., Helen M. Catlin and others vs. Aaron Burr, 1834-#282.
20. In Longworth's city directory, Burr's home address is given as "Jersey City" only once, in the 1833–34 edition, which would have been prepared in May or June 1833, after New

Yorkers had signed their leases for the year. After the breakup of the marriage, Burr moved into his office on Nassau Street. Later he lived with an illegitimate son, Aaron Columbus Burr.

21. Liber 368:371–72, 375–80, 379.

22. Ibid., 377.

23. Ibid., 370–72.

24. Ibid., 372–74.

25. Ibid., 374–76.

26. Ibid., 377.

27. Ibid., 349–50, 365–68, 381–82; NYHS-JP, box 1, folder 13, timeline of the hearings in chancery (1836).

28. Liber 368:381–82.

29. Parton, 677–78.

30. New York City Municipal Archives, Minutes of the Court of General Sessions, MN 10016, roll 16, fol. 204–205, 242; New York City Municipal Archives, D.A. Indictment Records, MN 5166, roll 166, The People vs. Maria Johnson; "Courts," *Mercury*, July 7, 1836, [2].

31. Liber 368:383.

32. Parton, 682.

33. Liber 368:373–74.

34. Nelson Manfred Blake, *The road to Reno: A history of divorce in the United States* (New York: The Macmillan Company, 1962), 119, 199.

35. For the effect that the reputations of the concerned parties could have on results of divorce proceedings, see Basch, *In the eyes of the law*, 94 (see chap. 21, n. 10); Norma Basch, "Relief in the premises: divorce as a woman's remedy in New York and Indiana, 1815–1870," *Law and History Review* 8, no. 1 (Spring 1990): 23n58.

36. Donald M. Roper, "The elite of the New York Bar as seen from the bench: James Kent's necrologies," *New-York Historical Society Quarterly* 56, no.3 (July 1972): 224.

37. N.Y. Ct. Ch., Alexander L. Botts vs. Aaron Burr, BM 1710B, Part 2.

38. N.Y. Ct. Ch., Alexander L. Botts vs. Aaron Burr, BM 1710B, Part 1; N.Y. Ct. Ch., Aaron Burr vs. John Pelletreau and others, BM 2759B, with additional details in the bill of complaint of a subsequent suit, N.Y. Ct. Ch., Aaron Burr vs. Benjamin Waldron and Sally his wife, John L. Wilson and Rebecca his wife, BM 2758B. On September 20, 1833, Pelletreau sold a valuable property on Long Island—a racecourse and adjoining farm—to a man named Alexander Botts. The sale was performed under Burr's supervision, with the purchase price to go to Burr himself: he would receive a five-hundred-dollar payment every six months for life. Allegedly Pelletreau made the arrangement in favor of Burr to compensate him for legal work and monetary advances during a lengthy lawsuit in which Burr had represented him. This explanation is suspicious, however, since Burr had been fighting unsuccessfully since before his marriage to Eliza to obtain additional fees for the work from Pelletreau and others. Suddenly he had succeeded, when his client was dependent on him and in failing health (Pelletreau would die in late 1833 or early 1834).

39. N.Y. Ct. Ch., Alexander L. Botts vs. Aaron Burr, BM 1710B, Part 2, deposition of Robert White, March 18, 1836.

40. Parton, 665.

CHAPTER 29: FINANCIAL SHENANIGANS

1. *Tresor de la langue française* 12:503; Andrew J. Counter, *Inheritance in nineteenth-century French culture: Wealth, knowledge and the family* (London: LEGENDA, 2010), 62–63, 69.
2. 1876 Bill of Complaint, letters 2, 15; ADL, 4 Q 1 445 (May 22, 1821).
3. 1876 Bill of Complaint, letters 17, 18, 19, 21, 23, 24, 46.
4. PUL Fuller, box 2, folder 83, Eliza Jumel to Stephen Jumel, December 1, 1826; 1876 Bill of Complaint, letter 28.
5. 1876 Bill of Complaint, letter 36A.
6. BM 710-J.
7. Ibid.
8. Crane, *Ebb tide in New England*, 172 (see prologue, n. 7).
9. Wilson, *Life after death*, 31, 42–44, 58 (see chap. 27, n.2).
10. 1876 Bill of Complaint, letters 31, 33, and 34.
11. NYHS-AHMC, Jumel, Madame Stephen, Eliza Jumel to Jean Lesparre Jeantet, June 30, 1833. Eliza addressed the letter to "Monsieur Lesparre Sante" [sic], a roughly phonetic spelling of Jeantet.
12. NYHS-AHMC, Jumel, Madame Stephen, Eliza Jumel to Jean Lesparre Jeantet, June 30, 1833.
13. Ibid.
14. BM 710-J, first account of the administratrix, filed January 20, 1836; NYHS-JP, folder 1, copy of the opinion of the chancellor in Eliza B. Jumel, administratrix, appellant, vs. François Jumel and Magdalen [*sic*] Lagadere, respondents.
15. NYHS-AHMC, Jumel, Madame Stephen, Eliza Jumel to Jean Lesparre Jeantet, June 30, 1833.
16. 1876 Bill of Complaint, letters 31, 34, 35.
17. BM 710-J.
18. Ibid. In Eliza's defense, many of the assets had become collectible only recently. She and Stephen had been trying to collect reimbursement for the *Prosper* since the 1820s (MJM 4.7, two English translations of a letter from Eliza Jumel to Stephen Jumel). Reparations only became possible after February 1836, when the French Chamber of Deputies began to carry out an 1831 treaty to compensate Americans for losses incurred during the Napoleonic Wars. Payments from the two marine insurance companies were made possible by the treaty's implementation as well (BM 710-J). That said, the indemnification treaty had been a political football for several years (Carl Cavanagh Hodge and Cathal J. Nolan, eds., *U.S. presidents and foreign policy: From 1789 to the present* [Santa Barbara, CA: ABC-CLIO, 2007], 68–69). The claims should have been revealed as potential assets.
19. NYHS-JP, folder 1, copy of the opinion of the chancellor in Eliza B. Jumel, administratrix, appellant, vs. François Jumel and Magdalen [sic] Lagardere, respondents; NYHS-JP, box 2, folder H, copy of decree and receipt.
20. BM 710-J, examination of Eliza B. Burr, December 17, 1836; 1876 Bill of Complaint, letter 34.

21. BM 710-J, examination of Eliza B. Burr, December 17, 1836.
22. Ibid.
23. Ibid.
24. T. F. Thiselton Dyer, *Folk-lore of Shakespeare* (New York: Griffith & Farran, [1883]), 314.
25. *Diary of James Gallatin*, 71, 262 (see chap. 15, n. 15); Hugh Stokes, *The Devonshire House circle* (New York: McBride, Nast & Company, 1916), 249.
26. 1876 Bill of Complaint, letter 37A.
27. BM 710-J.
28. Ibid.

CHAPTER 30: THE WIDOW'S MITE

1. Hartog, *Man and wife*, 145 (see chap. 21, n. 10).
2. NYHS-JP, box 2, folder A, Eliza B. Jumel vs. George Pramer, Circuit Roll; Eliza B. Jumel vs. George W. Clause, Circuit Roll; and subpoenas in Jumel vs. Pramer, August 15, 1837; box 3, folder B, subpoena to Dewit C. Bates, August 15, 1837; subpoena to Dan Martin, attorney of George Prunier, July 28, 1837; box 3 folder C, Eliza B. Jumel vs. George Pramer et al., stipulation, July 31, 1838; box 3, folder F, subpoenas in Eliza B. Jumel vs. George W. Clause, August 15, 1837; box 3, folder H, copy of proposition to settle dower suit of Eliza B. Jumel vs. George Pramer and others, after an original of March 8, 1838; N.Y. Ct. Ch., Eliza B. Jumel vs. Abraham Maynard, BM J-708; N.Y. Sup. Ct., Eliza B. Jumel vs. John Maynard and Phebe Maynard, Judgment Record, 1838 M-93 (after Abraham Maynard died, Eliza filed suit against his heirs, John and Phebe, but I have counted the two suits as a single case in totaling the number of her suits for dower rights).
3. NYHS-JP, box 3, folder H, copy of proposition to settle dower suit of Eliza B. Jumel vs. George Pramer and others, after an original of March 8, 1838; box 3, folder C, Eliza B. Jumel vs. George Pramer et al., stipulation, July 31, 1838. The property in Westchester occupied by the Maynards was an exception. In that case, a settlement was not forthcoming. She went to trial, her right to dower was affirmed, and she was awarded damages.
4. NYHS-JP, box 2, folder H, petition from Eliza B. Jumel to the Chancellor of the State of New York (copy); N.Y. Ct. Ch., Eliza Jumel vs. Catherine Ottignon and others, BM J-709.
5. Hartog, *Man and wife*, 145 (see chap. 21, n. 10).
6. N.Y. Ct. Ch., Eliza Jumel vs. Catherine Ottignon and others, BM J-709.
7. Basch, *In the eyes of the law*, 53 (see chap. 21, n. 10).
8. N.Y. Ct. Ch., Eliza Jumel vs. Catherine Ottignon and others, BM J-709.
9. NYHS-JP, box 2, folder H, copy of decree and receipt.
10. 1876 Bill of Complaint, act of notoriety 1 (for Francois's death); letters 40 to 44.
11. Ibid., letter 42.
12. Ibid., letters 42–44.
13. Ibid., letter 41; ADL, 4 Q 1 445 (May 22, 1821).
14. 1876 Bill of Complaint, letter 42; "Madame Jumel's will," *New York Herald*, February 8, 1866, 8 (the appearance of a legacy to Felicie in Eliza's will indicates that a compromise was reached).

15. N.Y. Ct. Ch., Magdalen [*sic*] Lagardere vs. Eliza B. Jumel, BM L-45.
16. Ibid.
17. Ibid.
18. Ibid.
19. 1876 Bill of Complaint, act of notoriety 1.
20. This was Old Saint Patrick's Cathedral on Barclay Street, completed in 1815 (later super-seded as the seat of the diocese by Saint Patrick's Cathedral on Fifth Avenue).
21. NYHS-AHMC, Jumel, Stephen, copy of an April 22, 1846, letter from Bishop Fenwick to Bishop Hughes.
22. New York County Clerk's Office, Division of Old Records, Water Commissioners of the City of New-York, #52-1836 (1839).

CHAPTER 31: A SECOND FAMILY

1. NYPL, Jumel family miscellany, NYGB Fam 2008-2482.
2. 1873 Transcript of Record, 306; B-779, box 113, deposition of Eliza J. Caryl.
3. 1873 Transcript of Record, 306.
4. According to *Doggett's New-York City Directory*, the Chases lived at 63 Chambers Street in Manhattan in 1834; 339 Greenwich St., also in Manhattan, in 1835 and 1836; and in Hoboken in 1837. A home address is not indicated for them between 1838 and 1841, but Nelson is again listed in Hoboken in 1842, and other documentation that includes his home address indicates that he was still there in the interim. For example, see his 1839 signature, with the indication that he lived in Hoboken, in the record relating to land taken from Eliza for the building of the Croton Aqueduct: New York County, County Clerk's Office, Division of Old Records, Water Commissioners of the City of New-York, 52-1836 (1839).
5. 1873 Transcript of Record, 307; B-779, box 112, deposition of Nelson Chase.
6. This discussion of women's involvement in business is based on the findings of Joyce W. Warren, *Women, money and the law* (Iowa City: University of Iowa Press, 2005), 10, 115, 153.
7. New York County, Land and Property Records, Liber 379:415–16; NYHS, Jumel Papers, box 3, folder D, indenture between Eliza B. Jumel and Francis Philippon, January 6, 1838.
8. NYHS-JP, box 2, folder I, agreement with respect to a party wall, December 1836.
9. NYHS-JP, box 1, folder 14, agreement between Eliza B. Jumel and Lucius Smith, January 16, 1846; box 2, folder I, agreement between Eliza B. Jumel and Michael Werckmeister, May 1, 1844; box 3, folder D, copy of lease, William L. Burdick to Eliza B. Jumel, February 26, 1850.
10. Pessen, *Riches, class, and power*, 17 and n26 (see prologue, n. 6).
11. Edgar W. Martin, *The standard of living in 1860: American consumption levels on the eve of the Civil War* (Chicago: University of Chicago Press, 1942), 395, table 11.
12. 1873 Transcript of Record, 306. Nelson dated Pell's tenancy from fall 1834, but indicated conversely that it was after the birth of his daughter, which occurred in 1836. Evidence in the Jumel/Burr divorce case (testimony of John Hopwood) placed Eliza at the mansion in the fall of 1834 and spring of 1835, supporting an 1836 rather than 1834 dating for Pell's arrival.

13. N.Y. Super. Ct., Eliza B. Jumel vs. James Monroe, 1839-#722.

14. NYHS-JP, box 3, folder B, agreement between Eliza Jumel and James Pheigan, April 6, 1842. If Pheigan's wife took care of the cows and dairy, they would be allowed to keep half of the profits from the milk and butter as well.

15. 1873 Transcript of Record, 308; Martin, *Standard of living*, 395, table 11.

16. New York County, Land and Property Records, Deeds, Liber 109:306–309.

17. N.Y. Ct. Ch., Stephen Jumel vs. John R. Murray et al., BM 713-J.

18. NYHS-JP, box 2, folder A, agreement between Michael Werckmeister, Eliza B. Burr, and James L. Curtis, April 27, 1835; N.Y. Ct. Ch., Eliza Jumel vs. Peter R. Wickoff and others, D. CH 91-J; New York County, Land and Property Records, Liber 377:425–26.

19. New York County, Land and Property Records, Liber 493:415–16.

20. NYHS-JP, box 3, folder D, articles of agreement between Eliza B. Jumel and Ambrose C. Kingsland, February 26, 1850.

21. Over the years, this lot was referred to as encompassing anywhere from 94 to 100 acres. I have chosen to refer to it consistently as the 96-acre lot, the size most often assigned to it.

22. NYHS-JP, box 3, folder A, lease of a farm from Eliza Jumel by Peter Lestrange, 1842; N.Y. Com. Pl., Martin C. Clancy vs. Eliza B. Jumel, 1861-#226.

23. N.Y. Com. Pl., Eliza B. Jumel vs. Philip A. Levy, 1841-#1245; N.Y. Com. Pl., Martin C. Clancy vs. Eliza B. Jumel, 1861-#226.

24. New York County, Land and Property Records, Liber 391:291–93.

25. N.Y. Com. Pl., Eliza B. Jumel vs. Philip A. Levy, 1841-#1245.

26. N.Y. Sup. Ct., Philip A. Levy vs. Eliza B. Jumel, 1841-#645.

27. Warren, *Women, money and the law*, 133–34.

28. N.Y. Sup. Ct., Philip A. Levy vs. Eliza B. Jumel, 1841-#645.

29. Ibid.

30. B-779, box 112, deposition of Nelson Chase.

31. N.Y. Sup. Ct., Philip A. Levy vs. Eliza B. Jumel, 1841-#645.

32. Warren, *Women, money and the law*, 10, 318n37.

33. Ibid.

34. NYHS-JP, box 3, folder B, summons in the case of Antoine Soil [*sic*] vs. Eliza Jumel, March 14, 1849; NYHS-JP, box 3, folder G, release, Antoine Soel [*sic*] to Eliza B. Jumel, March 22, 1849. The plaintiff signed himself variously "Soili" and "Soil."

35. N.Y. Com. Pl., John Rogers, an Infant, by William Wordsworth his next friend, vs. Eliza B. Jumel, Judgment Record, 1844-#864.

36. Ibid.

37. B-779, box 112, deposition of Nelson Chase; for the address, 255 West 19th Street, see the 1845 edition of *Doggett's New-York City Directory*.

38. New York City Municipal Archives, Manhattan Deaths, vol. 14; B-779, box 112, deposition of Nelson Chase; 1873 Transcript of Record, 303. The record of the death lists the location of the deceased as 253 West 19th Street. As this differs from the Chase's house number as given by Doggett's (255), one number may have been wrong or, alternately, Eliza Tranchell may have lived next door. If she had been taking care of Mary, the death could have occurred in the Tranchells' lodgings.

39. B-779, box 112, deposition of Nelson Chase.
40. NYHS-AHMC, Jumel, Mary E., Mary Jumel to Maria Jones, N.d. (beginning with the words "Dear Mother") vs. Shelton, 156 (beginning with the words "My Dear Mama").
41. She is buried in lot 222, section 111 (www.green-wood.com; accessed June 26, 2012).
42. B-779, box 112, deposition of Nelson Chase.
43. Ibid.
44. Ibid.
45. B-779, box 113, deposition of Eliza J. Caryl.
46. MJM 4.14, photocopy of a letter from Nelson Chase to Eliza Jumel and Eliza Jumel Chase, February 10, 1852.
47. 1873 Transcript of Record, 307.

CHAPTER 32: MADAME JUMEL

1. NYPL, MssCol 510, Thomas Chamberlain diary, 1835–1860, entries for July 17 and July 30, 1842; Barnes F. Lathrop, "A Southern girl at Saratoga Springs, 1834," *North Carolina Historical Review* 15, no. 2 (April 1938): 160.
2. Thomas Chamberlain diary, entries for July 30, August 1, and August 4, 1842; "High Life at Saratoga—1837," *American Heritage* 18, no. 4 (June 1967): 107; Field Horne, *The Saratoga reader: Writing about an American village 1749–1900* (Saratoga Springs: Kiskaton Publishing, 2004), 167.
3. Thomas Chamberlain diary, entries for summer 1842 (for attendance at various churches); "The late Daniel D. Benedict's diary," *Supplement to the Saratoga Sentinel*, May 19, 1881, [1], entry for August 20–22, 1846.
4. *Saratoga Sentinel*, June 25, 1833, 3; *Saratoga Sentinel*, July 9, 1833, 3.
5. *Saratoga Sentinel*, July 14, 1835, 3.
6. Salvatore Mondello, *The private papers of John Vanderlyn (1775–1852) American portrait painter* (Lewiston, NY: The Edward Mellen Press, 1990), 96–98, 112, 116. The painting is in the Metropolitan Museum of Art today.
7. E.g., *Philadelphia Inquirer*, February 9, 1830, 2 (in this report indicating that two of her horses were stolen, she is referred to as Madame Jumel).
8. "The Jumel estate case," *New York Herald*, January 29, 1873, 5; MJM 4.14, photocopy of a letter from Nelson Chase to Eliza Jumel and Eliza Jumel Chase.
9. Saratoga County Clerk, Deeds Book LL, 499–501, and Deeds Book CC, 224–25; NYHS-JP, box 2, folder I, conveyance from William L. F. Warren to Eliza B. Jumel, August 29, 1836; Saratoga County Clerk, Deeds Book CC, 250–51; NYHS-JP, box 3 folder C, indenture between Eliza B. Jumel and Isaac Taylor, September 3, 1836. She paid $13,343 in total for the farmlands.
10. J[ames] S[ilk] Buckingham, *America, historical, statistic, and descriptive* (London: Fisher, Son, & Co., [1841]), 2:435.
11. Buckingham, *America*, 2:431; Stuart, *Three years in North America* (see chap. 24, n. 5), 1:131.
12. Thomas Chamberlain diary, entry for August 5, 1842; also see entry for July 24; Horne, *Saratoga reader*, 128.

13. Lathrop, "A Southern girl," 160; Buckingham, *America*, 2:430–31.

14. Buckingham, *America*, 430; Horne, *Saratoga reader*, 166.

15. Horne, *Saratoga reader*, 95.

16. "A scene at Saratoga," *Alexandria Gazette*, September 8, 1846, [2] (for all of the quotations in this paragraph).

17. Ibid.; "Disgraceful affair at Saratoga," *New-Bedford* (Massachusetts) *Mercury*, September 4, 1846, [2] (reprinting an article published in the *Springfield Gazette*); "Daniel D. Benedict's diary," [1], entry for August 26, 1846.

18. "A scene at Saratoga," [2]; "Daniel D. Benedict's diary," [1], entry for August 26, 1846.

19. "A scene at Saratoga," [2].

20. Ibid.

21. Ibid.

22. "Disgraceful affair at Saratoga," [2]; "Daniel D. Benedict's diary," [1], entry for August 26, 1846; *Albany Evening News*, August 29, 1846, [2].

23. "Disgraceful affair at Saratoga," [2].

24. "A scene at Saratoga," [2].

25. "Daniel D. Benedict's diary," [1], editorial note to the August 26, 1846, entry.

26. *Albany Evening News*, August 29, 1846, [2]; Myra Beth Young Armstead, "The history of blacks in resort towns: Newport, Rhode Island and Saratoga Springs, New York 1870–1930" (PhD diss., University of Chicago, 1987), 41; Saratoga County Clerk, Deeds Book cc, 250–51.

27. "A scene at Saratoga," [2].

28. *Bellows Falls Gazette*, September 18, 1846, [2].

29. "A scene at Saratoga," [2].

30. *Bellows Falls Gazette*, September 18, 1846, [2].

31. Nigel Cliff, *The Shakespeare riots: Revenge, drama, and death in nineteenth-century America* (New York: Random House, 2007), 208, 245–46.

32. Cliff, *The Shakespeare riots*, 246.

33. Daniel E. Sutherland, *Americans and their servants: Domestic service in the United States from 1800 to 1920* (Baton Rouge: Louisiana State University Press, 1981), 10; [Thomas Hamilton], *Men and manners in America* (Edinburgh: William Blackwood, 1833, 1:106–107.

34. Holly V. Ivard and Caroline Fuller Sloat, "A teenager goes visiting: The diaries of Louisa Jane Trumbull (1835, 1837)," in *Children and youth in a new nation*, ed. James Martin (New York: New York University Press, 2009), 222; John Hope Franklin, *A Southern odyssey: travelers in the antebellum North* (Baton Rouge: Louisiana State University Press, 1976), 131, 133.

35. Sutherland, *Americans and their servants*, 15.

36. "A scene at Saratoga," [2].

37. "Fancy ball at Saratoga," *Daily Evening Transcript* (Boston), August 24, 1850, [2], quoting the *Saratoga Whig*.

38. "The courts," *New York Herald*, March 1, 1872, 11.

39. In 1865 Eliza's family said that the comtesse Tascher de la Pagerie, whose husband was a cousin of the Empress Josephine, sold jewelry and furniture owned by Josephine to

the Jumels (Shelton, 155). However, it is highly unlikely that the comtesse would have possessed such items. Neither she nor her husband, Henri, was on intimate terms with Josephine by the time of the empress's death (unsurprising, since Henri had become a royalist; see chapter 14, p. 73), although earlier, at the time of their marriage, Josephine had purchased a thirty-thousand-franc diamond parure for the new comtesse (Macleod, "Eliza Bowen Jumel: Collecting and cultural politics," 66 [see chap. 16, n. 39]). Possibly the comtesse sold the diamonds she had received from Josephine to the Jumels, and that is where the story that they had been worn by Josephine originated.

40. NYPL, Jumel Family Miscellany, NYBG Fam 2008-2482, transcription by Josiah C. Pumpelly of a clipping from an unnamed newspaper.

41. Ibid.

42. *Massachusetts Plowman and New England Journal of Agriculture*, October 12, 1850, 4.

Chapter 33: Eliza Burr Abroad

1. B-779, box 113, deposition of Eliza J. Caryl.

2. Ancestry.com, *U.S. Passport Applications, 1795–1925* (see chap. 6, n. 17).

3. MJM 4.8, two slightly different English translations of a letter from Eliza Jumel to Charles Louis [*sic*] d'Orléans, prince de Joinville (the addressee's given names were actually François Ferdinand; he had a brother named Louis Charles).

4. Ibid. A high-ranking naval officer, Joinville was staying in New York while his ship was refitted. See "Intelligence," *Army and Navy Chronicle* 12, no. 40 (October 7, 1841), 317; *Memoirs (Vieux Souvenirs) of the prince de Joinville*, trans. Lady Mary Loyd (New York: Macmillan and Co., 1895), 220.

5. *The Collector*, no. 1 (November 1922): 5.

6. "Sailing of steamers," *New-York Tribune*, October 13, 1851, 6; "Passengers arrived," *New York Daily Times*, June 14, 1852, 4, "The Jumel will case," *The World*, November 13, 1866, 5 (letter from Eliza Burr to Nelson Chase, Nice, Italy, February 6, 1852).

7. "The Jumel will case," 5.

8. NYHS-AHMC, Jumel, Mme. Stephen, Eliza J. Chase to Nelson Chase, May 21, 1852.

9. Ibid.

10. The original drawing is in the collection of the New-York Historical Society, acc. no. 1956.125.

11. The print was listed in the July 17, 1852, issue of *Bibliographie de la France*, an indicator that two copies had been deposited at the Bibliothèque nationale de France, as required by law.

12. She had an additional phrase added to the caption of a copy that would remain in the family, dubbing herself fantastically, "The heroine of New York" (MJM 80.467).

13. "Arrival of the Asia," *Weekly Herald*, April 24, 1852, 131; "Death of Prince Torlonia," *Clarence and Richmond Advertiser* (Grafton, New South Wales, Australia), March 30, 1886, 4; NYHS-AHMC, Jumel, Mme. Stephen, Eliza J. Chase to Nelson Chase, May 21, 1852.

14. "The Jumel will case," 5.

15. Ibid.

16. Ibid.

17. Eliza may have been referring to the explosion of the boiler of the steamer *L'Industrie*, which took place at Marseille on December 14, 1852. Two or three people were killed and ten or twelve seriously wounded ("Later from Europe," *New York Times*, January 3, 1852, 1).

18. "The Jumel will case," 5.

19. "The Jumel estate case," *New York Herald*, January 28, 1873, 8; 1873 Transcript of Record, 294–95.

20. "The Jumel estate case" (for the itinerary). Today the portrait is at the Morris-Jumel Mansion in New York City.

21. "Aaron Burr's wife," *Kenosha Democrat*, March 17, 1854, 2.

22. Ibid.

23. Greatorex, 181.

24. "The Jumel estate case," *New-York Tribune*, January 28, 1873, 2.

25. 1876 Bill of Complaint, letter 15.

26. NYHS-JP, box 1, folder 5, Eliza Burr to Jean E. Pery, May 22, 1854.

27. Ibid.

28. Ibid.

29. ADG, 3 E 45740.

30. 1873 Transcript of Record, 297.

31. Ibid.; NYHS-JP box 1, folder 5, Power of attorney from Eliza Burr to Levi K. Bowen; Archives Municipales de Bordeaux, 2 MI D 4/62, no. 373; "State news," *Albany Argus*, January 31, 1873, [2].

32. "State news"; *New York Post*, July 27, 1854 (marriage notice); "The Jumel estate case," *New York Herald*, January 28, 1873, [8]. According to the *Albany Argus* ("State news"), they had a fourth marriage performed by the American consul at Bordeaux, but this seems to be an error. The consul was present for the signing of the marriage contract and the legal registration of the marriage, but did not perform the ceremony (ADG, 3 E 45740; Archives Municipales de Bordeaux, 2 MI D 4/62, no. 373).

33. "State news."

34. Ancestry.com, *New York Passenger Lists, 1820–1957* [database online] (Provo, UT: Ancestry.com Operations, Inc., 2010).

35. *Daily Union* (Washington, DC) July 25, 1854, 3. The story was probably published first in one of the New York evening papers the day before. It was picked up by several other newspapers as well. The June 25 dating given to the so-called "letter from Bordeaux" confirms that it was concocted later. The "letter" refers to provisions in the marriage contract, but the contract wasn't signed until July 5.

CHAPTER 34: A ROMANTIC WIDOW

1. They are listed as passengers on the *Atlantic* from Liverpool, arriving in New York on August 7, 1854. See Ancestry.com, *New York Passenger Lists, 1820–1857* (see chap. 33, n. 34).

2. "The Jumel estate case," *New York Herald*, January 25, 1873, 11.

3. NYHS-JP, box 1, folder 5, Eliza Burr to "Monsieur Pery père," January 22, 1855.

4. NYHS-JP, box 1, folder 5, Eliza Burr to Paul Pery, January 21, 1855.

5. NYHS-JP, box 1, folder 5, Eliza Burr to Eliza Jumel Pery, January 21, 1855.

6. NYHS-JP, box 1, folder 5, Eliza Burr to Eliza and Paul Pery, February 7, 1855.

7. Ibid.

8. She was present at the mansion when the New York State census was taken on June 4, 1855. Ancestry.com, *New York, State Census, 1855* [database online] (Provo, UT: Ancestry.com Operations, Inc., 2013).

9. NYHS-JP, box 2, folder I, Nelson Chase to Jean Edouard Pery, March 22, 1856.

10. Ibid.

11. ADG, 4 M 738/268.

12. "A personal sketch of Madame Jumel, wife of Aaron Burr," *Pioneer and Democrat* (Washington Territory), November 14, 1856, [1], reprinted from an 1855 article in the *Albany Express*.

13. Ibid.

14. NYHS-JP, box 2, folder D, agreement between John Hodgman and Eliza B. Jumel, August 30, 1851.

15. NYHS-JP, box 3, folder D, agreement between Eliza Jumel and James H. Darrow & Co., September 1, 1853.

16. "Madame Jumel's estate," *New York Herald*, November 13, 1866, 4.

17. Ibid.; *Gleason's Pictorial Drawing-Room Companion*, June 18, 1853, 399.

18. "Madame Jumel's estate."

19. "Madame Jumel's estate"; *Daily Saratogian*, August 31, 1857, in *Chronicles of Saratoga*, ed. Evelyn Barrett Britten (Saratoga Springs, 1959), 195.

20. Ibid.

21. *Saratogian*, October 1, 1857, [2].

22. Parton, 661. The 1861 edition published by Mason Brothers bears the words "14th edition" on its title page.

23. Parton, 661.

24. Ibid., 660.

25. Ibid., 665.

26. Ibid., 664–65.

27. Ibid., 665.

28. NYHS-JP, box 3, folder E, letters between Samuel A. Pugh and Nelson Chase, dated from May 31, 1862, to May 7, 1863.

29. NYHS-JP, box 3, folder A, agreement between Samuel A. Pugh and Nelson Chase, May 12, 1862.

30. NYHS-JP, box 3, folder E, Samuel A. Pugh to Nelson Chase, June 8, 1862.

31. There is such a document in NYHS-JP (box 1, folder 13), with the header "July 8, 1836," but with the vice chancellor's signature dated September 14, 1836.

32. Liber 368:387-88; Isenberg, *Fallen Founder*, 403 (see chap. 25, n. 21).

33. Liber 368:381–82.

34. E.g., N.Y. Ct. Ch., Eliza Jumel vs. Peter R. Wickoff and others, D. CH 91-J.

35. NYHS-JP, box 3, folder E, Samuel A. Pugh to Nelson Chase, May 7, 1863.

CHAPTER 35: THE END OF AN ERA

1. *Michigan Farmer*, October 22, 1859, 342, quoting the *Saratoga Sentinel*.

2. Mathilde, born April 13, 1855, appears to be four or five years old. Her date of birth is given in the 1875 passport application for her in Ancestry.com, *U.S. Passport Applications 1795–1925* (see chap. 6, n. 17), although the event is wrongly stated to have occurred in New York. The large buttons on the central placket of Eliza Pery's bodice also suggest that the photograph was taken c. 1860, when that style was in fashion.

3. Eliza Jumel, Eliza and Mathilde Pery, and Nelson and William Chase are identified in NYHS-AHMC, Mauer, Charles Arthur, unsigned letter (probably from Mauer) to Dorothy C. Barack, February 3, 1950. None of the other figures are named. Paul's 1856 passport described him as one meter seventy centimeters tall (just under five foot seven inches), with reddish brown hair, a blond beard, an uncovered forehead, an oval face, a small mouth, and a round chin (ADG, 4 M 738/268).

4. "Madame Jumel's estate," *New York Herald*, November 13, 1866, 5.

5. N.Y. Sup. Ct., Eliza B. Jumel vs. John Flinn, 1860 F-12.

6. *New York Times*, April 11, 1861, 6 (advertisement).

7. "The widow of Aaron Burr has her farm surveyed—the surveyor's bill," *New York Times*, November 12, 1863, 2.

8. They are listed in *Trow's New York City Directory . . . for the year ending May 1, 1859* (New York: John F. Trow, 1858). 1873 Transcript of Record, 308. The property remained in Eliza Jumel's possession at the time of her death (N.Y. Sup. Ct., William Ingles Chase vs. Nelson Chase and others, 1878 (-36).

9. See *Trow's New York City Directory* for the years ending May 1, 1860, and May 1, 1864; 1873 Transcript of Record, 308.

10. Ancestry.com, *1860 United States Federal Census* [database online] (Provo, UT: Ancestry .com Operations, Inc., 2009).

11. 1873 Transcript of Record, 308. His address continues to be given as "Washington Heights" (or equivalent names for upper Manhattan) in city directories throughout this time period.

12. "Madame Jumel's estate," 5.

13. Ibid.

14. Ibid.

15. MJM 4.8, two slightly different English translations of a letter from Eliza Jumel to Charles Louis [sic] d'Orléans, prince de Joinville (the addressee's given names were actually François Ferdinand; he had a brother named Louis Charles).

16. Ibid.

17. Ibid.

18. "Madame Jumel's estate," 4.

19. "Local news . . . Jumel will case," *The Sun*, November 13, 1866, 4.

20. "Madame Jumel's estate," 5.

21. Ibid.

22. "Madame Jumel's estate," 4.

23. Ibid., 4–5.

24. Frederick David Bidwell, *Taxation in New York State* (Albany: J. B. Lyon, 1918), 264; Ancestry.com, *U.S. IRS Tax Assessment Lists, 1862–1918* [database online] (Provo, UT: Ancestry.com Operations, Inc., 2008).

25. "Madame Jumel's estate," 4. Dr. Alonzo Clarke, a kidney specialist, first visited her in 1863.

26. Ibid., 5.

27. *The World*, July 18, 1865, 5 [death notice].

28. "Obituary. Madam Eliza B. Jumel," *New York Times*, July 18, 1865.

29. "Funeral of Madam Jumel," *The World*, July 19, 1865, 4.

30. New York City Department of Health, Borough of Manhattan, Register of Deaths, 1798–1865 (available on microfilm at the New York Public Library).

31. "Obsequies. Funeral of Madame Jumel," *New York Herald*, July 19, 1865, [1].

32. Ibid.

33. "Funeral of Madam Jumel"; "Obsequies. Funeral of Madame Jumel." The lesson began with 1 Corinthians 15:20.

34. Ibid.

35. Ibid.

36. Plot 498, Westerly Division of Trinity Cemetery and Mausoleum.

CHAPTER 36: A DISPUTED INHERITANCE

1. "The widow of Aaron Burr," *New York Observer and Chronicle*, July 20, 1865, 230.

2. "The contest about the alleged will of the late widow of Aaron Burr—motion to settle the issues—over $1,000,000 of property involved," *New York Times*, February 8, 1866, 2; "The Jumel will case," *New York Times*, November 13, 1866, 8; "Madame's Jumel's will," *New York Herald*, February 8, 1866, 8.

3. "Madame Jumel's estate," *New York Herald*, November 13, 1866, 5.

4. Ibid.; "Madame's Jumel's will." Some of the sources indicate that Rev. Smith was to share in the residuary estate, but the will—at least as reproduced in the February 8 article in the *Herald*—barred him from doing so. The accuracy of the *Herald*'s transcript cannot be verified, because the original will is missing from the probate files in Manhattan.

5. Initial estimates of the value of the Jumel estate, made within a year or two of Eliza's death, ranged from "$700,000 or $800,000" to "over a million of dollars" ("The benefit of kindness—the will of Madame Jumell [*sic*] Burr," *New-York Tribune*, August 14, 1865, [8]; "Madame Jumel's estate"). As time passed, the value of the estate was exaggerated, with estimates reaching up to six million dollars ("Current topics," *Albany Law Journal*, December 7, 1872, 380). It is difficult to pin down an exact figure, and the estate was worth more when it was finally settled than in 1865, due to increasing real estate values. By adding up land sales made in the years after Eliza's death and money received for parcels taken by the City of New York under its power of eminent domain, my best estimate is that the estate was worth approximately one million dollars when Eliza died.

6. NYHS-JP, box 2, folder A, copy of Eliza B. Jumel's will, July 23, 1851.

7. N.Y. Sup. Ct., William Inglis Chase vs. Nelson Chase and others, 1878 C-36 (contains a copy of the October 12, 1865, agreement between Nelson and his children).

8. There were two agreements, the first for forty thousand dollars and the second, drawn up seventeen months later, for thirty thousand dollars; see "The Jumel will case" and "Law reports," *New York Times*, October 22, 1870, 3; "The Jumel estate," *New York Herald*, October 23, 1870, 10. Although it appears that the second agreement was designed to supersede the first, virtually all later references to the deal with the Joneses indicate that forty thousand dollars was the sum paid. William and Eliza would not have been considered Eliza Jumel's legal heirs without these transactions, as their relationship to her was through their mother, Mary, who was the illegitimate daughter of Eliza's sister, Maria. The descendants of a bastard child, even if legitimate themselves, could not inherit from maternal relatives who died intestate. In the absence of a will, they could only inherit from their own mother. The Joneses, in contrast, were Maria's legitimate children, so they could inherit from their mother's sister.

9. "The Jumel will case."

10. Ibid.; B-779, box 112, deposition of Nelson Chase.

11. "Madame Jumel's will"; B-779, box 112, deposition of Nelson Chase, and box 113, deposition of Eliza J. Caryl. Eliza left Felicie two thousand dollars. Possibly the extra five hundred was negotiated during the litigation after Stephen's death when the delay in payment was agreed upon (the money should have been paid within a year after his decease).

12. "Charles O'Conor," *Eclectic Magazine of Foreign Literature* 20, no. 1 (July 1874), 117.

13. Liber 368:313, 316, 327, 343, 350, 367, 383–84.

14. N.Y. Ct. Ch., Eliza Jumel vs. Catherine Ottignon and others, BM 709-J; BM 710-J.

15. Henry Ellsworth Gregory, "Charles O'Conor. 1804–1884," in *Great American Lawyers*, ed. William Draper Lewis, vol. 5 (Philadelphia: John C. Winston Company, 1908), 92–93.

16. "Charles O'Conor, Esq., to defend the great state prisoner," *The Daily Age* [Philadelphia], June 8, 1865, 1.

17. MJM 4.14, photocopy of a letter from Nelson Chase to Eliza Jumel and Eliza Jumel Chase, February 10, 1852.

18. "Two will cases," *New York Observer and Chronicle*, September 14, 1865, 43.

19. "Madame Jumel's estate," 4.

20. Ibid.

21. Ibid.

22. Ibid.

23. Ibid.

24. Ibid.

25. Ibid.

26. James C. Mohr, "The paradoxical advance and embattled retreat of the 'unsound mind': Evidence of insanity in the adjudication of wills in nineteenth-century America," *Historical Reflections* 24, no. 3 (Fall 1998): 426–27; Yvonne Pitts, *Family, law, and inheritance in America: The social and legal history of nineteenth-century Kentucky* (New York: Cambridge University Press, 2013), 84.

27. Mohr, "The paradoxical advance," 417–18.
28. Ibid., 420–21.
29. Pitts, *Family, law, and inheritance*, 54.
30. "Madame Jumel's estate," 5.
31. Ibid., 4.
32. "The Jumel will case," *New-York Tribune*, November 13, 1866, 8. The *Tribune* indicated that Wetmore only "got her to give away about fifty thousand dollars' worth of her property," but the *Herald*'s figure of one hundred thousand dollars appears to be more accurate, considering the individual bequests.
33. There is no evidence as to whether Nelson would have shared in the residuary estate in Wetmore's draft of the will.
34. NYHS-JP, box 2, folder H, agreement between Eliza Jumel and Thomas Connolly.
35. "Madame Jumel's estate," 4.
36. Charles Dickens, *Great Expectations*, intro. by Stanley Weintraub (Signet Classic, 1998), 67. A document purporting to be an extract from the diary of Anna Parker, later Mrs. John V. L. Pruyn, appears to have been inspired by *Great Expectations* also (NYHS-JP, "From the diary of Miss Anna Parker"). Supposedly it recorded a visit Parker and acquaintances had paid to Eliza in October 1862. In the entry, Parker portrayed Eliza as a mad old woman: rambling on about the past, living in an unkempt house, and keeping her dining room table set with moldering items placed there decades before. However, the likelihood that Parker paid the visit as described is slim, because in 1862 she was already married and had a young son, whereas the diary was said to have been that which she kept as a girl. Anna's son, John V. L. Pruyn Jr., was born in Albany on March 14, 1859, as documented by a record for him in Ancestry.com, *U.S. Passport Applications, 1795–1925* (see chap. 6, n. 17). Probably the purported diary entry was prepared for use in the will case, but ultimately not submitted as evidence. It became part of Eliza's legend nonetheless, after being published by her first biographer (Shelton, 188–94).
37. "The Jumel estate case," *New York Herald*, January 31, 1873, 11.
38. "The Jumel estate case"; "Special correspondence. Our New York letter," *Troy Weekly Times*, June 14, 1873, [1]. Nollston's name is listed on the birth certificate of their daughter Ella (born March 25, 1870), available on www.FamilySearch.org (accessed December 27, 2011). Her age comes from the 1880 census; she was then thirty-nine and William was forty. See Ancestry.com and the Church of Jesus Christ of the Latter-Day Saints, *1880 United States Federal Census* [database online] (Provo, UT: Ancestry.com, Inc., 2010).
39. "The Jumel estate case."
40. "Special correspondence. Our New York letter."
41. Leslie's age was given as five when the census takers arrived at the mansion on July 11, 1870; see the 1870 United States Census on www.FamilySearch.org. Ten years later, in June 1880, census takers on Long Island reported that Louisa was fifteen; see Ancestry.com, *1880 United States Federal Census*.
42. Ibid.
43. See the entry for William J. [*sic*] Chase in *Trow's New York City Directory . . . for the year ending May 1, 1857* (New York: John F. Trow, 1856).

44. "The Jumel estate case." Nelson indicated that William was keeping the grocery around the winter of 1864–65, but that dating is belied by the city directories. W. I. Chase & Co., grocers, is listed only once in *Trow's New York City Directory*, for the year ending May 1, 1860.

45. "The Jumel estate case."

46. MJM 98.13, Nelson Chase to Samuel J. Tilden, Esq.

Chapter 37: Proliferating Pretenders

1. "The Jumel will case," *New-York Tribune*, January 25, 1868, 7; "The Jumel estate—card from Mr. Nelson Chase," *New York Times*, February 1, 1868.

2. Irving Browne, "Count Johannes," *The Green Bag* 8, no. 11 (November 1896): 435–39; Willis Steell, "Acting 'Hamlet' behind a net," *The Theater* 10, no. 103 (September 1909): 80.

3. "The Jumel estate, *New York Herald*, October 23, 1870, 10; Browne, "Count Johannes," 436; "The Jumel estate," *New York Herald*, October 22, 1870, 8.

4. "The Jumel estate," *New York Herald*, October 22, 1870, 8.

5. Ibid.

6. Ibid.

7. "The Jumel estate," *New York Herald*, October 23, 1870, 10.

8. Ibid.

9. Ibid.

10. Ibid.; "The Jumel estate, *New York Herald*, October 22, 1870, 8.

11. "The Jumel estate," *New York Herald*, October 23, 1870, 10.

12. "Law reports," *New York Times*, October 22, 1870, 3.

13. 3-466, deposition of Ellen Bullock.

14. 3-466, deposition of John Bullock.

15. Ibid.

16. 3-312, deposition of John Hicks Bullock.

17. 3-466, deposition of John Bullock.

18. 3-312, deposition of John Hicks Bullock.

19. 3-466, deposition of Juliana Pearce.

20. 3-312, deposition of John Hicks Bullock.

21. Ibid.

22. Ibid.; 3-466, deposition of John Bullock.

23. 3-466, cross-interrogatory that was intended to be addressed to Elizabeth Salisbury (but not posed because of her sudden illness).

24. 3-466, deposition of Elizabeth Salisbury.

25. Ibid.

26. "The courts," *New York Herald*, April 23, 1871, 10.

Chapter 38: Enter George Washington

1. "The Jumel estate. Further testimony on behalf of the supposed son of Mme. Jumel," *New York Times*, March 21, 1871, 8.

2. J. W. Gerard Jr., *Titles to real estate in the State of New York: A digested compendium of law applicable to the examination of titles* . . . (New York: Baker, Voorhis & Co., 1869), 118, 123. The law was limited in its scope. Although an illegitimate child was eligible to inherit from an intestate mother, the privilege stopped with the child. His or her descendants were not legal heirs in cases of intestacy; see chap. 36, n. 8.

3. "The Jumel estate. Further testimony on behalf of the supposed son of Mme. Jumel."

4. Ibid.

5. Ibid.

6. Ballou, *Elaborate History*, 85, 202, 218–19; see chap. 6, n. 21.

7. TCMR 6:334–35.

8. Rhode Island State Archives, Providence County Jail, Gaol Book, December 1789–April 1794, entry for December 22, 1792.

9. TCMR 6:334–35, 338, 346; "The courts," *New York Herald*, February 13, 1872, 8.

10. TCMR 7:404; Linda L. Mathew, "Gleanings from Rhode Island town records: Providence Town Counsel Records, 1789–1801," *Rhode Island Roots*, Special Bonus Issue 2007 (April 2007): 91–92, 97, 101.

11. TCMR 8:171.

12. TCMR 8:258.

13. "Scandalum magnatum," *Albany Argus*, March 28, 1871, [1].

14. Ibid.; "The courts," *New York Herald*, February 10, 1872, 11.

15. "The courts," *New York Herald*, February 10, 1872, 11.

16. "The Jumel estate. Further testimony on behalf of the supposed son of Mme. Jumel."

17. "Madame Jumel's millions," *Albany Argus*, January 27, 1871, [2] (for all quotations in the paragraph).

18. Ibid.

19. "The courts," *New York Herald*, January 27, 1872, 11; "The courts," *New York Herald*, March 16, 1872, 11.

20. "The courts," *New York Herald*, February 17, 1872, 11; February 23, 1872, 11; and March 15, 1872, 8; 1873 Transcript of Record, 220.

21. Ibid.

22. "The courts," *New York Herald*, February 6, 1872, 5; "The courts," *New York Herald*, January 25, 1872, 11; "The courts," *New York Herald*, March 16, 1872, 11; 1873 Transcript of Record, 246–47. Among those who testified for George Washington Bowen were Elizabeth Price and Margaret A. Stanton, daughters of Solomon Northrup (author of the memoir *Twelve Years a Slave*, which detailed his captivity after being kidnapped from Saratoga Springs in 1841). Additionally, their mother Anne Northrup gave a deposition for Bowen. According to the statements by these members of the Northrup family, Eliza took Elizabeth, then a young girl, to work for her shortly after the kidnapping; placed Margaret, also a child, with Mary Chase; and briefly had Anne working for her as well. Eliza was claimed to have spoken of having a son on one occasion to Anne, on a second occasion to Elizabeth in Anne's presence, and on a third occasion to Elizabeth and Margaret, temporarily both at the mansion. However, much of the relevant testimony was suspiciously vague, and there is no indication that Anne (or her son Alonzo, also briefly mentioned) ever worked at the mansion, or that Elizabeth and Margaret were ever there

together. It is possible, however, that Elizabeth worked briefly for Eliza and Margaret for Mary Chase and then were sent back to Saratoga. Most of the individuals who testified for Bowen had some grounds for disgruntlement with Eliza, and the Northrop girls' time with her may not have been happy.

The main source for the testimony by Northrop family members is the 1873 Transcript of Record, 246–50.

23. "The courts," *New York Herald*, February 23, 1872, 8.

24. "The Jumel estate. Further testimony on behalf of the supposed son of Mme. Jumel."

25. Ibid.

26. Ibid.

27. "The courts," *New York Herald*, February 27, 1872, 5.

28. "An interesting episode in Rhode Island history," *Providence Evening Press*, January 25, 1872, [2].

29. "The courts," *New York Herald*, March 15, 1872, [8].

30. "Personal, political, and general," *New York Times*, March 30, 1871, 2.

31. "The Jumel estate—Gen. Washington not Bowen's father," *Providence Evening Press*, March 31, 1871, [2]; "An interesting episode in Rhode Island history."

32. "The courts," *New York Herald*, February 7, 1872, 8.

33. *New York Times*, January 27, 1872, 8.

34. "The courts," *New York Herald*, February 16, 1872, 11; "The courts," *New York Herald*, February 17, 1872, 11.

35. "The courts," *New York Herald*, February 14, 1872, [8].

36. "The Jumel estate—Gen. Washington not Bowen's father"; "The Jumel estate—further testimony, *New York Times*, March 29, 1871; "The Jumel estate. Further testimony on behalf of the supposed son of Mme. Jumel," *New York Times*, March 21, 1871; "The Jumel estate—further testimony," *New York Times*, March 22, 1871.

37. "The Jumel estate," *New York Times*, March 25, 1871.

38. "The courts," *New York Herald*, February 17, 1872, 11; February 23, 1872, 11; March 15, 1872, 8.

39. "The courts," *New York Herald*, March 16, 1872, 11. This was not even Bowen's first attempt at obtaining a share of the Jumel estate. He was one of the claimants in the suit brought by the descendants of James Bowen, before pursuing his own case on the grounds that he was Eliza's son. See "Law reports," *New York Times*, February 22, 1870, 3; and also 3-312 for the names of the thirty-three plaintiffs in the former suit, a "George W. Bowen" among them.

40. "An interesting episode in Rhode Island history."

41. "The courts," *New York Herald*, March 17, 1872, 10.

42. 3-466, notice from Commissioner Metcalf to James C. Carter, Esq., of the examination of Henry Nodine as a witness.

43. 3-466, deposition of Henry Nodine.

44. Ibid.

45. "A scene at Saratoga," *Alexandria Gazette*, September 8, 1846, [2].

46. "The Jumel estate case, *New York Herald*, January 15, 1873, 8; 3-466, deposition of Henry Nodine. Pension records show that his brothers served in the militia, but he did not. See

Ancestry.com, *War of 1812 Pension Application Files Index, 1812–1815* [database online] (Provo, UT: Ancestry.com Operations, Inc., 2010). Nodine gave his age as forty-eight in the 1850 census and as sixty in the 1860 census, making him only ten or twelve years old at the outbreak of the War of 1812 (see the 1850 and 1860 United States Federal Census databases in Ancestry.com).

47. NYHS-JP, box 1, folder 1, Eliza Jumel to Stephen Jumel, received October 4, 1826; N.Y. Ct. Com. Pl., Stephen Jumel vs. Lewis Nodine and Peter Nodine, 1824-#292.

48. "The Jumel ejectment suit," *New York Herald*, June 20, 1872, 4.

49. E.g., 1873 Transcript of Record, 197, 227. 260.

50. Ibid., 267, 322–23; "The courts," *New York Herald*, January 17, 1873, 11.

51. "New York; Boston," *Hartford Daily Courant*, January 15, 1873, 1, reprinting a report from the *Boston Journal*.

52. "The Jumel will case," *Daily Evening Bulletin* [San Francisco], March 5, 1873, [2].

53. "The courts," *New York Herald*, February 11, 1873, 8; 1873 Transcript of Record, 305.

54. "The courts," *New York Herald*, January 15, 1873, 8.

55. 1873 Transcript of Record, 310–11. A later deposition by this witness, John G. Caryl, makes it clear that his evidence should not be trusted (B-779, box 113).

56. "The great Jumel case," *New York Herald*, February 21, 1873, 5.

57. Ibid.

58. "The Jumel will case," *Boston Morning Journal*, March 1, 1873, [2].

CHAPTER 39: ON THE HOME FRONT

1. Record of the marriage of Nelson Chase and Hattie Crombie Dunning, available at www.FamilySearch.org; record for William Dunning and household at Ancestry.com, *1860 United States Federal Census* (see chap. 35, n. 10).

2. "Died," *New York Herald*, July 16, 1869, 7; New York City, Municipal Archives, Manhattan Death Certificates, no. 30903.

3. 1870 United States Census, accessed on www.familysearch.org.

4. Ibid.

5. "Another phase of the Jumel suit," *New York Times*, February 29, 1872, 8; NYHS-JP, box 2 folder D, agreement between Nelson Chase and John McBain Davidson.

6. N.Y. Sup. Ct., Nelson Chase vs. William Inglis Chase et al., 1880 C-3, schedule A.

7. N.Y. Sup. Ct., William Inglis Chase vs. Nelson Chase and others, 1878 C-36.

8. N.Y. Sup. Ct., Nelson Chase vs. William Inglis Chase et al., 1880 C-3, exhibit D.

9. Ancestry.com, *1880 United States Federal Census* (see chap. 36, n. 38).

10. New York City, Municipal Archives, Manhattan Death Certificates, no. 200348; NYHS-AHMC, Mauer, Charles Arthur, untitled notes relating to Eliza Jumel.

11. New York City, Municipal Archives, Manhattan Death Certificates, no. 200348.

12. Ancestry.com, *U.S. Passport Applications 1795–1925* (see chap. 6, n. 17), passport application for Mathilde Pery (wrongly indicating that she was born in New York State).

13. "Married," *New York Herald*, June 25, 1878, 8.

14. New York City, Municipal Archives, Manhattan Marriage Certificates, no. 3015.

15. NYPL, NYGB AZ Fam 09-78, Caroline Winslow Crippen, "Silas Crippen of Worcester, New York, and some of his descentants [*sic*]," typescript, 1824, 8–9, 25–26.
16. "The Jumel estate case," *New-York Evening Post*, May 3, 1873, [2].
17. "United States Supreme Court," *New York Herald*, January 12, 1877, 8.
18. *Bowen v. Chase*, 98 U.S. 254 (1878).
19. Ibid.; *Bowen v. Chase*, 94 U.S. 812 (1876).
20. 94 U.S. 812.
21. 98 U.S. 254.
22. Ibid.
23. E.g., Marianne Hancock, *Madame of the Heights: The story of a prostitute's progress* (Mt. Desert, ME: Windswept House Publishers, 1998).
24. Gilfoyle, *City of eros*, 70 (see chap. 1, n. 8).
25. In the early to mid-1790s, her mother and stepfather had wandered among at least four Massachusetts towns, but the documents do not show whether she traveled with them. See Duncan, *The amazing Madame Jumel*, 29–35, 39–40 (see chap. 3, n. 12).
26. Providence Ct. Com. Pl., Samuel W. Greene vs. Betsey Bowen, (Rhode Island Supreme Court Judicial Records Center, Pawtucket).
27. Ibid.; *State Gazette and Town and Country Advertiser*, January 25, 1796, 28 (advertisement); *Providence Gazette*, February 13, 1796, [3] (advertisement).
28. Providence Ct. Com. Pl., Samuel W. Greene vs. Betsey Bowen.
29. Ibid.
30. Ibid.
31. Ibid.
32. 1873 Transcript of Record, 128, 131–32, 153.
33. *New-York Tribune*, September 11, 1876, 4.

CHAPTER 40: MURDER MOST FOUL?

1. The Knickerbocker Brothers, "Life in New York," *Cincinnati Daily Gazette*, September 22, 1876, 5.
2. 1876 Bill of Complaint, 23–25. Strictly speaking, the suit was filed by the grandchildren. Madelaine's great-grandchildren were added after her last grandchild died in 1878 (B-779, box 113, deposition of François Henry Jumel).
3. 1876 Bill of Complaint, 26–27.
4. Ibid., 27
5. Ibid., 27–28.
6. United States Circuit Court for the Southern District of New York (in equity), *François Henry Jumel, et al., complainants, vs. Nelson Chase, et al., defendants. Amendments to the bill of complaint* (New York, 1878), 8, in NARA-NY-RG21, François Henry Jumel et al. vs. Nelson Chase et al., United States Circuit Court for the Southern District of New York, equity cases, vol. A-216, 1876.
7. B-779, box 113, deposition of John G. Caryl.
8. Ibid.

9. Ibid.

10. B-779, boxes 112 and 113, depositions of Nelson Chase.

11. Ibid.

12. B-779, box 112, deposition of Nelson Chase.

13. Supreme Court, City and County of New York, *William Inglis Chase and Isabella A. Chase, his wife, plaintiffs, against Nelson Chase and Hattie C. Chase, his wife, and others, defendants. Abstract of title to premises nos. 150 Broadway, 71 and 73 Liberty Street; and also to premises between 159th Street, 175th Street, Kingsbridge Road, and Harlem River* (New York: M. B. Brown, Printer and Stationer, 1881), 37–40.

14. *William Inglis Chase and Isabella A. Chase, his wife, plaintiffs, against Nelson Chase and Hattie C. Chase, his wife, and others, defendants. Abstract of title to premises.*

15. "Fifteen years in the courts," *New York Times*, July 1, 1881.

16. Supreme Court, City and County of New York, *William Inglis Chase and wife against Nelson Chase and Hattie C., his wife, and others. (Copy). Amended and supplemental judgments* (New York: Charles S. Hamilton & Co., Printers, 1882).

17. "Last of the Jumel suits," *New-York Tribune*, April 3, 1883: 1.

18. They would not share in the profits from the house and lands in Saratoga, since those had never belonged to their relative Stephen Jumel. Eliza had purchased them after his death. Nelson, Eliza, and William would receive one-third each of the Saratoga real estate. See *William Inglis Chase and Isabella A. Chase, his wife, plaintiffs, against Nelson Chase and Hattie C. Chase, his wife, and others, defendants. Abstract of title to premises*, 142–43.

19. 1876 Bill of Complaint, letters 34 and 35.

20. *Bowen v. Chase*, 94 U.S. 812 (1876).

21. 1876 Bill of Complaint, letter 34.

22. United States Circuit Court for the Southern District of New York, *François Henry Jumel, Louise C. L. Jumel Plante, Marie R. M. Jumel, Madeline R. Texoeres Marrast, Marie C. F. Lesparre Tauçiede vs. Nelson Chase, Amended bill of complaint and exhibits* (New York: Benj. H. Tyrrell, 1877), in NARA-NY-RG21, François Henry Jumel et al. vs. Nelson Chase et al., United States Circuit Court for the Southern District of New York, equity cases, vol. A-216, 1876.

23. *William Inglis Chase and Isabella A. Chase, his wife, plaintiffs, against Nelson Chase and Hattie C. Chase, his wife, and others, defendants. Abstract of title to premises*, 107.

24. "Unfortunate good fortune," *Sun* [Baltimore, MD], November 30, 1887, Supplement; "The courts. A decree for the sale of the Jumel estate," *New-York Tribune*, January 12, 1888, 3; "Bits of legal news," *New-York Tribune*, March 23, 1888, 3; "General term decisions," *New York Herald*, May 25, 1889, 4; "The courts," *New-York Tribune*, April 3, 1890, 5. The French heirs had made a deal with the marquis de Chambrun, legal counsel for the French legation in Washington, DC, to pursue their case. He was to receive 47.5 percent of the monies recovered. Subsequently Chambrun subcontracted much of the work to other lawyers, promising them smaller percentages of the recovered sums. Some of these subcontractors sold their interest in the case to third parties. By the time Nelson and his children settled with Stephen's relatives, an astonishing number of people, lawyers and otherwise, were awaiting payment out of the monies awarded to the French heirs. Many

of the details may be found in NARA-NY-RG21, Stephen M. Chester vs. François Henry Jumel et al., United States Circuit Court for the Southern District of New York, equity cases, vol. I-4062 (Archives Box No. 545A).

25. "The courts," *New-York Tribune*, April 3, 1890, 5.

26. "The Jumel estate," *New York Herald*, May 23, 1883, 4; *Springfield Daily Republican*, May 24, 1883, 4; "Asking for an accounting," *New York Herald*, August 25, 1891, 11; "Why a French marquis sued his lawyer," *New York Herald*, September 10, 1891, 8.

27. MJM 26.19, statement of William Luby, April 6, 1912; Stillwell, *History of the Burr portraits*, 71 (see chap. 25, n. 5).

28. William P. Schweickert Jr., "A seance at the Jumel Mansion," *Westchester Historian* 41 (Spring 1965): 28.

29. Parton, 661.

30. Flint, *Letters from America*, 18 (see chap. 2, n. 28).

31. B-779, box 112, deposition of Nelson Chase.

32. Ibid.

33. Ibid. For the practice of bloodletting after injuries, see, for example, Stuart, *Three years in North America*, 1:205 (see chap. 24, n. 5).

34. B-779, box 112, deposition of Nelson Chase.

35. B-779, box 112, deposition of Nelson Chase; also see BM 710-J, first account of the administratrix (for the doctors' bills).

36. Ibid. Berger received a staggering $150, an amount implying daily attendance on his patient. For medical fees at the time, see George Rosen, *Fees and the bills: Some economic aspects of medical practice in 19th century America*, Supplement to the *Bulletin of the History of Medicine*, no. 6 (Baltimore: The Johns Hopkins Press, 1946): 3, 11.

37. NYPL, Coroner's Inquisitions, 1823–1898. No inquest for Stephen was recorded in May or June 1832.

38. New York City Municipal Archives, Manhattan Deaths, vol. 8.

39. Greatorex, 243.

40. Ibid.

41. Ibid., 177–181 and 243 for the stories later embellished by Hopper Striker Mott in *The New York of yesterday*, 87–89 (see chap. 9, n. 1).

42. Greatorex, 244.

43. "A May Day Tramp," *New York Herald*, May 8, 1882, 5; Benson J. Lossing, "The Roger Morris House (afterward the residence of Madame Jumel), *Appleton's Journal of Literature, Science, and Art* 10, no. 228 (August 2, 1873), 129.

44. Greatorex, 244.

45. "Domestic news," *Sacramento Daily Union*, August 15, 1871, [1] (citing a report from New York's *World*).

46. Ibid.

47. Ibid.

48. Mme. Jumel's estate. The entire property disposed of and $1,092,452 realized," *New York Herald*, November 19, 1882, 11; *New York Herald*, December 8, 1882, 9; "The last of the

Jumel estate," *New York Herald*, March 12, 1886, 8; "The great Jumel sale," *New York Herald*, April 4, 1888, 8.

49. See NYHS-JP, box 3, folder E, for receipts showing that Nelson and Julius Caryl shared equally in paying taxes and insurance premiums on the mansion and homestead lot through the mid-1880s.

50. For Lizzie's presence in the household, see Ancestry.com, *1880 United States Federal Census* (see chap. 36, n. 38).

EPILOGUE

1. "Historic lands sold," *New York Times*, May 5, 1887, 4.

2. "Saratoga Springs," *New York Times*, July 30, 1899, 12.

3. "Death of Nelson Chase," *New York Times*, March 19, 1890. Nelson died on March 18.

4. "Mother and uncle accused by a boy," *New York Herald*, June 2, 1892, 7; "Dynamiter Tynan's charges," *New York Times*, June 4, 1894; "Tynan's 'revelations,'" *Saturday Review of Politics, Literature, Science and Art* 82, no. 2135 (September 26, 1895): 345–46.

5. "Mother and uncle accused by a boy."

6. New York City, Municipal Archives, Manhattan Death Certificates, no. 30903. He died on September 12, 1894.

7. "Mrs. Eliza J. P. Caryl dies," *New York Times*, April 29, 1915, 13 (wrongly giving her age as eighty-two and identifying Agnes Gourreau as her sister rather than granddaughter). She died on April 27, 1915.

8. Surrogate's Ct., Westchester County, N.Y., Estate of Julius H. Caryl, 148-1911. Caryl died on March 27, 1911.

9. "To manage Caryl estate," *New York Times*, May 2, 1915, 5; "Dr. Hampton weds a Caryl heiress," *New York Times*, March 5, 1916, 21; Surrogate's Ct., Westchester County, N.Y., Estate of Eliza Jumel Caryl, 1915-134 (for Agnes's four children, referred to in error as three in the newspapers).

10. "Dr. Hampton weds a Caryl heiress."

11. N.Y. Ct. Ch., Esther Cox v. Alexander G. Cox, BM 1847-C; "Plot and counter plot," *Burlington* [VT] *Free Press*, March 31, 1837.

12. Hudson, *Mistress of Manifest Destiny*, 46, 61 (see chap. 27, n. 15).

13. Obituary notes," *New York Herald*, February 7, 1885, 10 (wrongly indicating that he was ninety-one). He died on February 6.

14. "Fighting for big stakes," *Washington Post*, August 5, 1889, 2.

15. *Daily People*, October 12, 1900, 4.

16. "Claim to Jumel estate," *New York Times*, July 14, 1903, 14.

17. Ibid.; "Lays claim to all the Jumel estate," *Evening World*, July 13, 1903, 3.

18. "Arrests for selling part of the Jumel tract," *New York Times*, October 1, 1903, 16.

19. "Exhibit at Jumel Mansion," *New-York Tribune*, May 29, 1907, 4.

20. New York, Silo's Fifth Avenue Art Galleries, *Catalogue of the Jumel Collection* (see chap. 17, n. 25).

ACKNOWLEDGMENTS

1. William H. Shelton, *The Jumel Mansion: being a full history of the house on Harlem Heights built by Roger Morris before the Revolution; together with some account of its more notable occupants* (Boston and New York: Houghton Mifflin Co., 1916).

2. Constance Greiff, *The Morris-Jumel Mansion: A Documentary History* (Rocky Hill, NJ: Heritage Studies, Inc., 1995).

A NOTE ON THE SOURCES

1. All of the examples in this paragraph are taken from PUL Fuller, Eliza Jumel to Stephen Jumel, September 21, 1826.

2. For example, he took particular care in writing a letter in which he discussed numerous business matters that concerned them both (NYHS-JP, Stephen Jumel to Eliza Jumel, October 14, 1826).

3. 1876 Bill of Complaint.

IMAGE CREDITS

01. Detail of a photograph by Tom Stoelker. Courtesy of the Morris-Jumel Mansion.

02. G. Haywood, *Col. Roger Morris' House, Washingtons [sic] Head Quarters Sep.ʳ 1776. now known as Madame Jumel's Res..ᶜᵉ*, 1854. Lithograph. Courtesy of the Morris-Jumel Mansion.

03. *Gate at 160th Street*, ca. 1875. Vintage photograph, 2 5/8 x 3 3/4 in. MJM P.1.2.2. Collection of the Morris-Jumel Mansion.

04. Henri Courvoisier-Voisin (1757–1830) (after), *The Place Vendôme*, ca. 1815-20. Color engraving. Bibliotheque des Arts Decoratifs, Paris, France / Archives Charmet / Bridgeman Images.

05. Jean-Marc Nattier (1685–1766). *Portrait of an Aristocratic Youth (possibly the Duc de Chaulnes) as Bacchus*. Oil on canvas, 57 1/2 x 45 1/4 in., SN380. Bequest of John Ringling, 1936 Collection of The John and Mable Ringling Museum of Art, the State Art Museum of Florida.

06. Jean-Frédéric Schall (1752–1825). *A Lady with a Dog*. Oil on canvas, 11 3/4 x 8 3/4 in. Private Collection / © Arthur Ackermann Ltd., London / Bridgeman Images.

07. Simon Vouet (1590–1649). *King David Playing the Harp*. Oil on canvas, 36 3/4 x 47 3/8 in., P.62.278. From the Bob Jones University Collection.

08. Francesco Trevisani (1656–1746) (attributed to). *Hagar and Ishmael in the Desert*. Oil on canvas, 31 3/4 x 51 1/2 in. Current location unknown. Image courtesy of Sotheby's, London.

09. *Madame Stephen Jumel*. Watercolor on ivory, 4 1/8 x 3 5/8 in., 1957.35. Photography © New-York Historical Society. Collection of the New-York Historical Society, Gift of Mr. Thomas W. Streeter.

10. James van Dyck (active 1825–1843), *Aaron Burr*, 1834. Oil on wood panel, 9 5/8 x 7 3/4 in., 1931.57. Photography © New-York Historical Society. Collection of the New-York Historical Society, Gift of Dr. John E. Stillwell.

11. Augustin Amant Constance Fidèle Édouart (1788–1861), *Silhouette of Eliza Jumel*, 1843. Cut-paper silhouette on a lithograph, 12 3/4 x 9 3/4 in., MJM 1980.423.2.1.97. Collection of the Morris-Jumel Mansion.

12. Emily Jackson Photograph Collection of Édouart's American Silhouette Portraits, PR 101 (photograph of four of Augustin Amant Constance Fidèle Édouart's cut-paper silhouettes). Photography © New-York Historical Society. Collection of the New-York Historical Society.

13. *Eliza Jumel Burr*, 1852. Lithograph, image 14 1/4 x 10 7/8 in., MJM 1980.467. Collection of the Morris-Jumel Mansion.

14. Alcide Ercole, *Jumel Family Portrait* (detail), 1854. Oil on canvas, 97 x 68 in., MJM 1980.429.1. Collection of the Morris-Jumel Mansion. Photograph by Trish Mayo.

15. Photograph by Peter Flass. This work is licensed under a Creative Commons Attribution 2.0 Generic license.

16. Abraham Hosier, *Hall of the Roger Morris or Jumel Mansion*. Watercolor on paper, 11 3/4 x 9 1/4 in., 48.129.7. Collection of the Museum of the City of New York.

17. E. Bierstadt, *Eliza Jumel and others outside the Jumel Mansion* (detail), ca. 1860. Artotype. Photography © New-York Historical Society. Collection of the New-York Historical Society, Gift of Charles Mauer.

18. Photograph by Trish Mayo.

19. George Gardner Rockwood (1832–1911), *George Jones, the Count Johannes*, New York, 1878. Silver gelatin photograph, 2 1/2 x 4 in., UW36467. 19th Century Actors Carte-de-visite Collection, PH Coll 75. University of Washington Libraries, Special Collections.

20. *Charles O'Conor*, between 1865 and 1880. Wet collodion glass negative. Brady-Handy Photograph Collection, LC-DIG-cwpbh-05062. Courtesy of the Library of Congress.

21. George Washington Bowen, the most determined claimant to Eliza's fortune. Current location unknown. Image courtesy of the Morris-Jumel Mansion.

INDEX